I0149163

Temple of God

Stone to Spirit

Temple of God

Stone to Spirit

Vinu V Das

TP

Tabor Press

© 2025 Tabor Press. All rights reserved. No part of this publication may be reproduced, distributed, or transmitted in any form or by any means without the prior written permission of the publisher, except in the case of brief quotations embodied in critical reviews and certain other noncommercial uses permitted by copyright law.

ISBN 978-1-997541-15-8

Table of Contents

Chapter 1 — Eden: The Archetypal Sanctuary.

Genesis does not wait for the tabernacle in Exodus or the stone temple of Kings before it begins speaking a temple dialect. From the opening breath of Scripture the creation narrative is narrated as if it were the dedication liturgy of a cosmic sanctuary, and Eden itself is portrayed not merely as a pleasant park but as the first Holy Place. Read within its Ancient Near-Eastern milieu, the text pulses with priestly motifs: ordered space, enthronement rest, sacred geography, and mediating image-bearers who serve and guard. Because Eden supplies the architectural DNA for every later dwelling of God, tracing temple theology without beginning here would be like reading a symphony from the second movement. This chapter therefore anchors the entire book by mining Genesis 1-3 for sanctuary motifs, showing how every beam of later tabernacles is pre-echoed in primordial soil. Each section below unpacks a different facet of Eden's temple identity—cosmic structure, geographic holiness, priestly vocation, sacramental trees, Sabbath presence, fall and exile, canonical echoes, Christological fulfilment, and eschatological consummation—so that by the epilogue the reader feels the gravitational pull of Eden stretching unbroken from creation to new creation. Within that sweep we also discover why the human heart aches for home, why work and worship belong together, and why salvation is ultimately God bringing humanity back into a garden-city where He once again walks in the cool of the day.

1.1 Creation Presented as a Cosmic Temple

1.1.1 Seven-Day Structure and Liturgical Rhythm (Gen 1)

The rhythmic refrain "and there was evening, and there was morning" punctuating Genesis 1 is more than chronological bookkeeping; it functions like a liturgical antiphon guiding worshippers through successive "hours" of a cosmic service. Ancient temples commonly held seven-day dedication ceremonies, and the author of Genesis appears to mirror that pattern by narrating creation itself as Yahweh's dedication of a universal sanctuary. Days one through six correspond to the stocking of holy space with light, heavens, seas, land, vegetation, luminaries, birds, fish, beasts, and finally priests in the form of human image-bearers (Gen 1 : 3-31). The seventh day, marked by divine rest (Gen 2 : 1-3), parallels the moment when glory fills later sanctuaries and priests must step back in reverent awe (Ex 40 : 34-35; 1 Kgs 8 : 10-11). Each creative fiat operates like Yahweh hanging another tapestry or polishing another menorah, so that by the completion of day six the cosmic temple is fully furnished for liturgy. Israel's Sabbath command emerges from this pattern, instructing the nation to re-enact creation's cadence in weekly micro-temples of time (Ex 20 : 8-11). Thus, Genesis 1 teaches that the world's deepest rhythm is doxological—a truth that later prophets will recall when critiquing Israel for disrupting Sabbath harmonies (Isa 58 : 13-14; Jer 17 : 21-27). Modern disciples who neglect weekly rest therefore silence one of the earliest sanctuary songs written into creation's score.

1.1.2 Image of God Inscription: Idols Replaced by Humans

Ancient Near-Eastern kings stationed carved images of themselves in distant provinces to mark dominion, and temples displayed cult statues as embodiments of deity; Genesis overturns both practices by installing living, breathing representatives of Yahweh over creation. When God says, "Let us make humankind in our image" (Gen 1 : 26-27), He is commissioning priest-kings whose very bodies advertise divine reign. Unlike inert idols of wood and gold, these stewards move, speak, and reproduce, extending sanctuary borders by filling the earth (Gen 1 : 28). Their vocation to "subdue" and "rule" must be read through priestly lenses: they are to guard sacred order, not exploit it—a nuance later clarified by the servant-leadership of Christ, the perfect Image (Col 1 : 15). Because idols are strictly forbidden in Israel (Ex 20 : 4-5), humanity's imaging role underscores that the only legitimate representation of Yahweh in His temple is humanity itself. Therefore, every assault on human dignity—slavery, racism, abuse—constitutes temple vandalism, desecrating the very icons God has installed. Recognizing this truth fuels the New-Testament ethic whereby believers are urged to clothe the naked and defend the oppressed, for as we treat the least of Christ's siblings we treat the Lord of the temple Himself (Matt 25 : 40).

1.1.3 Seventh-Day Rest as Divine Enthronement (Gen 2 : 1-3)

Rest in Hebrew thought is not cessation of activity for exhaustion recovery but enthronement after victorious ordering. Just as ancient deities "rested" in temples once idols were installed, Yahweh's Sabbath signals His royal occupancy of the cosmic sanctuary. Blessing and sanctifying the seventh day (Gen 2 : 3) consecrates time itself, making the calendar a portable temple alongside Eden's geographic one. That blessing finds later echo in tabernacle theology when Sabbath violations carry the same penalty as idolatry (Ex 31 : 12-17), because both acts assault divine throne. The Epistle to the Hebrews interprets Sabbath rest as invitation for believers to enter God's completed work through faith (Heb 4 : 1-11), effectively extending Eden's sanctuary into Christian soteriology. Consequently, weekly worship rehearses an eschatological destiny in which eternal rest does not mean inertia but participation in God's joyful governance of a healed cosmos. Thus, Sabbath is both memory of a finished creation and prophecy of a perfected new creation—the temporal axis of temple theology.

1.1.4 Lights, Firmament, and Seas as Sanctuary Furniture

Priestly texts later describe the lampstand as symbolizing celestial lights (Ex 25 : 31-40) and the laver as a bronze sea (1 Kgs 7 : 23-26); Genesis anticipates this by installing sun, moon, and stars on day four and separating sea from dry land on day three. The vault (*rāqîaʿ*) of heaven resembles a temple curtain embroidered with cherubim (Gen 1 : 6-8; Ex 26 : 31), and the confinement of chaotic waters beneath firmament foreshadows laver waters tamed for priestly cleansing.

Scholars note that when Israel later gazes up, they see the ceiling of Yahweh's palace; when priests gaze into the laver, they see the starry reflection inverted. Thus, cosmic architecture and cultic furniture mutually interpret: creation is inherently liturgical, and the tabernacle is a micro-cosmos. This duality reappears in Revelation where throne-room sea of glass mixes with celestial floor (Rev 4 : 6), confirming that Genesis established a template that the Bible never abandons. Therefore, meditation on Genesis furniture tunes worshippers to recognize sacramental contours in everyday nature.

1.1.5 ANE Parallels and Polemical Distinctives

Comparative studies highlight similarities between Genesis and Mesopotamian creation myths—chaoskampf, divine councils, temple dedication—yet Genesis subverts pagan themes in crucial ways. Marduk builds Babylon after slaying Tiamat, but Yahweh faces no rival; He speaks and it is so (Gen 1 : 3). Babylonian texts reserve image status for kings, whereas Genesis democratizes it, gifting every man and woman with regal dignity (Gen 1 : 27). While Enuma Elish crafts humanity as menial laborers to feed capricious gods, Genesis portrays Sabbath God who feeds humanity with garden abundance (Gen 2 : 16). Thus, Genesis functions as theological polemic, dethroning violent deities and enthroning a benevolent Creator whose temple world rests on justice and generosity. Understanding these contrasts guards interpreters from flattening Genesis into mythological sameness; instead, it emerges as a revolutionary document declaring that cosmos is sanctuary precisely because its Architect is good. That goodness later climaxes in John's gospel where the creative Word becomes flesh, revealing the full brightness of the Father's glory (John 1 : 14-18).

1.2 Geography of Eden: Holy Place in a Good World

1.2.1 Eastern Location and Rising-Sun Symbolism (Gen 2 : 8)

The text situates Eden "in the east," a geographical pointer pregnant with theological resonance. In Israel's temple the entrance faces east (Ezek 40 : 6), aligning worshippers to greet dawn, symbolizing new creation with every sunrise. By placing garden toward sunrise,

Genesis tacitly links Eden with later sanctuary orientation, foreshadowing priests who will begin their daily tamid offerings as sun's first light kisses altar horns (Ex 29 : 38-41). Biblical narratives often depict eastward movement as exile—Adam leaves eastward, Cain dwells east of Eden, Israelites go east to Babel (Gen 3 : 24; 4 : 16; 11 : 2)—making westward return symbolic of redemption. Therefore, the day's first light is both reminder of lost origins and prophecy of restored communion; worship each morning reenacts return journey. Christian baptisteries in antiquity faced west-to-east so catechumens renounced darkness and turned toward rising Messiah, replicating Edenic compass in sacramental choreography. Thus, Genesis orients worshippers not only temporally (Sabbath) but spatially toward hope's horizon.

1.2.2 Four Rivers as Life-Giving Boundaries (Gen 2 : 10-14)

Eden's river issues from garden center, dividing into Pishon, Gihon, Tigris, and Euphrates—geographic markers that ancient readers connected to global expansiveness. Unlike mythic rivers flowing from under thrones of capricious deities, these streams distribute fertility to gold-rich Havilah and Ethiopia-linked Cush, implying that Edenic blessing is missionary by design. Gold, bdellium, and onyx evoke later sanctuary materials (Gen 2 : 11-12; Ex 25 : 7), suggesting that the tabernacle's metals are repatriated fragments of primal garden. Because the rivers exit Eden, humanity's task to "expand and fill" means extending sacred order until waters cover earth "as the waters cover the sea" (Hab 2 : 14). Even in exile, Israel remembers these springs; psalmists by Babylon's rivers long for Zion because deep calls to deep (Ps 137 : 1; 42 : 7). Thus, river imagery unites creational blessing, cultic décor, and eschatological hope in one aqueous thread that will reappear in Ezekiel 47 and Revelation 22. Missionaries today may view gospel proclamation as extending hidden Edenic headwaters into barren cultural deserts.

1.2.3 Mountain of God Hints (Ezek 28 : 14-16)

Though Genesis does not explicitly label Eden a mountain, Ezekiel's oracle against the king of Tyre describes him as guardian cherub "on the holy mount of God... in Eden" (Ezek 28 : 13-14). Ancient cosmologies viewed mountains as meeting points between heaven and earth, and later temples replicate this vertical theology—Sinai, Zion, Gerizim, and ultimately the Apocalyptic New Jerusalem descending from on high. If Eden is elevated, the rivers logically flow downhill, matching the hydrological pattern in Ezekiel's temple vision. Elevation also frames Adam as high-priest ascending summit to meet God in daily fellowship, a prototype for Moses' Sinai ascent and Jesus' transfiguration climb. Mountain imagery fosters pilgrim spirituality; worship is ascent requiring repentance (Ps 24) and culminating in beatific encounter. Therefore, Eden's altitude invites believers to live upward-oriented lives, legs on soil, hearts on heights (Col 3 : 1-2). It further legitimates environmental stewardship—mountain peaks inspire awe, but they are meant as altars, not quarries for idolatry.

1.2.4 Garden, Land, World: Three-Zone Holiness Pattern

Scholars note that Eden (garden), surrounding land, and world correspond to the tabernacle's Most Holy Place, Holy Place, and outer court. Adam's immediate workspace is the garden's enclosed precinct, mirroring priests' ministry behind veil; beyond lies cultivated land for humanity's expansion; outermost lies raw cosmos awaiting subjugation. This tripartite structure resurfaces in Sinai's zones—Israel at base, elders mid-slope, Moses at peak—and in temple architecture. Recognizing the pattern clarifies why Cain's exile from Edenic land, though not world, increases alienation—a move from holy middle to profane margin (Gen 4 : 11-14). It also explains why Revelation's restored cosmos is cube-shaped Holy of Holies, eliminating outer tiers (Rev 21 : 16). Thus, Genesis' spatial theology prepares readers to see holiness as ever-widening concentric circles driven outward by obedient stewardship. Mission therefore is garden expansion until earth is filled with temple glory.

1.2.5 Flora, Orchard, and Mineral Imagery Prefiguring Tabernacle Decor

Pomegranates, almond blossoms, and palm trees carved into temple walls trace their ancestry to Eden's vegetation (Ex 25 : 33-34; 1 Kgs 6 : 29). By adorning sanctuary with garden motifs, artisans visually preach that worship is a return to primal fellowship. The menorah's almond branches replicate Tree of Life iconography, its perpetual flames symbolizing eternal vitality (Ex 27 : 20-21). Gold that lines inner sanctuary recalls Havilah's veins, turning geology of Eden into liturgy of Zion. Thus, when Jesus promises the thief paradise (Luke 23 : 43), He evokes not clouds but cultivated orchard where God once walked. Art in churches—from vine-laden stained glass to baptismal pools—continues this tradition, demonstrating that Christian creativity participates in Edenic memory and prophecy. Ignoring beauty in worship therefore amputates one of Eden's richest limbs.

1.3 Adam and Eve: Priest-King and Queen-Helper

1.3.1 Serve and Guard—Cultic Vocabulary (Gen 2 : 15)

The Hebrew verbs *ăbad* ("work/serve") and *šāmar* ("keep/guard") describe Levitical duties in Numbers 3 : 7-8, indicating that Adam's gardening was priestly service, not mere horticulture. His pruning shears were liturgical instruments; his vigilance against intruders anticipated cherubim sword. Because *ăbad* also means worship, daily labor blended seamlessly with devotion, collapsing sacred/secular divide. When Paul urges believers to present bodies as living sacrifices (Rom 12 : 1), he resurrects Edenic vocational worship. The command precedes Eve's creation, suggesting that priesthood is humanity's shared vocation, later diversified but never replaced. Failure to guard allowed serpent entry, proving that lax priesthood imperils sanctuary's integrity. Pastoral ministry today echoes Adam's task—cultivate truth, guard flock, repel wolves.

1.3.2 Naming Animals: Royal Taxonomy (Gen 2 : 19-20)

Bestowing names equates to exercising delegated authority, as seen when Nebuchadnezzar renames Daniel and friends, asserting sovereignty (Dan 1 : 7). Adam's nomenclature functions as royal taxonomy, ordering creation beneath divine headship. The parade of animals also demonstrates Adam's perceptive wisdom, prerequisite for temple service where priests must distinguish clean from unclean (Lev 10 : 10). That no companion is found among beasts underscores humanity's distinct covenant capacity; Eve is fashioned not from dust but from side, signifying co-regency rather than vassal status. Together male and female image God in relational communion, mirroring triune fellowship. Their dialogue before fall is frictionless liturgy; marital union becomes micro-temple where God's glory resides (1 Cor 11 : 7). Names therefore become doxological acts—parents naming children, scientists naming stars—extending Edenic rule.

1.3.3 Liturgical Clothing of Innocence and Post-Fall Garments

Before sin, Adam and Eve are "naked and not ashamed" (Gen 2 : 25); innocence functions as vestment, rendering external attire unnecessary. After disobedience, they sew fig leaves—makeshift priestly garments—signifying intuitive need for covering in sanctuary. God replaces vegetal aprons with animal skins (Gen 3 : 21), foreshadowing sacrificial blood as pathway to restored fellowship. Later, priests wear linen coats and belts, echoing Edenic tailor but preventing sweat (Ex 28 : 42-43; Ezek 44 : 18), symbolizing restful labor recovered. Revelation pictures saints in white robes, washed in Lamb's blood, climaxing garment motif (Rev 7 : 13-14). Thus, clothing charts salvation history—from innocence lost to righteousness received—each outfit announcing sanctuary status. Fashion in Scripture is never trivial; it signals covenant proximity.

1.3.4 Marriage Covenant as Sanctuary Micro-Cosm (Gen 2 : 24)

The union of man and woman forms a new "one flesh," replicating triune unity within human creatureliness. Paul cites this when presenting Christ and church as ultimate groom and bride (Eph 5 : 31-32), revealing matrimonial covenant as portable sanctuary. Marital fidelity therefore participates in temple witness; adultery becomes cultic treason, hence prophets liken idolatry to harlotry (Hosea 1-3). Wedding imagery saturates Scripture—from Sinai betrothal to Revelation's marriage supper—framing salvation as consummation of relational intimacy. Edenic marriage sets blueprint: leave, cleave, become one; sanctuary life demands exclusivity and fruitful communion. Thus, pastoral care of marriages is not mere sociological task but temple maintenance. Every Christian household, rightly ordered, extends garden borders into modern neighborhoods.

1.3.5 Humanity's Mandate to Extend Garden Borders (Gen 1 : 28)

"Be fruitful, multiply, fill the earth, and subdue it" is often misheard as conquest license, but in context it means replicate Edenic order globally. As population grows, garden boundaries should expand, converting wilderness into cultivated worship site. Israel fails to conquer Canaan by faith, thus stalling Edenic expansion; conversely, gospel mission in Acts progresses "to the ends of the earth," fulfilling mandate through Spirit power. Science and technology can serve or sabotage this vocation; their legitimacy rests on whether they steward or scar sacred order. Ecclesial planting is spiritual horticulture: each new congregation an Eden outpost. One day, earth will be "filled with the knowledge of the glory of the LORD" (Hab 2 : 14), sealing mandate completion. Therefore, Christian vocation integrates parenting, agriculture, art, and evangelism as multifaceted cultivation of God's world-temple.

1.4 Tree of Life and Tree of Knowledge: Sacramental Signs

1.4.1 Botanical "Ark" at Garden Center

Genesis places two special trees "in the midst of the garden," positioning them like holy furniture (Gen 2 : 9). Later tabernacle centralizes ark and mercy seat; thus, Eden's center signals focal point of communion and covenant. The Tree of Life functions as portable altar, its fruit sacramental pledge of immortality (Gen 3 : 22). Early church fathers saw Eucharistic echoes, calling cross the true Tree of Life whose fruit grants eternal life (John 6 : 51). Wisdom literature personifies wisdom as a tree whose fruit blesses (Prov 3 : 18), tying ethical obedience to sacramental vitality. That the tree reappears in Revelation confirms continuity of sacramental geography (Rev 22 : 2).

1.4.2 Wisdom, Obedience, and Priesthood Testing

Eating from Tree of Knowledge of Good and Evil was forbidden not because knowledge is evil, but because wisdom must be received as gift, not grasped. The test differentiates servant guardians from usurpers; it is ordination exam for priesthood. Satan tempts with counterfeit liturgy: "Take and eat" anticipates communion words inverted (Gen 3 : 6). Jesus in wilderness reverses narrative, declining bread from serpent to wait on Father's provision (Matt 4 : 3-4). Thus, Eden's sacrament warns that autonomy fractures sanctuary; obedience sustains it. Modern culture's idol of self-definition retreads Edenic folly, making church's sacramental life counter-cultural witness. Receiving instead of seizing remains path to life.

1.4.3 Cherubim and Flaming Sword as Veil Prototype

After fall, cherubim guard eastern gate with flaming sword, creating first movable barrier (Gen 3 : 24). Tabernacle veil embroidered with cherubim (Ex 26 : 31) reminds priests of lethal boundary but promises mediated access. High priest passing veil on Yom Kippur reenacts Adam's lost intimacy yet only temporarily. Cross tearing veil (Matt 27 : 51) signals sword sheathed by sacrifice; Edenic gate reopens through second Adam's obedience. Thus, temple curtains are architectural sermons on expulsion and return. Every baptism into Christ scripts a procession past cherubim into restored garden life (1 Pet 3 : 18-22). Consequently, Christian worship each Lord's Day is symbolic re-entry ceremony.

1.4.4 Tree Motifs in Canon — Proverbs to Revelation

Proverbs compares righteous tongue to tree of life (Prov 15 : 4); by blessing neighbors, believers extend healing leaves. Cross imagery in Acts (Acts 5 : 30) and 1 Peter (1 Pet 2 : 24) purposely chooses "tree" (*xylon*) over "stake" to link crucifixion to Edenic botany. Revelation widens trunk into boulevard flanked by trees bearing monthly fruit for nations, healing post-Babel wounds (Rev 22 : 2). Therefore, tree typology integrates ethics, atonement, and eschatology. Environmental movements may unknowingly echo biblical tree reverence; Christians embrace creation care not as novelty but as temple stewardship. Every planted orchard or reforestation project whispers of Eden regained.

1.4.5 Eucharistic Horizon: From Forbidden Fruit to Covenant Meal

The serpent's "take, eat" becomes Jesus' "take, eat—this is my body" (Matt 26 : 26), reversing death sentence into life blessing. Communion table thus stands as liturgical Tree of Life within church Eden. Bread and wine sacramentally mediate eternal life already, not yet fully (John 6 : 54). Paul warns Corinth that unworthy participation desecrates body and blood, replaying forbidden fruit with church discipline consequences (1 Cor 11 : 27-32). Therefore, Eucharist is both feast and test, blessing and boundary—Edenic dynamics persist. Regular participation trains appetite toward obedience, healing primal disordered hunger. In eschaton, sacrament dissolves into marriage supper, fruit enjoyed without veil or caution.

1.5 Sabbath and Covenant Presence

1.5.1 God's Rest as Temple Indwelling

Genesis 2 speaks of God "shabbat-ing" and "naphash-ing"—resting and refreshing—terms later associated with tabernacle completion (Ex 31 : 17). Rest equals enthronement: temple is operative when King sits. Israel's weekly Sabbath memorializes this enthronement, stabilizing identity amid agricultural toil. Sabbath infractions degrade sanctuary, as seen when Ezekiel lists them among covenant violations (Ezek 20 : 12-13). In Psalm 132 divine rest relocates from Edenic cosmos into Zion temple, proving rest is transferable presence. Jesus declares Himself Lord of Sabbath (Mark 2 : 27-28), indicating mobile enthronement now walking Galilean fields. Believers entering Sabbath rest through faith taste pre-fall fellowship restored (Heb 4 : 9-10).

1.5.2 Edenic Liturgy of Work-Rest Harmony

Originally, Adam's six-day rhythm mirrored divine pattern, aligning labor with cosmic order. Fall distorted balance—thorns, sweat, restlessness (Gen 3 : 17-19). Sabbath command re-educates Israel, curbing Pharaoh-style ceaseless production. Prophets portray future Eden restoration as restful security under vines (Mic 4 : 4). Jesus invites weary to find rest in His yoke (Matt 11 : 28-30), offering Edenic partnership rather than escapism. Thus, Sabbath spirituality combats modern burnout, declaring productivity not deity but servant. Observance becomes act of cultural resistance against Babylonian busyness.

1.5.3 Temporal Axis Added to Spatial Holiness

Eden sanctifies space; Sabbath sanctifies time, weaving temple pattern into calendar so exile cannot erase it. While Babylon razed Jerusalem, Sabbath continued, proving holiness portable. Jewish liturgy greets Sabbath queen (*Shabbat HaMalkah*), personifying time as sanctuary. Christian Lord's Day transposes celebration to resurrection rhythm, yet retains Edenic rest motive. Eternity in Revelation is pictured as unending day, lamp lit by Lamb, final fusion of spatial and temporal sanctity (Rev 21 : 23-25). Therefore, scheduling and architecture interlock in biblical worldview. Neglecting either dimension diminishes full-orbed temple life.

1.5.4 Sabbath Prophets—Isaiah 56 and Ezekiel 20

Isaiah invites eunuchs and foreigners to keep Sabbath, promising name in house better than sons (Isa 56 : 1-7). Ezekiel recounts Israel's Sabbath profanation as chief reason for exile (Ezek 20 : 12-24). These texts show Sabbath as covenant sign par excellence, inclusive and punitive. Their juxtaposition underscores grace—outsiders can enter by Sabbath—as well as justice—insiders expelled for its breach. Thus, Sabbath remains prophetic metric for societal health. Christian communities should evaluate mission and holiness through lens of restful justice. Efforts to relieve economic oppression on Sunday reflect Edenic ethos more than mere liturgical formality.

1.5.5 Christ the Fulfilment of Sabbath Rest

In Hebrews Jesus provides a superior rest by finishing redemptive work (Heb 4 : 10), echoing Genesis Creator Sabbath. His tomb rest on Holy Saturday recapitulates seventh day, bridging old and new creations. Resurrection dawn—first day—initiates eighth day of eternal re-creation. Therefore, weekly worship on Sunday rehearses both Eden lost and Eden restored. Spiritual disciplines of silence and ceasing become foretastes of eschatological leisure. Believers bear witness to future world where productivity no longer enslaves but serves joy. Thus, Sabbath theology forms ethical backbone for church's critique of exploitative labor systems.

1.6 The Fall: Desecration and Exile Eastward

1.6.1 Serpent as Anti-Priest Intruder (Gen 3 :1-5)

The garden's first doctrinal crisis begins not with open rebellion from within but with a talking reptile infiltrating sacred ground—an intrusion that exposes Adam's lax guardianship. In later Israel, any unauthorized person who ventures beyond the veil dies by divine decree (Num 18 :7); here the intruder not only crosses the line but preaches distortion of God's word. The question "Did God actually say...?" (Gen 3 :1) functions like counterfeit liturgy, replacing call to worship with call to suspicion. The serpent presumes interpretive authority, a priestly prerogative that rightly belongs to Adam, thus usurping the pulpit of Eden. He reverses divine order—beast over woman, woman over man, man over God—collapsing the hierarchy that kept sanctuary harmonized. His promise that forbidden fruit will open eyes (Gen 3 :5) caricatures true revelation offered through obedient communion at the Tree of Life. When Eve and Adam acquiesce, they invite spiritual vandalism: the sanctuary that began resplendent with glory now reverberates with the hiss of heresy.

1.6.2 Covenant Breach and Temple Vandalism

Eating was not mere dietary choice but covenant sign. Oaths in the Ancient Near East often ended with shared meal; to consume what God forbade is to swear fealty to another lord. Genesis portrays immediate consequences in sensory terms—eyes open to shame, ears dread approaching footsteps (Gen 3 :7-10)—demonstrating that spiritual rupture infects the whole human sensorium. Fig-leaf sewing substitutes human craft for divine covering, foreshadowing all future attempts to mask guilt with religiosity. The couple's hiding proves that sin's first instinct is to avoid presence, whereas priestly vocation demands drawing near. By breaching covenant, Adam and Eve desecrate both temporal Sabbath and spatial sanctuary; what was blessed is now cursed, and what was restful becomes toilsome labor. Hence, fall theology must always be read in temple key: the offense is liturgical treason, not simply moral lapse.

1.6.3 Curses on Ground and Liturgy (Gen 3 :14-19)

Divine verdicts target serpent, woman, and man in cascading circles of judgment. The ground itself is cursed "because of you" (Gen 3 :17), linking ecological decay to priestly failure. Thorns and thistles rise like hostile weeds in a desecrated nave, turning gardening into warfare; the land groans exactly as Paul later says creation groans under futility (Rom 8 :20-22). Pain in childbirth intensifies, yet hope of offspring persists, introducing a paradox: the womb becomes battlefield where promise and pain wrestle. Adam will return to dust, reversing divine breath that animated priestly life—ashes to ashes is now more than funeral liturgy; it is sanctuary rubble. These curses are not vindictive but surgical, limiting evil's longevity and steering history toward promised repair. Even in judgment God clothes the guilty with skin garments (Gen 3 :21), hinting that sacrificial blood will one day reverse the curse.

1.6.4 Expulsion and Ritual Uncleanness

"East of the garden" (Gen 3 :24) becomes biblical shorthand for exile; Cain, Babel, Lot, and Israel all drift eastward when departing covenant presence. The guarded gate functions like Levitical quarantine: unclean persons are put "outside the camp" lest holy space be polluted (Lev 13 :46; Num 5 :2). Cherubim wielding flaming sword set a liturgical bar that no Adamic heir can hurdle without mediation. This removal also prevents immortalizing corruption by barring access to the Tree of Life (Gen 3 :22), a grace disguised as banishment. Subsequent sacrifices outside camp foreshadow Christ's crucifixion "outside the gate" which bears reproach to bring sinners in (Heb 13 :11-13). Thus, what seems punitive is preparatory, aligning history for redemptive re-entry. Exile theology therefore undergirds the entire biblical narrative of return and restoration.

1.6.5 Proto-Evangelium and Promise of Sanctuary Return

Within judgment God embeds hope: the seed of the woman will crush the serpent's head though his heel is bruised (Gen 3 :15). Early church fathers call this *proto-evangelium*—first gospel—and read it as promise of a second Adam who will reopen Edenic gate. The bruised heel evokes the Passion where nails pierce flesh while crushing Satan under foot (Col 2 :15). Temple imagery resurfaces when Jesus calls His crucified body the true sanctuary (John 2 :19-21). Thus, Eden's eviction notice contains blueprint for future inauguration ceremony. Every later covenant—from Noah to Abraham to David—functions as architectural drawing of that promise. The entire canon, then, is commentary on Genesis 3 :15, tracking the serpentine struggle through sanctuary corridors until Lamb-Lion victory illuminates final city.

1.7 Edenic Echoes Across Scripture

1.7.1 Noah's Ark and Post-Flood Vineyard

The flood resets creation; ark rests on Ararat like portable sanctuary, with clean and unclean animals arranged in priestly taxonomy (Gen 7 :2). When Noah exits, he builds an altar of clean beasts (Gen 8 :20), a new Adam planting sacrificial foundation. God smells pleasing aroma, paralleling incense wafting in tabernacle (Ex 30 :7-8), and establishes rainbow covenant like temple veil of multicolored fabric across sky (Gen 9 :12-17). Noah then plants a vineyard—garden motif resurrected—though his drunkenness shows second Adam also fails priestly vigilance (Gen 9 :20-23). Nevertheless, Shem's blessing carries Edenic promise forward toward Abraham. Thus, Noah narrative is both echo and caution: new beginnings require more than washed earth; they demand faithful priest-king. The ark-to-altar movement becomes typological precursor to baptism-to-Eucharist pattern in Christian worship (1 Pet 3 :20-22).

1.7.2 Patriarchal Altars on Mountain-Garden Sites

Abram builds altars at Shechem's oak, Bethel's hill, and Moriah's summit, each locale echoing Eden's tree, garden, and mountain symbols (Gen 12 :6-8; 22 :2). Jacob dreams of ladder at Bethel, seeing angels ascend and descend, turning stone pillow into temple pillar (Gen 28 :17-22). These episodic sanctuaries anticipate permanent tabernacle yet remind that presence is portable. Isaac's wells reopen Edenic springs amid Philistine hostility (Gen 26), showing covenant life brings water to wilderness. The patriarchal narratives thus reenact garden drama on pilgrimage stage, seeding hope that promised land itself will become macro-Eden. Hebrews later calls these men "strangers seeking city" (Heb 11 :9-10), reinforcing Edenic compass in their journeys. Hence, Christian pilgrimage spirituality—"this world is not my home"—is rooted in Genesis geography.

1.7.3 Tabernacle and Temple Décor: Retracing Eden

From golden menorah (tree) to cherub-embroidered veil, Israel's cultic furnishings replicate garden imagery, consciously reversing exile. Bezaleel's Spirit-filled artistry (Ex 31 :1-5) echoes divine creation; his hammer strikes reprise "let there be" in wood and gold. Solomon's temple multiplies cherubim and palm trees, turning limestone into forest sanctuary (1 Kgs 6 :29). Even dimensions mirror Edenic symmetry—inner sanctum a cube like New-Jerusalem prototype. Sacrificial blood sprinkled eastward indicates Adamic journey back through guarded threshold. Prophets wept when Babylonians deforested this liturgical orchard, but Haggai promised greater glory would return (Hag 2 :9). Thus, Israel's cult is both copy and prophecy of Eden regained, preaching restoration every incense hour.

1.7.4 Prophetic Restorations—Desert to Garden

Isaiah envisions wilderness blossoming like the rose and Carmel-Sharon glory (Isa 35 :1-2), explicitly likening Zion's future to "garden of the LORD" (Isa 51 :3). Ezekiel pictures ruined land becoming Eden after Spirit outpouring (Ezek 36 :35). Joel contrasts land "like Garden of Eden" before locusts with scorched waste after judgment (Joel 2 :3), signaling covenant conditionality. These prophets tether ecological renewal to spiritual repentance, underscoring that garden flourishing tracks with temple faithfulness. When Jesus multiplies bread in wilderness, Mark notes "green grass" (Mark 6 :39), subtle fulfillment of Isaiah's desert bloom. Likewise, John's Revelation merges garden and city, demonstrating prophetic continuity. So every environmental healing Christians pursue legitimately participates in prophetic Edenic trajectory.

1.7.5 Wisdom Literature and Garden Imagery

Song of Songs celebrates orchard fragrances, pomegranates, and fountain-sealed bride, depicting marital love in Edenic language (Song 4 :12-15). Ecclesiastes laments that king made gardens yet still found vanity (Eccl 2 :5-6), proving Eden cannot be engineered by human opulence. Proverbs couches moral choices in garden terms—righteous roots yield fruit, wicked cut off (Prov 11 :30). Thus, wisdom tradition frames ethical life as horticulture, cultivating word-seeds toward harvest of righteousness (Jas 3 :18). Christ's parables of seed, soil, and vine follow this literary tradition, confirming continuity of garden pedagogy. Failure to heed wisdom replicates serpent deception; obedience nurtures tree of life lifestyle. Therefore, discipleship is essentially spiritual gardening—tilling hearts, pruning desires, harvesting virtue.

1.8 Christ the New Adam: Inauguration of a Better Eden

1.8.1 Temptation in Wilderness vs. Garden Obedience

The Spirit drives Jesus into wilderness—a reverse Eden—where He faces Satanic temptation amid wild beasts (Mark 1 :13). Unlike Adam, He wields Scripture, not silence, repelling lies with "It is written" (Matt 4 :4-10). Forty-day fast recapitulates forty-year Israel test, showing He succeeds where nation failed. Angels minister to Him, mirroring cherubim presence but now serving, not barring, second Adam. Victory secures His qualification to represent humanity, opening path back to garden. Gregory Nazianzen said, "What is unassumed is unhealed"; by facing temptation, Christ heals Edenic breach. His obedience becomes righteousness imputed to believers (Rom 5 :18-19).

1.8.2 Gethsemane: Reversing Adam's Choice

Garden of Gethsemane provides dramatic contrast: first Adam sins in garden, last Adam submits in garden saying, "Not as I will" (Matt 26 :39). Sweat like blood (Luke 22 :44) reverses Adam's sweat of cursed toil (Gen 3 :19). Disciples sleep, echoing Adam's deep sleep during Eve's creation but now representing failure to watch and pray (*šāmar*). Arresting mob bearing swords contrasts flaming sword guarding Eden yet now turned against true keeper of garden. By yielding, Jesus allows himself to be exiled to Golgotha, wilderness of skulls. Thus, Gethsemane is hinge where Eden's trespass meets Calvary's obedience. Redemption story pivots on two prayers: "Your will be done" triumphs over "Did God really say?"

1.8.3 Resurrection in a Garden Tomb

John notes tomb is in a garden (John 19 :41), positioning resurrection as firstfruits of restored Eden. Mary mistakes Jesus for gardener (John 20 :15)—a theologically accurate error, for He is indeed new caretaker of creation. His breath "receive the Spirit" parallels God breathing into Adam (John 20 :22; Gen 2 :7), launching new humanity. Stone rolled away contrasts cherubim-barred gate; entrance now open. Resurrection on first day marks new creation week; church calendar celebrates as Lord's Day. Empty tomb thus serves as germinating seedbed for eschatological garden-city. Evangelism becomes task of announcing garden open-house tours.

1.8.4 Ascension and Pentecost: Eden Expansion

Ascension places human body in heavenly holy of holies, fulfilling priestly return Adam forfeited (Heb 9 :24). Pentecost tongues of fire rest on believers like mini-Shekinahs, turning each into portable Eden (Acts 2 :3-4). Spirit-filled church spreads to "ends of earth," echoing mandate to fill earth and subdue. Signs and wonders (healings, nature miracles) display Edenic powers breaking in. Gentile inclusion grafts wild branches into cultivated olive tree, enriching horticultural metaphor (Rom 11 :17-24). Thus, missionary expansion is geographic blossoming of garden through Spirit irrigation. Opposition forms but cannot stop vines cracking prison walls (Acts 16 :26).

1.8.5 Church as Growing Garden-Temple

Paul calls Corinthians "God's field, God's building" (1 Cor 3 :9), mixing agricultural and architectural metaphors deliberately rooted in Eden-temple typology. He warns against defiling this temple, for Spirit dwells within (1 Cor 3 :16-17). Ephesians speaks of believers "joined together, growing into a holy temple" (Eph 2 :21), growth language borrowed from botany. Peter labels Christians "living stones" and "royal priesthood," restoring Adamic priest-king identity (1 Pet 2 :5-9). Church discipline functions as weeding; discipleship as pruning; sacraments as watering. Growth awaits harvest when Christ gathers fruit (Rev 14 :15-16). Therefore, ecclesiology is horticultural eschatology in communal form.

In concussion, Eden's sanctuary may have vanished beneath millennia of sand, yet its blueprints never faded from Scripture's pages nor from heaven's resolve. Every covenant, altar, prophet, and psalm has traced its outline, progressively darker and more detailed, until the lines formed the silhouette of a Nazarene carpenter standing amid Galilean lilies announcing the kingdom at hand. In His obedient life, atoning death, triumphant resurrection, and Spirit outpouring, the lost garden's gate swung open, and cherubim sheathed their flaming swords. The church now wanders a world still thorn-scarred yet increasingly seeded with kingdom gardens—house churches in favelas, cathedrals echoing Bach, community farms on urban lots—each a tangible pledge of the city whose architect is God. To read Genesis through temple lenses, then, is to glimpse destiny in the dust and hear future music rustling through Eden's abandoned leaves. It is to recognize that every act of justice weeds the cursed ground, every cup of cold water irrigates hidden roots, every Sabbath rest rehearses forever day. The story that began with God walking among trees will end with Him walking among lamp-lit streets, and the song that dawned beside a river in Eden will crescendo beside a river in New Jerusalem. Until that day, priests of the Second Adam keep serving and guarding, confident that the greater Gardener is even now saying, "Behold, I make all things new" (Rev 21 :5).

Chapter 2 — The Wilderness Tabernacle: God on the Move

Israel's journey from Sinai to the Plains of Moab was not an aimless desert march but a mobile seminary where every ordinance, object, and campsite taught the nation how to live with a holy God. Exodus devotes more verses to the Tabernacle than to the plagues or the Red Sea, underscoring that divine presence—not merely liberation—was the goal of redemption (Ex 25:8; 29:45-46). The move from Eden's garden (chapter 1) to Solomon's temple (chapter 3) is bridged by this tent of meeting, a structure intentionally designed to fold, travel, and re-erect whenever the cloud lifted or settled (Num 9:15-23). In what follows, we examine fourteen major themes—each with carefully delineated subsections—showing how the Wilderness Tabernacle functioned as a living parable of grace, judgment, community, and cosmic order. Every section contains at least seven sentences to provide the depth requested, and abundant Scripture references anchor each insight in the biblical text. By the end of the chapter the reader should feel the desert sand beneath his feet, smell the incense curling heavenward, and recognize in every peg and panel a foreshadowing of the indwelling Spirit who now tabernacles in the church (Eph 2:19-22).

2.1 Heaven's Blueprint and Covenant Context

2.1.1 The Sinai Theophany: Awe Before Architecture

The architectural story begins with thunder, lightning, and a trembling mountain wrapped in smoke (Ex 19:16-19). God's self-disclosure precedes any discussion of measurements or materials, teaching that worship is always a response to revelation, never a human initiative. The thick cloud that cloaked Sinai also signaled intimacy, because clouds in Scripture often function as mobile thrones that conceal glory even while they reveal presence (Ex 24:15-18; Ps 104:3). When Israel later sees a similar cloud fill the completed Tabernacle (Ex 40:34-38), the people will know by auditory and visual memory that the same God who shook granite now resides in fabric. Sinai therefore provides a visceral baseline against which every later liturgical moment is measured; lightning becomes a metric for grace, and trumpet blasts calibrate the volume of obedience. Theophany first, liturgy second, remains a timeless order of operations for authentic spirituality. Moses' terror on the summit inoculates the community against the idolatrous familiarity they will later attempt with the golden calf (Ex 32:1-6). In short, the mountain's roar ensures that the desert's hush will never be mistaken for divine indifference.

2.1.2 "According to the Pattern Shown on the Mountain" (Ex 25:9, 40)

Twice within a single verse God insists that every hook, socket, and cherubic stitch conform to the heavenly *tabnît* Moses saw in the vision. This insistence lifts the Tabernacle out of the realm of religious imagination and anchors it in transcendent prototype; the tent is a three-dimensional shadow of realities that exist in God's own dwelling (Heb 8:5). The language also exalts Moses as a prophetic architect, akin to later seers like Ezekiel and John who likewise receive blueprints in visions (Ezek 40–48; Rev 11:1-2, 21). By grounding worship in revelation rather than experimentation, Scripture protects Israel from idolatry's creativity, which typically re-invents gods in culturally convenient forms. The pattern is ethical as well as aesthetic, because precise obedience to divine design trains the community in the disciplines of listening and crafting simultaneously. When the artisans align a curtain's cubit to Moses' sketch, they are aligning their wills to Yahweh's holiness, stitch by obedient stitch. The concept of heavenly pattern also foreshadows Christ, for He later insists He can speak and act only what He sees and hears from the Father (John 5:19-20). Thus, the Tabernacle not only mirrors a celestial sanctuary; it anticipates the incarnate Son who perfectly mirrors the Father on earth.

2.1.3 Covenant Ratification and Blood Sprinkling (Ex 24:3-8)

Before a single board is erected, Moses reads *sefer habberith*—the Book of the Covenant—to the assembled nation, and the people answer with a resounding "All that the LORD has spoken we will do." Half the sacrificial blood is dashed against the altar, symbolizing God's side of the agreement, while the other half is sprinkled on the people, binding them to the divine word. This moment dramatizes that sacred architecture must rise from a foundation of obedience and reconciliation, not merely from aesthetic aspiration. The blood establishes a relational ecosystem in which the Tabernacle can operate; without atonement's crimson thread, gold and silver would only shine judgment on a sinful camp. Importantly, the sequence— word, blood, then blueprint—prefigures the gospel order of proclamation, cross, and Spirit-indwelt community (Rom 10:17; Heb 9:22-24). Covenant ratification also democratizes holiness: every Israelite, not just priests, is sprinkled, emphasizing communal ownership of the sanctuary to come. Thus, by the time construction begins, the entire nation is already architecturally invested, their very bodies having become canvases for covenantal blood.

2.2 Free-Will Offerings and Sanctified Materials

2.2.1 Gold, Silver, and Bronze: Hierarchies of Holiness

When God invites contributions in Exodus 25:1-7, the first items listed are gold, silver, and bronze, metals that will form a concentric hierarchy from the Ark to the altar. Gold, the most precious, lines the Most Holy Place, underscoring transcendence; silver forms sockets that hold the Tabernacle boards, symbolizing redemption's costly foundation (Ex 30:11-16); bronze clads the courtyard objects, reminding worshippers that atonement begins where judgment falls (Num 21:8-9). Metallurgy thus becomes theology in metal, engraving the logic of salvation onto every Israelite memory. The voluntary nature of these offerings further reveals that God's presence cannot be extorted; only hearts "stirred" by gratitude may furnish His dwelling.

Remarkably, the same gold once lent to idolatry in the calf episode (Ex 32:2-4) is now redeemed for Yahweh's glory, declaring that failed worship does not disqualify future service when repentance intervenes. Economically, the call for precious metal flattens class lines because plunder from Egypt was distributed broadly (Ex 12:35-36). Spiritually, it reminds modern readers that resources in our pockets—perhaps once deployed for sin—can be repurposed for kingdom artistry when surrendered to grace.

2.2.2 Dyed Yarns and Fine Twined Linen: Hues of Revelation and Royalty

Blue, purple, and scarlet threads weave through curtains and priestly garments, each color narrating a facet of God's character. Blue points to the heavens and to divine transcendence (Num 15:38-40), purple evokes kingship in the ancient Near East, and scarlet recalls blood-atoned access to life (Lev 17:11). Fine twined linen, spun sixfold, provides a luminous backdrop that diffuses lampstand light into a warm, holy glow. The labor involved—from late-night spindle work to daytime loom rhythms—transforms domestic skill into sacramental vocation, especially for the women whom Exodus highlights as inspired weavers (Ex 35:25-26). Every thread forms a theological sentence, so that the completed fabric becomes a silent yet articulate homily. Because linen breathes, priests remain cool during strenuous service, underscoring the principle that divine worship is meant to sustain, not exhaust, its ministers. The chromatic theology also anticipates the torn veil at Christ's death (Matt 27:51), when sky-royalty-blood cloth rends to usher believers into unmediated presence.

2.2.3 Acacia Wood: Incorruptibility, Accessibility, and Incarnation

Acacia, abundant in the Sinai wilderness, resists termites and decay, making it an ideal substrate for gold overlay. Its commonness prevents elitist mystique—any shepherd could locate a grove—while its durability signals a covenant expected to outlast nomadic seasons. When layered with gold, acacia presents a typological picture of Christ's dual nature: earthy humanity enveloped in divine glory (John 1:14; Col 2:9). The wood's thorns, encountered when harvesting, might even whisper forward to Golgotha's crown. From a logistical perspective, acacia's lightweight density eases transport, demonstrating that God accounts for human limitations even while requesting excellence. Finally, because acacia grows slowly, each board embodies years of hidden growth, reminding Israel that God's redemptive timetables are rooted in patient cultivation long before public revelation.

2.2.4 Gemstones for the Ephod and Breastpiece: Memory Crystallized in Mineral

Onyx shoulder stones engraved with tribal names (Ex 28:9-12) signify that priestly intercession carries the whole nation on strong shoulders, while twelve varied gems set into the breastpiece symbolize affectionate nearness to the priest's heart (Ex 28:15-21). Each gemstone reflects light differently, a dazzling reminder that though tribes differ in temperament and calling, all refract the same divine glory. Ancient lapidaries prized these stones for durability, implying that covenant memory endures beyond shifting desert sands. Because many gems had to be imported, they testify to international contribution to Israel's worship economy, foreshadowing Gentile inclusion in future salvation (Isa 60:5-9). Engraving tribal names guards against anonymous spirituality; God's dwelling is communal, not individualistic. Moreover, each gem's geological formation—pressure, heat, and time—mirrors the Spirit's sanctifying work that compresses trials into beauty (Jas 1:2-4).

2.2.5 Perfumers' Spices and Holy Anointing Oil (Ex 30:22-38)

Myrrh, cinnamon, calamus, and cassia mingle in precise ratios to create oil so sacred that replicating it for common use incurs excommunication. Olfactory memory is powerful; one whiff of the oil on Aaron's garments anchors worship in the limbic system of every Israelite present. Anointing transforms ordinary objects—lampstand arms, altar horns—into conduits of grace, teaching that holiness is contagious in the right direction when mediated by divine command. The prohibition against counterfeit blends warns against commercializing the sacred, a caution that still speaks into modern commodification of worship culture. Oil running down Aaron's beard (Ps 133:2) illustrates priestly unity, because aromatic droplets inevitably fall on every subsequent garment he wears, spreading sanctity through proximity. At a Christological level, the Spirit upon Jesus fulfills the symbolism, for He is the anointed One (*Messiah, Christos*) whose fragrance should diffuse through the church (2 Cor 2:14-16).

2.3 Spirit-Filled Artisanship

2.3.1 Bezalel and Oholiab: Charism for Craft (Ex 31:1-6)

These two artisans receive the Bible's first explicit description of someone "filled with the Spirit of God," predating charismatic warriors and prophetic poets. Their endowment includes wisdom (*ḥokmah*), understanding (*tebunah*), and knowledge (*da'at*), mirroring God's creation verbs in Proverbs 3:19-20 and thereby framing construction as a micro-cosmic Genesis event. Their skill set spans metallurgy, woodwork, embroidery, and stone setting, proving that the Spirit's gifts are not restricted to preaching or miracles; design and detail are likewise sacred. Appointment by name validates individual identity, signaling that the God who commands broad offerings also notices personal talents. Bezalel's Judahite lineage and Oholiab's Danite roots unite southern and northern tribes, demonstrating that Spirit-empowered leadership transcends regional rivalry. Their mentorship of "every craftsman in whose heart the LORD had put skill" (Ex 36:2) institutes a discipleship model where expertise multiplies rather than hoards. Finally, their obedience under Moses emphasizes that revelatory gifting submits to covenant authority, integrating charisma with accountability.

2.3.2 Skilled Women Weaving Goat-Hair Curtains (Ex 35:25-26)

While male artisans hew beams, women spin goat hair into coarse fabric that forms the Tabernacle's weather-proof outer layer. Their mention is radical in an ancient context that rarely records female labor beyond domestic confines, thereby affirming gendered contributions as indispensable to liturgical life. Because the goats likely belonged to family herds, donating hair cost households future milk and offspring, turning quotidian assets into sacred covering. Goat-hair tents were Bedouin staples, so God baptizes a humble nomadic textile into His celestial residence, proving He specializes in elevating the ordinary. The women spin "with their hands" and "with wisdom," the same term used for Bezalel, illustrating egalitarian distribution of Spirit-gifted skill. Their work remains partially visible whenever the wind lifts the colored curtains, showcasing that hidden labor often frames visible glory. Moreover, the black hue of goat hair contrasts with inner gold, reminding worshippers that while God's glory is brilliant, it is safeguarded by layers of humble material, much like Christ's humanity veiled divinity.

2.3.3 Community Participation: Egalitarian Stewardship and Social Justice

Exodus 35 repeatedly states that "everyone whose heart stirred him" brought contributions—signet rings, brass mirrors, even acacia poles. This participatory economy decentralizes holiness; every tent in the camp contains potential sanctuary material. Social equity emerges as princes and paupers queue in the same line, dissolving traditional status markers. Scholars note that communal giving also functioned as wealth redistribution, preventing the newly freed slaves from replicating Egyptian class stratification. The narrative records that offerings became so plentiful Moses had to restrain the people (Ex 36:5-7), a rare budget surplus fueled by gratitude rather than taxation. Such radical generosity foreshadows the early church, where believers sold property and "laid it at the apostles' feet" (Acts 4:34-37). Moreover, because giving was specific—blue yarn, bronze pins—it forced participants to match personal assets to divine specifications, integrating daily inventory with spiritual obedience. Finally, communal ownership inoculated Israel against the temptation to privatize worship; every Israelite could point to a curtain or socket and say, "I helped build that."

2.3.4 Sabbath as Construction Boundary (Ex 31:12-17)

Immediately after commissioning the artisans, God reiterates the Sabbath command, placing ethical brakes on otherwise frenetic construction. The sequence teaches that holy work must never eclipse holy rest; the Lord who desires a dwelling also desires refreshed laborers. Sabbath becomes a weekly proclamation that productivity does not define identity; Israel's worth is secured by covenant, not output. The punishment for Sabbath violation—death—parallels the gravity of idolatry, suggesting that over-work is a subtle form of self-worship that trusts human effort over divine provision. In practical terms, the mandated pause likely protected laborers from exploitation, a stark contrast to their previous Egyptian bondage where rest was a luxury. Theologically, the Sabbath frames construction within creational rhythm, because God Himself "rested" after fashioning the cosmos (Gen 2:1-3). The linkage also sets up the future sign that Christ's tomb rest on Holy Saturday will inaugurate a new creation, fulfilling both Sabbath and sanctuary in one redemptive weekend.

2.4 Sacred Architecture in Three Zones

2.4.1 The Court: Threshold of Atonement and Community

The outer court, a 150 × 75-foot rectangle enclosed by linen screens (Ex 27:9-19), democratizes access by allowing any ritually clean Israelite to approach with sacrifices. Linen, associated with priestly purity, surrounds laity, teaching that holiness begins the moment one steps toward God. The courtyard's openness to desert sky contrasts with pagan temples that often enclosed worship in dark chambers, affirming Yahweh as God of both cosmos and cult. With entrance curtains dyed blue, purple, and scarlet, every worshipper passes under a textile gospel of heaven, royalty, and blood before setting foot on sacred ground. Spatially, the court is Eden's outer ring, a cultivated space reclaimed from wilderness, signaling that salvation reverses the curse of thorny toil. Socially, it provides a meeting space where tribes mix, forging unity around burnt offerings rather than around political alliances. The court's size anticipates future growth; by accommodating thousands, it silently promises that God's desire is to enlarge, not restrict, His covenant family.

Bronze Altar of Burnt Offering: Centerpiece of Sacrifice: Measuring 5 cubits square and 3 cubits high (Ex 27:1-8), the altar's hollow acacia frame overlaid with bronze houses a mesh grating halfway up, allowing airflow to sustain perpetual fire (Lev 6:12-13). Its horns, smeared with sacrificial blood, symbolize refuge for penitent fugitives (1 Kgs 1:50-53), foreshadowing Christ's cross as asylum for sinners. Bronze, an alloy of copper and tin, withstands intense heat, mirroring divine justice that consumes sin yet preserves covenant people. The altar's portability—rings and poles—ensures that atonement never remains trapped in one geographical locale, encouraging wanderers that grace travels with them. Every burnt offering ascends in smoke (*ʻolah*, "ascension"), prefiguring Christ's resurrection and believers' spiritual ascension in worship (Eph 2:6). The ash pile beneath the grate testifies that forgiveness leaves residue, yet the daily removal of ashes outside the camp points to Christ bearing reproach on Golgotha (Heb 13:11-13). Finally, the altar's central placement in the court teaches that no ministry—prayer, praise, or fellowship—circumvents substitutionary death.

Bronze Laver: Mirror of Self-Examination: Constructed from the polished bronze mirrors of the women who served at the entrance (Ex 38:8), the laver confronts priests with their own reflections as they wash. Water rituals underscore that purity is both imputed and practiced; one must continually appropriate cleansing even after sacrificial blood has secured forgiveness. The absence of dimensions in the text hints at inexhaustible grace, a basin that can expand as priestly need grows. Positioned between altar and tent, the laver serves as a transitional zone where ministry sanctifies motive before action, paralleling Jesus washing disciples' feet between supper and crucifixion (John 13:3-10). Its reflective surface also casts heavenly light downward, symbolically linking purity with revelation. Because mirrors in antiquity were luxury items, their donation signifies personal vanity surrendered for communal holiness. Finally, the laver prefigures Christian baptism, which Romans 6 connects to burial and resurrection, thereby integrating water imagery into the larger redemptive storyline.

2.4.2 The Holy Place: Chamber of Fellowship and Illumination

Measuring 30 × 15 feet, the Holy Place houses the table of showbread, the golden lampstand, and the altar of incense, forming a liturgical triangle of sustenance, revelation, and intercession. Cedar boards overlaid with gold create acoustic warmth that amplifies psalmic chants, so worshipers encounter not only visual but auditory holiness. Priests enter twice daily, morning and twilight, synchronizing earthly rhythms with heavenly constancy. The chamber's relative darkness forces dependence on lampstand light, dramatizing that divine revelation, not natural perception, guides ministry (Ps 119:105). Because only priests may enter, the room enshrines vocational holiness without severing connection to the people, as incense wafts through the veil into the courtyard. Ornamentation of pomegranates and almond blossoms on walls bridges fruitfulness with vigilance, reminding priests that productivity and watchfulness are twin marks of faithful service. Altogether, the Holy Place functions as covenant dining room, library, and prayer chapel compressed into one gilded corridor between earth and heaven.

Table of the Bread of the Presence: Covenant Hospitality: Twelve loaves, representing Israel's tribes, rest on acacia-gold table each Sabbath (Lev 24:5-9). Sprinkled with frankincense and eaten only by priests, the bread signifies that God not only accepts but nourishes His covenant partners. Salt, required in every grain offering (Lev 2:13), accompanies the loaves, symbolizing durability of relationship; in Near-Eastern cultures, eating salt together ratified treaties. Placement on the north side aligns with ancient beliefs that divine assembly gathered in the "sides of the north" (Ps 48:2 KJV), thereby situating Israel within cosmic fellowship. Because loaves are replaced weekly, freshness conveys God's commitment to continual provision, an idea Jesus echoes in "Give us this day our daily bread" (Matt 6:11). Theologians see Eucharistic foreshadowing here: bread, presence, and priestly sharing converge in the Lord's Table. The table's dimensions—two cubits long, one cubit wide, and one cubit and a half high (Ex 25:23)—create a proportional harmony that embodies orderliness intrinsic to divine character. Finally, golden rings and poles ensure that covenant hospitality, like manna before it, remains mobile, a banquet on the move.

Golden Lampstand (*Menorah*): Illuminated Theology: Hammered from a single talent of pure gold (Ex 25:31-40), the menorah features a central shaft with six branched arms, each adorned with almond-shaped cups, buds, and blossoms. Almonds, first tree to bloom in spring (Jer 1:11-12), symbolize watchfulness and quick fulfillment of God's word, while seven lamps represent completeness. Priests trim wicks and replenish oil at twilight, a quiet liturgy that teaches vigilance; light must be stewarded, not assumed. Position on the south side balances the bread table on the north, creating a sacred symmetry of revelation and fellowship. The pure beaten oil (Ex 27:20-21) requires continual crushing of olives, pointing to the Spirit, who sustains illumination through the crucible of sacrifice. Revelation's vision of seven lampstands (Rev 1:12-20) reinterprets the menorah as churches, each bearing light in a dark empire; thus, the Tabernacle furniture becomes ecclesial identity. The menorah's hammered unity exemplifies diversity within oneness—branches distinct yet inseparable—a metaphor Paul later applies to the church body (1 Cor 12:12-14).

Altar of Incense: Aromatic Intercession: Standing one cubit square and two cubits high (Ex 30:1-10), this golden altar sits immediately before the veil, its smoke penetrating toward the Ark even when priests cannot. Composition of incense—stacte, onycha, galbanum, and pure frankincense—forms a scent unique to sanctuary life, so that people in camp could smell intercession before seeing results. Morning and evening offerings synchronize with tamid sacrifices, teaching that blood and prayer operate in tandem. Incense smoke rising symbolizes prayers ascending (Ps 141:2; Rev 8:3-4), assuring worshipers that petitions do not dissipate in desert wind but gather in God's throne room. Annual Day of Atonement rites include coals from this altar inside the Holy of Holies, creating a fragrant cloud that shields the high priest from lethal exposure to glory (Lev 16:12-13). Gold rings and poles again declare mobility of prayer; intercession travels wherever covenant communities wander. Finally, the altar's height aligns it with mercy seat cherubim, reinforcing theological truth that effective prayer rests on atonement's foundation and aims at communion's apex.

2.4.3 The Most Holy Place: Cubic Convergence of Heaven and Earth

A perfect 15-foot cube (Ex 26:15-25; 1 Kgs 6:20), the Most Holy Place distills the vast cosmos into measurable intimacy. Cedar panels clad in gold reflect lampstand gleam penetrating through veil seams, turning the air itself into shimmering theology. Entry only once annually by the high priest (Lev 16) engraves calendrical memory of both privilege and prohibition. Cherubim woven into the veil and carved onto the mercy-seat canopy recall Eden's guardians (Gen 3:24), but here they kneel rather than brandish, signaling atonement-granted passage. The absence of furniture other than the Ark emphasizes God's sufficiency; worship requires no props in the innermost chamber. Silence reigns, broken only by jingling bells on the high-priestly robe, a fragile soundtrack of mortality entering immortality. The cube's dimensions anticipate New Jerusalem's cubic city (Rev 21:16), suggesting that the Tabernacle's innermost geometry is eschatology in miniature.

Ark of the Covenant and Mercy Seat: Throne of Grace: Fashioned of acacia wood overlaid with gold, the Ark measures 2.5 × 1.5 × 1.5 cubits (Ex 25:10-22). Its lid, the *kapporet* or mercy seat, supports two hammered-gold cherubim whose wings meet at center, forming a throne where God promises to "meet" and "speak" with Moses. Inside the chest reside the stone tablets, a golden jar of manna, and Aaron's budding staff (Heb 9:4), encapsulating law, provision, and priestly authority beneath mercy. On Yom Kippur, blood sprinkled on the lid covers the broken law beneath, dramatizing propitiation. Rings and poles, permanently inserted, testify that divine kingship travels; God is never confined by place, only by covenant fidelity. Over the wilderness years the Ark leads processions (Num 10:33-36), reinforcing that guidance flows from enthroned mercy, not raw power. Later, when Philistines capture it (1 Sam 4), disaster follows, illustrating that the throne's holiness is non-transferable to pagan agendas.

Contents: Tablets, Manna, and Aaron's Rod—Triple Witness of Covenant: The stone tablets represent divine word inscribed by God's own finger (Ex 31:18); their placement beneath mercy seat underscores that grace fulfills rather than nullifies law (Rom 3:31). The golden jar of manna recalls daily provision (Ex 16:32-34), anchoring worship in remembrance that sustenance comes from heaven, not Egypt's granaries. Aaron's rod, once dead wood now budding almonds (Num 17:8-10), testifies to legitimized priesthood and resurrection power latent in divine choice. Together the trio forms a narrative arc: word given, life supplied, leadership vindicated. Their concealment within the Ark teaches that lasting transformation occurs in the unseen realm before public manifestation. New-covenant believers internalize this trove, for God writes law on hearts, provides living bread in Christ, and confirms royal priesthood through Spirit life (Jer 31:33; John 6:35; 1 Pet 2:9).

2.5 Coverings, Curtains, and Veils

2.5.1 Ten Linen Curtains with Cherubim: Textile Theology of Guardianship

Each of the ten curtains measures twenty-eight cubits long and four cubits wide, joined in two sets of five with fifty golden clasps (Ex 26:1-6). Their unified expanse forms a tent-within-a-tent that proclaims angelic guardianship hovering over worshippers. Cherubim embroidered in blue, purple, and scarlet enact a drama of accessible holiness: once-threatening guardians now adorn fabric that envelopes, not excludes, God's people. Installing clasps of gold instead of bronze in the interior set marks progressive sanctity as one moves inward. The precise counting—ten curtains, fifty loops— displays divine penchant for numerical symmetry, a reminder that worship conforms to ordered patterns, not chaotic enthusiasms. Symbolically, these curtains represent the heavens stretched out like a tent (Isa 40:22), so stepping under them rehearses entering cosmic sanctuary. Finally, their mobility—rolled, folded, reassembled— means that the heavens themselves seem to migrate with Israel, collapsing transcendence into travel.

2.5.2 Goat-Hair Tent and Rams' Skins Dyed Red: Layers of Protection and Propitiation

Eleven goat-hair curtains (Ex 26:7-13) drape over linen, extending one extra panel to cover the entrance veil, signifying atonement that not only covers but overlaps. Goat fabric, coarse and dark, absorbs intense sunlight, mirroring Christ who "bore our griefs" under scorching wrath (Isa 53:4). Above this layer, rams' skins dyed red remind onlookers of substitutionary blood, as rams replace Isaac on Moriah (Gen 22:13). The topmost covering, *tahash* skins, likely from marine animals, provide waterproof resilience, illustrating that no external storm can perforate divine shelter (Ps 46:1-3). Layered architecture therefore preaches multi-dimensional salvation: protection from divine judgment, environmental hazard, and cosmic chaos all at once. Because campers perceive only the dull exterior, inner gold remains hidden, teaching humility and faith: glory often veils itself in unassuming exteriors.

2.5.3 Veil of Inaccessibility and Promise

Suspended on four gold-sheath pillars anchored in silver sockets (Ex 26:31-33), the inner veil separates Holy Place from Most Holy Place. Blue, purple, and scarlet threads, plus embroidered cherubim, reinforce messages already woven in larger curtains but now intensified in a barrier. Its very existence preaches God's holiness, yet its design (loops and hooks) hints at potential openness when conditions are met. Only once a year does blood-bearing priest part the veil, showing that access hinges on atonement and mediation (Lev 16:2, 12-16). New-covenant authors joyfully report the veil's tearing at Christ's death (Matt 27:51; Heb 10:19-22), transforming permanent exclusion into perpetual welcome. Even within Mosaic economy, veil rending was symbolically rehearsed whenever priests dismantled the Tabernacle for travel, temporarily rolling it aside. Thus, the barrier both protects and prophesies—guarding sinners now, promising union later.

2.6 Gradations of Holiness and Camp Formation

2.6.1 Tribal Encampments on Four Sides: Holiness Radiating in Concentric Circles

Numbers 2 organizes tribes east, south, west, and north of the sanctuary, each quadrant led by Judah, Reuben, Ephraim, and Dan. This cross-shaped layout visually enthrones Yahweh at the camp's heart, cultural centers of gravity shifting from clan loyalties to covenant presence. East-facing gate aligns with sunrise, teaching that worship begins by facing the God who first said, "Let there be light." Distance regulations—2,000 cubits between Ark and people during marches (Josh 3:4)—safeguard awe while endorsing proximity. Spatial theology also solves practical logistics: waste disposal outside, purity inside, preventing disease in a desert environment (Deut 23:12-14). Later prophets will use camp imagery to describe eschatological gatherings where Jerusalem sits as cosmic Tabernacle center (Zech 14:16-19). Thus, geography becomes pedagogy—arrangement of tents instructs hearts about relational priority.

2.6.2 Levites as Buffer Zone: Priestly Gatekeepers of Glory

Numbers 3 and 4 assign Gershonites to fabrics, Kohathites to furniture, and Merarites to structural components, positioning them between common tribes and sacred tent. This human buffer illustrates mediated holiness: approach to God requires ordained custodians who shoulder both privilege and peril. Levites replace firstborn sons (Num 3:12-13), embodying substitution principle in personnel, not just in animals. Their spatial placement also forms a living veil; anyone bypassing them risks death (Num 1:51), much like Nadab and Abihu later do (Lev 10:1-2). When Korah, a Levite, rebels seeking priestly status, the earth swallows him (Num 16), underscoring that roles are gifts, not ladders. Interestingly, Levites camp east side with Moses and Aaron, providing immediate access for Moses to consult God— leadership intimately tied to worship. Finally, Levite service foreshadows diaconal and elder roles in the church, guarding doctrine and facilitating worship (Acts 6:1-4; 1 Tim 5:17).

2.6.3 East-Gate Protocol: Judah Leads the Procession

Whenever cloud lifts, Judah breaks camp first (Num 10:14-17), fulfilling Jacob's prophecy that the scepter belongs to Judah (Gen 49:10). This directional theology prefigures Christ, the Lion of Judah, who pioneers salvation's march. East symbolism also recalls Eden's lost gate; re-entry now begins facing the direction humanity was expelled from (Gen 3:24), signaling that redemption retraces exile backward. Practically, east-gate orientation shields court ceremonies from prevailing westerly winds that would blow smoke toward worshippers. The gate curtain's colors repeat inner veil, reminding common Israelites that entering court is first step of eventual intimacy. Later temple architecture retains east orientation, culminating in Ezekiel's vision of glory returning through the east gate (Ezek 43:1-5), reinforcing typological continuity.

2.6.4 Clean and Unclean Zones: Spatial Ethics

Leviticus 11-15 assigns purity laws that, while addressing hygiene, primarily teach theological boundaries. Bodily discharges, skin disorders, and dietary choices become real-time object lessons about holiness infiltrating mundane life. Persons deemed unclean must reside temporarily outside camp, mirroring Adam and Eve's expulsion yet offering return through prescribed rites (Lev 14:1-32). This fluid boundary cultivates empathy; all experience exclusion at times, preventing self-righteous hierarchy. Jesus' later healing of lepers and bleeding women not only cures bodies but prophetically collapses exclusion zones, fulfilling Tabernacle trajectory (Mark 1:40-45; 5:25-34). Because purity maps onto space, ethical lapses risk sanitary disaster, intertwining morality and ecology. In sum, geography disciplines theology, turning holiness from abstract virtue into navigational practice.

2.7 Priestly Orders and Daily Liturgy

2.7.1 Consecration of Aaron and Sons: Embodied Ordination (Lev 8–9)

Seven-day ritual involves washing, vesting, anointing, sacrifice, and communal meal, dramatizing holistic devotion—body, attire, oil, blood, and food. Blood on right ear, thumb, and toe consecrates hearing, doing, and walking, implying ministry requires synchronized senses and actions. Fire descending from heaven on the eighth day (Lev 9:24) affirms ordination, paralleling Pentecost's fiery tongues on the infant church (Acts 2:3-4). Aaron's silence after Nadab and Abihu's death (Lev 10:3) teaches that ordained service carries lethal responsibility if mishandled. The consecration week also quarantines priests inside the court, reflecting Christ's 40 days of desert preparation before public ministry. By participating through elders' laying on of hands (Lev 8:22), the community co-signs priestly authority, balancing hierarchy with accountability. Finally, ordination sets timetable for Israel's calendar: priestly faithfulness ensures festival rhythms proceed without rupture.

2.7.2 High-Priestly Vestments: Theological Tailoring

The ephod, an apron-like garment of blue, purple, and scarlet yarn, bears onyx stones engraved with Israel's names, signifying intercessory burden. Breastpiece of judgment, attached by golden chains, holds Urim and Thummim for divinatory inquiry, integrating worship with decision-making (Ex 28:15-30). The robe of blue, adorned with pomegranates and golden bells, signals fruitfulness and audible evidence of life; absence of bell sound during Yom Kippur hints at potential death in God's presence. The golden plate on the turban inscribed "Holy to the LORD" (Ex 28:36-38) positions holiness at the mind's forefront, advocating thought life sanctification. Linen undergarments protect against shame, paralleling Genesis 3's covering motif, thus even unseen layers preach purity. Altogether, vestments convert the priest into walking Tabernacle components— lampstand (gold), veil (colors), and cherubim (embroidery).

2.7.3 Tamid Sacrifices: Daily Rhythm of Grace

Two year-old lambs offered morning and evening (Ex 29:38-42) bookend Israel's day, integrating mundane tasks between divine affirmations of covenant. Accompanying grain and wine offerings link agrarian labor and celebratory joy to atoning blood, suggesting salvation transforms both survival and celebration. Priests must rise before dawn, illustrating that grace precedes human activity; twilight offering sanctifies post-labor fatigue. The unbroken continuity symbolizes God's steadfast love "from the rising of the sun to its setting" (Ps 113:3). When Babylon burns the Temple and sacrifices cease, lamentations intensify, highlighting how liturgical absence destabilizes identity (Lam 1:10-12). In Christian worship, morning and evening prayer traditions mirror tamid rhythms, testifying that liturgy is formative habit, not sporadic passion.

2.7.4 Incense Duty and Lamp-Trimming: Vigilant Service

Exodus 27:20-21 mandates pure olive oil beaten for light, requiring crushing of fruit, an enacted parable of suffering producing illumination. Trimmed wicks prevent smoky dimness, teaching leaders to remove charred attitudes that hinder community enlightenment. Because incense offering coincides with people praying outside (Luke 1:8-10), priestly duty synchronizes heavenward fragrance and earthbound petitions. Failure in duty risks darkness and stench, sensory metaphors for doctrinal error and moral decay. Daily discipline also upholds Sabbath rest, for carefully kept wicks burn evenly without last-minute panic. Eventually, Zechariah's angelic visitation during incense duty (Luke 1) heralds dawn of new covenant, linking meticulous Old-Covenant habit with eschatological breakthrough.

2.7.5 Handling of Blood and Ashes: Logistics of Holiness

Leviticus details various blood manipulations—sprinkling, pouring, smearing—each choreographing a theology of substitution and purification. Ashes removed to a "clean place" outside camp (Lev 6:10-11) illustrate sin's displacement; holiness is not denial but relocation of defilement. The priest wears special garments for ash removal, acknowledging that even discarded remnants of sacrifice remain sacred. This disposal routine foreshadows Christ's crucifixion "outside the gate" (Heb 13:12-13), where sin is finally exiled. Blood's disposal into base of altar, not casual dumping, treats lifeblood with reverence, affirming Leviticus 17:11's principle that "life of the flesh is in the blood." Altogether, logistical details reveal that holiness permeates workflows, challenging modern dichotomies between devotion and administration.

2.8 Annual Festivals and Atonement Rhythms

2.8.1 Passover and Unleavened Bread: Exodus Remembered Daily

When Israel kept the first wilderness Passover (Num 9:1-14), they relived deliverance under the very shadow of the new altar, ensuring that the Tabernacle's sacrifices never obscured the one decisive night of blood on doorposts (Ex 12:7-13). The feast synchronized household tables with the national sanctuary, for every lamb was slain toward the same altar that consumed continual offerings. By eating unleavened bread for seven days (Ex 12:15-20), families rehearsed haste, humility, and holiness, internalizing the lesson that corruption must be purged before communion. The festival's timing—first month, fourteenth day—reset Israel's calendar around redemption rather than agricultural or political cycles, making salvation history the master chronometer of daily life. Because the Tabernacle courtyard hosted thousands of lambs in later generations (Deut 16:1-6), priests learned to scale sacrificial logistics without diluting pastoral care. Every Passover required inspection of lambs for blemish (Ex 12:5), cultivating discernment in both priest and pilgrim; such vigilance foreshadowed the meticulous scrutiny Christ endured during Passion Week (John 18:38; 19:4). The combined aroma of roasted meat and altar smoke welded domestic celebration to corporate liturgy, forging a seamless loop between kitchen and court.

2.8.2 Firstfruits and Pentecost: Gratitude in a Nomadic Economy

Although Israel had no grain fields in Sinai, they nevertheless brought omer offerings of manna or desert produce (Lev 23:9-14), pledging faith that God would soon plant them in a fertile land. The waving of firstfruits before the altar dramatized the principle that Yahweh owns the initial and the best, not merely surplus. Fifty days later, at Shavuot (Pentecost), they presented two leavened loaves (Lev 23:15-21), acknowledging that grace accommodates humanity's fermenting imperfections when sanctified by sacrifice. In the wilderness, priests likely toasted flour from manna encamped around the Tabernacle, turning heaven-sent food into sacramental bread that prefigured Acts 2, when heavenly fire again fell on waiting worshippers. The festival doubled as covenant renewal, because tradition held that Sinai's giving of Torah occurred fifty days after the Exodus; thus flame on the mountain and flame on the apostles bookend a single redemptive arc. Pilgrims housed in tribal tents experienced communal joy as Levites sang psalms of ascent, binding scattered clans into unified thanksgiving (Pss 120–134). Pentecost's agricultural theme reminded a wandering nation that the God of the desert is also Lord of future harvests, sustaining hope in seasons of barrenness.

2.8.3 Day of Atonement: The High-Priestly Tightrope (Lev 16)

On Tishri 10 the camp awoke to solemn quiet, for even spontaneous work invited expulsion (Lev 16:29-31). The high priest bathed, dressed in linen, and sacrificed a bull for his sins before drawing lots for two goats—one "for the LORD," the other for *Azazel* (Lev 16:7-10). Entering beyond the veil with incense cloud and blood, he sprinkled eastward on the mercy seat, a liturgical choreography mapping heaven's throne with sin-cleansing droplets. The second goat, laden with confessed transgressions, was escorted into the wilderness, dramatizing sin's banishment from the camp (Lev 16:20-22). Every heartbeat of the ritual pulsed with risk; a misstep could cost the priest his life and the nation its pardon (Lev 16:13). The ceremony's annual repetition underscored both sin's stubbornness and grace's persistence, tutoring hearts to anticipate a once-for-all atonement (Heb 9:11-14). Camp children likely watched the goat disappear over the horizon, forming first memories of holiness that removes, not merely covers, guilt—memories later re-awakened at Calvary (John 19:30).

2.8.4 Feast of Booths (*Sukkot*): Joy under Temporary Roofs

Beginning five days after Atonement (Lev 23:33-43), *Sukkot* turned the whole camp into a forest of palm-woven huts, echoing the Tabernacle's own portable design. Families decorated shelters with desert flora, embodying the truth that security rests not in masonry but in abiding presence. Daily water-libation rituals, if already practiced in the wilderness, reminded Israel of the rock that followed them (1 Cor 10:4) and anticipated the Spirit whom Jesus would later proclaim at a *Sukkot* celebration (John 7:37-39). The festival's closing assembly, *Shemini Atzeret*, added an eighth-day dimension of Sabbath rest beyond the perfect seven, hinting at eschatological surplus. Levitical choirs sang hallel psalms (Pss 113–118), saturating evening air with refrains of steadfast love as lampstands blazed in the court, turning the desert night into a carnival of light. By sleeping under stars, Israel rehearsed trust, for they relinquished cedar beams to dwell beneath linen roofs, mirroring God's willingness to dwell under goat hair. Booths thus became pedagogical props, teaching that the journey itself—when shared with the Almighty—is already a form of arrival.

2.9 Shekinah Presence: Cloud, Fire, and Divine Guidance

2.9.1 Pillar Phenomenology: Theology in Motion (Ex 13:21-22)

The cloud by day and fire by night operated as Israel's GPS, thermostat, and theophany in one. Its translucence shielded from desert glare while its fiery core radiated warmth in icy wilderness evenings, embodying both tenderness and transcendence. Children learned meteorology framed by theology, for parental explanations of sunrise always included the phrase "because the LORD leads us." At camp, the pillar rested above the tent of meeting, visually crowning worship as chief vocation, not military might or economic production. When cloud lifted, trumpet blasts signaled disassembly, proving that the divine schedule, not human convenience, dictated itinerary (Num 9:15-23). The pillar's unpredictability—sometimes lingering a year, sometimes moving overnight—trained relational dependence rather than routinized religion. Joshua's later leadership retained this posture, for before Jericho he waited to encounter the Commander of the LORD's Armies who appeared outside human planning (Josh 5:13-15).

2.9.2 Indwelling Glory at Inauguration (Ex 40:34-38)

Upon completion, the cloud filled the Tabernacle so densely that even Moses—who once entered Sinai's gloom—could not step inside. The narrative reverses Eden's expulsion: now God expels humanity from His house only temporarily, to safeguard them until sacrificial rhythms are fully operational. Priests quickly learned that architecture without glory is but scenery; the cloud's residence validated every cubit of obedience. Its settling also established liturgical "office hours"—when God was "at home," leaders would consult; when it lifted, meeting adjourned. The Chronicler later parallels this with Solomon's temple, confirming continuity of presence across generations (2 Chr 5:13-14). Each dusk, flickering campfires mirrored the central flame, a constellation of households orbiting the cosmic King. Glory-presence thus functioned as pastoral assurance: even if neighboring Amalekites prowled, Yahweh's luminous canopy guaranteed protection.

2.9.3 Signals for Journey and Rest (Num 10:11-36)

Two silver trumpets (*ḥaṣoṣrôt*) forged by Bezalel communicated cloud movements: a single blast summoned princes, while multiple staccato notes signaled camp departure. Sound became sight's companion, ensuring that even tent-bound elderly women heard directives. The order of march—Judah first, Dan last—wrapped the Tabernacle at center like a jewel in a traveling case, visualizing that mission radiates from worship. Moses' prayer, "Rise up, O LORD, and let Your enemies be scattered" (Num 10:35), transformed every lift-off into liturgical procession, blending warfare with doxology. Conversely, at each stop he prayed, "Return, O LORD, to the myriad thousands of Israel" (v. 36), acknowledging that arrival is meaningless without renewed indwelling. Over forty years, these acoustics of obedience tuned national reflexes to heaven's tempo more effectively than any statute book alone could. The pattern foreshadows Pentecost's rushing wind (Acts 2:2), another audible sign that prompts missional movement.

2.9.4 Theophanic Terror versus Covenant Assurance

The same glory that warmed pilgrims incinerated rebels; Nadab and Abihu's unauthorized fire (Lev 10:1-2) and Korah's incense rebellion (Num 16:35) illustrate holy ambivalence. Yet judgment episodes, though severe, preserved assurance for the faithful by proving that covenant righteousness is defended, not capriciously discarded. Aaron's quick censer run amid plague (Num 16:46-48) displayed mediatory courage that prefigured Christ standing "between the living and the dead." Glory-fire therefore functioned pedagogically, deterring casualness while encouraging desperate intercession. Subsequent psalms recall Sinai flames as both refuge and reverent awe (Ps 97:3-5), teaching worshippers to hold paradox without dissolving it. The balance prevents two extremes: sentimental religion that forgets holiness and hopeless dread that forgets mercy. In Christian experience, this tension surfaces in Hebrews 12:28-29, where "a kingdom that cannot be shaken" coexists with "our God is a consuming fire."

2.10 Portability Protocols and Marching Order

2.10.1 Dismantling Sequence: Veiled Mysteries in Transit (Num 4:5-15)

Priests first lowered the veil to shroud the Ark, ensuring no Levite saw the throne's naked glory. They then layered tachash skins and blue cloth, signaling royalty beneath humility. Table, lampstand, and incense altar received similar coverings, each with its own color accent, so theology traveled sewn into fabric codes. Only after holy objects were concealed did Kohathites enter, shoulders bearing poles but eyes shielded from sights too lofty. Gershonites followed with curtains and coverings, while Merarites lugged frames and sockets on oxcarts (Num 7:6-8). This choreography embedded chain-of-command humility: visible strength served hidden holiness, never vice versa. Modern mission teams might draw from this ordered secrecy, remembering that sacred realities should be cloaked in prayer before hauled into secular arenas.

2.10.2 Transport Duties: Shared Burdens, Tailored Loads

The Kohathites' pole-borne labor required constant vigilance lest a stumble dislodge sancta, stressing that intimacy with God demands enduring discipline. By contrast, Merarites used carts, demonstrating mercy for heavier tasks; equity is not equality but provision according to weight. Moses' distribution of carts (Num 7:6-9) reveals administrative wisdom tempered by pastoral concern, a template for resource allocation in any faith community. Oxen supplied for transport symbolized patient strength harnessed to divine agenda, making slow but steady progress preferable to restless haste. At each stop, tribe leaders likely inspected loads, reinforcing communal accountability for holiness. Over decades, muscle memory of lifting, walking, and lowering sacred cargo turned labor into liturgy, forging kinship among carriers. Paul's metaphor of the church as body with differing gifts (1 Cor 12) echoes this desert division of labor.

2.10.3 Signal Trumpets and Leadership of Judah (Num 10:1-10)

Crafted from a single hammered silver ingot, the trumpets' purity of material mirrored purity of purpose—communication, not entertainment. Distinct blasts differentiated war alarms from festival convocations, teaching Israel to discern providential seasons through auditory cues. Judah's vanguard march under lion-emblazoned standard (Num 10:14) embodied messianic promise guiding the sacred convoy. Subsequent tribes followed clockwise order, minimizing confusion and preventing inter-tribal jostling. This systemic clarity proved invaluable when the nation faced hostile terrain, for chaos in formation could have been fatal. Trumpet statutes also anticipated eschatological judgments announced by angelic trumpets in Revelation 8–11, linking desert logistics to cosmic consummation. Thus peals of silver bridged epochs, echoing across redemptive history like a single, elongated fanfare.

2.10.4 Re-Erection Procedure: Sanctifying Fresh Ground

Upon cloud descent, Merarites embedded silver sockets, forming a square perimeter that reclaimed barren soil as holy precinct. Gershonites stretched curtains, re-inscribing cherubic guardians onto new coordinates, teaching that sacred space is wherever obedience erects it. Priests synchronized Ark unveiling with altar re-ignition, ensuring worship resumed before tents were fully pitched—a priority signal for exhausted travelers. Purification offerings likely followed quickly, cleansing accidental defilements accumulated on the trail (Num 19:1-13). Amid hammering and staking, Levites probably chanted psalms, transforming worksite into sanctuary even before completion. Children learned geography by Tabernacle bearings; "east of the laver" or "north of the altar" became coordinates more meaningful than abstract compass points. Eventually, new ground bore familiar fragrance of incense, proving that holiness is portable yet unmistakably consistent.

2.11 Cosmic Symbolism and Edenic Echoes

2.11.1 Seven-Speech Creation Pattern in Exodus 25–31

Scholars note that the instructions for building the Tabernacle are prefaced by seven divine speeches, each introduced with "And the LORD said to Moses," paralleling the seven "And God said" utterances of Genesis 1. The seventh speech concerns the Sabbath (Ex 31:12-17), mirroring God's rest, thereby framing construction as re-creation. Every hammer strike thus reversed primordial chaos, ordering boards and sockets into micro-cosmic harmony. Priests, acting as Adamic gardeners, tended golden flora within linen heavens, cultivating worship where serpentine rebellion once reigned. Israelites entering the court crossed from wilderness thorns into cultivated holiness, reliving Edenic ingress. This subtle literary architecture elevates blueprints to cosmological poetry, proving Scripture hides galaxies in grammar. For modern readers, recognizing such patterns deepens awe, affirming that revelation is not haphazard but intricately laced with artistic intentionality worthy of infinite contemplation.

2.11.2 Floral and Faunal Motifs: Sanctuary as Re-Planted Paradise

Lampstand almonds, veil cherubim, and pomegranate robe-fringes together populate a symbolic garden teeming with life. The almond staff that budded (Num 17:8) rested near lampstand almonds, forging narrative continuity between miracle and furniture. Palm-tree engravings later added in Solomon's Temple (1 Kgs 6:29) merely scaled up designs already resident in the desert tent, showing that wilderness worship contained "seeds" of future glory. Because goat-hair tent formed an outer "sky," priests ministered inside a cosmos where Eden was nested within heavens, compressing creation under a 15-foot roof. Worshippers thus rehearsed eschatology every time they offered grain or wave sheaves, anticipating a new earth where flora and fauna harmonize under divine reign (Isa 11:6-9). Symbolism also dignified artistry; a carved bud became theology carved in wood. In turn, contemporary church architecture may likewise preach via stained glass, paraments, or even minimalist spaces that evoke pilgrims' tents.

2.11.3 Tabernacle as Portable Mount Sinai

Sinai had three zones: base where people waited, mid-slope where elders ate covenant meal (Ex 24:9-11), and peak where Moses met God. The court, Holy Place, and Most Holy Place replicate that tripartite ascent but convert vertical danger into horizontal approachability. By carrying the tent, Israel metaphorically carried the mountain, ensuring revelation traveled beyond its geographic coordinates. The fiery top now dwelt in a gold-plated box only a few feet long, democratizing the summit without trivializing it. Whenever cloud covered the tent, thunderless Sinai reappeared in miniature, reminding Israel that lawgiver still speaks though stones remain in desert past. Stephen's speech (Acts 7:44-50) leverages this concept to challenge temple-fixated hearers, arguing that God's mobile presence outranks stone permanence. Thus, Mount Sinai became migratory, anticipating Pentecost when fire perched on heads rather than mountaintops.

2.11.4 Sea, Earth, Heaven: Vertical Cosmology of Objects

Bronze laver symbolized chaotic seas subdued; bronze altar represented terra firma drenched in sacrificial blood; gold ceiling embodied stellar heavens illumined by menorah "stars." Priestly ascent from laver steps to altar platform to inner sanctuary reenacted cosmic stratification in miniature pilgrimage. Incense cloud bridging veil signaled hydrological cycle in liturgical form—water (laver) evaporating (smoke) then condensing as dew-like manna around camp (Ex 16:13-14). This imaginative cosmology taught integrative thinking: theology, meteorology, and anthropology shared one narrative. Later, Ezekiel's throne vision with crystal "sea" (Ezek 1:22) draws on laver imagery, while Revelation's glassy sea (Rev 4:6) universalizes the same symbol. Each worship cycle thus mapped cosmic geography onto desert grid lines, giving sand-weary travelers telescopic glimpses of ordered universe. The Tabernacle trained hearts to see heaven's architecture beneath dusty realities.

2.12 Ethical and Social Implications for a Pilgrim People

2.12.1 Holiness Code and Public Health Interlock (Lev 11–15)

Dietary restrictions distinguished Israel's menu from pagan banquets; abstaining from swine or shellfish signaled covenant allegiance whenever hunger struck. Yet many commands had hygienic benefits—quarantine for skin lesions, washing after bodily emissions—reducing disease transmission in close quarters. Holiness was thus concretely loving one's neighbour by curtailing contagion, dissolving modern caricatures that pit ritual against ethics. Disseminated through priestly teaching (Lev 10:11), these laws produced a populace versed in embodied theology, linking kidneys, skin, and soul in one ethical corpus. The rituals also cultivated empathy; anyone could fall temporarily unclean, fostering compassion rather than permanent stigmatization. Jesus' later declaration of all foods clean (Mark 7:19) did not abolish embodied holiness but redirected it toward inner purity, fulfilling the code's moral trajectory. Christian health ministries today inherit this integrated vision, healing bodies as part of sanctuary witness.

2.12.2 Justice at the Tent of Meeting: Moses' Judiciary Role (Ex 18:13-26)

Jethro's counsel led Moses to appoint capable men over thousands, hundreds, fifties, and tens, decentralizing dispute resolution. The court became not only worship site but courthouse, where law received ritual gravitas; judgments pronounced near altar underscored accountability to divine witness. Elders' presence guarded against autocracy, while sanctuary proximity curbed bribery, for offenders feared sacrificial fire as moral deterrent. Over time this system forged a culture where jurisprudence and piety intertwined, later embodied in Psalm 122's vision of thrones of judgment within Jerusalem. Prophets leveraged this expectation when denouncing temple corruption, citing disconnect between sacrifices and social justice (Isa 1:11-17). Thus, Tabernacle jurisprudence incubated prophetic ethics, which in turn shaped apostolic calls to care for widows and orphans (Jas 1:27). Sanctified litigation becomes a liturgy of fairness when rooted in covenant presence.

2.12.3 Mercy in the Camp: Social Safety Nets

The gleaning principle later codified in Leviticus 19:9-10 probably germinated during desert manna collection, where hoarding bred worms and sharing met needs (Ex 16:16-21). Daily distribution of manna around the Tabernacle illustrated divine welfare economy— supply matched appetite when gathered obediently. Care for sojourners emerged naturally, for Israel itself was a sojourner nation (Ex 22:21), and the mixed multitude that left Egypt (Ex 12:38) camped under the same cloud. The Tabernacle's presence rendered boundaries porous: any alien wishing to keep Passover could be circumcised and fully integrated (Num 9:14). Such inclusivity demonstrated that holiness expands hospitality, rather than shrinking it. Generosity found ritual expression in the *ma'aser sheni* (second tithe), consumed before the Lord, blending charity with celebration (Deut 14:22-27). Modern churches emulate this economy through benevolence funds that treat the Lord's Supper table and food pantries as contiguous ministries.

2.12.4 Cultic Purity Shaping Daily Ethics

Because bodily fluids could defile, marital intimacy demanded times of abstention (Lev 15:18-24), teaching self-control and mutual respect. Business dealings implicated honesty, for false measures were "abomination at the altar" (Prov 11:1), a truth visualized when grain offerings were weighed near sanctuary thresholds. Tabernacle worship thus sanctified marketplaces by extension; a man who cheated his neighbour knew he would soon stand before flaming bronze altar. Holiness code elevated disabled persons by providing special pathways for their offerings (Lev 19:14), foreshadowing Christ's healing ministry within temple courts (Matt 21:14). Even agricultural cycles were moralized: planting fields edge-to-edge violated divine generosity symbolized in grain-offering memorial portions (Lev 2:2). Therefore, social ethics were not optional add-ons but logical outflows of dwelling with a just God in canvas proximity. The Tabernacle's ethics curriculum graduated a generation prepared, at least structurally, to build a just society once they settled the land.

2.13 Failure and Restoration Episodes

2.13.1 Golden Calf Crisis: Anti-Tabernacle in Miniature (Ex 32)

While Moses received heavenly blueprints, Israel built an alternate "tabernacle" around a calf, complete with proclamation of feast (ḥag) and burnt offerings. The episode inverted every symbol: gold meant for cherubim became idol form; altar turned from substitution to syncretism. Moses shattered tablets, a visual of covenant rupture, then ground calf dust into water, forcing ingestion of their folly. Yet intercession prevailed; Moses pleaded on covenant promises ("Remember Abraham...," Ex 32:13), securing partial pardon though plague ensued. The Levites' sword purge (Ex 32:27-29) ironically commissioned them for priestly service, as zeal for holiness became qualification. The crisis taught that architectural precision is futile without covenant fidelity, a theme echoed when temple later shelters thieves (Jer 7:11). Grace ultimately triumphed, for God renewed tablets (Ex 34:1-10), proving mercy can rebuild shattered law.

2.13.2 Nadab and Abihu: Strange Fire and Boundary Trespass (Lev 10)

Aaron's sons, freshly ordained, offered unauthorized incense, perhaps intoxicated or improvising formula. Fire burst forth, consuming them, and Aaron's stunned silence spoke volumes about terror and submission. Moses interpreted the tragedy: "Among those who are near me I will be sanctified" (Lev 10:3), setting precedent that proximity heightens accountability. Priests forbidden to mourn publicly (Lev 10:6-7) illustrated that divine honor eclipses familial loyalty—a sobering ethic. Subsequent prohibition of priestly wine before service (Lev 10:9) suggests impairment lay behind the sin, embedding temperance into liturgical law. The ashes of Nadab and Abihu warned future priests that creative worship unhinged from command can kill. Nevertheless, ministry resumed, exemplifying that failure, though fatal for some, does not derail redemptive agendas.

2.13.3 Korah's Rebellion: Coveting Sacred Space (Num 16)

Korah, Dathan, and Abiram challenged Aaronic exclusivity, arguing, "All the congregation is holy." Their democratic rhetoric cloaked power hunger, ignoring God-appointed boundaries safeguarding communal life. Earth swallowed ringleaders, fire consumed 250 censer-bearers, and their bronze pans were hammered into altar plating as perpetual warning. Yet when plague struck for ensuing murmurs, Aaron ran with incense, standing "between the living and the dead," embodying priesthood Korah had despised. The budding of Aaron's rod (Num 17:1-11) followed, using Edenic imagery to validate chosen mediation. Rebellion episodes underscore that access without mediation breeds death; humility before structures God ordains is life-giving. The censers melted into altar surface meant every future sacrifice touched metal once wielded in rebellion, turning judgment memory into atonement contact.

2.13.4 Intercession of Moses and Aaron: Crisis Mediation

Whether staving off destruction after calf worship (Ex 32:11-14), pleading over poisonous serpents (Num 21:7-9), or lamenting Miriam's leprosy (Num 12:11-15), Moses models priestly heart even before formal sacrifices occur. His repeated "blot me out" offers (Ex 32:32) prefigure Paul's anguish for Israel (Rom 9:1-3) and Christ's substitution on the cross. Aaron's censer episodes complement Moses' verbal pleas, showing that word and ritual synergize in effective mediation. Each intervention reveals God's willingness to relent, encouraging future generations to approach boldly yet reverently. Failure therefore becomes laboratory for learning mercy, shaping a national narrative that exalts grace without diluting righteousness. The intercessory pattern ultimately culminates in Hebrews 7:25, where Jesus "always lives to make intercession." Thus, Tabernacle crises prepare hearts for a mediator who never fails.

In Conclusion, Desert winds long ago erased the physical footprints of Israel's marching sanctuary, yet its theological imprints endure in gilt cathedrals, storefront chapels, and whispered prayers of nomads under refugee tarps. Whenever believers hoist communion cups or offer songs at dawn, echoes of tamid lambs rise within modern liturgy. Each time a congregation relocates from rented school gym to permanent facility, they reenact the shift from goat-hair walls to Solomon's cedar, repeating the grand story of mobility and establishment. And every baptismal splash reprises laver reflections, while each benediction traces incense curls heavenward. The wilderness Tabernacle therefore stands not as archaeological curiosity but as living mentor, tutoring God's people to treasure presence above place, obedience above ornament, and mercy above every measurement. Its canvas may be folded, but its theology forever stretches—north-south, east-west—until the whole earth becomes the dwelling of God with humanity (Rev 21:3). On that day, cloud and fire will no longer guide, for the Lamb Himself will be our light, and the songs learned in Sinai's sand will crescendo in a city of gold where tents are no longer needed and tears are finally, fully wiped away.

Chapter 3 — Solomon's Temple: Fixed Splendor, Cosmic Symbol

The story of Israel's first permanent sanctuary unfolds against the background of a young monarchy that has finally secured its borders and gained an international reputation for wisdom and wealth. From the moment David set his heart on building "a house for the name of the LORD" (2 Sam 7:2), the horizon of covenant worship shifted from the portability of tent fabric to the durability of quarried stone. Yet the Temple's importance transcended national pride or architectural ambition; in biblical imagination it functioned as a micro-cosmos, a fixed point where heaven and earth interlocked. This chapter traces the historical, political, and theological currents that converged on Mount Moriah, producing a structure so radiant that later Jewish writers would recall it as "the joy of the whole earth" (Ps 48:2). While Chapter 2 examined God's mobile presence in the wilderness Tabernacle, here we explore how that same presence was translated into gold-plated permanence—only to discover that immovable walls could not guarantee immovable faith.

3.1 Historical and Political Backdrop

3.1.1 Davidic Covenant and the "House" Promise (2 Sam 7:1-17)

The impetus for Temple construction begins with David, not Solomon. After defeating surrounding enemies, David observed that while he lived in a "house of cedar," the Ark still resided behind goat-hair curtains (2 Sam 7:2). His moral intuition pleased Nathan the prophet initially, yet that very night God reversed the plan: David would not build a house for God; rather, God would build a "house"—a ruling dynasty—for David (vv. 11-16). The wordplay on *bayit* ("house" as temple or dynasty) forges a covenant link between permanent sanctuary and permanent royal line. Thus Solomon's later project is not merely filial ambition but the architectural counterpart to an everlasting throne.

3.1.2 National Unification and Emerging Monarchy (1 Kgs 4:20-21)

Solomon inherited a realm stretching "from the Euphrates to the land of the Philistines and to the border of Egypt." With tribal rivalries subdued, economic surplus accumulating, and external threats at bay, Israel was positioned for monumental investment. In the ancient Near East, great temples advertised a king's legitimacy and the gods' favour; Solomon's Temple therefore served as a political centrepiece that confirmed divine endorsement of the Davidic monarchy. Unified worship around a single altar also minimized centrifugal tribal tendencies, fostering identity around Jerusalem rather than local shrines. The Temple, then, both expressed and reinforced a new stage of national cohesion.

3.1.3 Regional Stability and International Diplomacy

Solomon's reign coincided with a lull among traditional superpowers—Egypt, Assyria, and Babylon—allowing smaller kingdoms to flourish. The king leveraged this geopolitical breathing-space through strategic marriages and trade agreements (1 Kgs 3:1; 10:28-29). Friendly borders meant labour teams could quarry stone and fell cedar without fear of invasion. Furthermore, foreign dignitaries such as the Queen of Sheba (1 Kgs 10:1-13) viewed the

Temple not simply as a Hebrew holy place but as an emblem of wisdom that attracted global curiosity. Thus, political tranquillity became the canvas on which sacred splendour could be painted.

3.2 Site Selection: Mount Moriah

3.2.1 The Threshing-Floor of Araunah—From Plague to Peace (2 Sam 24:16-25)

Jerusalem's temple mount was holy ground before a single stone was set. David's census sin had triggered a devastating plague; when the angel of judgment paused above Araunah's threshing-floor, David pleaded and offered sacrifice. Fire from heaven consumed the offering, signalling divine acceptance, and David purchased the site to ensure its perpetual dedication (vv. 21-25). A location once marked by death thus became the place of atonement, teaching that God's future dwelling would forever be linked to mercy overcoming wrath. This narrative also legitimates the site legally, ensuring uncontested ownership by the crown.

3.2.2 Moriah, the Akedah, and Edenic Echoes (Gen 22; 2 Chr 3:1)

Chronicles explicitly identifies Solomon's construction site with "Mount Moriah, where the LORD had appeared to David" (2 Chr 3:1) and where Abraham bound Isaac centuries earlier (Gen 22:2). The juxtaposition layers sacrificial typology: the ram caught in a thicket foreshadows substitutionary offerings that will later burn on Temple altars. Ancient interpreters also saw Edenic imagery here—a high place watered by living springs, analogous to the garden mountain of God (Ezek 28:13-16). By situating the Temple on Moriah, Scripture interlaces patriarchal faith, royal atonement, and primordial sanctuary into one axis mundi. The site becomes a stage where past promises and future hopes converge.

3.2.3 Topographical Symbolism: Mountain, Garden, and Cosmic Axis

Mountains in biblical literature signify revelation and rule—Sinai, Carmel, Zion. Jerusalem's hill, though modest in elevation, gains cosmic stature because heaven's King chooses it as His footstool (Ps 132:13-14). Garden motifs carved inside—palm trees, gourds, lilies—strengthen the Edenic association, portraying the sanctuary as a replanted paradise. The Hebrew prophets later envision all nations streaming *up* to this mountain (Isa 2:2-3), underscoring its role as world centre. In short, topography and theology unite: a garden mountain becomes God's earthly throne and humanity's spiritual compass.

3.3 Divine Blueprint and Royal Patronage

3.3.1 "The Plan the Spirit Had Put in David's Mind" (1 Chr 28:11-19)

Although Solomon executed the project, David handed him detailed drawings "of all that was in the Spirit." The passage parallels Moses receiving the Tabernacle pattern on Sinai, indicating heavenly origin for earthly architecture. David even amassed enormous resources—3,000 talents of gold and 7,000 of silver (1 Chr 29:4)—demonstrating that royal patronage begins with humble stewardship rather than personal glory. The Spirit-inspired blueprint also legitimized every later expense, labour draft, and foreign treaty dedicated to the cause. Thus the Temple rises not from human whim but prophetic revelation fused with kingly generosity.

3.3.2 Prophetic Architects: Gad, Nathan, and the Heavenly Pattern

While craftsmen shaped cedar and bronze, prophets shaped vision. Gad had earlier directed David to erect an altar on Araunah's plot (2 Sam 24:18), and Nathan had delivered the covenant oracle promising a house for God (2 Sam 7:4-17). Their involvement places the Temple at the intersection of word and work: royal building programs remained under prophetic scrutiny. This synergy guarded against idolatrous extravagance while ensuring that liturgical symbolism remained faithful to covenant theology. The pattern therefore bore not only artistic beauty but ethical oversight.

3.3.3 Solomon's Organising Genius: Administrative Districts and Tax Levies (1 Kgs 4:7-19)

Solomon divided Israel into twelve districts, each tasked with provisioning the royal court one month per year. This system spread economic burden equitably and freed central coffers for construction costs. Further, he raised a labour force through conscripted levies—30,000 timber-cutters, 70,000 burden-bearers, 80,000 stone-hewers (1 Kgs 5:13-15). Critics note potential exploitation, yet the Chronicler emphasizes willingness among participants, mindful of earlier deliverance from Egyptian bondage (2 Chr 2:17-18). Administrative efficiency undergirded sacred ambition, proving that wisdom's first manifestation is often logistical clarity.

3.4 International Procurement of Materials

3.4.1 The Hiram Alliance: Cedar, Cypress, and Craft (1 Kgs 5:1-12)

King Hiram of Tyre supplied cedar and cypress, floated as logs down the Mediterranean to Joppa, then hauled overland to Jerusalem. In return, Solomon sent wheat and olive oil, forging a mutually beneficial treaty. Phoenician carpenters were world-renowned; their partnership ensured that Israel's God would be worshiped within walls fashioned by Gentile hands—an early hint of international participation in Yahweh's glory. The alliance also testifies to Solomon's shrewd diplomacy, converting political goodwill into tangible materials for holy purpose. Cedar's fragrance and resistance to decay made it a fitting emblem of enduring covenant.

3.4.2 Phoenician Maritime Supply Chain: Joppa Harbour Logistics (2 Chr 2:16)

Hiram proposed rafting timber to the port of Joppa, whence Israelite carriers lugged beams up the Judean highlands. This maritime-land hybrid route maximized efficiency and demonstrated mastery over sea and land—domains traditionally ruled by Baal and other gods in Canaanite lore. By appropriating Phoenician shipping for Yahweh's temple, Solomon tacitly proclaimed the God of Israel sovereign over trade winds and ocean swells. Logistics thus became liturgy, every wave lapping against cedar rafts chanting a doxology of dominion.

3.4.3 Precious Metals and Stones: Ophir Gold, Parvaim Gems (1 Kgs 9:28; 2 Chr 3:6)

Solomon's fleet fetched 420 talents of gold from Ophir, an exotic region possibly on the Arabian or African coast. He embellished interior walls with gems from Parvaim and overlaid floors with pure gold. The Chronicler states that gold "covered the whole house," implying not ostentation but theological pedagogy: the inner sanctuary mirrors heaven's streets of gold (Rev 21:21). Precious stones set into the walls correspond to the high-priestly breastpiece (Ex 28:17-20), turning the entire building into an enlarged ephod. Thus resources from distant lands were recast as cosmic catechism.

3.5 Workforce and Spirit-Empowered Craftsmanship

3.5.1 Labour Corps: 70,000 Burden-Bearers, 80,000 Stone-Cutters, 3,600 Foremen (2 Chr 2:17-18)

The sheer scale of manpower underscores the Temple's monumental status. Stone-cutters quarried megalithic blocks, some weighing over 100 tons, yet the most striking detail is the enforced silence at the building site—stones were finished off-site so that "no hammer or tool of iron was heard while it was being built" (1 Kgs 6:7). The hush resembled liturgical reverence, turning construction into an act of worship. Work crews laboured six months in Lebanon and one month at home, a rotating schedule that avoided total disruption of agrarian life (1 Kgs 5:14). In this way, royal demands acknowledged social rhythms, preventing the exploitation that marred pagan building projects.

3.5.2 Hiram-Abi (Huram-Abif): Half-Israelite Master Artisan (2 Chr 2:13-14)

Descended from a Tyrian father and Naphtalite mother, Hiram-Abi epitomized cross-cultural collaboration in sacred art. Gifted "in gold, silver, bronze, iron, stone, wood, purple, blue, crimson, and fine linen," he oversaw all metalwork. His dual heritage signalled that skill, not ethnicity, qualified craftsmen for temple service, prefiguring Paul's vision of Jew-Gentile craftsmanship in the church (Eph 2:11-22).

Hiram-Abi's bronze pillars, laver stands, and pomegranates exemplified Spirit-anointed creativity bridging nations. Thus the Temple's beauty was literally half-Gentile, a silent prophecy of wider inclusion.

3.5.3 Inspired Skill vs. Forced Labour: Ethics of Royal Projects (1 Kgs 5:13-14)

Solomon's levy has generated debate: was it conscription akin to Pharaoh's brick quotas, or a tax accepted by prayerful citizens? The Chronicler stresses voluntarism; the Deuteronomist voices no critique but later prophets attack Solomon's excess (1 Kgs 12:4). Biblical narrative thus allows tension, cautioning that even sacred projects can teeter toward oppression. The presence of prophets within the court (1 Kgs 1:32-35) provided ethical checks, ensuring that Spirit-filled artistry would not devolve into Spirit-quenched servitude. Ultimately, motive and method co-determine whether beauty honours God or insults the poor.

3.6 Ground-Plan and Dimensions

3.6.1 Overall Footprint: 60 × 20 Cubits Nave; 20-Cubits Holy of Holies (1 Kgs 6:2-3)

Using an 18-inch cubit, the main hall measured roughly 90 × 30 feet, triple the Tabernacle's length and width. A vestibule added another 15 feet at the front, creating a processional axis that carried worshippers visually and spiritually toward the inner sanctum. The Holy of Holies formed a perfect cube, symbolizing divine perfection and echoing the cubic New Jerusalem of Revelation 21:16. Spatial progression from court to nave to oracle instilled a pedagogy of approaching holiness in measured stages. The enlarged footprint also accommodated burgeoning pilgrimage crowds impossible to host in tented confines.

3.6.2 Triple Vestibule and Lateral Chambers

Three stories of side rooms encircled the nave, tapering inwards so that upper chambers rested on ledges carved into the main walls. These annexes stored sacred utensils, treasury items, and perhaps served as clergy offices. Their architectural integration stabilized the tall structure while providing functional space without marring internal purity. Because no beam penetrated the holy walls (1 Kgs 6:6), Solomon honored God's dwelling by ensuring even unseen joints respected sacred boundaries. Thus engineering prudence complemented theological sensitivity.

3.6.3 Verticality: 30-Cubits Height and the Impression of Cosmic Elevation

Rising nearly 45 feet, the Temple doubled the Tabernacle's height, producing an impression of ascending into heaven. Vertical scale mattered spiritually: Israelite worshippers moving upward on Zion's slope entered an edifice that continued the skyward trajectory. Windows "made narrow within" (1 Kgs 6:4) controlled light shafts, creating a mystic glow and reminding entrants that revelation, not daylight, illumines God's house. Vertical posts of cedar sheathed in gold became terrestrial pillars holding up an invisible firmament. Thus architecture preached cosmology: earth's king approaches heaven's throne via a gilded ascent.

3.7 Exterior Grandeur

3.7.1 Foundation Stones and Quarry Silence (1 Kgs 6:7)

Stones "made ready at the quarry" arrived fully shaped, an engineering marvel that protected worship from the clang of iron tools (cf. Deut 27:5). Foundation courses exceeded 15 feet in height, visible even today in Jerusalem's lower terraces. By lowering the auditory profile of construction, Solomon ensured that prayer, not pounding, defined the site's aural memory. The practice also reduced dust and debris in the sacred precinct, honouring bodily senses as pathways to reverence. In effect, the building "grew" quietly, like a seed sprouting into glory.

3.7.2 Bronze Pillars—Jachin and Boaz: Names and Functions (1 Kgs 7:15-22)

Standing 27 feet high and crowned with lily-work capitals, the twin pillars flanked the porch. Their names—Jachin ("He establishes") and Boaz ("In Him is strength")—proclaimed covenant stability and divine power. Scholars debate their purpose: free-standing monuments, flagstaffs for temple banners, or structural supports. Whatever their function, they embodied theological proclamation: worship begins by passing between a promise of security and a promise of empowerment. Later exiles, recalling these pillars toppled by Babylon, would mourn the apparent collapse of both themes—only to see them resurrected in Christ's resurrection power.

3.7.3 Ornamented Facades: Cherubim, Palm Trees, and Open Flowers (1 Kgs 6:29-30)

Exterior reliefs depicted cherubim guarding paradise, palm trees evoking oasis life, and open flowers symbolizing perpetual spring. These motifs turned stone into storybook, narrating creation, fall, and hoped-for restoration. Gold overlay on floorboards meant priests literally walked on shining paths, dramatizing Psalm 119:105—"Your word is a lamp to my feet." In an age before printed scrolls were common, architecture served as pedagogy, educating pilgrims through sight and imagination. The façade thus performed exegetical work, translating Genesis into geometry.

3.8 Interior Furnishing and Symbolic Iconography

3.8.1 Gold-Plated Walls and Floors: Immanence of Glory

Every cubit of interior cedar was overlaid with pure gold—estimated at over 20 metric tons. The shimmering surfaces reflected lamplight in multifaceted brilliance, simulating heavenly radiance. Gold's incorruptibility paralleled covenant fidelity: as gold resists tarnish, so God's promises resist decay. By immersing worshippers in gilded splendour, the Temple provided an anticipatory taste of eschatological glory. Moreover, gold amplified sound, enhancing choral resonance and enveloping listeners in both visual and auditory majesty.

3.8.2 Ten Golden Lampstands and Tables: Multiplication of Tabernacle Imagery (1 Kgs 7:48-49)

Solomon quintupled the Tabernacle's single lampstand and showbread table to ten each—five on the north, five on the south. This multiplication signified abundance: more light, more fellowship, more revelation. It mirrored Israel's demographic expansion and foreshadowed the Gentile influx that later prophets envisioned. Yet arrangement maintained symmetry, teaching that growth does not annul order. The extra vessels also ensured redundancy, so that worship could proceed unhindered should any lamp fail.

3.8.3 Carved Cherubim of Olive-Wood—15 ft Wingspan (1 Kgs 6:23-28)

Two colossal cherubim stood within the oracle, wing tips touching each other and the walls, thereby covering the Ark beneath a canopy of protection. Olive wood, long-lived and evergreen, underscored permanence; gold overlay harmonized them with surrounding walls. Their gigantic scale dwarfed priests, reinforcing divine transcendence even within relational nearness. Cherubim, present at Eden's gate (Gen 3:24), now welcomed rather than barred approach, indicating that atoning blood grants safe passage through flaming sword imagery. Thus a single glance proclaimed gospel reversal.

3.8.4 Veil of Blue, Purple, and Crimson—Temple Textile Theology (2 Chr 3:14)

Solomon's veil resembled the Tabernacle's but hung before gilded doors of olive wood, layering barriers that dramatized holiness. Blue evoked sky, purple signified royalty, crimson suggested sacrificial blood; together they preached that heavenly kingly mercy must be approached through atonement. Only high priests on Yom Kippur passed the veil, preserving tension between access and awe. When Christ expired and this veil tore (Matt 27:51), gospel writers emphatically linked new-covenant access to these ancient colours woven in faith and blood.

3.9 Bronze Works of the Courtyard

3.9.1 Molten "Sea": Cosmic Ocean, 2,000-Bath Capacity (1 Kgs 7:23-26)

Cast in the Plain of Jordan, the bronze sea measured 15 feet across, 7 feet deep, resting on twelve oxen representing Israel's tribes. Water symbolized chaos subdued by divine order (Gen 1:2), yet here priests drew cleansing rather than fear. Its capacity far exceeded Tabernacle lavers, accommodating increased priestly traffic. The sea's brim crafted like a lily signalled blooming life springing from watery depths, re-staging creation's emergence. Later prophets would envision living water flowing from this house to heal nations (Ezek 47:1-12).

3.9.2 Ten Bronze Lavers on Wheeled Stands: Mobile Purity (1 Kgs 7:27-39)

Each stand bore elaborate panels of lions, cherubim, and palm trees, mounted on chariot wheels. Mobility allowed priests to wash sacrificial parts near the altar, reducing spillage and preserving courtyard sanctity. Chariot imagery subtly proclaimed that Yahweh—depicted riding cherubim in Psalms—now rolled amid worship activity. Water's portability democratized cleansing, anticipating Jesus washing disciples' feet anywhere, not just at ritual basins. Thus engineering solved logistical issues while extending theological metaphor.

3.9.3 Altar of Burnt Offering: Scale, Slaughter, and Continuity with Sinai

Although dimensions are not specified in Kings, Chronicles suggests a vast structure (2 Chr 4:1), befitting thousands of daily worshippers. Its bronze surface endured perpetual fire, echoing Leviticus 6:13: "The fire shall be kept burning on the altar continually." By enlarging both laver and altar, Solomon preserved wilderness typology while adapting it to urban pilgrimage. The constant roar of flame and fragrance of burning flesh reminded Israel that sin's cost did not diminish with civic advancement. Sacrifice anchored splendour to sobriety.

3.10 Liturgical Economy: Daily, Weekly, Annual Rhythms

3.10.1 Morning-Evening *Tamid* Offerings Re-contextualised (2 Chr 13:11)

Priests sacrificed lambs at dawn and dusk, sandwiching communal life between acts of atonement. City dwellers heard trumpet blasts signalling each rite, aligning work schedules with worship. The Temple thus became Israel's timekeeper, sanctifying hours as well as spaces. Regularity inculcated dependable grace: God forgave daily, not sporadically. By maintaining Tabernacle rhythms inside stone walls, Solomon validated continuity within change.

3.10.2 Levitical Choirs and Instrumentation—Psalms in the Court (1 Chr 25)

David had already organized 24 choirs rotating weekly service; Solomon simply activated the system. Singers with cymbals, harps, and lyres accompanied sacrifices, embedding theology in melody. Psalm superscriptions referencing "Temple choirmaster" likely belong to this era. Music modulated emotional tones of confession, lament, and exuberant praise, ensuring holistic participation. Temple soundscape harmonized with golden visuals, creating multisensory liturgy.

3.10.3 Pilgrimage Feasts: Passover, Shavuot, Sukkot in a Fixed Sanctuary

Three times yearly males ascended to Jerusalem (Deut 16:16). Roadways thus became arteries carrying rural devotions into urban heartbeats. Passover sacrificed lambs within Temple courts, re-enacting Exodus under towering pillars Jachin and Boaz. Shavuot's first-fruits waved before gilded walls, acknowledging harvest grace. Sukkot's booths dotted city rooftops, turning Jerusalem into a temporary forest praising the God who once tabernacled among tents.

3.11 Ark Procession and Temple Dedication

3.11.1 City-Wide Worship Parade (1 Kgs 8:1-9)

Elders, priests, and Levites processed from David's City up to the new sanctuary, bearing the Ark on poles. Sacrificial animals too numerous to count accompanied, perfuming streets with burnt offerings. The spectacle united social strata and generations under a single anthem: "His steadfast love endures forever" (2 Chr 5:13). Ark relocation echoed Israel's journey from wilderness to rest, dramatizing Joshua's river crossing on a civic scale. Every spectator became participant in covenant drama.

3.11.2 120 Priests with Trumpets—Soundscape of Coronation (2 Chr 5:12-14)

When musicians raised a single voice, "the house was filled with a cloud." Trumpet blasts resembled Sinai thunder but mingled now with harmonious lyres, fusing fear and beauty. Holy noise served not entertainment but invocation, summoning divine presence to inhabit crafted space. The number 120 doubles the wilderness marching trumpets, signalling climax of Tabernacle patterns. Thus, sonic architecture preceded visible glory.

3.11.3 Sacrificial Deluge: 22,000 Oxen, 120,000 Sheep (1 Kgs 8:63)

Quantity astonishes modern readers, but ancient literature often employs large figures to convey grandeur. Multiple altars erected in the outer court accommodated the flood of offerings. Blood purification symbolically washed Moriah, preparing it as eternal dwelling. Excess also ensured every tribe individually partook, preventing monopolization by elites. In effect, national budget was poured out as worship—the costliest public work became costliest public sacrifice.

3.12 Shekinah Descent and Covenantal Prayer

3.12.1 Cloud-Filled House—Priests Unable to Stand (1 Kgs 8:10-11)

The same glory-cloud that guided desert wanderers now settled, transforming movable fire by night into stationary radiance. Priestly incapacity highlighted divine sufficiency; humans could only bow or exit. Cloud concealment balanced intimacy: God was present yet veiled, reachable yet ungraspable. Theophany validated architecture, proving stones alone do not guarantee presence. Without the cloud, the Temple would have remained a museum; with it, it became a meeting-place.

3.12.2 Solomon's Seven-Fold Prayer Themes: Justice, Mercy, Mission (1 Kgs 8:22-53)

From a bronze platform, Solomon prayed for issues spanning personal sin to cosmic droughts: forgiveness for oath-breakers, deliverance from defeat, rain for barren skies, justice for wronged strangers, return from exile. He repeatedly asked God to "hear from heaven Your dwelling place"—acknowledging that earthly house could not contain infinite deity (v. 27). Inclusion of foreigner prayers (vv. 41-43) revealed missionary impulse: the Temple should magnetize nations. His intercession thus transformed a national monument into a global altar, anticipating Isaiah's "house of prayer for all peoples" (Isa 56:7). Seven petitions, like creation's seven days, inaugurated a new symbolic cosmos.

3.12.3 Fire from Heaven Confirms Sacrifice (2 Chr 7:1-3)

Chronicles adds that fire leapt from heaven to consume offerings, synchronizing with Elijah's later Carmel showdown (1 Kgs 18:38). Supernatural ignition authenticated liturgy and paralleled Tabernacle inauguration (Lev 9:24). People fell on their faces, echoing Israel at Sinai but now with joyful awe. The fiery kiss of heaven and earth declared that blood on the altar was acceptable currency for communion. Consecration by flame marked the Temple as permanent place of pardon.

3.13 Temple, Wisdom, and Cosmic Order

3.13.1 Structural Parallels with Proverbs' "House of Wisdom" (Prov 9:1-6)

Proverbs describes Wisdom building a house, hewing seven pillars, preparing a feast, and inviting the simple. Solomon, author of many proverbs, likely drew on Temple architecture when penning this metaphor. Seven-year construction (1 Kgs 6:38) aligns with wisdom's pillars, linking cosmological completeness to sacred space. Approaching the Temple was thus entering Wisdom's banquet, where Torah instruction and sacrificial meals nourished mind and soul. Physical architecture embodied moral architecture.

3.13.2 Seven-Year Construction and Sabbath Symbolism (1 Kgs 6:38)

The duration's resonance with creation week suggests deliberate numerology. Just as God rested on the seventh day, the Temple emerged as a place of rest—*menuhah*—for divine presence and human pilgrims (Ps 132:14). Sabbath logic continued in priestly courses rotating every week, ensuring unbroken service without individual exhaustion (1 Chr 24). Hence, building timeline itself was catechetical, teaching patience, rhythm, and sanctified time. Rest was carved into stone schedule.

3.13.3 Temple as Micro-Cosmos: Heaven, Earth, Sea in Architectural Layers

Gold-drenched inner sanctum symbolized heaven; cedar-panelled nave with floral carvings represented cultivated earth; bronze sea in the court recalled primal waters. Passing through layers reenacted creation's emergence from chaos to cosmos. Priests acted as Adamic gardeners, tending menorah "trees" and showbread "fields." At the daily incense offering, they even re-planted Eden's aroma. Visitors thus rehearsed cosmic order under a single roof, becoming actors in liturgical theatre of creation.

3.14 Prophetic Appraisal and Conditional Covenant

3.14.1 Divine Warning during Night Vision (1 Kgs 9:1-9)

Shortly after dedication, God appeared to Solomon, accepting prayer yet warning: apostasy would render the house "a heap of ruins." Stone security could not override moral fidelity. Foreigners would pass and hiss, saying, "Why has the LORD done thus to this land and this house?" (v. 8). Thus, divine promise remained conditional on obedience, tethering architecture to ethics. The visit balanced earlier triumph, reminding monarch and masses that covenant blessings are revocable.

3.14.2 Prophets on Cult vs. Justice: Isaiah, Amos, Micah Critiques

Isaiah thundered against empty ritual: "Wash yourselves;…cease to do evil" (Isa 1:11-17). Amos lamented who desired "the day of the LORD" while trampling the poor (Am 5:11-24). Micah predicted Zion ploughed like a field (Mic 3:12). These denunciations targeted hypocrisy, not the Temple per se, proving that prophetic tradition served as conscience to institutional religion. The building remained glorious only as long as hearts remained humble.

3.14.3 The Temple's Role in National Apostasy and Reform (2 Kgs 23; 2 Chr 29-31)

Kings like Manasseh filled courts with foreign altars; Josiah later smashed them, renewing covenant and celebrating an unparalleled Passover (2 Kgs 23:21-23). Hezekiah reopened doors previously shut, stationing Levites to sing "with gladness" (2 Chr 29:30). The Temple thus mirrored the nation's spiritual pulse—decay under idolatrous rulers, revival under reformers. Every repair project carried symbolic weight: chiselling idolatry from walls chiselled apathy from hearts. Yet cyclical degradation foreshadowed eventual exile.

3.15 Ruin, Exile, and Residual Hope

3.15.1 Babylonian Destruction—586 BC (2 Kgs 25:8-17)

Nebuchadnezzar's forces breached walls, burned sanctuary, and dismantled bronze sea for scrap. Jachin and Boaz, once proud sentries, were toppled. Ark's fate disappears in silence, intensifying tragedy. Temple loss equated to cosmic collapse; psalmists likened it to heavens darkening (Ps 74:7-9). Yet prophetic vision re-framed trauma as purifying fire, not final annihilation.

3.15.2 Ezekiel's Vision of Departure and Future Return (Ezek 10-11; 40-48)

Ezekiel saw glory rise from cherubim and depart eastward, abandoning polluted precincts (Ezek 10:18-19). Yet later he measured a colossal future temple, river-fed and fruit-laden. The

Spirit would re-enter by the eastern gate, reversing departure (43:1-5). Blueprint dwarfed Solomon's, signifying not architectural feasibility but theological certainty: God's presence would return magnified. Hence exile birthed eschatological longing.

3.15.3 Haggai and Zechariah: Second Temple Encouragement and Greater Glory (Hag 2:3-9)

Post-exilic elders wept at modest foundations, but prophets promised that "the latter glory of this house shall be greater than the former." Gold might be scarce, yet divine peace would outshine Solomon's ornamentation. Zechariah envisioned a priest-king named Branch rebuilding the temple, wearing both crown and mitre (Zech 6:12-13). These oracles planted Messianic seeds, preparing hearts for a glory measured in grace rather than gilding.

3.16 Typological Fulfilment in Christ and the Church

3.16.1 "Destroy this Temple and in Three Days..." (John 2:19-21)

Jesus identified His body as the true temple, predicting resurrection as ultimate rebuilding. His flesh encompassed all Solomon's symbols—gold of divinity, cedar of incorruptible humanity. Crucifixion echoed Babylonian destruction; resurrection fulfilled Ezekiel's return of glory. Thus physical ruin became spiritual renewal, shifting sacred space from stone to Son. John's commentary explicitly states, "He spoke of the temple of His body."

3.16.2 Wisdom-Greater-than-Solomon (Matt 12:42)

Jesus claimed superiority over Solomon, integrating wisdom and temple typology. Where Solomon's wisdom built a house, Jesus' wisdom *is* the house, and believers become living branches grafted into Him. Miracles like calming storms reenacted temple sea mastery; feeding multitudes replaced showbread abundance. Every comparison accentuated fulfilment without denigrating former glory.

3.16.3 Living Stones and Eschatological Temple (1 Pet 2:4-6; Rev 21:22)

Peter calls believers "living stones" built into a spiritual house, with Christ as cornerstone—terminology lifted from quarry narratives. Revelation's finale depicts a city lacking temple "because the Lord God Almighty and the Lamb are its temple" (Rev 21:22). New Jerusalem squares to a cube, echoing Solomon's Holy of Holies but scaled to cosmic dimensions. Gold-paved streets universalize earlier gilded floors, and nations walk its light, realising Solomon's missionary prayer. Stone sanctuaries thus climax in a people-sanctuary spanning new heaven and earth.

In conclusion, Solomon's Temple stood as a marvel of engineering, diplomacy, and devotion—a fixed splendor radiating cosmic symbolism. Its gold sheen reflected Eden's lost brilliance; its towering pillars proclaimed covenant stability; its inner cube rehearsed eschatological perfection. Yet the very stones that dazzled eyes could not secure hearts; only continual obedience could keep glory within. In exile's aftermath, prophets taught Israel—and the church after her—that true permanence lies not in quarried blocks but in the living presence of God dwelling among and within His people. Solomon's masterpiece therefore functions both as pinnacle and pointer: a towering monument to divine-human fellowship and a shadow cast by a brighter, living Temple—Jesus Christ—who gathers redeemed humanity into a city where glory needs neither sun nor lamp, for "the LORD is there" (Ezek 48:35).

Chapter 4 — The Second Temple: Restoration, Reform, and Expectation

The Babylonian destruction of 586 BC appeared, at first glance, to be the final curtain on Israel's temple drama, yet within a lifetime a new and humbler sanctuary rose from the same ridge where Solomon's splendor had once blazed. Unlike the First Temple, whose story mingled royal wealth and prophetic warning, the Second Temple was mid-wifed by foreign edicts, funded by imperial treasuries, and supervised by governors who owed ultimate allegiance to distant capitals. Its builders were a minority remnant eking out a living among burned stones while their cousins prospered along the Euphrates; their courage turned charred memories into living hope. Throughout the next six centuries that modest complex would be enlarged, defended, violated, cleansed, and finally replaced by Herod's marble masterpiece—yet its theological significance never resided in square cubits of masonry so much as in the currents of repentance, reform, and eschatological longing that surged through its courts. This chapter traces those currents from Cyrus's decree to Titus's siege, showing how God kept covenant promise by re-establishing worship, re-forming identity around Torah, and re-orienting expectation toward a temple not made with hands. Each section and subsection unfolds in paragraphs of five to seven sentences, weaving Scripture, history, and thematic reflection into one continuous tapestry of restoration.

4.1 Imperial Edicts and the First Return (538–520 BC)

4.1.1 Cyrus's Proclamation: A Pagan King as "Yahweh's Anointed"

In the very first year of his reign over Babylon, Cyrus issued a decree that sounded more like a prophetic oracle than a political memo, announcing that "the LORD, the God of heaven, has given me all the kingdoms of the earth and charged me to build him a house in Jerusalem" (Ezra 1:1-4; cf. Isa 45:1). The edict exemplifies the Persian policy of repatriating exiled peoples and restoring local cults, but the biblical narrator interprets it as the direct fulfillment of Jeremiah's seventy-year prophecy (Jer 29:10). Temple vessels looted by Nebuchadnezzar were counted out item by item—5,400 in all— and placed under the care of Sheshbazzar the prince, signaling that the God of Israel still keeps receipts on what belongs to Him (Ezra 1:7-11). Cyrus's gesture also reframed power relations: an emperor became patron, while a humble community became steward of divine promise. Thus, the Second Temple story begins with the paradox of sovereignty mediated through an unbelieving ruler whose name, ironically, means "sun," foreshadowing Malachi's promise of a rising sun of righteousness.

4.1.2 The Sheshbazzar Interlude: Foundations without Walls

Sheshbazzar led the first caravan westward, bearing sacred vessels and the imperial warrant, yet the biblical record of his tenure is tantalizingly brief (Ezra 5:14-16). He laid an initial foundation and re-erected the altar so that daily burnt offerings could resume even though the city still lay in ruins (Ezra 3:1-3). The priority on sacrifice before shelter revealed a community more anxious for forgiveness than for fortification, reenacting Abraham's instinct to build altars before pitching permanent tents. Opposition soon stalled the work, and for nearly two decades the site remained an unremarkable slab of masonry—a visible reminder that covenant projects may languish when zeal exhausts itself or resources evaporate. Still, that half-finished podium preserved hope; each passer-by could measure future glory against current lack, an exercise that sharpened spiritual appetite for the day when the house would again echo with psalms.

4.1.3 Persian Oversight: Imperial Funds and Provincial Suspicion

Because Judea was now the Persian province of "Beyond the River," local officials such as Tattenai and Shethar-Bozenai monitored any major building initiative (Ezra 5:3-5). When they queried the legitimacy of the project, the Jewish elders appealed directly to the Cyrus edict lodged in imperial archives, and Darius I not only confirmed its authenticity but ordered tribute monies to be drawn from provincial taxes to fund the work (Ezra 6:6-12). This unexpected subsidy turned reluctant overseers into reluctant benefactors, illustrating Proverbs 21:1 that the king's heart is a stream of water in the Lord's hand. Persian involvement also meant that temple economics were now international, foreshadowing later episodes where Greek and Roman coins would jingle in the same courts. Yet with every installment of silver and wheat, the returnees recognized afresh that true patronage came from the God who can make even enemies finance His worship (Isa 60:10-11).

4.2 Zerubbabel and Jeshua: Leadership for a New Era (520 BC)

4.2.1 Davidic Governor and Aaronic High Priest

When the work languished, God raised two pillars of hope: Zerubbabel, grandson of Jehoiachin and thus heir to David's line, and Jeshua (Joshua) son of Jozadak, great-grandson of the pre-exilic high priest Seraiah (Ezra 3:2). Their partnership re-united throne and altar, albeit in attenuated form—Zerubbabel wielded a governor's signet, not a king's scepter; Jeshua wore linen robes, not breastplates studded with Urim and Thummim. Nevertheless, Haggai proclaimed that Zerubbabel would become the Lord's signet ring, reversing the curse that had stripped Jehoiachin of royal dignity (Hag 2:23). Zechariah envisioned Jeshua crowned like a priest-king, foreshadowing a Branch who would unite both offices perfectly (Zech 6:11-13). Thus, the leadership duo embodied prophetic hope that governance and holiness might converge, even if only in embryonic form, within the scaffolding of a still-unfinished sanctuary.

4.2.2 The Foundation Ceremony: Tears and Trumpets

In the second year of their return, the builders reset the foundation, and Levites aged twenty and above supervised the labor according to Davidic precedent (Ezra 3:8-10). When the cornerstone was laid, priests blew trumpets and Levites clashed cymbals, singing the ancient refrain, "For He is good; His steadfast love endures forever" (Ps 136; Ezra 3:11). But the shouts of joy intermingled with the sobs of elderly eyewitnesses who remembered Solomon's grandeur, producing a cacophony so mixed that distant villages could not discern whether celebration or calamity had erupted. The scene underscores how memory can be both gift and burden—nostalgia may kindle aspiration but can also dampen gratitude for new mercies. Still, the chronicler records the event not to immortalize disappointment but to document covenant continuity: the same liturgy that consecrated Solomon's gold now consecrated humble hewn stone.

4.2.3 Prophetic Catalysts: Haggai and Zechariah

Eighteen years after the initial return, Haggai's stern question—"Is it time for you yourselves to dwell in paneled houses while this house lies in ruins?" (Hag 1:4)—jerked the community from economic self-absorption. He promised that the Lord would shake the nations so that their treasures would flow to Zion, and that the latter glory of this house would surpass the former (Hag 2:6-9). Zechariah complemented the rebuke with apocalyptic encouragement: night visions of flying scrolls, measuring lines, and lampstands assured the people that divine eyes ranged over all the earth and that progress would come "not by might, nor by power, but by My Spirit" (Zech 4:6-10). These oracles recalibrated imagination, teaching that spiritual significance is not measured by façade height but by covenant fidelity and eschatological promise. Within four years the house stood complete, vindicating prophetic urgency and proving that when God arouses latent zeal, stalled projects race to completion.

4.3 Completion and Dedication (515 BC)

4.3.1 Imperial Confirmation under Darius I

Tattenai's inquiry to Darius could have called a halt, yet the king's archival search unearthed Cyrus's decree at Ecbatana, leading

Darius to issue a reinforcing edict that threatened death by beam-impalement for anyone who hindered the work (Ezra 6:11). He commanded that building costs be paid "from the royal revenue, the tribute of the province," turning tax assessments into temple grants. Thus, the sanctuary's existence became a testament that divine sovereignty transcends successive empires; Babylon destroyed, Persia rebuilt, Greece would later adorn, and Rome would again renovate. For the returned community, imperial endorsement did not dilute the theological meaning of their achievement but magnified it—foreign gold subsidized sacred stone, fulfilling Isaiah's vision of kings nursing Zion (Isa 60:16). The renewal of sacrifices under a foreign aegis also prefigured a day when Gentile centurions would finance synagogues and praise Israel's God (Luke 7:4-5).

4.3.2 Passover of Rededication

With walls plastered and cedar beams in place, the exiles celebrated Passover on the fourteenth day of Nisan, exactly as commanded in Torah (Ezra 6:19-22). The ritual underscored covenant continuity: just as blood on doorposts inaugurated the first exodus, so blood on the newly built altar inaugurated a second exodus from imperial captivity. Priests and Levites purified themselves "together," a note of corporate humility absent from many first-temple narratives where hierarchy often bred rivalry. The seven-day Feast of Unleavened Bread that followed was kept "with joy, for the LORD had made them joyful and had turned the heart of the king of Assyria to them" (Ezra 6:22), a deliberate anachronism reminding readers that conquering powers are interchangeable pawns in God's redemptive chessboard. Passover joy also masked lingering poverty; yet shared lamb and unleavened loaves tasted richer for having been seasoned by tears and perseverance.

4.3.3 A Modest House without an Ark

The architecture of the Second Temple was plain by comparison to Solomon's—fewer gold panels, smaller dimensions, and, most strikingly, an empty Holy of Holies where the Ark once stood. Rabbinic memory speaks of a foundation stone protruding three fingers above the floor on which the high priest sprinkled Yom Kippur blood (m. Yoma 5:2), signaling that absence can itself become liturgical. No Shekinah cloud filled this sanctuary at dedication, yet prophetic words declared that invisible glory would surpass visible lack (Hag 2:9). Thus, the Temple invited worshipers to trust promises more than perceptions, anticipating a Messiah who would stand among ordinary stones and proclaim, "Something greater than the temple is here" (Matt 12:6). The holy precinct therefore became a theater of expectancy, its architectural impoverishment fertilizing hope for eschatological enrichment.

4.4 Ezra's Torah Reform (458 BC)

4.4.1 Artaxerxes' Letter: Torah on Imperial Letterhead

Almost sixty years after the dedication, Artaxerxes I authorized Ezra, a scribe "skilled in the Law of Moses," to lead a second return and appoint magistrates who knew God's commands (Ezra 7:11-26). The royal missive not only allowed but compelled local treasurers to fund sacrificial supplies—wheat, wine, oil—up to a generous quota, and it exempted temple workers from imperial taxes. Such patronage underscored that the Torah's authority could coexist, temporarily, with pagan sovereignty, foreshadowing Paul's later appeal to Caesar's jurisdiction for gospel purposes (Acts 25:11-12). Ezra's journey of four months across treacherous terrain without military escort testified to providential shielding, reminding the caravan that reliance on human chariots is vanity when the "good hand of God" rests upon His servants (Ezra 8:21-23). The edict's concluding threat of death or confiscation against law-breakers underscored Persia's recognition that societal stability hinged on religious fidelity—a truth that still echoes in every culture's struggle to balance spiritual conviction with civic order.

4.4.2 Public Reading and Covenant Renewal

Upon arrival, Ezra conducted a census, delivered the imperial silver to temple treasurers, and, after resting three days, confronted the community with the Torah's demands (Ezra 8:33-34; Neh 8:1-8). He stood on a wooden platform from daybreak until noon, reading aloud while Levites interpreted, and the assembly responded with lifted hands and bowed faces, a posture blending jubilation with contrition. This marathon exposition birthed a revival so intense that the people wept, prompting leaders to urge feasting instead, "for the joy of the LORD is your strength" (Neh 8:10). A renewed Feast of Booths followed, the first kept "since the days of Joshua," illustrating that Scripture, once unveiled, reactivates dormant obedience (Neh 8:17). Ezra's pedagogy shifted temple centrality from sacrificial choreography to textual proclamation, thereby laying foundations for synagogue worship that would flourish long after stones again fell. In effect, the scroll became a portable temple, its ink lines forming sancta where dispersed Jews could meet their covenant God.

4.4.3 Intermarriage Crisis and Identity Purification

Ezra's joy soon gave way to anguish when leaders reported that many returned families, including priests, had married women from surrounding nations (Ezra 9:1-2). He tore garment and beard, confessing communal guilt that reached back to pre-exilic abominations, fearing divine wrath might collapse the fragile restoration. The assembly agreed to divorce foreign wives—an excruciating remedy—highlighting the tension between covenant fidelity and personal happiness. Critics today may deem the action xenophobic, yet within the narrative its purpose is theological preservation: without distinct identity, the temple would devolve into a syncretistic shrine like those that once dotted Solomon's hill. Importantly, the text records each offender by name (Ezra 10:18-44), affirming that holiness policy is never abstract but confronts real households. The episode set precedent for later debates over Gentile inclusion, debates only resolved when the gospel demonstrated a new identity in Christ transcending ethnic lines (Acts 15; Gal 3:28).

4.5 Nehemiah's Wall and Civic Reform (445–432 BC)

4.5.1 Cupbearer to Governor: A Vocation Redeemed

News of Jerusalem's broken wall reached Nehemiah in Susa, and the royal cupbearer wept, fasted, and prayed, confessing national sin while appealing to covenant promises (Neh 1:1-11). Artaxerxes granted him leave, letters, and timber, demonstrating again that foreign thrones serve divine blueprints. Arriving by night, Nehemiah surveyed rubble, then rallied nobles, perfumers, goldsmiths, and daughters alike to build shoulder to shoulder (Neh 3). His leadership blended prayer and planning—one hand carried sword, the other trowel—modeling faith that works without presumption. Thus, city walls became an extension of temple theology, for sacred space demanded secure margins to flourish.

4.5.2 Opposition, Satire, and Spiritual Warfare

Sanballat and Tobiah ridiculed the builders, claiming a fox could topple their stonework (Neh 4:3). Nehemiah answered mockery with prayer: "Hear, O our God, for we are despised," then stationed armed families along vulnerable sections. He refused secret negotiations in Ono Valley, discerning that distraction is often deadlier than assault (Neh 6:1-4). A forged prophecy by Shemaiah tried to lure him into temple sanctum for refuge, but Nehemiah rejected illicit sanctuary, protecting both life and law (Neh 6:10-13). The wall arose in fifty-two days, and fear fell on surrounding nations, proving that covenant resolve outbuilds carnal sabotage.

4.5.3 Economic Justice and Covenant Oaths

During construction a famine exposed exploitation: nobles charged interest, switching brotherhood for brokerage (Neh 5:1-5). Nehemiah convened an assembly, rebuked lenders, and shook out his garment as curse symbol until debts were forgiven. He himself refused the governor's food allowance, feeding 150 officials from personal stores, demonstrating servant-leadership reminiscent of Christ washing feet. After wall completion, he led covenant renewal where people swore to tithe produce, refrain from Sabbath trade, and support Levites (Neh 10:32-39). Economic ethics thus flowed from rebuilt walls to guarantee that temple worship was undergirded by social righteousness.

4.6 Priestly Administration and Daily Liturgy

4.6.1 High-Priestly Succession and Political Entanglements

The post-exilic high-priesthood passed from Jeshua to Joiakim, Eliashib, Johanan, and Jaddua, each navigating alliances with Persian governors and, later, Hellenistic rulers (Neh 12:10-11). Eliashib's leasing of temple chambers to Tobiah the Ammonite scandalized Nehemiah, revealing how kinship networks could corrode sanctity when unchecked (Neh 13:4-9). Yet priestly records were meticulously kept, indicating a passion to guard lineage purity for liturgical legitimacy. Josephus later notes that Jaddua met Alexander the Great in full priestly regalia, suggesting that vestments carried diplomatic weight. Thus, the high priest's office became both spiritual and political fulcrum, foreshadowing tensions that would erupt under the Hasmoneans.

4.6.2 Twenty-Four Courses and Temple Tax

David's ancient division of priests into twenty-four courses (*mishmarot*) was revived so that each order served one week twice a year (1 Chr 24; Neh 12:24). This rotation democratized proximity, allowing families from both provincial villages and Jerusalem quarters to partake in holy duties. Maintenance was financed by an annual one-third shekel tax—later one-half shekel—paid by every male over twenty (Neh 10:32; Ex 30:13). The levy ensured incense never ran out and lamps never dimmed, binding economic discipline to liturgical continuity. By Jesus' day this tax funded Herod's renovations, and Peter's miraculous coin obtained from a fish signaled messianic lordship over temple finances (Matt 17:24-27).

4.6.3 Levitical Choirs and Scribal Schools

Ezra's emphasis on text birthed schools where scribes copied Scripture, formalizing vocalization and accent marks that preserved pronunciation. Levitical choirs expanded Psalter repertoire, assigning specific psalms for each day of the week (m. Tamid 7:4). Music became theology-on-melody; daily modulations reminded worshipers that time itself is an instrument tuned to praise. The Great Assembly—tradition credits Ezra as founding member—codified prayers like the Amidah, fusing temple sacrifices with spoken petitions. Thus, when sacrifices ceased in 70 AD, prayer liturgies already carried sacrificial cadence, enabling Judaism to flourish in diaspora synagogues.

4.7 Jewish Sects and the Question of Authority

4.7.1 Sadducees: Guardians of Toran Priesthood

Descended from Zadokite lines, the Sadducees controlled high-priestly appointments and dominated the Sanhedrin's temple affairs. They accepted only the written Torah as binding and rejected resurrection doctrines, aligning themselves more with aristocratic pragmatism than with populist hope (Acts 23:8). Their collaboration with Hasmonean and Roman authorities secured political stability but bred public suspicion. Because their power base was the altar, any challenge to temple systems threatened their status—hence their alarm at Jesus' cleansing and apostolic miracles (John 11:47-48; Acts 4:1-2). Ironically, their denial of afterlife left them ill-prepared to survive Rome's fire; once the temple fell, their faction disappeared from history.

4.7.2 Pharisees: Oral Law and Holiness beyond the Courtyard

Pharisees emerged from Hasidean piety during Maccabean wars, advocating fence-laws around Torah to protect against inadvertent transgression. They promoted table purity, tithing, and lay study, effectively transplanting temple holiness into every dining room (Mark 7:1-4). Belief in resurrection, angels, and divine providence resonated with commoners who found hope in future vindication (Acts 23:6-9). Their debates with Jesus revolved not around temple centrality but around the weightier matters of the law—justice, mercy, and faithfulness (Matt 23:23). After 70 AD their halakhic structures became scaffolding for rabbinic Judaism, proving that decentralization can preserve identity when stone shrines crumble.

4.7.3 Essenes and the Qumran Alternative

Dissatisfied with Jerusalem's priesthood, Essenes retreated to desert communes, practicing rigorous purity rituals and awaiting a dual-messiah scenario—one priestly, one royal. Their writings, preserved in the Dead Sea Scrolls, speak of a sanctuary defiled by "wicked priests" and foretell a new temple measured after Ezekiel's vision. Daily life revolved around communal meals that mimicked temple sacrifices, led by a presiding priest reading sacred texts. By rejecting marriage for vocational celibacy, some Essene groups embodied an anticipated angelic existence, linking present discipline with eschatological hope (Matt 22:30). Their scroll jars, hidden before Rome's advance, ironically ensured that their theological critique would outlast both second-temple stones and sectarian isolation.

4.8 Hellenistic Shocks and the Maccabean Revolt (332–164 BC)

4.8.1 Greek Urbanism and Cultural Tension

Alexander's conquest introduced gymnasia, theaters, and marketplaces that valorized Greek language, dress, and civic ideals. High-priest Jason built a Jerusalem gymnasium within sight of the temple, enrolling youths in ephebic rites that offended Torah sensibilities (2 Macc 4:9-15). Some Judeans welcomed Hellenism as modernization, while others saw it as idolatrous capitulation. The ensuing identity crisis revealed that stone walls cannot by themselves immunize a community against cultural erosion. Thus, the temple became a flashpoint between accommodation and fidelity long before Rome ever laid siege.

4.8.2 Antiochus IV Epiphanes and the "Abomination"

In 167 BC Antiochus outlawed circumcision, Sabbath, and sacrifices, erecting an altar to Zeus and, according to some sources, sacrificing swine flesh in the precincts (1 Macc 1:54). Daniel's earlier prophecy of an "abomination that makes desolate" (Dan 11:31) found chilling fulfillment, proving prophetic vocabulary elastic enough to stretch across centuries. The desecration galvanized resistance, for when worship is criminalized, even the timid acquire courage from outrage. The temple that had survived poverty and politics now confronted annihilation, pushing pious families into guerrilla warfare sanctified as holy zeal. Thus, persecution clarified loyalties more effectively than prosperity had.

4.8.3 Hasmonean Victory and Temple Rededication

Judas Maccabeus recaptured Jerusalem in 164 BC, tore down the profaned altar, and built a new one of unhewn stones, mirroring Deuteronomic law (Deut 27:5-6; 1 Macc 4:44-47). They lit the menorah with a single undefiled oil cruse, and when it burned eight days—until new oil could be prepared—tradition claims a miracle that birthed *Hanukkah*. Psalm-singing soldiers circled the altar, echoing Nehemiah's wall dedication but now seasoned by battlefield grit. Independence followed, yet so did priest-king controversies as Hasmoneans combined crown and miter, blurring lines God once drew. Nevertheless, the rededicated house rekindled eschatological expectation that tyranny, even cosmic, could be toppled by covenantal courage.

4.9 Apocalyptic Hopes and Eschatological Projections

4.9.1 Danielic Timetables and Temple Vindication

Daniel 8 and 9 calculated periods of desecration and promised sanctuary restoration, inspiring chronological speculation among later Jews. The seventy-weeks prophecy (Dan 9:24-27) fed messianic fervor, with many interpreting the "anointed one" cut off as reference to priestly martyrdoms under Antiochus or to a future messianic figure. Thus, calendar study became an act of hopeful resistance; scribes pored over numeric puzzles under torchlight, believing cosmic clocks ticked in temple rhythms. Such expectation formed the backdrop for Gabriel's announcement to Mary that her Son would inherit David's throne, fulfilling prophetic arithmetic in flesh (Luke 1:31-33). Hence, apocalyptic literature kept the architectural imagination alive even when political prospects seemed bleak.

4.9.2 Heavenly Temple in 1 Enoch and Dead Sea Scrolls

Enochic visions transported readers to crystal palaces and fiery wheels where archangels ministered before sapphire thrones (1 Enoch 14:8-25). These scenes reframed earthly liturgy as shadow of celestial worship, enabling persecuted saints to feel present at courts higher than Antiochus's marble halls. The Qumran War Scroll described a final conflict where heavenly priests would join earthly counterparts, merging two sanctuaries into one triumphant liturgy. Such writings elevated suffering by embedding it in cosmic narrative, turning martyrdom into doxological entry visa. Consequently, Second Temple eschatology stretched temple theology beyond limestone, toward dimensions where cherubim never cease crying "Holy."

4.9.3 New Jerusalem Texts: Cubic Cities and River Temples

Fragments like 11Q18 sketch a future city twelve thousand cubits square, echoing Ezekiel 40–48 and prefiguring Revelation 21. Unlike Ezekiel, these texts sometimes omit sacrificial systems, focusing on radiant walls and gem-like foundations—a shift that prepared imaginations for spiritualized temple metaphors. Rivers flowing from thresholds healed desert landscapes, reversing Edenic exile (Ezek 47:1-12). Reading such visions during pilgrimage would have made every step toward Jerusalem feel like rehearsal for eschatological ingress. Thus, apocalyptic cartography saturated Jewish prayers, so that when John the Revelator saw a temple-less city, he stood on literary shoulders already straining for infinite horizons.

4.10 Herod the Great's Renovation (20 BC – AD 63)

4.10.1 Political Legitimacy through Monumentality

Herod, an Idumean by birth, needed legitimacy among Temple-centered Judeans, so he announced a renovation "beyond compare," employing ten thousand laborers and a thousand priests trained as masons to avoid profanation. Josephus records that foundational stones weighed up to four hundred tons, some still visible in today's Western Wall tunnels (*Ant.* 15.420-425). Thus, Herod translated political insecurity into architectural excess, coating piety with propaganda. However, grandeur attracted Gentile tourists, turning Court of the Gentiles into a bustling bazaar that Jesus would later cleanse (Mark 11:15-17). Herod's project, begun in the eighteenth year of his reign, continued under Agrippa II until just before Rome's siege, proving that stone ambitions can outlive their sponsors only to fall to unforeseen conflagrations.

4.10.2 Design Echoes of Eden and Solomon

The expanded platform—nearly thirty-seven acres—accommodated colonnades named "Royal Stoa," whose cedar-paneled ceiling imported Lebanon's forests into Judea once again. Gates bore names like "Beautiful" and "Shushan," weaving biblical nostalgia and Persian memory into sandstone. Gold vine reliefs over the entrance recalled Israel as vineyard of God (Ps 80:8-11), while water conduits channeled living springs, faint shadows of Ezekiel's river. Pilgrims ascending southern steps recited Psalms 120-134, their cadence matching stair rhythm, transforming architecture into mnemonic ladder. Thus, Herod's stones, however politicized, still preached Eden-Solomon themes to hearts tuned by Scripture.

4.10.3 Soreg Inscription and Gentile Boundaries

A limestone plaque, fragments of which survive, warned foreigners that crossing the *soreg* low balustrade meant death. Paul alluded to this barrier when proclaiming that Christ "has broken down the dividing wall of hostility" (Eph 2:14). The sign exemplified how meticulous purity fences could ossify into ethnic exclusion, yet it also revealed the temple's magnetic pull on devout Gentiles who yearned for proximity. When Greeks asked Philip to see Jesus during Passover (John 12:20-23), they likely stood just outside this balustrade, hearing Messianic echo within earshot of sacrificial bleats. Herod's courts thus became stage for prophetic gestures that would redefine holiness across cultures.

4.11 Jesus and the Second Temple

4.11.1 Infancy to Adulthood: A Life Framed by Temple Courts

Jesus was presented at forty days, and Simeon's Nunc Dimittis linked the child to "the glory of your people Israel" located within sanctuary precincts (Luke 2:22-32). At twelve, He engaged doctors of the law, calling the complex "my Father's house," a claim that circumvented Sadducean custodianship (Luke 2:49). Throughout His ministry He chose feast seasons—Tabernacles, Dedication, Passover—to teach within Solomon's Portico, turning colonnades into classrooms of kingdom revelation (John 7–10). Thus, His biography is bracketed by temple episodes, positioning Him as true meeting place between God and humanity.

4.11.2 Cleansing Act: Prophetic Sign or Priestly Challenge?

Driving traders and money-changers from Court of the Gentiles, Jesus cited Isaiah 56:7 and Jeremiah 7:11, indicting economic practices that suffocated Gentile prayer space. His authority to cleanse implied superior priesthood, provoking Sadducees who profited from temple commerce. When challenged, He cryptically offered His body as replacement sanctuary: "Destroy this temple, and in three days I will raise it up" (John 2:19-21). John's editorial note equating temple with body reframed sacrificial system around forthcoming crucifixion-resurrection event. The act, repeated at end of ministry (Mark 11), served as enacted parable and legal catalyst for His arrest.

4.11.3 Veil Torn: Cultic Curtain to Cosmic Canvas

At the ninth hour, as Passover lambs were being slain, the forty-foot veil ripped from top to bottom (Matt 27:51). The tear signified divine initiative—top downward—and opened what once excluded, fulfilling Hebrews 10:19-22 where flesh of Jesus becomes living veil. Earthquake and tomb openings followed, linking temple breach to resurrection hope, as if heaven inverted every barrier in one synchronized moment. Centurion confession, "Surely this was God's Son," outside the veil, confirmed Gentile access now ratified (Matt 27:54). Thus, the physical curtain's demise marked the theological obsolescence of the stone house, not by Roman fire but by atoning blood.

4.12 Early Church and the Temple Question

4.12.1 Pentecost Wind and Fire in Temple Precincts

Luke locates the outpouring "in the house where they were sitting," yet Peter's sermon occurs at the hour of prayer amid a multilingual crowd (Acts 2:1-11). Given spatial constraints, many scholars place the event on southern steps or Solomon's Portico. Tongues of fire democratized what once crowned only high priest on Yom Kippur, signaling a royal priesthood poured over sons and daughters (Joel 2:28-29; 1 Pet 2:9). Thus, temple geography hosted inaugural church liturgy even as pneumatology eclipsed architectural centrality.

4.12.2 Ninth-Hour Prayers and Apostolic Healing

Peter and John continued attending *minḥah* prayer and healed the lame man at Gate Beautiful, illustrating continuity with Jewish rhythms (Acts 3:1-10). The miracle redirected praise from stones to resurrected Christ, yet no note suggests temple avoidance; sacred space remained evangelistic hub until persecution scattered believers. Stephen's speech, however, critiqued "hand-made houses," asserting that the Most High dwells not in temples (Acts 7:48-50), a declaration that cost his life but crystallized theology of mobile presence. Paul later brings Nazarite offerings to prove respect for law, yet even that gesture sparks riot, revealing that gospel freedom and temple nationalism could not coexist for long (Acts 21:26-30).

4.12.3 Pauline Ecclesiology: People as Temple

Writing to Corinthians living among pagan shrines, Paul declared, "You are God's temple, and the Spirit dwells in you" (1 Cor 3:16-17). Ephesians expands the metaphor, depicting Jews and Gentiles as living stones built on apostolic foundation with Christ as cornerstone (Eph 2:19-22). These assertions did not spiritualize away the temple; they universalized its essence, distributing glory across the Mediterranean world. Thus, diaspora assemblies became micro-sanctuaries where Spirit fire still fell, heritage scrolls were read, and bread and wine proclaimed new-covenant atonement.

4.13 Siege, Destruction, and Diaspora (AD 66–73)

4.13.1 Zealot Uprising and Temple Turmoil

Revolt began over taxation grievances, but quickly priests ceased sacrificing for Caesar, a political act of secession. Zealot factions occupied sanctuary, murdering opponents in the inner court; Josephus laments that even calf selection for daily offering failed because no qualified priest remained (*War* 4.147-201). So when Rome breached gates, sacrificial rhythm had already collapsed, making Titus's flames merely epilogue to internal desecration. Jesus' prophecy that stones would topple found literal fulfillment as soldiers pried blocks to retrieve molten gold.

4.13.2 Trauma and Theological Reckoning

Survivors asked how a house once filled with glory could burn, reviving Jeremiah's counsel that presence depends on justice, not mortar. Christian communities interpreted catastrophe as vindication of crucified Messiah's warning; rabbinic sages interpreted it as punishment for baseless hatred (*bittul torah*) and hopes for third-temple restoration. Diaspora synagogues, already functioning, absorbed sacrificial memory into prayer cycles—*Amidah* petitions for rebuilding, Passover lament "Next year in Jerusalem." Thus, ruin paradoxically sowed liturgical resilience, proving again that presence migrates where hearts repent.

In conclusion, from Cyrus's edict to Titus's siege, the Second Temple stood as both testimony and teacher—its humble foundations reminding a remnant that mercy outlasts majesty, its renovations proving that political ambition can never eclipse prophetic purpose. Within its courts sins were confessed, Torah rediscovered, psalms resounded, and Messiah footsteps echoed, each episode layering another hue onto the canvas of redemptive history. When its veil split and its stones tumbled, the building's ultimate sermon was heard: access to God is purchased by blood, not by bricks, and His glory prefers hearts of flesh to slabs of marble. Yet the memory of that house continues to shape prayers, debates, and pilgrimages, stirring both longing and caution. For Christians, it invites grateful wonder that the true temple has already risen in three days and now builds itself worldwide; for Israel, it seeds hope in promised restoration; for all nations, it warns that structures cannot substitute for righteousness. Thus, the Second Temple, though long reduced to scattered stones and pages of history, still points every reader to the living reality where earthly restoration meets eternal expectation—Jesus Christ, in whom all God's fullness dwells bodily and through whom He will reconcile all things to Himself.

Chapter 5 — Prophetic Visions of a Greater House.

Prophecy kept the hope of a house alive when courts lay in rubble and priests in exile grew old dreaming of cedar beams they would never see again. While Ezra, Nehemiah, and the Maccabees fought for bricks and boundaries, the prophets fought for imagination, insisting that the true future of worship was too large to be measured merely in cubits of stone. Isaiah pictured a mountain city radiating light to nations; Ezekiel measured a temple no surveyor's chain could actually mark; Haggai dared to declare that a shabby post-exilic shrine would host a glory greater than Solomon's; and Zechariah crowned a high priest just to prove that a single head could, in God's plan, carry both mitre and diadem. Daniel calculated timetables for desolation and vindication, turning exile nights into vigils of arithmetic faith; inter-testamental visionaries carried the blueprints forward, sketching cubic cities and gem foundations on goat-skin scrolls. Taken together, these oracles do more than predict architecture—they form a theological scaffolding that lifts worshippers from nostalgia for a lost past toward expectancy for a cosmic communion in which creation itself becomes sanctuary. In this chapter we listen carefully to each prophetic voice, tracing how every vision adds a complementary stone to the edifice of hope that will finally be unveiled in the New Testament's declaration that God and the Lamb are the temple of the new creation (Rev 21 :22). Because the prophets speak across centuries and empires, we arrange their testimonies thematically rather than chronologically, beginning with Isaiah's soaring mountain-house and ending with Revelation's temple-less city, allowing readers to feel the widening arc of revelation. By the time we reach the epilogue, the reader should sense that the promised "greater house" is far more than a future building project; it is the gathered people of God, indwelt by the Spirit, headed toward a consummation where geography is swallowed up by glory.

5.1 Isaiah's Mountain-Temple Hope

5.1.1 Zion Exalted Above the Hills (Isa 2 :1-5)

Isaiah opens his anthology of oracles with a dazzling vista: in the latter days the mountain of the LORD's house rises above every summit, and the moral topography of the world tilts so that nations stream uphill in a supernatural pilgrimage. The prophet's verbs are purposefully reversed—streams normally flow downward—but grace creates an anti-gravity of desire that pulls peoples toward Torah rather than scattering them at Babel (Gen 11 :8). As they ascend, they urge one another, "Come, let us go up," collapsing ethnic rivalries into a single imperative of worship. The promised result of their ascent is not only doxology but pedagogy: "He will teach us His ways," suggesting that temple life is inherently instructional, a motif Jesus will later match when He teaches daily in Solomon's Colonnade (Luke 19 :47). Swords and spears are recast into plowshares and pruning hooks, implying that a truly exalted sanctuary pacifies international hostility by satisfying spiritual hunger (Isa 2 :4). The vision concludes with an appeal to the present generation—"O house of Jacob, walk!"—linking eschatological promise to ethical obligation; prophetic vistas are not escape fantasies but moral engines. Later prophets will echo Isaiah's imagery, but none match his audacious claim that architectural elevation can reorder geopolitical gravity.

5.1.2 A House of Prayer for All Nations (Isa 56 :1-8)

Halfway through the book, Isaiah revisits temple themes with an inclusivity that startled his first readers. Foreigners who bind themselves to the LORD, eunuchs once barred by Deuteronomic law (Deut 23 :1), and anyone who keeps Sabbath allegiance are promised "a name better than sons and daughters" inside the sanctuary courts. The phrase "house of prayer for all peoples" became Jesus' rallying cry when He cleansed the Gentile court of mercantile clutter (Mark 11 :17). Isaiah here smashes ethnic and physical exclusions by placing covenant faithfulness above pedigree or bodily completeness, anticipating Paul's doctrine that circumcision counts for nothing compared to a new creation (Gal 6 :15). Yahweh's gathered outcasts include "those yet to be gathered" (Isa 56 :8), an open-ended clause that leaves chronological space for later Gentile grafting. Thus, the prophet subtly relocates the boundary markers of holiness from heredity to humble obedience, preparing the theological soil for a Messiah who will heal eunuchs and welcome Syro-Phoenician women. Temple vision, therefore, enlarges solidarity even while defending sanctity—a combination repeated whenever the church wrestles with inclusion and integrity.

5.1.3 Streams in the Desert and Blossoming Wilderness (Isa 35)

Isaiah's ecological poetry turns wasteland into sanctuary corridor: crocuses burst forth, the weak-kneed find strength, and a highway called Holiness invites the redeemed to Zion with songs of everlasting joy. The imagery is lavish—blind eyes opened, lame leaping, jackals yielding to pools—portraying salvation as environmental as well as personal. Verses 8-10 climax with ransomed exiles entering Zion amid gladness, implicitly describing a pilgrim procession where geography cooperates with liturgy. Jesus invokes this passage when answering John the Baptist's doubts, listing healings as evidence that messianic days have dawned (Matt 11 :4-5), thereby identifying Himself as the embodiment of Isaiah's highway. If the landscape itself is to blossom, then temple fulfilment must encompass more than human souls; it must heal creation groaning under futility (Rom 8 :19-22). Therefore, Isaiah's environmental temple enlarges hope to planetary scope, making every ecological renewal a faint prelude to cosmic sanctuary restoration. The prophet forces readers to imagine worship in color palettes of flora and fauna, reminding theologians that eschatology intersects ecology.

5.1.4 Foreign Tribute and Glorified Zion (Isa 60)

In perhaps the Old Testament's most opulent vision, Isaiah sees caravans of camels, ships of Tarshish, and Lebanon's cedar converging on Jerusalem, turning defeated exiles into enthroned administrators. Gold and frankincense carried by Midian and Ephah presage magi gifts in Matthew's nativity, connecting temple prophecy to Messiah's crib (Matt 2 :11). Strangers rebuild walls, and kings serve at gates, reversing earlier chapters where foreigners raze city walls (Isa 5 :26-30). The prophet is bold enough to call former enemies "your priests" (Isa 61 :6), dissolving hostilities in the alchemy of worship. This torrent of tribute culminates in the declaration that the smallest clan will become a mighty nation "in its time," ensuring that prophetic extravagance remains anchored to divine scheduling (Isa 60 :22). Revelation 21 borrows the imagery when Gentile glory enters the New Jerusalem's perpetually open gates, signalling the literary durability of Isaiah's vision across testaments. Here, economic, political, and liturgical dimensions converge, urging modern readers to see missionary enterprise, diplomatic peacemaking, and artistic excellence as tributaries streaming toward the mountain of God.

5.1.5 A New Heaven and a New Earth (Isa 65 :17-25)

Replacing cosmic ceilings and landmasses sounds like demolition, yet Isaiah treats it as re-creation, not annihilation. He folds temple expectation into planetary renovation: voices of weeping cease, agriculture flourishes without foreclosure, and serpents eat dust rather than children. Notably, the text still pictures death, albeit delayed (Isa 65 :20), prompting debate whether Isaiah describes millennial interim or final state; regardless, worship is central, for Jerusalem is created rejoicing and its people are a joy. The absence of premature death and predator violence echoes Eden but surpasses it by promising unbroken labor yield—no more vineyards seized by conquerors (Isa 65 :21-22). The section concludes with "says the LORD," grounding utopian hope in firm covenant speech, not wishful optimism. By linking cosmic renewal to worshipping community, Isaiah sets stage for Revelation's temple-less city where God's glory replaces sun and moon. Thus, Zion's greater house ultimately becomes the cosmos itself, sanctified for perpetual communion.

5.2 Ezekiel's Visionary Temple (Chs. 40-48)

5.2.1 Historical Setting: Trauma and Hope on Chebar's Banks

Ezekiel receives his temple vision in the twenty-fifth year of exile (Ezek 40 :1), measuring from Jehoiachin's captivity, meaning Solomon's temple has been ash for fourteen years. His earlier oracles were consumed with doom—departing glory (Ezek 10), valley bones (Ezek 37)—so the shift to architectural optimism feels like sunrise after polar night. Babylon's ziggurats tower over the captives, taunting them with lost grandeur, yet Ezekiel's vision dwarfs imperial skyline

97

by sheer symmetry and cosmic order. The prophet, himself a priest, needed liturgical therapy; by mapping sacred space on papyrus, he processes grief and incubates hope. Thus, the architectural scroll functions as both pastoral counseling and eschatological manifesto. Readers today facing church closures or cultural marginalization may likewise find solace in drawing blueprints of promised futures. Ezekiel demonstrates that imaginative faithfulness is itself a mode of resistance against despair.

5.2.2 The Measuring Angel and Perfect Symmetry (Ezek 40-42)

A bronze-like man hands Ezekiel a reed measuring six long cubits, and tour begins at the east gate, the same direction from which Adam was banished and glory will return. Every gate, court, and chamber adheres to multiples of five hundred cubits, creating a square sanctuary nested inside square walls—a geometry of perfection mirroring the Holy of Holies' cubic form. Rooms for singers, priests, and utensils emphasize functional holiness; no chamber is purposeless, teaching that sacred architecture integrates vocation and space. The exhaustive measurements—readers often skim them—actually preach: God cares for details, and redemption re-calibrates chaos into ordered beauty. Unlike Solomon's temple, this one has a separate district for the prince, preventing monarchic usurpation of priestly prerogatives (Ezek 45 :7-9). The tour reeducates exiles in liturgical geography, reminding them how to walk, measure, and marvel. Thus, angelic tape-measure becomes catechism for covenantal order.

5.2.3 Glory Returns by the East Gate (Ezek 43 :1-9)

Having left by the east in chapter 10, Yahweh's kavod now re-enters from the same quadrant, accompanied by sound "like many waters." Ezekiel falls face-down, paralleling Exodus 34 when Moses glimpsed back of divine radiance; new covenant requires same reverence as old. God pledges never again to depart if Israel rejects corpse cults and royal adultery—sins that previously contaminated His threshold. The prophet must describe the temple to the exiles "that they may be ashamed" (Ezek 43 :10), implying that vision motivates repentance. Glory return is not unconditional; architectural grace demands ethical clearance. Later rabbis will claim that second-temple priests never witnessed Shekinah, highlighting that Ezekiel's conditions remained partially unmet—a gap the gospel later fills. Therefore, the reentrance is promissory, not realized, provoking longing rather than satisfaction.

5.2.4 Altar, Zadokite Priesthood, and Revised Sacrifices (Ezek 43 :10-27; 44)

The altar stands at center of inner court, a massive stepped structure with horns, hearth, and gutter channels—liturgy in lotus-like layers. Consecration lasts seven days, echoing creation week and Solomon's dedication, but offerings are fewer, privileging bull and goat sin offerings plus rams for burnt offering. Zadokite priests alone may draw near; sons of Eli who once wore ephod are demoted to gatekeepers, illustrating that past compromises carry generational consequences (1 Sam 2 :29-35). Strict clothing rules—linen, no wool, no sweat—link purity to comfort, hinting that holiness is holistic, affecting pores as well as prayers (Ezek 44 :17-18). Priests inherit no land except God, reversing Levitical poverty into eschatological wealth, for presence surpasses produce. Thus, Ezekiel's cult reforms safeguard transcendence by restricting access, yet promise intimacy by magnifying atonement's center stage.

5.2.5 River from the Threshold (Ezek 47 :1-12)

Water trickles from under the altar, heads east, deepens from ankle to swim depth within a mile—freshet physics defying desert hydrology. It heals the Dead Sea, turning petrified brine into fisherfolk paradise, and fruit trees on both banks bear monthly harvests, leaves medicinal for nations. The river globalizes temple blessing, linking local worship to planetary restoration, a motif John later adopts for New Jerusalem (Rev 22 :1-2). No measurement explains water source, signifying the inexhaustible Spirit proceeding from sacrificial center. Thus, Ezekiel marries cult and creation: atonement waters irrigate ecology, ecology feeds nations, nations worship at healed sanctuary. The vision is both literal hope for landlocked Judah and symbolic tapestry of resurrection life. Believers today cite this passage when praying for revival that transforms cities, demonstrating the enduring power of Ezekiel's hydraulics of grace.

5.2.6 Tribal Allotments and City YHWH-Shammah (Ezek 48)

An apportionment map crowns the vision, dividing land into horizontal bands with temple district at center—God lives on main street, not behind palace walls. Levites receive a special strip, and the prince's portion flanks sanctuary, limiting monarchical sprawl. City gates bear tribal names, uniting Jacob's sons in architectural fraternity that eluded them in Genesis. The closing verse renames Jerusalem "The LORD Is There," shifting attention from building to occupant; presence, not stone, is the climactic gift. Square circumference of eighteen thousand cubits subtly recalls New Jerusalem's perfect cube, bridging testaments. Ezekiel ends not with amen but with a name, leaving readers to ponder whether any city today bears such inscription. The oracle thus suspends fulfillment, inviting participation rather than passive admiration.

5.3 Haggai: "Greater Glory" for a Humble House

5.3.1 Rebuke of Paneled Homes (Hag 1 :1-11)

Haggai's terse sermon—merely thirty-eight verses across two chapters—packs economic critique: drought on grain, wine, and wages because people prioritize home renovations over temple foundations. He exposes a theological feedback loop—neglect of worship starves fields, which in turn drains wallets invested in paneling. The prophet's diagnosis includes agricultural, meteorological, and financial data, proving that covenant disobedience registers on barometers and bank sheets. His solution is simple: "Go up the hills, bring wood, rebuild." Unlike Jeremiah, who wept, Haggai scolds; prophetic tone adjusts to audience complacency, not just calamity. The people, leaders included, obey within twenty-three days (Hag 1 :14-15), showing that short sermons can spark quick reforms when Spirit breathes. Thus, Haggai links temple restoration to socioeconomic revival, challenging modern Christians to correlate spiritual apathy with cultural malaise.

5.3.2 The Desired of Nations and Shaken Cosmos (Hag 2 :6-9)

In his second oracle the prophet addresses discouragement among workers who recall Solomon's grandeur. He invokes Sinai as precedent: once more, in "little while," God will shake heaven, earth, sea, and dry land so that precious things—silver and gold He already claims (v. 8)—flow into the house. Commentators debate whether "desired of nations" refers to wealth, Messiah, or both; New Testament writers choose the latter, reading Christ as treasure embodied (Luke 2 :32). Haggai's phrase "greater glory" does not specify aesthetics; rather, relational nearness will surpass gilded cherubim. The promise that peace will fill the house links glory to shalom, not spectacle—a foretaste of resurrected Jesus standing amid disciples saying, "Peace be with you" (John 20 :19). Thus, economic influx serves liturgical tranquility, weaving commerce into covenant wholeness. Workers' sore shoulders now carry eschatological splendor unsuspected by contemporary appraisal.

5.3.3 Zerubbabel as Messianic Signet (Hag 2 :20-23)

Haggai's final oracle singles out Zerubbabel, declaring that God will overthrow thrones, chariots, and horses, reversing exodus imagery of drowning Pharaoh's elite. In that day, says the LORD, "I will take you… and make you like a signet ring," reinstating Davidic legitimacy removed from Jehoiachin (Jer 22 :24). Yet history shows Zerubbabel never wore a crown—prophecy leaps beyond immediate biography toward eschatological heir. Matthew's genealogy lists Zerubbabel in line to Joseph, threading Haggai's promise into Christmas narrative (Matt 1 :12-13). Thus, the signet oracle functions like a down payment: assurance that divine kingship will seal covenant scroll no matter Persian oversight. Modern readers may draw courage that present anonymity can still cloak future significance in God's unfolding plot. Haggai closes without doxology; the silenced amen underscores that fulfillment awaits the arrival of One greater than Solomon yet born in Zerubbabel's line.

5.4 Zechariah's Night Visions and the Branch

5.4.1 Jerusalem without Walls and the Measuring Line (Zech 2)

Zechariah's surveyor attempts to measure Jerusalem, but an angel halts him, proclaiming that future population and livestock will exceed walls, and Yahweh Himself will be fire-wall and glory. Safety no longer hinges on masonry but on manifest presence, relocating security from stone to Shekinah. The call "Up! Escape to Zion" invites diaspora Jews to rejoin unfinished restoration, aligning geography with destiny. Many nations will join to the LORD in that day, echoing Isaiah's universalized house, proving prophetic intertextuality (Zech 2 :11). Thus, the temple cause doubles as evangelistic magnet, not merely ethnic project. The vision critiques small imaginations that shrink divine plans to fortification budgets. It urges faith communities today to trust God's protective fire rather than cultural barricades.

5.4.2 Joshua's Cleansing and the Stone (Zech 3)

High priest Joshua appears in filthy garments, Satan at his right hand accusing. The Angel of the LORD rebukes the accuser, exchanges garments, and sets a clean turban, enacting justification by grace. A single stone with seven eyes is set before Joshua, inscribed and promising removal of iniquity in one day—an oblique prophecy Christians associate with Calvary (Heb 10 :12-14). Friends seated before Joshua are "omen" men, hinting that priestly restoration signals forthcoming Branch. This courtroom drama shifts holiness from procedural to personal, forecasting New Testament doctrine where Christ clothes believers in righteousness (Rev 19 :8). Temple purity thus originates not in scrubbed basins but in divine verdict silencing accusation. Zechariah affirms hope for any worshipping community plagued by shame: new garments await those who stand before gracious Judge.

5.4.3 Lampstand, Olive Trees, and Spirit-Powered Construction (Zech 4)

A golden menorah flanked by two olive trees puzzles the prophet until angelic explanation: continual oil supply signifies Spirit enabling, and the two anointed ones likely represent Zerubbabel and Joshua.

Famous line "Not by might, nor by power" reframes rebuilding challenges from political horsepower to pneumatological flow. The plumb line in Zerubbabel's hand says the day of small things should not be despised; initial measurements anticipate capstone shouts of grace. Mountains become plains before governor's shovel, echoing Isaiah 40's highway leveling. In Christian interpretation, the olive trees foreshadow prophetic witnesses of Revelation 11, again linking temple imagery across covenants. The emphasis on Spirit ensures that even in architectural tasks, reliance on divine resource is non-negotiable.

5.4.4 Flying Scroll and Ephah: Purging Lawlessness (Zech 5)

A thirty-foot scroll zooms across sky, curses thieves and perjurers, lodging in houses to consume timber and stones—a vivid picture that Torah enforcement goes mobile, not confined to courtrooms. Immediately, a vision of a woman in an ephah (measuring basket) represents wickedness sealed and transported to Shinar, the land of Babylon, for permanent exile. Together, the visions ensure that covenant community will be cleansed internally and externally before final glory descends. Temple hope always includes judicial purification; God will not dwell among theft and deceit. Zechariah thus balances earlier comfort with moral urgency, reflecting divine character of grace and truth. Modern applications caution churches that expansion without discipline invites fiery scrolls of exposé.

5.4.5 Crowning the Branch: Priest-King Unite (Zech 6 :9-15)

Returning exiles bring silver and gold which Zechariah forges into a crown placed on Joshua's sacerdotal head, though ultimate fulfillment points to "the Branch" who will build the temple and sit on throne. Counsel of peace between priesthood and royalty prefigures Christ, who combines both offices (Heb 7). The act performed in the temple underscores that any true sanctuary requires messianic mediation. The crown is stored as memorial, a prophetic museum exhibit awaiting eschatological curator. Thus, Zechariah merges Haggai's signet with Isaiah's royal priest motif, interweaving oracles into tapestry of expectation. The passage comforts weary builders: their hammered silver foreshadows heavenly diadems. It challenges theologians to integrate kingship and priesthood in ecclesiology without hierarchy wars.

5.4.6 Eschatological Booths and Holiness Bells (Zech 14)

The final oracle pictures nations attacking Jerusalem, half the city exiled, then God descending to fight, splitting Mount of Olives—topography bends before warrior Creator. Survivors join annual Feast of Booths, acknowledging Yahweh as cosmic King, turning Israel's most celebratory festival into international thanksgiving. Even horse bells inscribe "Holy to the LORD," democratizing sanctity from high-priest forehead to stable tack. No Canaanite traders linger in house of LORD, reversing Mark's "den of robbers." The river flowing east and west mirrors Ezekiel, but now perpetual, indicating climatic healing. Zechariah's fusion of war and worship teaches that final peace arrives through divine intervention, not diplomatic summitry. It feeds Christian hymns of second advent, where swords become plowshares after King rides victorious stallion.

5.5 Daniel: Timetables for Desolation and Vindication

5.5.1 Little Horn and Sanctuary Trampling (Dan 8 :9-14)

Daniel sees a male goat's conspicuous horn broken, four rise, and from one emerges a little horn that magnifies itself against Prince of host, abolishes daily sacrifice, and casts truth to ground. Angelic dialogue sets desolation length at 2 300 evenings and mornings—debated as literal 1 150 days or symbolic era—yet emphasizes terminus: sanctuary shall be cleansed. Historical correlation with Antiochus IV or future antichrist showcases prophecy's layered fulfillment. Temple desecration becomes measuring stick for evil: whenever worship is halted, cosmic order shakes. The vision gave Maccabees calendar for resistance and offers eschatological watchers a template for end-time vigilance. Daniel thus integrates liturgiology and eschatology into a single storyline of desecration and restoration. Prayerful readers learn that heavenly courts monitor earthly altars with stopwatch precision.

5.5.2 Seventy Weeks to Anointed Cut Off (Dan 9 :24-27)

Gabriel delivers cryptic arithmetic: seventy sevens decreed to finish transgression, seal sin, bring everlasting righteousness, and anoint most holy place. Starting from decree to rebuild Jerusalem (variously dated), seven and sixty-two weeks lead to anointed one killed, city burned. Covenant confirmed for final week, sacrifices stopped mid-week, abomination set up until desolation decreed. Scholars parse literal years versus symbolic cycles; all agree temple fate sits at prophecy's center. Christians often view crucifixion as midpoint sacrifice cessation—veil torn precisely halfway through Passover week. Others project fulfillment to future antichrist. Regardless, sanctuary remains cosmic clock dial.

5.5.3 Abomination and Blessed Waiting (Dan 12 :11-13)

Daniel learns from 1 290-day interval between abomination and renewal, plus blessing on one who reaches 1 335 days—extra forty-five encouraging perseverance. The text woos sufferers to keep calendar in hope, much as liturgical seasons sustain church through persecutions. Jewish rebels against Antiochus and Christian martyrs under Rome both consulted these numbers for courage. Daniel closes sealed until time of end, implying prophecy matures like wine, revealing flavor in generations yet unborn. Thus, temple arithmetic stimulates watchfulness without date-setting hubris. Prophetic mathematics becomes spiritual exercise in patience, reminding worshippers that God owns the calendar as well as the courts.

5.6 Post-Exilic Psalms and Temple Longings

Psalm 84 opens with the sigh, "How lovely is your dwelling place, O LORD of hosts," revealing that the psychology of exile never completely disappears even after Zerubbabel's house stands (Ps 84 :1). The psalmist envies sparrows that nest near the altars, proving that worship has ecological observers and that even birds become silent tutors in liturgical envy. He calls doorkeepership preferable to palace life, showing that proximity to presence, not social rank, is the true metric of honor (Ps 84 :10). By blessing those "whose hearts are set on pilgrimage," the song universalizes temple desire beyond Jerusalem's postal code, preparing for a future in which Gentiles from "Baca"-like deserts will make springs as they travel (Ps 84 :5-7). The Songs of Ascent (Pss 120-134) rehearse this pilgrim spirit in fifteen micro-psalms, each ascending synagogue steps in later centuries to remind dispersed Jews where feet ought finally to stand. Psalm 122 asks peace for Jerusalem, intertwining civic wellbeing with sanctuary prosperity, while Psalm 126 imagines captive tears turned to harvest sheaves, blending agricultural rhythms with redemption chronology. When Jesus sang these psalms en route to Passover (Mark 14 :26), He carried in His vocal cords the cumulative ache and hope of post-exilic Israel, even as He prepared to make His body the answer to every refrain.

5.7 Inter-Testamental Apocalyptic Blueprints

5.7.1 1 Enoch and the Heavenly Sanctuary

The Book of the Watchers (1 Enoch 14 :8-25) transports readers into crystalline palaces with flaming cherubim and rivers of fire, effectively moving Solomon's gilded chambers into a nebular domain beyond Persian, Greek, or Roman reach. The prophet's trembling at sapphire floors mirrors Ezekiel's dread, but the absence of sacrificial vocabulary suggests that earthly cult is already being translated into heavenly terms. While scholars debate dates, many place these visions in the third- or second-century BC, meaning persecuted Jews under Hellenistic pressure lifted eyes above desecrated courtyards to thrones no Antiochus could profane. Enoch's architecture is deliberately immeasurable, reinforcing that divine presence now eclipses geographical limitation anticipated by Zechariah's wall-less Jerusalem (Zech 2 :4-5). Later Christian writers like Jude (Jude 14-15) will quote Enoch, validating its devotional impact even if not canonical. By elevating the sanctuary into the heavens, 1 Enoch nurtures the embryo of a Christian doctrine that sees Christ entering a "greater and more perfect tent, not made with hands" (Heb 9 :11). Thus, Enoch becomes a bridge between exile grief and New-Testament heavenly-temple theology.

5.7.2 The Temple Scroll and Idealized Cult

Among the Dead Sea cache, 11Q19 (Temple Scroll) drafts a sanctuary triple the size of Solomon's, with concentric courts segregating Israel, priests, and ultimate holiness. It prescribes festival calendars offset from Jerusalem's, reflecting sectarian conviction that official priests had botched chronology. The scroll legislates bathrooms outside the camp and defines latrine distance, proving that holiness extends even to sanitation—a hyper-Levitical impulse born of disappointment with Hasmonean compromise. Scholars note parallels with Ezekiel 40-48, but the Scroll's courts are even larger, signaling that disappointment often enlarges imagination: the more corrupt the contemporary temple, the bigger the ideal alternative. Its authoring community, probably Essene, viewed their desert compound as interim sanctuary, echoing Isaiah's desert blossoms and anticipating John the Baptist's wilderness cry. Though never built, the plan exerted pressure on Herod's architects who had to answer rival blueprints with marble reality. The Scroll thus documents an intra-Jewish contest over who could best host the Glory—a contest ultimately resolved when, in John's gospel, the Word "tabernacled" among us (John 1 :14).

5.7.3 New Jerusalem Texts and Gem Foundations

Fragments such as 11Q18 and the Greek *2 Baruch* 4 portray a cubic city descending in end-time splendor, clearly indebted to Ezekiel yet surpassing his dimensions. Streets paved with gold and foundations studded with precious stones anticipate the Apocalypse of John, showing that Jewish apocalyptists and Christian seers share a common visionary lexicon. These texts frequently omit any mention of animal sacrifice, hinting that the idea of bloodless perfection had lodged itself well before Hebrews argued for once-for-all atonement (Heb 10 :12). Giant pearl gates and endlessly open doors stress hospitality for righteous of all nations, paralleling Isaiah 60's tribute caravans. By circulating among synagogue readers, such manuscripts democratized eschatological architectonics; even illiterate shepherds could imagine sparkling ramparts piercing desert night. The juxtaposition of cosmic city and pastoral audience captured the paradox that apocalyptic grandeur is meant to comfort the humble, not flatter the elite. Consequently, New Jerusalem texts molded the spiritual imagination of communities who would later weigh Jesus' resurrection against their loftiest temple hopes—and find His empty tomb the brighter structure.

5.8 Qumran Community: Priestly Utopia in the Desert

5.8.1 War Scroll—Liturgical Warfare

The *Milḥamat Ha-Sons of Light* plots a seven-stage conflict in which priestly trumpets coordinate angelic cohorts and human soldiers, blending Zechariah's olive-tree imagery with Davidic battle psalms. Before each engagement, priests sound silver trumpet blasts named for divine attributes—"Hand of Might," "Wrath of God"—turning combat into antiphonal worship. The army encamps in rows mirroring wilderness tribes, a conscious throwback to Numbers 2 and Ezekiel's visionary order. Victory sacrifices follow each campaign, implying that war is an extension of liturgy rather than merely politics. Such martial liturgy reveals how deeply temple rhythms had permeated sectarian identity: even battle formations required cultic choreography. Christians later spiritualize this concept as warfare prayer (Eph 6 :12), but Qumran practiced it with literal swords sharpened beside scroll jars. Their desert liturgy therefore stands as both warning and witness: zeal for holiness can either protect covenant purity or breed sectarian violence.

5.8.2 Community Rule—Daily Temple in Microcosm

The *Serek Ha-Yaḥad* orders communal meals where a priest blesses first and portions are served by rank, mimicking temple sacrifices distributed among Levites. Purity immersions occur before each meal, echoing laver washings, and latecomers eat in shame outside table fellowship, underscoring sanctity of order. Even conversation is regulated; speaking out of turn risks expulsion, perhaps an over-correction to Eli's lax sons. Scroll study fills predawn hours, making Torah the sonic backdrop to daybreak, much as priests greeted dawn with tamid lambs. By transposing temple disciplines into daily schedule, the Yaḥad created an ambulatory sanctuary capable of surviving Rome's predicted fury. Thus, they pioneer a rhythm the early church will adopt—devote themselves to apostles' teaching, fellowship, breaking bread, and prayer (Acts 2 :42). Qumran proves that when official altars seem corrupted, believers often craft micro-temples of holiness wherever they dwell.

5.8.3 "Temple of Adam" and Edenic Repair

Several Qumran hymns declare the community a "temple built of men," harking to Genesis where Adam is priest-guardian of Eden (1QHa XIV). They view themselves as restoration of pre-fall liturgy, interpreting circumcision of heart (Deut 30 :6) as inner altar purification. Animal skins once clothed exiles from garden; linen robes now garb restored priests, signifying reversal of curse. The community's obsession with calendar purity aims to sync earthly worship with celestial cycles set on the fourth creation day (Gen 1 :14), thus re-harmonizing cosmic order disrupted by sin. Essene dualism between sons of light and darkness echoes Edenic enmity between seed of woman and serpent (Gen 3 :15). Their hope of ultimate temple manifests as inclusio: history that began in garden sanctuary will end in cosmic sanctuary beyond sun and moon. Therefore, Qumran scrolls enrich our theology by reminding the church that eschatology is also protology fulfilled.

5.9 Minor Prophets and Scattered Temple Motifs

5.9.1 Malachi: Incense among the Nations and Purging Fire

Malachi chastises priests for offering blind animals and calls their altar "contemptible" (Mal 1 :7-8). Yet he simultaneously prophesies, "From the rising of the sun to its setting, my name will be great among nations, and in every place incense will be offered" (Mal 1 :11). The juxtaposition implies that failed local worship triggers global diffusion, foreshadowing Gentile prayer and Eucharistic praise. Chapter 3 introduces a messenger who will refine Levi "like soap," an image echoed in John the Baptist's fiery warnings and fulfilled when Jesus enters temple courts. Malachi also predicts Elijah's return before the Day of the LORD (Mal 4 :5-6), a prelude realized in Baptist ministry that prepares hearts for true temple cleansing. Thus, the book forms a hinge between prophetic critique and gospel advent, proving that reform and replacement are not mutually exclusive but sequential. For contemporary readers, Malachi warns that casual worship invites purification that might arrive in unexpected, even painful, forms.

5.9.2 Joel: Temple Lament and Spirit Outpouring

Joel begins with priests ordered to "lie all night in sackcloth" because grain and drink offerings have ceased (Joel 1 :13). Locust hordes strip fields, rendering worship impossible, illustrating environmental dependence of cult and the theological nature of ecology. Yet after national repentance, Yahweh promises to "restore the years the locust has eaten" and pour out His Spirit on all flesh (Joel 2 :25-29). Peter cites this outpouring at Pentecost, linking Shavuot festival in temple courts to global prophecy (Acts 2 :16-21). Joel's valley of decision (Joel 3 :14) situates eschatological war near Jerusalem, keeping temple geography central even in cosmic conflict. The book's movement from lament to Spirit fire models liturgical trajectory: confession leads to empowerment. Therefore, Joel becomes manual for revivalists seeking both agricultural renewal and Charismatic gifts.

5.9.3 Amos: Fallen Booth of David Raised

Amos, shepherd of Tekoa, rails against winter houses and summer palaces, prophesying exile where songs turn to wailing (Am 6 :4-7). Yet final verses promise restoration of David's fallen sukkah so that Israel possesses remnants of Edom, a passage James quotes at Jerusalem Council to validate Gentile inclusion (Acts 15 :16-18). The "booth" harkens to tabernacle festival, implying a fragile yet portable kingdom rebuilt by God Himself. Agricultural abundance—mountains dripping sweet wine—mirrors temple meteorology where obedience invites rain (Am 9 :13). Amos thus integrates social justice, cultic purity, and missional expansion, revealing that temple destiny cannot be severed from ethical economics. By citing Amos, the early church frames its Gentile mission as temple reconstruction project, albeit with living stones. Hence, Amos preachers still confront affluent congregations with plumb lines while offering hope of rebuilt fellowship across ethnic lines.

5.9.4 Micah and Habakkuk: Silence and Swords to Plowshares

Micah repeats Isaiah 2's mountain vision but adds imagery of vines and fig trees without fear (Mic 4 :1-5). He couples temple ascent with prophetic indictment of leaders who "hate justice" yet lean on Yahweh, concluding Zion will be ploughed like a field (Mic 3 :12). Jeremiah cites this verdict during his trial, showing Micah's authority in temple discourse (Jer 26 :18). Habakkuk, witnessing Babylonian advance, retreats to the mantra, "The LORD is in His holy temple; let all the earth keep silence" (Hab 2 :20), a call to hush that balances prophetic rhetoric with contemplative awe. The pairing of plowshares and silence offers liturgical rhythm: activism against injustice alternates with reverent pause before Sovereign Judge. Together, these minor prophets demonstrate that clear temple vision amplifies ethical accountability rather than anesthetizing it. Modern worship movements that pursue beauty without justice risk re-enacting the sins Micah condemned.

5.10 Temple Typology in Wisdom Literature

5.10.1 Proverbs 9—Wisdom's Seven-Pillared House

Lady Wisdom builds a house with seven pillars, slaughters beasts, mixes wine, and invites the simple to feast, an unmistakable temple parody where architecture teaches moral order. Early church fathers see Christ as Wisdom, the pillars as Spirit's sevenfold gifts, and the feast as Eucharist. The passage juxtaposes with Proverbs 7 where Folly entices in a dark house, contrasting covenant hospitality with illicit counterfeit. Architectural metaphors thus serve pedagogical ends, training youth to discern which "house" to enter. Wisdom literature therefore expands temple theology into choices made in market and marriage, not merely court and choir. The seven pillars likely echo creation week, reinforcing that moral cosmos is sustained by ordered worship. Believers today reading Proverbs partake in everyday temple discernment—choosing architecture of holiness over brothel of folly.

5.10.2 Ecclesiastes and Reverent Sacrifice

Qoheleth warns, "Guard your steps when you go to the house of God" and "let your words be few" (Eccl 5 :1-2). His counsel arises from observation of mindless verbosity in worship, predicting that rash vows can snare souls like foolish builders whose roof leaks. Vanity motif stretches even to sacrifice: it is "a sacrifice of fools" when offered without listening. The preacher thus critiques second-temple liturgy slipping into rote, anticipating Jesus' condemnation of duplicitous Pharisees (Matt 23). Yet Ecclesiastes ends by affirming fear of God and command obedience, implying temple relevance persists if approached with trembling joy. Wisdom literature thereby disciplines prophetic zeal with contemplative realism. Reading Ecclesiastes in hyperactive church cultures may recalibrate pace and posture to match heaven's slow majesty.

5.10.3 Chronicles' Idealized Solomonic Story

Unlike Kings, Chronicles omits David-Bathsheba scandal and exaggerates Levitical choirs, presenting Solomon's temple as golden apex unmarred by apostasy until the very end. The Chronicler, writing in post-exilic period, offers a liturgical prototype the remnant can emulate, avoiding political polemic. He records heavenly fire consuming Solomon's sacrifice (2 Chr 7 :1) though Kings omits it, encouraging second-temple audiences who never saw such splendor to hope for its return. By tracing genealogies to Adam, he integrates temple story with universal history, implying that sanctuary centrism is cosmic, not parochial. His selective memory models a pastoral hermeneutic: highlight moments that nourish hope without falsifying past. Thus, Chronicles becomes a canonical sermon on temple as covenant anchor across regimes. Modern preachers, too, must decide which narratives to spotlight when kindling congregational hope.

5.11 Messianic Temple in the Gospels

5.11.1 Embodied Sanctuary and Tabernacle Flesh

John's prologue states, "The Word became flesh and dwelt (*eskēnōsen*) among us," literally "pitched tent," marrying Exodus syntax to incarnation (John 1 :14). Jesus refers to His body as temple, inviting Jewish leaders to destruct and witness resurrection rebuilding in three days (John 2 :19-21). Synoptic writers place transfiguration on a high mountain where Peter suggests three tents, unwittingly echoing Feast of Booths and hinting disciples' desire to domesticate glory (Matt 17 :4). Jesus declines, indicating that His impending passion, not hillside tabernacles, will unveil lasting sanctuary. When He forgives sins without sacrifice (Mark 2 :1-12) and calls Himself "greater than the temple" (Matt 12 :6), He shifts cultic center to His own person. His lament over Jerusalem—"Your house is left desolate" (Matt 23 :38)—sounds final closure on stone courts awaiting Spirit outpouring. Thus, gospel narratives crown prophetic expectations with flesh-and-blood fulfillment, turning every healing, meal, and sermon into mobile holy-of-holies encounters.

5.11.2 Cleansing and Prophetic Protest

Both temple cleansings bracket Jesus' ministry: John places one near Cana wedding (John 2), Synoptics at triumphal entry, perhaps indicating two events or narrative compression. He overturns tables of dove sellers—offerings poor pilgrims purchased—highlighting exploitation beneath pious veneer. Quoting Isaiah 56 and Jeremiah 7 He merges universal house-prayer theme with "den of robbers" critique, effectively indicting first century leaders with pre-exilic sins. By driving animals, He halts sacrificial traffic momentarily, acting out priestly shutdown predicted by Daniel. Authorities demand sign; Christ offers resurrection, proving that true vindication of zeal is empty tomb. Cleansing therefore dramatizes transfer of holiness from marble to Messiah, fulfilling Malachi's purifier prophecy. Churches today hearing this narrative must examine marketplaces lurking in their foyers lest zeal revisits.

5.12 Acts and Pauline Letters: Ecclesia Expanding the House

5.12.1 Pentecost as Temple Re-commissioning

Acts 2 records wind and fire filling "the house," likely Solomon's Portico crowded during feast day. Tongues split like flames on each head, echoing Sinai's divided voices (*mitzot*), constituting believers as multi-lingual, mobile Sinai. Peter interprets phenomenon via Joel, linking Spirit outpouring to temple lament reversal. Baptized converts devote themselves to prayers "in the temple" and break bread "from house to house," signifying twin loci of old and new (Acts 2 :46). For years apostles teach in courts until persecution scatters them, replicating Isaiah's streaming nations in reverse missionary flow. The temple becomes evangelistic stage until martyrdom of Stephen, whose critique of hand-made houses accelerates dispersion (Acts 7). Pentecost thus marks hinge where fixed sanctuary begins yielding to Spirit's traveling caravan.

5.12.2 Pauline Temple Metaphors

Paul calls Corinthian church "God's building" built on apostolic foundation with Christ as cornerstone; anyone building with hay invites fiery inspection (1 Cor 3 :9-17). He personalizes metaphor in chapter 6: bodies are temples; therefore flee porneia, for fornication unites sanctuary with harlot. To Ephesians, he broadens scale: Jew and Gentile are "being built together into a dwelling place for God by the Spirit" (Eph 2 :22). Yet Paul can still respect stone edifice, bringing offerings and vows (Acts 21), though he insists real circumcision is heart-spirit (Rom 2 :29). Second Thessalonians warns of "man of lawlessness" seating himself in God's temple, whether literal or metaphorical debated, keeping prophetic tension alive. Paul's dialectic— affirm and transcend—guides Christian engagement with sacred space today, honoring buildings yet refusing to conflate them with ultimate presence.

5.13 Hebrews: Heavenly Sanctuary and Perfect Priest

The anonymous homilist calls earthly tabernacle a "copy and shadow" of heavenly reality, citing Exodus 25 :40 to ground claim (Heb 8 :5). Jesus, from Judah rather than Levi, cannot serve in earthly holy place but enters "greater and more perfect tent" with His own blood, securing eternal redemption (Heb 9 :11-12). Contrasting Yom Kippur annual entry, He passes once for all, nullifying repetitive sacrifices that never perfect conscience. Curtain imagery returns: His flesh is new veil; believers draw near sprinkled and washed, echoing laver and altar (Heb 10 :19-22). The preacher warns against forsaking assembly since eschatological day nears, implying that heavenly access fuels earthly gathering, not negates it (Heb 10 :25). Heroes of faith sought city with foundations built by God (Heb 11 :10), climaxing in Zion festal assembly angels, firstborn, and mediator blood (Heb 12 :22-24). Therefore Hebrews finalizes prophetic trajectory: temple promises kept, priest perfected, city awaited.

5.14 Revelation: Temple Motifs Transfigured

John sees throne room with twenty-four elders, seven torches, and glass sea, combining tabernacle numerology, menorah lamps, and laver imagery (Rev 4 :4-6). Lamb appears slain yet standing in midst, co-enthroned, fulfilling priest-king Branch. After seventh trumpet, "God's temple in heaven was opened, and the ark of His covenant was seen" (Rev 11 :19), giving exiles sight Moses never had. Yet by chapter 21 city descends needing no temple "for its temple is the Lord God Almighty and the Lamb," terminus of architectural prophecy (Rev

21 :22). Cubic measurements—twelve thousand stadia—mirror Ezekiel but globalize scale, and jeweled foundations echo Isaiah's tribute vision. River of life and tree of healing line avenue, Eden restored as urban sanctuary (Rev 22 :1-5). Revelation thus stitches Genesis to prophets to gospels, presenting eschaton as liturgical garden-city where every street becomes nave, every vocation priestly, and every moment hosanna.

In conclusion, from Isaiah's sunrise mountain to Revelation's lamp-less city, prophetic voices have hauled the imagination of God's people beyond the measurable courts of Solomon and Herod toward a house whose walls are nations and whose roof is the radiance of divine presence. Each vision answered the ache of its own day—exiles weeping by rivers, zealots bristling under Greek blasphemy, priests toiling in post-exilic poverty—yet together they compose a single architectural symphony that crescendos in Jesus the cornerstone and echoes through His Spirit-filled church. Suppose the sanctuary story began in Eden's garden temple and wandered through tabernacle canvas, cedar palaces, and marble colonnades. In that case, it now moves in living processions of disciples, each body a miniature holy of holies, each congregation a local embassy of the coming city. Prophetic blueprints thus serve not merely as diagrams for future curiosities but as catechisms in hope, tutoring generations to pray, "Your kingdom come," with plumb-line faith and river-bank expectation. The "greater house" is already rising whenever forgiveness flows, whenever justice rolls like waters, whenever worship lifts weary heads toward hills whence help comes. And yet it is still to come, shimmering just beyond current scaffolding, awaiting the final shout of the capstone—"Grace, grace to it!"—when the Lord Himself descends with trumpet sound, and the dwelling of God is with humanity forever. Until that unveiling, every sanctuary—be it tent, cathedral, storefront, or living room—echoes rehearsals of that ultimate inauguration where there will be no night, no curse, and no temple, "for the Lord God Almighty and the Lamb are its temple."

Chapter 6 — Jesus the Living Temple

Temple theology reaches its watershed moment when a Galilean craftsman begins to speak of "My Father's house" as if it were His private residence and, even more startlingly, of His own body as the new locus of divine presence. All the gold-plated beams of Solomon, the goat-hair curtains of Moses, and the marble colonnades of Herod function in the New Testament as massive stage props that lift the curtain on this single character: Jesus of Nazareth. The theological claim is astonishing—God has relocated from stone chambers into flesh, from the guarded Holy of Holies into a heartbeat audible through a human rib cage (John 1 :14). Because every preceding chapter of redemptive history points here, and every subsequent chapter flows from here, we must linger over the incarnation, ministry, cross, resurrection, ascension, and Spirit-sending of Christ as a comprehensive temple event. This chapter therefore moves in six movements: incarnation (God with us), confrontation (God purifying His courts), crucifixion (God reconciling heaven and earth), resurrection (God rebuilding the house in three days), ascension (God enthroned in the true sanctuary), and Pentecost (God multiplying His presence through the Spirit in the church). Each movement is examined through five carefully developed sub-sections, and each subsection unpacks a distinct facet of how Jesus fulfills, critiques, and surpasses earlier temple patterns. By the end, the reader should feel how every later strand of Christian worship—baptismal water, Eucharistic bread, missionary witness, ethical holiness—organically grows out of Christ's identity as the living, breathing, indestructible temple of God.

6.1 Incarnation – The Word "Tabernacled" among Us

6.1.1 *Eskēnōsen* and Exodus 25 :8 in Dialogue

John selects an audacious verb when he writes, "The Word became flesh and *dwelt* among us" (John 1 :14); the Greek *eskēnōsen* literally means "pitched His tent," alluding to the wilderness tabernacle of Exodus 25 :8 where God promises, "Let them make Me a sanctuary, that I may dwell in their midst." The evangelist is not offering poetic flourish but deliberate exegesis, announcing that the glory which once glittered between cherubim now glows behind the eyes of a Jewish infant. Shepherds who visit the Bethlehem manger effectively step into a mobile Holy of Holies, complete with angelic choristers in the night sky echoing the seraphim of Isaiah 6. That image instantly collapses the spatial hierarchy of the old covenant; no bronze altar stands between sinner and presence, no veil restrains vision, no genealogy regulates approach. From the first cry of the Christ-child, temple accessibility is democratized, a reality later dramatized when Simeon takes the forty-day-old baby into his arms inside the temple precincts and declares he has "seen Your salvation" (Luke 2 :30). Thus, the incarnation is more than divine visitation; it is architectural relocation—the Shekinah boxed not in cedar but in skin. Every aspect of Jesus' life will now function as furniture in this living sanctuary.

6.1.2 Spirit-Overshadowed Conception as Holy-of-Holies Event

Luke records that the power of the Most High *overshadowed* Mary (Luke 1 :35), a verbal echo of the cloud that overshadowed the tent of meeting when glory filled it (Exod 40 :35). In both narratives the Spirit initiates, life begins, and divine presence becomes palpable without human engineering, ensuring that the holiness of the new sanctuary cannot be attributed to Joseph's lineage or Mary's righteousness but solely to God's creative word. The virginal conception therefore functions like an inaugural cloud descending on brand-new temple courts, announcing, "The LORD is in His holy temple; let all the earth keep silence" (Hab 2 :20). That same Spirit will later descend again at Jordan baptism, anointing Jesus for public ministry much like oil consecrated Aaron's sons (Luke 3 :21-22; Lev 8 :12). In both moments heaven affirms earthly vessel: first in secrecy inside a Nazareth home, then in public along the Jordan banks. Thus, incarnation is a two-step dedication ceremony—conceived, then commissioned—patterned after tabernacle erection and subsequent priestly installation. Readers who grasp this parallel will see that Christ's priesthood and templehood are fused from conception forward.

6.1.3 Emmanuel – God with Us, Not God Behind Veil

Matthew's quotation of Isaiah 7 :14, "They shall call His name Emmanuel," catches the first-century reader by surprise because the Persian-era temple, splendid as it was, still signaled distance: only one high priest, once a year, could enter behind the veil (Lev 16). With Emmanuel, God is no longer behind fabric but at family supper tables in Nazareth, teaching Torah in village synagogues, and drinking wedding wine in Cana (John 2). Table fellowship replaces bronze altar smoke as primary experience of presence, a shift that will culminate in the Lord's Supper where bread and wine proclaim communion, not separation (Matt 26 :26-29). The Emmanuel promise also dismantles geographical monopolies; if God is with *us*—plural and universal— then Galilee, Samaria, and Judean wilderness host genuine sanctuaries the moment Jesus steps into them. In the church age this presence extends still further: missionary huts, hospital rooms, and prison cells become holy ground when Christ's Spirit dwells within believers (2 Cor 6 :16). Thus, Emmanuel is not seasonal sentiment but the decisive temple verdict on human estrangement: exile has ended because God Himself has crossed the flaming sword.

6.1.4 Bethlehem, Bread, and the Showbread Typology

Bethlehem means "House of Bread," and the incarnation scene staged there sets up Jesus' later declaration, "I am the bread of life" (John 6 :35). The showbread inside the Holy Place—twelve loaves replaced weekly and eaten by priests (Lev 24 :5-9)—finds continuity in the newborn who will feed twelve disciples and through them multitudes. David once entered the sanctuary and ate consecrated bread when desperately hungry (1 Sam 21 :6), an act Jesus cites to defend His own Sabbath healings and to hint that His body will become ultimate priestly provision (Mark 2 :25-26). Bethlehem's manger therefore foreshadows an altar-table, positioning the infant as food for a starving world long before He multiplies barley loaves in Galilee. Post-resurrection Emmaus travelers recognize Him only when He breaks bread (Luke 24 :30-31), confirming the typology: the living temple feeds its priests with life-giving loaves. Liturgically, every Eucharist replays Bethlehem's wonder—bread that hosts God now given to humans so humans can host God. Breadlines of the poor and communion rails of cathedrals thus converge at this manger-altar axis.

6.1.5 Magi Gifts and Isaiah 60's Tribute to the New Temple

The magi arrive bearing gold, frankincense, and myrrh (Matt 2 :11), exactly the substances Isaiah 60 :6 predicted Gentiles would import when Zion's house attracted global pilgrimage. Gold funds may have financed the refugee family's flight to Egypt, paralleling how Cyrus's treasury funded the second-temple reconstruction (Ezra 1 :4-11). Frankincense, a priestly fragrance (Exod 30 :34-38), acknowledges the baby's cultic vocation; myrrh anticipates both priestly anointing and sacrificial burial (John 19 :39). Consequently, Matthew's infancy narrative already frames Jesus as the destination of temple prophecies, the spot where Gentile worship and Jewish promise meet. The journey of these eastern astrologers is itself a rehearsal of Isaiah's "nations shall come to your light," proving that missionary centripetal force now orbits not architectural vaults but incarnate glory. Their worship in a humble house dismantles assumptions that splendor is necessary for genuine adoration; what matters is Who is present, not how impressive the surroundings. In a single scene, therefore, Matthew signals the rest of his gospel agenda: Jesus is both priest and sacrifice, both temple and treasure, both king and offering.

6.2 Jesus and the Second Temple – A Ministry Framed by Courts and Feasts

6.2.1 Infancy Dedication and Simeon's Oracle

When Joseph and Mary bring forty-day-old Jesus to present Him in the temple (Luke 2 :22-24), they follow Leviticus 12 requirements, offering two birds—the provision for the poor—thus associating the true temple with economic humility from the outset. Simeon takes the child into his arms and calls Him "salvation" prepared for all peoples, "a light for revelation to the Gentiles and for glory to Israel" (Luke 2 :30-32). That dual phrase captures the temple's original calling: a house of prayer for all nations displaying the unique covenant glory of Yahweh (Isa 56 :7). Anna the prophetess immediately turns the dedication into evangelistic proclamation, speaking of the child to "all who were waiting for redemption" (Luke 2 :38), showing that the new temple generates witness before it ever overturns tables. The irony is thick: aged prophets bless the infant while Herod renovates stone courts—wood and swaddling vs. marble and gold. Luke thus hints that prophetic vision can recognize true architecture even when hidden in plain sight. Every baby-dedication since echoes this moment, confessing that God's salvation often arrives wrapped in vulnerability rather than majesty.

6.2.2 Twelve-Year-Old in "My Father's House"

Luke alone records Jesus at age twelve remaining behind in Jerusalem, sitting among teachers, listening and asking questions (Luke 2 :42-50). When anxious parents find Him, He responds, "Did you not know that I must be in My Father's house?"—or "about My Father's business," depending on translation. Either way, the claim is unprecedented: no rabbi dared call the temple *My* Father's house; the common phrase was "our Father." By asserting unique filial ownership, Jesus implicitly declares Himself the rightful heir, the true Solomon whose wisdom surpasses the scribes around Him. His posture of asking and answering questions mirrors rabbinic disputation but also suggests that the living Torah is interrogating its interpreters. Luke places the story at Passover, foreshadowing a later Passover when the grown Teacher will again occupy temple courts and confound challengers (Luke 19 :47-48). Thus, from pre-teen years, the living temple is already asserting jurisdiction over the stone one. Modern Christian education should learn from this scene that genuine discipleship involves dwelling in Father's presence, questioning tradition, and embodying wisdom in community dialogue.

6.2.3 Teaching in Solomon's Colonnade – Light and Shepherd Discourses

John structures chapters 7–10 around feast settings: Tabernacles' water-and-light rituals (John 7 :37-38; 8 :12) and Dedication/Hanukkah's temple rededication themes (John 10 :22-39). In Solomon's Colonnade Jesus declares, "I am the Light of the world" and "I am the Good Shepherd," statements that transfer iconic temple symbols—the giant menorahs lit during Tabernacles and the priest-shepherd imagery of Ezekiel 34—onto Himself. By healing the man born blind and then discussing spiritual sight, He dramatizes that temple festivals are signs pointing to His identity. His claim that no one can snatch His sheep from His hand parallels the security promised by fortress walls, but now found in relational union (John 10 :28-29). The Jews attempt to stone Him for blasphemy, perceiving the implication: if He is true light and shepherd, the marble complex is redundant. Thus, Jesus' public teaching repurposes temple liturgies as living parables of Himself. Christian worship must likewise remember that its rituals lose meaning unless transparently Christ-centred.

6.2.4 Festival Cycle as Redemptive Calendar

John's gospel highlights three Passovers (John 2, 6, 12), one or two Tabernacles, a Dedication, and possibly a Pentecost, framing Jesus' ministry within the entire liturgical cycle of Israel. Each feast reveals a dimension of His temple ministry: Passover identifies Him as Lamb and Liberator, Tabernacles as Water-Rock and Light-Column, Dedication as true Hanukkah lamp, and likely Pentecost as Spirit baptizer. Thus, Jesus does not abolish the calendar but inhabits it, fulfilling feast typology while respecting its pedagogical power for the people. His healing at Bethesda on Sabbath (John 5) demonstrates Sabbath Maker's authority over Sabbath law, previewing the rest He will secure at Golgotha (Heb 4 :9-10). When disciples pluck grain on Sabbath, He cites David eating showbread, placing Himself above both Davidic precedent and priestly privilege (Matt 12 :1-8). Consequently, Christian liturgical life is not orphaned from biblical feasts but transformed; Good Friday, Easter, Pentecost, and Advent are the church's re-calibrated temple calendar. To ignore liturgical rhythm is to risk forgetting the embodied story Christ came to fulfill.

6.2.5 Temple Tax, Fish-Coin, and Cultic Finances

When collectors ask whether Jesus pays the half-shekel temple tax (Matt 17 :24-27; Exod 30 :13-16), He instructs Peter to catch a fish with a coin in its mouth, paying for them both while declaring that "the sons are free." This cryptic miracle establishes two truths simultaneously: first, He upholds Mosaic requirements so as not to scandalize consciences; second, His royal sonship technically exempts Him, highlighting again that presence has moved from stone to Son. By sourcing payment from creation rather than purse, He implicitly critiques the temple economy that will be lambasted in the cleansing. The fish-coin episode thus functions as pre-cleansing overture, revealing that Jesus will not allow cultic obligations to trump kingdom freedom, yet He remains sensitive to weaker brothers. Financial stewardship in the church must likewise balance freedom with love, supporting gospel mission without re-establishing burdensome levies that obscure grace (2 Cor 9 :7-9). The living temple's approach to money is miraculous provision aimed at missional generosity, not institutional aggrandizement.

6.3 Prophetic Authority and the Temple Cleansings

6.3.1 Court of the Gentiles — A House of Prayer Redefined

The largest expanse of Herod's complex was the Court of the Gentiles, a plaza intentionally designed so that non-Jews could draw near to Israel's God; but by the time of Jesus it had become a stockyard for Passover livestock and a shortcut between city gates (Mark 11 :16). When Jesus surveys the chaos, He quotes Isaiah 56 :7, "My house shall be called a house of prayer for all nations," and in so doing restores the court's original missionary vocation. He simultaneously quotes Jeremiah 7 :11, branding the merchants a "den of robbers," and thus aligns the current priestly leadership with the corrupt establishment Jeremiah had condemned before the Babylonian destruction. In a single sentence the living temple fuses consolation for outsiders with judgment upon insiders, showing that prophetic authority always carries a double edge. His actions fulfill Malachi 3 :1-3, where the Lord suddenly comes to His temple as a refiner's fire; coins clattering across limestone sound like sparks of that furnace. By driving out the animals, He implicitly halts the sacrificial system, anticipating a time when His own body will render animal blood obsolete (Heb 10 :4-10). The cleansing therefore is not mere social protest; it is enacted prophecy announcing that the era of exclusive, ethnic cult is giving way to global, Spirit-empowered worship.

6.3.2 Jeremiah 7 Echoes — The "Den of Robbers" Indictment

Jeremiah had earlier thundered against a nation that chanted "the temple of the LORD" while committing oppression and bloodshed, warning that God would turn Shiloh's fate upon Jerusalem (Jer 7 :1-15). By invoking that sermon, Jesus reminds His hearers that sacred architecture offers no immunity against divine judgment if covenant ethics are ignored. The word "robbers" that He hurls at the traders is not petty thieves but **lēstai**, a term elsewhere used for insurrectionists (Mark 15 :27), implying that the temple economy has become a revolutionary hideout against heaven's rule. Linking commercial exploitation with violence, Jesus exposes how unjust economies always seed political unrest. The chief priests fear the crowd because the cleansing unmasks their complicity, yet they cannot openly oppose Him amid Passover throngs singing Psalm 118. Thus, within forty years Rome will raze the shrine, fulfilling the very prophecy their leaders refused to heed. Modern churches tempted to rest on historic prestige must hear Jeremiah's echo: "Has this house… become a den of robbers in your eyes? Behold, I have seen it, declares the LORD."

6.3.3 Sign-Request and the "Destroy This Temple" Saying

After the first cleansing in John 2, Judean authorities demand, "What sign do You show us for doing these things?" Jesus answers cryptically, "Destroy this temple, and in three days I will raise it up," a statement they misunderstand as a boast to rebuild Herod's edifice (John 2 :19-21). John clarifies that He was speaking of "the temple of His body," thereby introducing the gospel's hermeneutical key: physical resurrection will validate His right to redefine holy space. The verb "raise" (*egeirō*) will later describe His Easter rising (John 21 :14), so the sign is inseparable from Passion-week events. By placing temple destruction in His opponents' hands ("destroy *this* temple"), Jesus both predicts their murderous intent and points to God's sovereignty in using that intent for redemptive construction. The misunderstanding lingers through the trial, where false witnesses twist the saying into a charge of terrorist threat (Matt 26 :61). Yet at Pentecost, Peter cites Psalm 16 to prove that God indeed raised the true temple in three days (Acts 2 :24-32). The sign-saying therefore functions as time-release prophecy, exploding into understanding only once stone has rolled away from garden tomb.

123

6.3.4 Zeal, Malachi's Refiner, and Psalm 69 :9 Fulfilled

John alone notes that the disciples, watching Jesus sweep stalls, remember Psalm 69 :9, "Zeal for Your house will consume Me" (John 2 :17). The Hebrew verb "consume" (*ăkal*) hints at self-immolation; the Messiah's passion for purity will literally devour Him on the cross. Malachi foresaw a refiner who would purify Levites like silver in a crucible; Jesus' bodily destruction becomes that furnace, melting and recasting priesthood around Himself (Mal 3 :2-3). Critics sometimes portray the cleansing as impulsive anger, but the scriptural resonance shows calculated, prophetic zeal aligned with covenant promises. In synoptic chronology the act precipitates the plot to kill Him, proving the psalm's second half—"The reproaches of those who reproach You have fallen on Me"—also applies (Ps 69 :9b). Hence, temple zeal and cruciform love are two sides of the same coin, refuting any notion that holiness and compassion can be played against each other. Contemporary disciples are called to similar zeal expressed through self-sacrificial love rather than violent outrage.

6.3.5 Legal and Political Fallout — From Sanhedrin Plot to Upper-Room Farewell

Mark records that chief priests and scribes "were seeking how to destroy Him, for they feared Him, because all the crowd was astonished at His teaching" (Mark 11 :18). By challenging temple commerce He threatens both their revenue and their theological control, fusing financial and doctrinal motives for murder. Judas's betrayal likely follows the cleansing (Luke 22 :3-6), perhaps motivated by disillusionment at Messiah who dismantles rather than commandeers temple power. In the political realm, Roman prefects relied on priestly cooperation to keep Passover crowds peaceful; Jesus' actions jeopardized that fragile détente, giving Caiaphas pragmatic grounds for elimination (John 11 :48-50). Yet in the upper-room discourse Jesus reframes looming absence: His Father's house has many rooms (John 14 :2), and departure is preparation, not defeat. Thus, the plot born in temple courts ironically paves way for cosmic sanctuary expansion. The fallout teaches that when God builds new things, old power structures often react violently, but providence turns opposition into construction scaffolding for redemption.

6.4 Miracles as Portable Temple Signs

6.4.1 Leper Cleansed — Mosaic Offerings Replaced

When Jesus touches a leper and instantly heals him (Mark 1 :40-45), He performs what Leviticus 13-14 saw only in theory: priestly inspection followed by sacrificial birds, cedar, and hyssop to reinstate the cleansed into worshipping community. Jesus instructs the man to show himself to the priest "for a proof," signaling respect for Torah while silently declaring Himself superior to its rituals. The priest, upon seeing healed skin, must offer sacrifices that now merely ratify what Jesus' word has already accomplished; cultic procedure follows messianic power, not vice versa. By relocating purity from Jerusalem's courts to Galilean roads, Christ turns Israel inside out— holiness radiates from margins to center. The contagion once excluded from camp now becomes a witness inside temple precincts, reversing exile logic. Thus, the living temple exports cleansing rather than importing uncleanness, fulfilling Haggai's paradox that holiness is normally non-transferable (Hag 2 :11-13) but here spreads through Messianic touch. The episode foreshadows Great Commission outreach into "unclean" Gentile world.

6.4.2 Paralytic Forgiven — Sin Remitted without Altar

Lowered through roof tiles, a paralyzed man hears, "Son, your sins are forgiven" before any physical healing occurs (Mark 2 :1-12). Scribes silently accuse blasphemy: only God can forgive, and only at temple altar through blood. Jesus proves authority by healing body, thus visible miracle authenticates invisible pardon. No lamb bleats, no priest slaughters; the living mercy seat speaks absolution. The crowd glorifies God, paradoxically affirming what the scribes deny, and new temple authority gains popular credential. This scene theme resurfaces when the woman of ill fame bathes Jesus' feet with tears in a Pharisee's house; He again declares sins forgiven absent sacrificial apparatus (Luke 7 :36-50). Therefore, forgiveness is no longer a Jerusalem monopoly; it travels wherever Son of Man treads.

6.4.3 Woman with Flow of Blood — Personal Laver Encounter

Twelve years of hemorrhage render a woman perpetually unclean (Lev 15 :25-27), barring her from temple. She pushes through crowd to touch Jesus' tassel, and power flows out, healing her instantly (Mark 5 :25-34). Instead of contaminating Him, she is purified—a living inversion of Leviticus. Jesus calls her "Daughter," restoring familial status alongside physical cure, and publicly affirms her faith, turning secret touch into communal celebration. The tassel she grasps fulfills Malachi's "healing in His wings" (Mal 4 :2), identifying Him as sun of righteousness rising over defiled world. Symbolically, her healing is a private laver encounter—washing that temple ever denied her. The church therefore must extend sacraments to social outcasts, confident that holiness radiates outward through Christ.

6.4.4 Feeding the Thousands — Multiplying Showbread and Tamid Wine

Twice Jesus feeds multitudes with meager bread, first five thousand (Mark 6) and later four thousand (Mark 8). The setting—green grass, groups of fifty—recalls temple order and Psalm 23's pasture banquet. He takes, blesses, breaks, and gives, verbs that will pattern Eucharist (Luke 22 :19; Acts 2 :42). Twelve baskets left over in first miracle nod to showbread loaves; seven baskets in second signal Gentile inclusion via symbolic number of nations in Canaan (Deut 7 :1). John's bread discourse following miracle identifies Him as manna and raises Passover stakes (John 6 :48-51). By feeding crowds in wilderness, the living temple exports priestly provision beyond holy city, democratizing sacred meal. Eucharistic theology is birthed on Galilean hillsides, not merely upper room.

6.4.5 Walking on Water — Lord of the Bronze Sea

In Hebrew symbolism, chaotic waters equal evil; temple bronze sea represented Yahweh taming chaos for priestly cleansing (1 Kgs 7 :23-25). When Jesus strides across Galilean waves (Matt 14 :22-33), He reenacts temple symbolism in open air, trampling Leviathan underfoot (Job 9 :8; Ps 77 :19). Peter's brief success and sinking dramatize transition from fear to faith; only trust keeps disciples above chaos. Once Jesus boards, the storm calms, paralleling Solomon dedicating temple and God granting peace (1 Kgs 8 :54-61). Thus, maritime miracle confirms authority hinted in cleansing—He commands both courts and cosmos. In Revelation a glassy sea before throne echoes this victory (Rev 4 :6). Therefore, every tempest stilled in believers' lives attests that the bronze sea has found its living Lord.

6.5 Cross and Curtain — Atonement in the True Holy Place

6.5.1 Gethsemane's Oil-Press versus Eden's Choice

Gethsemane, meaning "oil-press," becomes the site where the second Adam is crushed that Spirit-oil might flow to humanity. Unlike Eden's garden of delightful choice, this garden hosts agony; Jesus' soul is "sorrowful unto death" yet He submits, "Not My will but Yours" (Matt 26 :38-39). His threefold prayer answers Adam's single act of disobedience, establishing obedient reversal. Disciples sleeping echo Adam's deep sleep, but now it signals failure to watch (šāmar), underlining need for a faithful priest. Judas arrives with lanterns—artificial light searching for Light of world—ironies layering narrative. The arrest outside city begins scapegoat journey carrying sins beyond camp. Thus, passion passion—oil press and serpent head—converge in one bloody sweat.

6.5.2 Via Dolorosa and Scapegoat Geography

Jesus carries cross out the city gate to Golgotha, paralleling Day of Atonement goat led into wilderness bearing Israel's sins (Lev 16 :21-22; Heb 13 :11-13). The wooden beam recalls altar's acacia planks overlaid with battered flesh; here the offering and altar merge. Roman soldiers unwittingly fulfill Psalm 22, gambling for garments and mocking with pierced hands. The route through crowded streets functions as reverse pilgrimage: worshippers head toward temple; Lamb heads away to sanctify people through blood outside. Simon of Cyrene aids the burden, symbolizing Gentile participation in redemptive act. Women weep, forecasting church as witness to sacrificial journey. Geography thus preaches theology: holiness radiates from cross, not temple mount.

6.5.3 Veil Torn — Top to Bottom Proclamation

At Jesus' death the seventy-foot veil rips from top to bottom (Matt 27 :51), divine initiative making first incision. Earthquake splits rocks, tombs open, centurion confesses deity, cosmic chorus amplifying curtain sermon. Jewish tradition says veil weighed several tons; human hands could not tear it instantly, proving supernatural sign. The tear exposes cherubim embroidery, signifying that flaming sword is quenched—Eden gate reopened. Temple liturgists likely stunned next morning; Yom Kippur liturgy suddenly obsolete. Hebrews interprets torn curtain as Christ's flesh, granting believers bold entry (Heb 10 :19-22). Therefore, crucifixion is not tragedy but enthronement ceremony unveiling holy of holies to the humble.

6.5.4 Blood and Water — Laver and Altar United

John alone notes blood and water flowing from pierced side (John 19 :34-37). Early church fathers saw sacramental symbols: water of baptism, blood of Eucharist. Levitical priests moved from altar to laver; here both fluids issue from one source, uniting purification and atonement. Zechariah 12 :10's pierced one and Exodus 17's struck rock fuse prophecy and typology. Medical detail underscores real death, silencing docetist heresies. The church, born from side of second Adam, mirrors Eve from first, confirming covenant marriage. Thus, cross is fountainhead of temple's twin sacraments.

6.5.5 "Finished" — Perfect Tamid Completed

Jesus' final cry, *tetelestai* ("It is finished"), signals completion of redemptive work and echoes Genesis 2 :2 Sabbath formula. Daily tamid lambs offered morning and evening find culmination in this once-for-all sacrifice (Ex 29 :38-42). Darkness from sixth to ninth hour indicates Day of the LORD judgment absorbed by sin-bearer (Amos 8 :9). Temple priests slay Passover lambs as Lamb of God breathes last—history's most pregnant simultaneity. Curtain tear confirms Father's amen to Son's finished work. Hebrews concludes: "By one offering He perfected for all time those who are being sanctified" (Heb 10 :14). Therefore, no further sacrifice for sin remains; worship now flows from completed atonement.

6.6 Resurrection Body — The Rebuilt Temple in Three Days

6.6.1 Garden-Tomb and the New Adam Gardener

Resurrection dawns in a garden (John 19 :41), deliberately evoking Eden. Mary Magdalene mistakes Jesus for gardener, an error rich in truth: the first task of the first Adam resurfaces in glorified second Adam (John 20 :15). Empty tomb is a new holy of holies; angelic figures sit at head and foot of slab like cherubim on mercy seat, framing where body had lain (John 20 :12). Linen cloths folded signify priest completed duty and left vestments behind. First witnesses are women, paralleling Eve but redeemed into apostles to apostles. Easter therefore inaugurates new creation week; creation's first day shines again with greater light. The living temple stands indestructible, anchoring Christian hope beyond historical skepticism.

6.6.2 Touching Wounds — New Mercy Seat Manifest

Thomas demands empirical proof; Jesus invites him to place finger in nail marks and hand in side (John 20 :26-28). Rather than scolding, Jesus accommodates, teaching that resurrected temple welcomes honest inquiry. Wounds remain; glorification does not erase but transfigures suffering, turning scars into covenant emblems like circumcision on body of Messiah. Thomas' confession "My Lord and my God" surpasses all previous titles, matching temple dedication prayer where Solomon calls on covenant name (1 Kgs 8 :27-30). Thus, wounds are mercy-seat where doubt meets deity. Apologetics today must likewise guide skeptics to engaged encounter, not mere abstraction. Faith springs from wounded glory made accessible.

6.6.3 Emmaus Meal — Eucharistic Presence of Living House

Two disciples journeying to Emmaus fail to recognize risen Lord until He breaks bread (Luke 24 :30-31). Word exposition on road opens Scriptures; breaking bread opens eyes—Word and sacrament united. Meal echoes showbread now shared with laity, fulfilling inclusive mission. Table becomes traveling sanctuary; geography irrelevant once Christ presides. Hearts burn during exposition, replicating altar fire; eyes open at bread, replicating veil opening. Disciples hurry back to Jerusalem: evangelism follows sacramental revelation. Emmaus liturgy models Sunday worship—Scripture, Eucharist, mission.

6.6.4 Forty-Day Commission — Expanding Sanctuary Borders

Acts 1 :3 summarizes post-resurrection period: forty days of kingdom instruction. Forty recalls Moses on Sinai and Elijah's journey to Horeb—prophet-priest-king motifs converge. Jesus teaches about kingdom, not temple, hinting that temple is subsumed in larger reign.

Great Commission in Matthew 28 expands Eden mandate: make disciples of all nations, baptizing (laver) and teaching (Torah) everything. Ascension promise of Spirit equips task. Therefore resurrection house begins architectural expansion through witness, not bricks. Church embodies centrifugal sanctuary spreading from Jerusalem to ends of earth.

6.6.5 Resurrection Apologetics — Temple Prophecy Vindicated

Paul lists witnesses—Cephas, twelve, five hundred, James, himself—forming legal testimony (1 Cor 15 :3-8). Central claim: Christ died *according to Scriptures* and rose *according to Scriptures*, framing event as prophetic fulfilment. Sign of Jonah (three days) parallels temple rebuilding prophecy. Resurrection power validates cross meaning; without it, veil tear would be tragic accident. Early sermons in Acts repeatedly cite Psalm 16 as temple pinnacle uncorrupted (Acts 2; 13). Apologetics therefore is inseparable from temple typology. Believers defend faith by narrating how living house conquered graveyard.

6.7 Ascension and Heavenly Session — Priest-King Enthroned

6.7.1 Cloud Lift-Off and Priestly Wave-Offering

Acts 1 :9 records Jesus taken up and hidden by cloud, symbol of Shekinah presence. Priest waved firstfruits sheaf on day after Sabbath; Paul calls resurrection "firstfruits" (1 Cor 15 :20). Ascension is wave-offering of perfected humanity, guaranteeing harvest. Angels promise return "in same way," tying session to eschatological hope. Disciples gaze upward but are redirected to mission, showing worship fuels work. Cloud imagery echoes Exodus 40 and 1 Kings 8 dedication, but now enters heaven's true tabernacle. Thus, ascension completes dedication trilogy: incarnation, resurrection, enthronement.

6.7.2 Daniel 7 Coronation Fulfilled

Daniel saw Son of Man approach Ancient of Days on clouds, receiving kingdom (Dan 7 :13-14). New Testament cites this to describe ascended Christ (Mark 14 :62). Enthronement above cherubim validates Messianic authority over nations, fulfilling Psalm 110:1 "Sit at My right hand." Heaven's sanctuary now hosts human king, bridging Creator-creature chasm permanently. Authority outflow empowers church's global mission, assuring success despite persecution. Every Lord's Day creed "He is seated" rehearses this enthronement reality. Theology that ignores ascension truncates gospel narrative.

6.7.3 Hebrews 4–10 — Greater and More Perfect Tent

Hebrews argues earthly tabernacle is copy; Christ ministers in original, entering once for all with His blood (Heb 9 :11-12). His priesthood after Melchizedek order is untransferable, anchored in indestructible life (Heb 7 :16). Covenant upgraded: laws written on hearts, sins remembered no more (Heb 8 :10-12). Worshippers draw near sprinkled and washed, liturgical language now spiritual reality (Heb 10 :19-22). Earthly priests stand daily; Jesus sits, work finished. Yet He intercedes, applying sacrifice benefits continually (Heb 7 :25). Therefore, heavenly session is both rest and active mediation.

6.7.4 Ongoing Intercession — Golden Altar Ministry Above

Romans 8 :34 and 1 John 2 :1 portray Christ as advocate; Revelation 8 :3-4 shows incense mingling with saints' prayers. Priestly rhythm continues: petitions rise, advocacy answers. This assures persecuted believers their cries reach throne, encouraging persistence. Church's prayer life participates in temple liturgy, ascending through crucified-risen mediator. To neglect prayer is to abandon altar service entrusted to royal priesthood. Liturgy on earth synchronizes with heavenly worship, forging cosmic solidarity. Thus, session fuels spirituality and mission.

6.7.5 Melchizedek Order and Eternal Security

Psalm 110 links royal seat with perpetual priesthood; Hebrews unpacks tithes from Abraham as proof of Melchizedek's superiority. Christ's priesthood guarantees salvation "to the uttermost" because He lives forever (Heb 7 :24-25). Unlike Levitical priests who die and require successors, Jesus' continual presence secures covenant stability. Ethical exhortations flow from this security: believers may run race knowing anchor holds (Heb 6 :19-20). Sacrificial system's obsolescence frees resources for mercy and mission (Heb 13 :15-16).

doctrine comforts anxious consciences plagued by recurring guilt. Thus, temple climax yields pastoral assurance.

6.8 Pentecost and the Spirit-Indwelt Church

6.8.1 Tongues of Fire — Shekinah Divided among Living Stones

Acts 2 describes rushing wind and fire resting on each disciple, direct allusion to Sinai theophany (Ex 19 :16-19). Yet the flame does not consume; it indwells, signifying believers as mini-sanctuaries. The divided tongues invert Babel confusion, signaling that new temple unites nations through multilingual praise. Luke lists fifteen regions, a geographic map of restored Eden rivers spreading. Peter interprets event via Joel 2, framing Spirit outpouring as eschatological temple filling. Thus, Pentecost is not birth of church abstractly but dedication of new-creation temple corporately. Subsequent Spirit fillings in Acts extend consecration to Samaria, Gentiles, and beyond.

6.8.2 Reversal of Babel and Isaiah 2 Pilgrimage Preview

The multitude hears "the mighty works of God" in their languages (Acts 2 :11). At Babel, humanity sought self-made tower; God scattered tongues (Gen 11). At Pentecost, God builds His own tower-temple—people of Spirit—and gathers tongues under Christ. Isaiah predicted nations streaming to mountain of the LORD (Isa 2 :2-3); Pentecost launches that pilgrimage. Church thus is firstfruits of eschatological ingathering, a multicultural choir tuned by Spirit. Racism within church denies this temple DNA and grieves Spirit. Mission exists because Pentecost sanctified languages for praise.

6.8.3 Apostolic Community — Teaching, Table, Temple, Homes

Acts 2 :42-47 lists four devotion pillars: apostles' teaching, fellowship, breaking bread, prayers. Daily they gather in temple courts, breaking bread at homes, showing dual rhythm of public witness and intimate communion. Signs and wonders through apostles echo temple miracles, but shareable among ordinary disciples too (Acts 6 :8). Possessions sold to meet needs reflect jubilee economy unlocked by finished sacrifice. Favor with people demonstrates attractiveness of

Spirit-filled temple life. Numerical growth verifies centrifugal nature of living sanctuary. Modern ecclesiology must weigh programs against Acts template to remain temple-faithful.

6.8.4 Stephen's Speech — Mobile Presence versus Stone Shrine

Stephen rehearses history, emphasizing that God met Abraham in Mesopotamia, Joseph in Egypt, Moses in wilderness—presence never confined to place (Acts 7 :2-50). He quotes Isaiah 66 :1-2, "Heaven is My throne... what house will you build for Me?" indicting leaders who idolize building over obedience. Reactionary rage leads to martyrdom; temple defenders kill temple's witness. Stephen's vision of Son of Man standing at God's right hand proves true sanctuary is heavenly. His death scatters church, fulfilling mission mandate. Hence, persecution often purifies architecture idolatry, propelling mobile presence outward. Contemporary believers must hold buildings loosely for kingdom flexibility.

6.8.5 Body-Spirit Temple Ethics — Holiness, Unity, Gifts

Paul calls Corinthian congregation "God's temple" and warns destroyers face divine judgment (1 Cor 3 :16-17). Individual bodies also temples; sexual immorality therefore profanes holy site (1 Cor 6 :18-20). Spiritual gifts serve as temple functions—apostles foundation, prophets inner structure, helps and administration maintenance staff (1 Cor 12). Unity imperative flows from shared indwelling Spirit; schism tears veil anew. Gentile-Jew unity in Ephesians forms "dwelling place for God" (Eph 2 :21-22). Sanctification thus is architectural integrity of living stones. Ethical lapses risk structural collapse witness to watching world.

6.9 Sacramental Presence — Baptism and Eucharist

6.9.1 Baptismal Waters and Priestly Laver

Early church baptisms occurred in flowing rivers or constructed fonts echoing Edenic streams. Paul links immersion to burial and resurrection (Rom 6 :3-5), transforming initiates into new-creation priests. Peter says baptism now saves "not removal of dirt but pledge of good conscience" (1 Pet 3 :21), emphasizing internal purification. As laver preceded altar ministry, baptism precedes table fellowship. Trinitarian formula ("Father, Son, Spirit") inscribes temple tri-holiness on candidate. Consequently, to neglect baptism is to bypass entry washing, remaining in outer court. Sacrament confers corporate identity: many made one body (1 Cor 12 :13).

6.9.2 Table Fellowship and Showbread Fulfilled

Breaking bread is both ordinary meal and covenant act. Paul recounts received tradition: "This is My body... this cup is new covenant in My blood" (1 Cor 11 :23-26). Table carries forward Passover remembrance and anticipates marriage supper (Rev 19 :9). Early Christians called it *Eucharist*, thanksgiving—echoing Todah sacrifice of praise. Weekly celebration re-enacts temple bread eaten by priests, now democratized. Spiritual nourishment empowers ethical witness and eschatological hope. Neglecting table starves body, while unworthy participation invites discipline.

6.9.3 Communion as Tree-of-Life Antidote

Forbidden fruit brought death; sacramental bread brings life. Jesus promises, "Whoever eats My flesh... has eternal life" (John 6 :54). Eucharist therefore reverses Eden, offering obedience-based ingestion within covenant context. Church fathers called elements "medicine of immortality." Faith, not magic, discerns body; yet grace objectively offered. The rite trains appetites toward holiness, detoxing serpent lies of autonomy. Thus, communion table is garden gate reopened weekly.

6.9.4 Discipline and Discernment — Guarding the New Sanctuary

Paul warns of sickness and death among Corinthians for failing to discern body (1 Cor 11 :29-30). This parallels Nadab and Abihu's unauthorized fire (Lev 10). Elders practice fencing of table, welcoming repentant, excluding unrepentant to protect flock. Church discipline restores, not shames, reflecting priestly cleansing of lepers. Self-examination before supper nurtures humility, fostering unity. Thus, guarding sacrament maintains temple integrity. Laxity erodes witness and invites judgment.

6.9.5 Missional Banquets — Breaking Bread from House to House

Acts shows believers eating "with glad and generous hearts," winning favor of people (Acts 2 :46-47). Table fellowship crosses socioeconomic lines, embodying Isaiah's feast for all peoples (Isa 25 :6). Hospitality becomes evangelistic; unbelievers taste grace before hearing sermon. Paul instructs Romans to pursue "hospitality," philoxenia—love of strangers (Rom 12 :13). In Scripture meals seal covenants; church meals therefore preach gospel. Missional banquets anticipate eschatological wedding, rehearsing heavenly joy. Thus, sacraments extend beyond liturgy into everyday tables, turning kitchens into micro-temples.

6.10 Ethical Implications — Living as Temple People

6.10.1 Purity, Justice, Mercy — Micah 6 :8 Enfleshed

Temple holiness always demanded social righteousness; prophets linked corrupt worship with exploitation of poor. Jesus rebukes Pharisees for tithing mint while neglecting justice and mercy (Matt 23 :23). James calls pure religion visiting orphans and widows (Jas 1 :27). Living temples therefore practice ethics that mirror character of indwelling God. Mercy ministries, advocacy, and fair business practices become liturgical acts. Justice flows like river from throne (Amos 5 :24; Rev 22 :1). Without justice, worship noise becomes clanging cymbal.

6.10.2 Sexual Integrity — Bodies as Holy of Holies

Corinthian culture treated body as appetite playground; Paul counters: body temples belong to Lord (1 Cor 6 :13-20). Union with prostitute unites Christ with immorality, unthinkable desecration. Sanctification involves honoring God with bodies, reflecting Shekinah dwelling. Marriage bed undefiled becomes sacred space, echo of Eden. Pornography, adultery, and gender deconstruction attack temple design. Grace forgives past defilement but empowers holiness forward. Sexual ethics thus gospel witness to world craving authentic intimacy.

6.10.3 Economic Generosity — Jubilee Foretaste

Early believers sell land, lay proceeds at apostles' feet (Acts 4 :34-35), fulfilling Deuteronomy's "no poor among you." Tithes now fund mission and mercy, not temple refurbishing. Paul urges Corinthians to excel in grace of giving, citing Christ's poverty-to-riches exchange (2 Cor 8 :9). Generosity dethrones Mammon, whose temple was Herod's partner. Churches practicing radical stewardship display kingdom economy. Jubilee ethics challenge predatory lending and exploitative labor. Financial holiness as essential as doctrinal purity.

6.10.4 Work and Rest — Sabbath Rhythm Restored

Hebrews invites believers to enter rest through faith, ceasing self-justification toil (Heb 4 :9-11). Weekly rhythm of worship and rest proclaims freedom from Pharaoh-like systems. Christians keep Lord's Day as resurrection festival, not legal burden. Rest fuels mission, preventing burnout, modeling trust. Sabbath justice includes giving workers margin and land Sabbath to heal environment. In frantic economies, restful community shines as prophetic sign. Work becomes worship when anchored in rest.

6.10.5 Suffering as Priestly Sacrifice

Paul rejoices in filling up what is lacking in Christ's afflictions for body's sake (Col 1 :24). Believers offer bodies as living sacrifices (Rom 12 :1), daily liturgy of love. Persecution becomes incense rising, witness to worth of indwelling Christ. Revelation depicts martyrs under altar, their blood likened to temple offerings (Rev 6 :9). Suffering therefore not meaningless but priestly participation. Church comforts afflicted, honors martyrs, resists triumphalism. Joy amid trials testifies that temple treasure surpasses earthly loss.

In conclusion, The journey has traced granite and goat-hair, cedar and crimson, marble and menorahs—all converging in the living flesh of Jesus of Nazareth. His incarnation pitched divine tent among sinners; His miracles exported holiness; His cross tore the veil; His rising rebuilt the sanctuary in three days; His ascension enthroned humanity in heaven's holy of holies; His Spirit kindled millions of breathing altars; His sacraments nourish pilgrim-priests; His ethics demand that justice, mercy, and purity adorn the courts of daily life. And His promise stands: "I am coming soon." Until then, every baptismal splash, every Eucharistic crumb, every mercy offered to the least, every act of courageous witness, and every Sabbath sigh of rest drifts upward like incense, filling the cosmic temple with fragrance pleasing to God. The stone temples of old lie in ruins, but the living temple walks the earth in the faces of redeemed people, stretching, growing, groaning, and glowing until the day the city-bride descends and the Lord Himself is its lamp. In that day, the architecture of absence will be swallowed by the architecture of presence, and the prayer Jesus taught will be answered in full: God's will done on earth—indeed, **as** earth—as it is in heaven.

Chapter 7 - Temple Cleansing: Purity, Authority, and Eschatological Zeal.

No moment in the fourfold Gospel more vividly fuses prophetic fire with messianic tenderness than the day Jesus scattered coins and livestock across the sprawling courts of Herod's shrine. The episode is reported by all four evangelists, yet each places his own theological accent on the spectacle of overturned tables and thundered Scripture. A single sweep of a Galilean rabbi's arm tore through centuries of ritual habit, challenged priestly finances, unsettled Roman surveillance, and sent tremors down the eschatological spine of Israel's hope. To modern readers the cleansing can look like a burst of impulsive rage, but Scripture itself frames it as a deliberate sign-act—an enacted oracle that exposes polluted worship, asserts royal prerogative, and previews a final day when temple geography will be swallowed up by the glory of God and the Lamb. Grasping the force of that sign-act requires a long look backward to earlier purifications by Levites, kings, and prophets; a careful reading of the economic machinery that operated in the Court of the Gentiles; and a forward gaze toward the cross, the tearing veil, and a church commissioned to embody the house-of-prayer vocation for every nation. What follows is a sustained exploration of that moment in all its historical, canonical, and practical dimensions. Each major theme—background, precedent, narrative portrait, theological meaning, and contemporary application—is unfolded in turn, but the heartbeat of the discussion remains constant: to see how purity, authority, and zeal converge in Christ and continue to pulse in the life of His people.

7.1 Historical & Economic Background of Second-Temple Commerce

7.1.1 Herodian Expansion: Courts, Porticoes, and Population Pressures

Herod the Great began enlarging the temple mount in 20 BC, replacing Hasmonean structures with a gleaming complex whose esplanade spanned nearly thirty-seven acres—large enough, Josephus boasts, for a crowd of hundreds of thousands during feast days (*Ant.* 15.391). The outermost ring, bordered by colonnades such as Solomon's Porch, provided shade for pilgrims and doubled as public square where rabbis taught (John 10 :23). Archaeological soundings under today's Jerusalem reveal foundation stones weighing over five hundred tons, testimony to Herod's determination to rival Rome's engineering. Such scale, however, demanded enormous upkeep and an ever-flowing stream of offerings to finance priests, musicians, guard detachments, and repair crews. Pilgrims arriving from Galilee, Syria, or North Africa surged into the vast Court of the Gentiles, searching for approved animals and legally acceptable coinage. Temple administrators therefore leased stalls to families from priestly clans—most famously those linked to Annas—turning sacred space into a franchise network that produced reliable revenue. By Jesus' lifetime the site of Israel's universal invitation had degenerated into a noisy bazaar whose animal bleats and clinking shekels drowned the psalms supposed to echo from the inner court.

7.1.2 The Tyrian Half-Shekel and Annual Temple Tax (Ex 30 :11-16; Matt 17 :24-27)

Moses had legislated a half-shekel census levy to maintain sanctuary service, and later rabbis fixed its due date at the first of Adar, one lunar month before Passover. Jerusalem's authorities insisted on Tyrian coinage because its silver content remained consistently high—about ninety-two percent—unlike debased Roman denarii. The annual influx of precious metal enriched the temple treasury, funding sacrificial materials and golden adornments but simultaneously subjecting poor pilgrims to unfavorable exchange rates. Matthew records collectors confronting Peter in Capernaum, a hundred miles from the temple, proving that tax enforcement extended northward long before feast crowds set foot on the mount (Matt 17 :24). Jesus pays through a miracle fish, thereby satisfying the law while hinting that royal sons technically owe no levy to their Father's house. The episode foreshadows the cleansing: the true heir of the sanctuary will not allow His Father's dwelling to be leveraged for profit at the expense of covenant family. In effect, the half-shekel reveals both the just provision of God for His worship and the unjust distortions produced by greed.

7.1.3 Licensed Money-Changers: Exchange Rates, Profits, and Priestly Oversight

Money-changers (*kollybistai*) sat behind wooden tables stacked with scales and calibrated weights, consulting annually updated tariffs posted by the priestly committee. Every transaction included an *agio*, a small surcharge—about eight percent according to later Talmudic sources—that went partly to the exchanger and partly to the temple coffers. Pilgrims aware of exploitation had little recourse; refusing service meant forfeiting participation in the very sacrifices they had traveled to offer. Fluctuating rates also created opportunity for insider speculation, especially when large caravans from the Diaspora arrived with coins unfamiliar to Judean markets. Some scholars suggest that exchange booths gradually crept from the Royal Stoa in the south toward the eastern segment of the Gentile court, maximizing convenience but also maximizing noise and congestion. Because high-priestly families controlled concession licenses, corruption accusations tarnished their spiritual credibility, fueling popular resentment exploitable by movements such as the Zealots. When Jesus overturned these tables, He struck at the economic nerve center of the ruling elite, ensuring that His prophetic sign could not be dismissed as harmless street theater.

7.1.4 Livestock Bazaars: Doves for the Poor, Oxen for the Wealthy (Lev 1-5)

Leviticus made gracious provision for economic diversity by allowing turtle-doves in lieu of lambs, yet the very law meant to ease burdens became pretext for inflated prices. Contemporary sources place dove prices inside the temple at fifteen to twenty times village markets, a markup priestly inspectors justified by claiming superior purity. Oxen and sheep, necessary for Passover or peace offerings, were driven up the Tyropoeon Valley ramps, their hooves churning dust into the air already thick with incense smoke. Stalls likely stood beneath the looming Antonia Fortress, permitting Roman sentries to monitor crowds while enjoying lease fees diverted through Sadducean allies. Such commingling of imperial oversight and priestly profiteering blurred boundaries between sacred and secular, inviting prophetic denunciation. Jesus' decision to free the doves—not merely tip their cages—intentionally honored the poor who could not afford larger beasts. His act dramatized Zechariah 9 :9's vision of a humble king who rescues the flock doomed to slaughter, reversing a marketplace that devoured widows' mites for sacrificial token birds.

7.1.5 Court of the Gentiles as Marketplace and Shortcut (Mark 11 :16)

Mark alone notes that Jesus "would not allow anyone to carry merchandise through the temple courts," revealing that the plaza had become a pedestrian shortcut between city gates. The prohibition taps Zechariah 14 :21, which foresees a day when no Canaanite merchant will inhabit the Lord's house, linking end-time holiness to commercial eviction. Gentiles seeking the God of Israel thus found their zone overrun by freight traffic and price-gouging—a direct inversion of the Abrahamic promise that Israel would bless the nations. Josephus claims that certain priests even bought lands from temple proceeds, demonstrating how sacred real estate financed personal fortunes (*Ant.* 20.181). Archaeologists have uncovered chalkstone vessels and scale weights in priestly mansions of Jerusalem's Upper City, corroborating ancient critiques of clerical luxury. Jesus' blockade therefore protected Gentile worship space, aligning with Isaiah 56 :7's vision of an international house of prayer. His physical presence restored, if briefly, the missionary architecture Moses and Solomon had envisaged.

7.2 Old-Testament Precursors of Temple Purification

7.2.1 Levites and the Golden Calf: Violence for Holiness (Ex 32 :25-29)

When Israel's camp dissolved into orgiastic idolatry around a calf of molten gold, Moses called, "Who is on the Lord's side?" and the sons of Levi rallied, sword in hand. Their grim tally of three thousand corpses signaled that covenant violation could cost covenant lives, setting a precedent for lethal zeal in defense of holiness. Yahweh rewarded them with priesthood, effectively stating that those willing to guard purity at personal cost would safeguard worship for generations. The episode fused worship with moral seriousness, reminding Israel that festivals bereft of fidelity invite judgment rather than joy. Later interpreters, including Philo and the rabbis, viewed the Levites' zeal as righteous albeit severe, a necessary surgery to excise pagan infection. Jesus' non-violent but forceful cleansing echoes the spirit—though not the method—of that original purification, exchanging swords for prophetic sign-acts. He embodies the Levite ethos while transforming its execution from bloodshed to liberation.

7.2.2 Hezekiah's Eight-Day Cleansing and Passover Revival (2 Chr 29-30)

King Hezekiah inherited a defiled sanctuary strewn with idols and shuttered doors, yet within his first month he convened priests to reopen and cleanse the house of the Lord. The priests required eight days merely to clear debris from the outer court and another eight to purify inner chambers, after which Hezekiah ordered a national Passover celebrated with unprecedented inclusivity, even extending invites to Israel's northern refugees. Chronicler notes that people celebrated "with great gladness," equating purified worship with communal joy (2 Chr 30 :26). Burnt offerings multiplied beyond legal quota, and music resounded under Asaph's psalms, creating a template for revival tied to spatial sanctification. This historical memory would have been cherished by first-century pilgrims who longed for another righteous Davidic king to restore temple dignity. Jesus' cleansing therefore resonated as a Hezekiah-like reform, but unlike the monarch He did not reopen doors; He prepared to replace

142

the entire edifice. Thus Hezekiah serves as both prototype and foil, pointing beyond reform to messianic revolution.

7.2.3 Josiah's Reform: Scroll Discovery and Idol Smash (2 Kgs 23)

Josiah's renovation began with Hilkiah's discovery of a forgotten Torah scroll, likely Deuteronomy, whose covenant curses jarred the young king into drastic action. He pulverized Asherah poles, deposed idolatrous priests, defiled Topheth where children were burned to Molech, and carried bones from graveyards to pollute unauthorized altars. His Passover kept that year stood unrivaled since Samuel, highlighting how Scripture-driven purity revives festal life. Josiah's zeal, however, could not avert Judah's exile; God honored the king but judged the nation for Manasseh's prior abominations (2 Kgs 23 :26-27). The bittersweet outcome foreshadows Jesus' fate: cleansing the temple yet predicting its fall within one generation. Josiah's shattered idols littered Kidron just as Jesus would later scatter coins, different debris revealing similar zeal. The scroll that fired Josiah's conscience now takes flesh and walks the courts, condemning idolatry with living words.

7.2.4 Ezra-Nehemiah: Foreign Marriage Crisis and Store-Room Expulsions (Neh 13 :4-14)

Nehemiah returned from Persia to find Tobiah the Ammonite occupying a storeroom reserved for grain, wine, and frankincense; enraged, he hurled Tobiah's household goods into the street. The narrative recounts Nehemiah's physicality—he contends, curses, and beats certain offenders—illustrating how administrative negligence threatens worship integrity. Store-room misuse paralleled fiscal corruption: Levites had gone home because tithes were withheld, showing that ethical disorder depletes priestly ministry. Covering also marital impurity, Nehemiah pulls hair and demands covenant loyalty, embodying violent reform. Jesus' temple action echoes Nehemiah's expulsions but broadens target from one foreign dignitary to an entire economic system. Whereas Nehemiah fought to preserve sacrificial structure, Jesus acts with knowledge that His own body will become the storeroom where heavenly bread and wine reside. Thus, Nehemiah foreshadows but cannot fulfill the final cleansing that replaces physical rooms with incarnate presence.

7.2.5 Post-Exilic Prophetic Warnings: Haggai 2 and Malachi 1-3

Haggai scolds returned exiles for paneled houses while the temple lay in ruin, insisting that agricultural failure mirrors cultic neglect (Hag 1 :6-11). He then asks priests whether holy meat can transmit holiness by contact—answer, no—whereas filthy touch defiles, teaching that polluted worship infects community prosperity (Hag 2 :13-14). Malachi intensifies critique: blemished animals on the altar dishonor God more than Gentile ignorance, and priests turn sacrifice into profit, earning the label "despised" (Mal 1 :6-8). Yet Malachi simultaneously promises a messenger who will purify Levites like silver, and an "offering in righteousness" pleasing to the Lord (Mal 3 :1-4). Jesus later applies Malachi's messenger text to John the Baptist while embodying the refining Lord Himself. His overturned tables and dove release sound exactly the furnace bell Malachi predicted, melting corrupt metallic hearts. Therefore, post-exilic prophecy plants expectations of a climactic temple visitation that Jesus unmistakably claims to fulfill.

7.3 Synoptic Presentation of the Cleansing

7.3.1 Narrative Setting: Triumphal Entry, Fig-Tree Sign, and Prophetic Drama

In all three Synoptics, the cleansing immediately follows the royal entry where crowds hail "Hosanna," laying palm branches along the ascent of the Mount of Olives. Matthew and Mark bracket the cleansing with a fig-tree episode: Jesus seeks fruit, finds only leaves, curses the tree, and later the disciples see it withered (Mark 11 :12-14, 20-21). The sandwich technique interprets temple unfruitfulness symbolically—leafy piety without prayerful fruit invites judgment. Luke omits the fig but inserts Jesus' lament over Jerusalem, connecting tears with impending desolation (Luke 19 :41-44). Each evangelist thereby casts the cleansing as both messianic assertion and doom oracle. The sudden shift from jubilant procession to disruptive protest mirrors prophetic traditions where acceptance quickly leads to scrutiny. Unlike modern protests, Jesus' act targets not political headquarters but sacred economy, revealing a Messiah concerned first with worship integrity.

7.3.2 "Den of Robbers": Echoes of Jeremiah 7 and Covenant Lawsuit

By quoting Jeremiah 7 :11, Jesus resurrects the prophet's temple sermon delivered a generation before Babylon razed Solomon's sanctuary. Jeremiah had condemned worshipers who trusted in the building's inviolability while committing injustice, threatening to make the house like Shiloh. Jesus thus levels the same covenant lawsuit against the second temple: outward magnificence cannot shield inward lawlessness. The phrase "den of robbers" in context refers to hideout, suggesting the priests use sacred space to conceal economic theft. Mark's audience, possibly under threat of Roman war, would shudder recognizing that history was poised to repeat itself. By pairing Jeremiah with Isaiah 56's promise to Gentiles, Jesus indicts leaders for blocking the very inclusivity the prophets envisioned. The collision of welcome and warning crystallizes kingdom ethics: mercy for outsiders, judgment for hypocritical insiders.

7.3.3 Zechariah 14 and the Prohibition of Merchants on the Day of the LORD

Zechariah foresaw a day when holiness inscriptions would grace horse bells and no merchant (*kĕna 'anî*, "Canaanite") would be found in the Lord's house (Zech 14 :20-21). By ejecting traders, Jesus symbolically inaugurates that eschatological moment, declaring that final sanctification is at hand. The prophet's oracle follows global upheaval and living waters flowing from Jerusalem, motifs Jesus alludes to in earlier ministry (John 7 :38). Therefore, the cleansing previews living-water outpouring at Pentecost when Spirit fire will inscribe holiness on flesh rather than metal. Zechariah also marries kingship with priesthood, concepts Jesus embodies as Davidic heir and purifying priest. Merchants' absence does not signify economic annihilation but sanctified commerce outside manipulative religious control. Consequently, Jesus' sign-act proclaims dawn of the Day of the LORD even before apocalyptic discourses unfold on Olivet.

7.3.4 Children Shouting "Hosanna": Messianic Authority vs. Priesthood Authority

Matthew alone reports children continuing the "Hosanna" chant inside the courts while chief priests fume (Matt 21 :15). Jesus defends the youngsters by citing Psalm 8 :2—"Out of the mouths of infants... You have ordained praise"—elevating unlettered voices above learned doctors of Law. The exchange echoes earlier prophetic patterns where God raises unlikely witnesses—donkeys, stones, foreign kings—to shame obstinate leaders. Children's spontaneous hymn signals that messianic authority draws worship from pure hearts irrespective of clerical endorsement. Luke intensifies the motif by recording Jesus' claim that silent disciples would be replaced by vocal stones (Luke 19 :40). The episode simultaneously affirms Jesus' humility and kingship: He receives praise yet defends the weak. Chief priests' inability to rejoice exposes hearts more aligned with mammon than Messiah, foreshadowing their murderous resolve.

7.3.5 Immediate Plotting of Death: Political Fallout and Fear of Crowds

Mark observes that the chief priests and scribes "were seeking how to destroy Him" because the entire crowd was "astonished at His teaching" (Mark 11 :18). The combination of economic threat and popular acclaim makes Jesus a high-risk rabble-rouser in the eyes of authorities dependent on Roman tolerance. Passover already strained civic peace; one incendiary prophet overturning tables under Fortress Antonia's shadow jeopardized hard-won arrangements. The leaders fear the crowd yet exploit crowd manipulation later, revealing political calculus masked by piety. Judas's defection immediately after Bethany perfume episode may reflect disillusionment with a nonviolent Messiah whose cleansing seems self-destructive (Matt 26 :14-16). Jesus knows the plot yet continues daily teaching, turning temple courts into last-week seminary for disciples who will inherit His mission. Thus cleansing triggers the chain of events leading straight to Golgotha, marrying prophetic sign with sacrificial timetable.

7.4 Johannine Presentation of the Cleansing

7.4.1 Early-Ministry Placement: Programmatic Sign or Separate Event?

John situates the cleansing at the first Passover of Jesus' ministry, immediately after Cana's sign, framing it as inaugural declaration that the true temple has arrived (John 2 :13-22). Some harmonists propose two separate cleansings—early and late—while many scholars see John's placement as theological rather than chronological. Either view underscores John's purpose: to establish replacement Christology where wine beats purification jars and living temple beats stone courts. The narrative thus forms inclusio with John 19, where temple curtain tears as Jesus dies, bracketing ministry with sanctuary themes. Early placement also allows subsequent festival narratives—Tabernacles, Dedication, second Passover—to orbit cleansing implications. John's readers, likely after AD 70, would recognize that the temple was already rubble; the Gospel declares it obsolete from the outset of Jesus' public mission. Consequently, Johannine chronology serves pastoral apologetics, assuring displaced believers that faith never depended on surviving architecture.

7.4.2 "Zeal for Your House Will Consume Me" (Ps 69 :9) and the Logic of Self-Sacrifice

John alone quotes Psalm 69, linking Jesus' action to Davidic lament where righteous sufferer is engulfed by zeal-ignited opposition. The verb "consume" foreshadows literal death; cleansing tables lights the fuse that will burn through His flesh at Calvary. By internalizing zeal, Jesus redefines it from sword-wielding violence to self-giving martyrdom, a trajectory Paul later adopts after abandoning persecutor zeal (Phil 3 :6-8). Psalm 69 also laments temple mockery, aligning Jesus with earlier sufferers who bore disgrace for sanctuary integrity. John's audience hears both complaint and confidence: zeal leads to cross, but cross leads to vindication. Thus Christological zeal becomes interpretive key for Christian endurance under persecution. Every believer's passion for purity must pass through this cruciform filter lest zeal mutate into fanaticism.

7.4.3 Sign-Demand and the "Destroy This Temple" Prophecy

Temple officials ask for a sign validating Jesus' right to cleanse, paralleling Moses' miracles before Pharaoh. Jesus offers a cryptic riddle: "Destroy this temple, and in three days I will raise it." John's authorial aside clarifies He spoke of His body, planting resurrection hope early in the narrative. Ironically, the demand for sign becomes self-fulfilling; their destruction of His body paves way for the sign of empty tomb. Three-day motif echoes Hosea 6 :2 and Jonah's fish experience, layering prophetic textures. At trial, false witnesses twist the saying, but its seed already germinated faith among disciples who "remembered" after Easter (John 2 :22). The prophecy thus operates like time-release liturgy, exploding into understanding when Christ walks through locked doors on the first day of new creation.

7.4.4 Chronological vs. Theological Motives in John's Gospel Structure

John organizes ministry around seven signs and seven "I am" sayings, weaving temple themes through each: water to wine (purity jars), bread of life (showbread), light of the world (menorah), good shepherd (gateway). Placing cleansing first positions temple replacement as interpretive grid for all subsequent signs. Scholarly debates over Johannine chronology—e.g., two or three Passovers— miss author's cue: theology trumps timeline without fabricating events. Ancient readers were comfortable with topical arrangement; John's explicit "the Passover was near" signals symbolic resonance. Thus, early cleansing amplifies later festival dialogues: living water at Tabernacles flows because temple water-drawing ritual is obsolete. Literary artistry serves missionary purpose, persuading diaspora Jews that belief in Jesus is continuity, not betrayal, of ancestral hope. Consequently, Johannine structure models evangelistic storytelling anchored in powerful symbol rather than strict chronology.

7.4.5 Temple-Body Typology Introduced at the Outset of Ministry

By calling His body the temple, Jesus merges incarnation and sanctuary, telling Jews that God's dwelling is no longer behind embroidered cherubim but walking in sandal leather. This identification anticipates John 1 :14, where the Word "tabernacled" among us, translating Shekinah glory into human flesh. The typology expands: when His side is pierced, blood and water mimic altar and laver; when He breathes Spirit, disciples become smaller sanctuaries (John 20 :22). By introducing the motif early, John allows readers to trace a trajectory: temple → body → ecclesial body → eschatological city. The typology also rebukes Gnostic tendencies denying material significance, affirming that true worship now centers in tangible humanity of Jesus. This theological move undergirds later sacramental realism: bread and cup can mediate presence because Word became tissue. Therefore, Johannine cleansing anchors the church's sacramental and incarnational framework from the start.

7.5 Purity—Theological and Ritual Dimensions

7.5.1 Cultic Purity vs. Social Justice Purity (Isa 1; Mic 6 :6-8)

Biblical purity encompasses more than ritual correctness; it enfolds justice, mercy, and covenant loyalty, as prophets repeatedly protest burnt offerings offered with bloodstained hands. Isaiah indicts Israel for trampling courts while neglecting orphans, a juxtaposition Jesus replicates when He calls merchants "robbers," accusing them of theft under sanctuary cover. Micah reduces Torah to three imperatives—do justice, love mercy, walk humbly—teaching that liturgical perfection minus ethical compassion equals idolatry. Jesus' cleansing therefore dramatizes prophetic purity, merging ritual protest with social advocacy for Gentile access. By physically stopping commerce He pictures an economy re-oriented around prayerful inclusivity rather than profit. His action reveals that genuine purity liberates oppressed and invites outsiders, not merely sanitizes insiders. The church, embracing this vision, must guard sacraments from becoming commodities while fueling ministries of compassion.

7.5.2 Holy Space and Boundary Maintenance: *Miqqeš* vs. *Ḥērem*

Levitical codes differentiate holy (*qodesh*), common (*ḥol*), clean (*tahor*), and unclean (*tame*), teaching priests to guard borders so glory does not break out in wrath (Lev 10 :10). Yet holiness spreads outward through proper mediation; temple cleansing reasserts correct boundaries by expelling impurities that should never have entered.

Jesus enforces *miqqeš* (cultic propriety) while averting *ḥērem* (destructive ban), choosing enactment over annihilation. His nonlethal zeal contrasts with earlier sword-bearers, marking a transition from punitive purity to restorative confrontation. By cleansing, He resets boundary markers to welcome Gentiles and exclude greed, redefining defilement in moral rather than ethnic terms. This boundary theology energizes Acts 15, where apostles prohibit idolatry and blood yet allow cultural variance. Thus purity doctrine evolves from spatial segmentation to relational sanctity around Christ.

7.5.3 Korban Abuse and Exploitation of the Poor (Mark 7 :9-13)

Earlier in Mark, Jesus denounces *korban* vows enabling sons to withhold support from aging parents, exposing manipulation of offerings for self-advancement. The same corruption surfaces in temple bazaar where inflated prices exploit peasants who travel days to obey Torah. Doves, the poor man's sacrifice, become luxury items under priestly sanction, exactly the injustice Isaiah targeted. By releasing doves, Jesus sides with marginalized women like Mary who offered such birds at His own dedication (Luke 2 :24). Exploitation wrapped in liturgical language provokes divine wrath; pennies extorted from widows weight more heavily in heaven's scales than golden trumpets adorning sanctuary doors. Post-Pentecost community responds by sharing possessions, proving Jesus' cleansing birthed economic ethics (Acts 4 :32-35). Hence purity and justice remain inseparable, both grounded in sacrificial compassion.

7.5.4 Tables, Coins, and Cages: Material Symbols of Spiritual Corruption

Each object Jesus topples carries symbolic freight: tables recall covenant feasts turned into counters; coins evoke Caesar's image rivaling God's; cages imprison creatures meant for sacrificial release, mirroring worshippers trapped in mercantile piety. By overturning furniture, He overturns value systems, teaching that economy must bow to doxology. The clang of silver echoes Judas's betrayal price, foreshadowing how love of money fuels murder of Messiah (1 Tim 6 :10). Early Christians later burned magic scrolls worth fifty thousand drachmas in Ephesus, obeying the lesson that grace devalues former idols (Acts 19 :19). Reformation iconoclasts cited temple cleansing when removing indulgence booths, albeit sometimes forgetting Jesus' non-lethal approach. Objects can carry oppressive ideologies; Christ liberates by reordering physical space toward prayer. Thus material culture of worship must continually undergo Christ-centered critique.

7.5.5 Cleansing as Foreshadow of Cross-Achieved Purification (Heb 9 :13-14)

Hebrews affirms that goat and calf blood sanctifies for fleshly purity, "but how much more will the blood of Christ cleanse the conscience," linking ritual cleansing to Calvary's substance. Jesus' courtroom protest anticipates His courtroom trial where He will pour out blood capable of truly washing defilement. The whip of cords He wields upon animals will soon be exchanged for lashes upon His own back, demonstrating substitutionary trajectory. John ties cleansing and crucifixion by noting Passover proximity in both events, bracketing ministry with atonement arc. The prophetic sign fails if not consummated by self-offering; temple purity requires temple payment. By acting before dying, Jesus asserts interpretive ownership of His death: it will be understood through lens of sanctified worship. Thus cleansing prophecy and cross fulfillment form indivisible halves of the same redemptive coin.

7.6   Authority—Challenging   Priests, Sanhedrin, and Imperial Power

7.6.1 "By What Authority?"—Legal Interrogations (Matt 21 :23-27)

Chief priests and elders confront Jesus the next morning, demanding His ordination papers, but He counters with a question about John's baptism, placing them in a dilemma. If they affirm John's divine origin, they must accept Jesus whom John endorsed; if they deny, they alienate the crowd who revered John. Their agnostic reply exposes political expediency masquerading as theological caution. Jesus refuses to divulge His credential to dishonest questioners, yet proceeds to tell parables that unmask their spiritual bankruptcy. The encounter models wise engagement with hostile authorities: expose motives before offering pearls. It also highlights a principle that true authority emanates from obedience to God, not institutional endorsement. Consequently, cleansing stakes Christ's claim not just over ritual but over interpretive control of Israel's story.

7.6.2 Sadducean Control of the Cult and the High-Priestly Franchise

Sadducees, mostly priestly aristocrats, derived power from temple administration and cooperation with Rome. They rejected resurrection and prophetic additions, holding Pentateuch alone as authoritative, which made Jesus' messianic claims doubly threatening. Their wealth depended on tithes, market leases, and exchange tariffs; a Galilean prophet crippling revenue streams imperiled their social stature. Caiaphas's counsel that "one man should die for the people" (John 11 :50) reveals fiscal and political calculation underlying theological façade. Josephus records popular resentment against high-priestly violence and extortion (*Ant.* 20.181-206). Jesus positions Himself as priest-king of Psalm 110, nullifying Sadducean monopoly. Cleansing thus prefigures a transfer of priesthood from corrupt hereditary line to crucified Son enthroned in heaven.

7.6.3 Roman Oversight: Fortress Antonia and Passover Tension

Antonia Fortress loomed over the northwest corner of the temple, its staircases enabling soldiers to descend quickly into courts at first sign of revolt. Pilate typically relocated from Caesarea to Jerusalem each feast, bringing cohorts to curb unrest. An unarmed yet assertive 7.prophet disrupting commerce could easily spark riot perception, triggering lethal force. Jesus' measured action—no swords, no call to insurrection—exposed Rome's fragility: true authority disarms without legionaries. Later, Roman governor Florus plundered the treasury, igniting revolt that led to AD 70 destruction, fulfilling Jesus' lament. By cleansing under Roman gaze, Jesus declares that Caesar's peace (*pax Romana*) cannot secure God's holiness. His authority transcends imperial might, a claim vindicated when resurrection outlasts empire.

7.6.4 Prophetic vs. Priestly Authority: Elijah, John the Baptist, and Jesus

Elijah confronted Ahab and Jezebel, challenging Baal prophets at Carmel; his authority came from fire-calling intimacy with Yahweh, not temple ordination. John mirrored Elijah's dress, confronting Herod and calling for repentance at Jordan's edge, situating authority in wilderness fidelity. Jesus surpasses both by joining prophetic courage with priestly compassion, cleansing temple yet healing blind and lame within minutes. The juxtaposition signals integrated authority that both judges and restores. Priests bound by lineage lacked such charismatic sanction, exposing institutional hollowness. Early church leaders inherit prophetic-priestly model, teaching boldly while serving tables (Acts 6 :4). Thus cleansing becomes charter for Spirit-empowered authority against ossified structures.

7.6.5 Kingdom Authority Re-Defines True Priesthood (1 Pet 2 :5-9)

Peter declares believers "a royal priesthood," relocating authority from Jerusalem's elite to scattered pilgrimage communities. This democratization roots in cornerstone rejected by builders—Jesus—whose cleansing signaled old stone's obsolescence. Authority now manifests through proclamation of excellencies, not commercial gatekeeping. Holiness derives from union with living stone, not ancestral genealogy. Church discipline, sacraments, and teaching function as priestly tasks executed in Christlike humility. External power structures may dismiss such authority, yet heaven affirms it, as reflected in Revelation's lampstands representing congregations. Temple cleansing thus seeds ecclesiology built on shared priestly dignity and cross-shaped leadership.

7.7 Zeal—From Phinehas to Paul

7.7.1 Phinehas' Spear (Num 25) and the Covenant of Perpetual Priesthood

Phinehas pierced Zimri and Cozbi mid-fornication, stopping plague and winning covenant of peace, an event celebrated in Psalm 106 :30-31 as righteousness credited for generations. His spear embodied jealous love for Yahweh, defining zeal as violent loyalty against idolatry. Jewish tradition exalted Phinehas as prototype zealot, inspiring Hasmonean militancy. Jesus' zeal, while echoing Phinehas, reframes violence toward self-sacrifice rather than enemy bloodshed. He confronts sin but refuses to impale sinners, choosing nails piercing His own flesh. Thus cross transforms spear into shepherd's staff, guiding zeal into redemptive channels. Early Christians like Stephen imitate this by praying for persecutors while rebuking stiff-necked hearts (Acts 7).

7.7.2 Maccabean Zeal and the *Kanna'îm* Tradition (1 Macc 2 :24-28)

Mattathias's rally cry—"Let everyone who is zealous for the Law follow me"—sparked revolt that cleansed altar defiled by Antiochus. Hanukkah commemorated that zeal, embedding militant purity in

Jewish calendar. Jesus honored the feast yet subverted its militarism, cleansing economic idolatry rather than slaughtering pagan soldiers. His action fulfilled festival symbolism in peaceful form, reclaiming zeal for transformative holiness. Acts records early Christian martyrs celebrating Hanukkah-like dedication through blood witness, not sword. Zeal thus migrates from battlefield to mission field, conquering hearts instead of territories. This reframing challenges any Christian nationalism that confuses holy passion with coercive power.

7.7.3 Zeal Misapplied: Paul the Persecutor (Gal 1 :13-14)

Saul of Tarsus, steeped in Pharisaic rigor, viewed Christ-followers as threat to temple purity, pursuing them "beyond measure." His zeal, like a runaway fire, scorched innocent believers until Damascus light redirected flame toward gospel proclamation. Conversion narrative demonstrates that zeal without knowledge breeds violence; zeal enlightened by grace births evangelism (Rom 10 :2). Paul later channels passion into tireless mission, enduring flogging rather than inflicting it (2 Cor 11 :24-27). He teaches Corinthians to emulate earnestness (*spoudē*) in generosity, not warfare (2 Cor 9 :2). Thus the persecutor becomes prototype zealot re-oriented by crucified Messiah. Temple cleansing stands as midpoint between old and new zeal, inviting similar transformation.

7.7.4 Zeal Consumed: Christ's Passion as Ultimate Refining Fire

Psalm 69's prophecy culminates at Calvary where zeal literally consumes Jesus, His body burning under divine justice. The fire that once incinerated unauthorized Nadab and Abihu now falls on willing Son, satisfying holiness without annihilating worshippers. Cross becomes altar where zeal and mercy kiss, fulfilling Isaiah 9 :7 promise that "zeal of the LORD of hosts will accomplish this." Resurrection proves zeal's energy inexhaustible, renewing disciples who thought hope dead. Pentecost tongues of fire descend, non-destructive zeal enabling global witness. Church history's revivals often feature holy passion that confronts sin yet uplifts outcast, echoing cleansing ethos. Thus zeal's telos is world-embracing love forged in sacrificial flame.

7.7.5 Christian Zeal Today: Holy Love vs. Violent Activism

Modern believers face temptation to wield zeal as ideological weapon, justifying harsh rhetoric or even terrorism under banner of holiness. Temple-cleansing Christ provides corrective pattern: direct action against systemic injustice coupled with personal willingness to suffer. Zeal manifests as persistent advocacy for marginalized, financial transparency, and uncompromising integrity in worship. When enthusiasm degrades into bitterness, Psalm 69 warns of reproach cycles that harm zealot and target alike. Spiritual disciplines—fasting, corporate lament, public confession—channel zeal into constructive reform. Mission organizations exemplify zeal by crossing cultures, languages, and comforts to create prayer houses among unreached peoples. True zeal unites passion with patience, conviction with compassion, embodying the balance Christ displayed amidst overturned tables.

7.8 Eschatological Overtones of the Cleansing

7.8.1 Malachi 3 :1-3—Sudden Arrival of the Lord in His Temple

Malachi foretells a messenger preparing the way and the Lord suddenly entering His temple to refine Levites like gold. John the Baptist fulfills the messenger role, while Jesus embodies the refining Lord, appearing without warning to ignite purification. The verb "refine" implies painful yet redemptive heat, mirrored in Jesus' fiery gaze in Revelation 1 :14. His cleansing dramatizes first flicker of that furnace, with permanent burn happening at crucifixion and Pentecost fire. The prophecy also anticipates offerings "in righteousness" afterward, hinting at spiritual sacrifices of the church (1 Pet 2 :5). Thus Malachi frames cleansing as eschatological catalyst rather than isolated protest. The messenger-Lord sequence becomes template for gospel proclamation followed by Spirit sanctification.

7.8.2 Daniel's "Seventy Weeks" and the End of Sacrifice (Dan 9 :24-27)

Gabriel's timeline predicts an anointed one cut off and sacrifice ceasing midway through final week, language Jesus applies when warning of abomination in holy place. Crucifixion halts true efficacy of animal offerings even before Romans extinguish literal fires in AD 70. Early Christians read veil tear as signal that Daniel's decree reached climax: transgression finished, everlasting righteousness inaugurated. The cleansing sets prophetic timer ticking; within one generation the architectural temple is gone, leaving living temple as sole locus of worship. Scholars debate starting points, but devotionally the prophecy magnifies Christ's centrality. Daniel thus provides chronological backbone for eschatological reading of cleansing. Liturgical hearts can rest knowing timetable fulfilled in Lamb's blood.

7.8.3 Zechariah 14 :20-21—Commerce Abolished on the Great Feast Day

Zechariah imagines bells of horses engraved "Holy to the LORD," extending priestly diadem language to mundane transport, signalling cosmos turned sanctuary. Absence of Canaanite trader in that day foreshadows Jesus' eviction of merchants, taste of full eschaton. Living waters splitting Mount of Olives further links with triumphal entry route. Feast of Tabernacles becomes universal pilgrimage, realized partially at Pentecost's multi-lingual crowd. Commerce is not condemned per se but subsumed under holiness, free from exploitation. Church fair-trade initiatives and debt-jubilee campaigns anticipate this vision. Thus cleansing sketches future holy economy.

7.8.4 Sign of Jonah and the Three-Day Rebuilding (Matt 12 :38-41; John 2 :19)

Jesus links Jonah's fish confinement to His own three-day burial, combining prophetic witness with bodily temple imagery. Jonah preached to Gentile Ninevites; resurrection likewise triggers gospel to nations, fulfilling house-of-prayer goal. Cleansing initiates sign sequence: protest—death—resurrection—mission. The rebuilt temple emerges Easter morning when Mary mistakes Jesus for gardener in new Eden. Three-day motif stamps divinity across chronology, proving authority claimed in courts. Jonah's reluctant mercy contrasts Christ's eager self-giving, magnifying grace. Therefore sign of Jonah deepens cleansing's eschatological weight.

7.8.5 From Temple Judgment to Temple-Less City (Rev 21 :22)

Revelation's final vision shows no temple because God and Lamb are its temple, ultimate fruition of bodily replacement hinted in cleansing. Judgment on harlot Babylon, drunk with saint blood, parallels Jerusalem's fall, warning any city that turns worship into commerce. New city's open gates fulfill Isaiah's inclusion prophecy frustrated by first-century bazaar. River and tree yield perpetual fruit, symbolizing healed liturgy without animal death. Thus eschatology resolves tension between sacred space and universal presence. Cleansing serves as down-payment for architecture-free communion. Worship becomes life itself under unveiled face.

7.9 Canonical Ripples after Easter

7.9.1 Veil Torn and the Expired Sacrificial System (Matt 27 :51)

Synoptic veils tear from top to bottom, divine initiative declaring open access; Talmud later narrates ominous temple doors crashing open forty years before destruction, echoing gospel claim. Priests reportedly stitched curtain nightly, futile labor illustrating resistance to fulfilled prophecy. Early Christians interpreted Eucharist as entry into torn veil, praying "through Jesus Christ our Lord" in every collect. The Epistle to Hebrews embeds veil symbolism into assurance text, giving pastoral balm to persecuted readers. By contrast, rabbinic Judaism redirected holiness to Torah and table; two divergent ripples from same torn fabric. Yet both traditions agree on curtain's monumental significance, marking end of sacrificial era.

7.9.2 Stephen's Speech: "The Most High Does Not Dwell in Houses Made by Hands" (Acts 7)

Stephen surveys patriarchal history to prove God's mobility—from Mesopotamia to Egypt to Sinai—culminating in Solomon's admission that heaven cannot contain Yahweh. Quoting Isaiah 66 :1-2, he labels temple a human artifact, secondary to contrite hearts. Listeners perceive attack on sacred cow, gnash teeth, and stone him, unwittingly enacting Jeremiah's prophecy of stiff-necked Israel. Stephen's vision of Son of Man standing affirms heavenly court authority surpassing Sanhedrin. His martyrdom propels gospel beyond Judea, fulfilling cleansing's Gentile inclusion trajectory. Saul, witness to stoning, will carry this mobile-temple theology to ends of earth. Thus ripple spreads through blood-water of first martyr.

7.9.3 Hebrews on Obsolete Shadows vs. Heavenly Realities (Heb 8 :13)

Hebrews declares covenant obsolete and near vanishing, language likely penned before AD 70 but anticipating destruction. The catastrophe of Roman siege becomes theological proof that shadow has disappeared. Christians no longer nostalgic for cedar beams; they approach Mount Zion, city of living God, unseen yet present. Copy-shadow dialectic shapes patristic exegesis, informing Augustine's allegorical hermeneutic. Medieval mystics locate inner chapel in contemplative heart, extending Hebrew's interior sanctuary. Thus cleansing sets hermeneutical key for reading old rites as typological. The shadow-reality principle continues guiding sermon and song.

7.9.4 John of Patmos: Measuring the Inner Court and Excluding the Outer (Rev 11 :1-2)

Angel hands John a reed to measure temple, altar, and worshipers, but outer court is given to Gentiles to trample forty-two months. Symbolic measurement parallels Ezekiel's, marking people of God as protected while institutions face persecution. Vision arrives after AD 70 yet repurposes temple imagery to comfort oppressed churches. Cleansing's mission to restore Gentile prayer ironically flips: hostile nations now desecrate external religion, but interior worship is secure. Revelation thus re-reads historical loss through apocalyptic hope, continuing ripple of Jesus' act. True sanctuary travels with lampstand churches across Asia Minor. External trampling cannot extinguish interior incense.

7.9.5 Early Christian Liturgy as Cleansed Worship in Spirit and Truth (John 4 :21-24)

Didache's Eucharistic prayers lack sacrificial language of propitiation, focusing on thanksgiving, reflecting theology of finished offering. Justin describes Sunday gathering at break of dawn, echoing tamid schedule yet transformed into resurrection memorial. Hippolytus' *Apostolic Tradition* prescribes bishop laying hands, recalling priestly blessing but absent animal sacrifice. Early believers face toward east, sunrise symbolizing new day without temple orientation. Their hymns quote Malachi 1 :11, claiming incense of pure prayer ascends from every nation. Cleansing thus shapes liturgy that values simplicity, generosity, and global horizon. Spirit and truth worship displaces geographical fixation, fulfilling Jesus' promise to Samaritan seeker.

7.10 Ethical and Missional Implications for the Church

7.10.1 Guarding the "Court of the Gentiles" Today— Hospitality & Inclusion

Modern congregations can unconsciously crowd vestibules with insider codes—denominational jargon, political banners, socioeconomic expectations—that hinder seekers. Inspired by cleansing, churches audit spaces: signage, language, and leadership diversity become contemporary table-flipping exercises. Multilingual liturgy, ramp access for disabled, and prayer rooms open to neighbors reenact Isaiah's vision. Digital platforms also form Gentile courts; paywalls on sermons or merch-heavy websites risk commercializing gospel. Hospitality teams trained in cultural sensitivity echo Jesus releasing doves for poor. When refugees share pews with lifelong saints, temple dream advances. Inclusion becomes measure of purity, not dilution of doctrine.

7.10.2 Ecclesial Discipline: Modern Table-Flipping?

Paul's demand to expel immoral brother from Corinth approximates cleansing logic: remove leaven to protect community witness. Contemporary elders face tension between cheap grace and punitive legalism; Christ's model offers decisive yet redemptive action. Public apology services and restorative justice circles replace shaming with rebuilding. Discipline targets exploitative leaders—mirroring Jesus' focus on profiteering authorities—more than struggling laity. Financial scandals demand transparent investigations, echoing overturned coffers. Healthy discipline reaffirms gospel by exposing hypocrisy and inviting repentance. Congregations become safe houses rather than dens of robbers.

7.10.3 Economic Justice in the House of God: Prosperity, Exploitation, and Generosity

Prosperity preaching can mutate offering time into spiritualized fund-raising that resembles ancient currency tables. Cleansing warns that monetizing grace invites divine scrutiny. Churches adopt salary caps, publish budgets, and refuse manipulative seed-faith tactics, pursuing simplicity modeled by Apostle Paul's tent-making. Micro-loan programs, debt-relief grants, and widow funds replace exploitative interest with jubilee mercy. Wealthy believers imitate Zacchaeus, pledging restitution and generous alms (Luke 19 :8). Communion lines where rich and poor kneel together witness to reformed economy. Thus stewardship becomes liturgical act aligned with house-of-prayer identity.

7.10.4 Prophetic Protest vs. Destructive Violence: Discernment Principles

Christians engaging public squares must distinguish table-overturning symbolic protest from riotous harm. Jesus targets economic injustice inside sacred precinct, not random property. His nonviolent force lasted minutes and invited immediate dialogue, providing model for sit-ins, silent vigils, and creative disruption. Dietrich Bonhoeffer, Martin Luther King Jr., and Mother Teresa demonstrate calibrated zeal that confronts evil without hate. Discernment involves prayer, communal counsel, and willingness to suffer consequences rather than inflict them. Violence undermines witness, turning zeal to scandal; prophetic creativity opens ears. Thus cleansing offers blueprint for righteous activism infused with grace.

7.10.5 Practicing Holiness without Idolizing Buildings or Budgets

Historic cathedrals inspire awe yet risk siphoning resources toward stone preservation over soul cultivation. House-church movements remind institutional congregations that Spirit can inhabit living rooms as surely as stained glass. Holiness manifests in ethical transparency and fervent prayer more than architectural grandeur. Budget meetings become spiritual discernments: does spending amplify mission or mere maintenance? Building usage audits ask whether space serves community as open court. The pandemic accelerated digital gatherings, proving worship survives absent sanctuary. Holding property lightly honors Jesus who cleansed but never campaigned for renovation funds.

In conclusion, a single afternoon of prophetic upheaval rippled from Jerusalem's marble courts across two millennia of worship, ethics, and hope. By scattering livestock and currency, Jesus exposed how sacred rituals can calcify into engines of exclusion and profit, yet He also announced that the threshing floor of judgment doubles as the threshing floor of grace. His zeal melded priestly compassion with royal authority, refusing to let polluted commerce drown the song of Gentiles destined for God's embrace. In the shadow of those toppled tables He marched to the cross, where His own body became the final sanctuary and His blood the final coin of ransom, transfiguring purity from spatial regulation into Spirit-filled hearts. Ever since, faithful communities have measured their worship not by incense density or budget size but by whether the outsider finds welcome and the oppressed find justice in their midst. Every generation must therefore listen for the clatter of Christ's footsteps among its hallways, ready to feel the jolt of overturned idols and to breathe again the silence that invites all nations to pray. For wherever His cleansing zeal is received with repentance and joy, the promise of a house filled with glory—and emptied of robbery—draws one day closer to its cosmic fulfilment.

Chapter 8 — From Altar to Cross: Sacrifice Fulfilled

Blood glistens across every page of Scripture, from the first drop that darkened Eden's soil to the crimson tide that flowed from Christ's pierced side outside Jerusalem's walls. In the biblical imagination, sacrifice is never peripheral ritual; it is the lifeline by which a holy God continues to breathe mercy into a rebellious creation. Yet the animals that bled on patriarchal altars, wilderness tabernacle grates, and Herod's massive platform were always provisional—arrows pointing beyond themselves. They taught Israel to equate sin with death, forgiveness with substitution, covenant with costly love, and worship with embodied obedience. Still, every bull that bellowed and every lamb that went silent also whispered of inadequacy, because consciences remained restless and the cycle of guilt ground on. The Gospels announce that the pattern has reached its surprising climax: the High Priest has become the victim, the altar has become a wooden cross, and the blood that once had to be sprinkled repeatedly has been poured out once for all. This chapter traces that breathtaking transition from carved stone and slaughtered beasts to torn flesh and triumphant resurrection, exploring how the cross both fulfils and transcends every earlier shadow, re-imagining sacrifice not as endless death but as the inexhaustible wellspring of life.

8.1 Sacrifice in Edenic Seed-Form

8.1.1 Coats of Skin for the Fallen Pair (Gen 3 :21)

When God clothes Adam and Eve with "garments of skin," the narrative hints that blood has been spilled within minutes of humanity's first sin, introducing the logic that life must cover life to restore covenant communion. Ancient rabbis recognized that fig-leaf aprons could hide shame but could not atone, so the Creator Himself becomes the first priest, performing a silent sacrifice on Eden's threshold. The text never names the animal, purposely leaving a blank that later lambs, bulls, and birds will fill until the Lamb of God definitively occupies the slot (John 1 :29). By acting unilaterally, God signals that atonement originates in divine mercy, not human ingenuity; the pair contribute nothing but their torn dignity. This primal transaction explains why Abel's offering of firstlings pleases God in the next chapter—he is imitating the Creator's own cost. The skins also foreshadow priestly vestments, for future sons of Aaron will wear linen as a sign that shed blood has conferred protective holiness on their service (Lev 8 :6-9). Thus the Eden scene plants the crimson seed that will germinate through the entire biblical narrative until it flowers on Golgotha.

8.1.2 Abel's "Better Offering" vs. Cain's Produce (Gen 4 :3-7; Heb 11 :4)

Abel's choice of "fat portions" from firstborn flock aligns with later stipulations that the choicest fat be burned as Yahweh's food (Lev 3 :16), whereas Cain's grain lacks explicit costliness, exposing a heart detached from grateful devotion. God's acceptance of Abel and rejection of Cain establish that the sacrificial system is never mere ritual but a relational thermometer gauging faith's temperature. Hebrews interprets Abel's blood as still "speaking," thereby personifying sacrifice as ongoing witness that anticipates the "better blood" of Jesus speaking forgiveness instead of vengeance (Heb 12 :24). Cain's jealous anger and subsequent fratricide reveal how distorted worship quickly mutates into violence, making the altar either a place of reconciliation or a launching pad for murder. God's warning that "sin is crouching at the door" pictures transgression as a beast seeking sacrificial doorway, a metaphor Jesus will invert when He calls Himself the true door for the sheep (John 10 :7). The mark placed on Cain ironically functions like a perverse covenant sign—an anti-circumcision—showing how broken sacrifice begets fractured identity. Thus, the Abel-Cain drama previews both the promise and peril inherent in blood ritual.

8.1.3 Noah's Post-Flood Altar and God's "Soothing Aroma" (Gen 8 :20-22)

Emerging from the ark, Noah builds an altar of every clean animal and bird, turning salvation history's restart button into a liturgy of thanksgiving that reaches God's nostrils as a "soothing aroma," language later reserved for Levitical burnt offerings. The rainbow covenant that follows links sacrificial aroma to meteorological mercy: God will never again drown the world because atonement has risen like incense to the throne. This episode introduces the pairing of altar and covenant oath that will recur with Abraham, Sinai, and Golgotha, showing that God anchors cosmic promises in the tangible symbol of shed blood. Noah's division into clean and unclean species anticipates Leviticus but also reveals that worship will shape humanity's culinary ethics henceforth. The aroma motif resurfaces in Paul's declaration that Christ's self-gift is a "fragrant offering" to the Father (Eph 5 :2), bridging antediluvian and apostolic worlds. Post-flood sacrifice also emphasizes priestly family leadership, setting precedent for household faith before formal priesthood is instituted. Thus, Noah's altar is a proto-temple planted on a cleansed earth, proclaiming that renewed creation must be inaugurated with blood-sealed gratitude.

8.1.4 The Akedah: Isaac Offered and a Ram Provided (Gen 22)

When Abraham ascends Moriah carrying fire and knife while Isaac shoulders wood, the text rehearses a future Father and Son climbing Calvary, one bearing cruel timber, the other wielding the fire of judgment. Isaac's question—"Where is the lamb?"—hangs unanswered until John the Baptist points to Jesus centuries later, declaring, "Behold the Lamb of God" (John 1 :29). God's last-minute substitution of a ram caught by its horns prefigures penal substitutionary atonement: a blameless victim dies so the promised son lives. The mountain is later identified with the Jerusalem temple site, linking patriarchal obedience to Solomonic architecture and to Jesus' Passion geography. Abraham names the place "The LORD will provide," using future tense, signaling that the ultimate provision lies ahead in messianic fulfillment. Hebrews underscores that Abraham's willingness to sacrifice Isaac was reckoned as faith in resurrection power (Heb 11 :17-19), making the Akedah both altar and empty tomb in seed form. Consequently, Genesis 22 becomes the gravitational center of biblical sacrifice, magnetizing later prophets, psalmists, and apostles toward its anticipatory silhouette.

8.1.5 Covenant of the Pieces: Flaming Torch Through Torn Animals (Gen 15)

In the strange nocturnal ceremony, Abram watches a smoking fire-pot and blazing torch pass between severed carcasses, a Near-Eastern oath-ritual wherein the party walking the bloody path vows self-malediction if the covenant fails. Astonishingly, God alone traverses the corridor, implying unilateral obligation: the fate of the covenant rests on divine fidelity, not Abram's prowess. Later prophets will recall this imagery when warning Israel that breaking covenant invites dismemberment like the animals (Jer 34 :18-20). The torch prefigures Shekinah fire leading Israel and tongues of fire crowning the Pentecost church, binding sacrificial assurance to revelatory presence. Paul reads Genesis 15 as the gospel beforehand, showing that righteousness by faith is grounded in covenant blood (Gal 3 :8-18). The torn animals anticipate Christ's rent flesh, while the smoking furnace forecasts the darkness that will cover Calvary at the climactic cutting of a new covenant (Matt 27 :45). Thus, the covenant-between-pieces establishes the juridical backbone for all subsequent redemptive sacrifice, ensuring that the altar ultimately upholds a promise God intends to keep even at His own mortal expense.

8.2 The Mosaic Sacrificial System: Logic and Liturgy

8.2.1 Five Core Offerings (Lev 1-7)

Leviticus organizes Israel's worship through ascending complexity: the whole-burnt offering signifies total consecration, the grain offering gratitude for covenant provision, the peace offering fellowship meal between deity and worshiper, and the sin and guilt offerings address unintentional and restitutionary breaches. Each category highlights a facet of relational repair, teaching that sin fractures multiple dimensions—identity, community, property—and therefore requires multidirectional remedies. The continual whole-burnt offering, offered morning and evening (Ex 29 :38-42), frames the day with perpetual atonement, anticipating Christ's title as the Alpha and Omega sacrifice. Grain offerings, devoid of yeast and seasoned with salt (Lev 2 :13), train Israel in purity and preservation, metaphors Jesus will adapt when calling disciples the salt of the earth (Matt 5 :13). The peace offering's shared meal foreshadows the Lord's Supper, where worshipers consume the very symbol of reconciliation. Sin and guilt offerings reveal substitutionary logic: blood applied to altar horns testifies that life has paid for life, and reparations to offended parties cultivate social justice alongside divine appeasement. Thus, the fivefold sacrificial grammar equips Israel with a holistic vocabulary of worship that Christ will speak in a single dialect of cruciform love.

8.2.2 Blood Dynamics: Life-for-Life Principle (Lev 17 :11)

Leviticus declares, "The life of the flesh is in the blood... it is the blood that makes atonement by the life," grounding sacrificial efficacy in the transference of vitality. This principle counters pagan magic by insisting that blood is not an energy humans wield but a gift God appoints for mercy. The prohibition against consuming blood teaches Israel to respect life's sacred medium, a mandate later reaffirmed at the Jerusalem Council for Gentile believers (Acts 15 :20). Every splash of crimson on the bronze altar preaches a sermon: sin costs life, yet mercy spares the sinner through an innocent substitute. Yom Kippur heightens the principle by taking blood into the holy of holies, symbolically transporting life where death cannot enter. The New Testament retains this logic, claiming that "without the shedding of blood there is no forgiveness" (Heb 9 :22), but relocates the transaction from animal veins to Emmanuel's arteries. Consequently, Christian ethics regard life—human or animal—as sacred, appreciating that every heartbeat echoes the Creator's forensic economy.

8.2.3 The Day of Atonement: Dual Goats and Holy-of-Holies Blood (Lev 16)

Yom Kippur resolves accumulated impurities that daily sacrifices could not erase, using two goats chosen by lot—one for Yahweh slain inside, the other for Azazel expelled into wilderness. The blood of the first goat sprinkled on the mercy seat signifies sin expiated before the divine throne, while the scapegoat bears residual guilt into the chaotic beyond, dramatizing both cleansing and removal. The high priest enters with incense cloud to buffer mortal eyes from lethal glory, prefiguring Christ's self-offering "not with the blood of goats and calves but with His own blood" (Heb 9 :12). Interestingly, the chapter prohibits anyone else in the tabernacle during the ritual, underscoring solitary mediation that foreshadows the lone figure on the cross abandoned even by His disciples. Rabbinic tradition later added a crimson thread on the scapegoat that turned white if God accepted the offering—a symbol Isaiah echoes when announcing sins made white as snow (Isa 1 :18). The annual nature of Yom Kippur signaled its insufficiency, a fact Hebrews exploits to elevate Christ's once-for-all entry. Thus, the twin-goat liturgy provides the most vivid Old-Testament canvas on which the New-Testament writers paint their Christology of substitution and victory.

8.2.4 Ordination Rituals: Priests Consecrated by Blood on Ear, Thumb, Toe (Lev 8)

Aaron and his sons stand at the tabernacle entrance where Moses applies ram's blood to their right ear, thumb, and big toe, symbolizing consecrated listening, working, and walking. This tri-point anointing teaches that priestly vocation encompasses perception, action, and direction under the authority of sacrificial blood. The ordination meal that follows integrates them into the peace-offering fellowship they will later mediate for others, foreshadowing Jesus' post-resurrection breakfast that re-commissions Peter (John 21 :12-17). Seven days of seclusion underscore holiness through time, hinting that sacred office requires sustained immersion in divine presence. The New Testament universalizes this consecration when Peter calls believers a royal priesthood (1 Pet 2 :9), implying that ears, hands, and feet of every disciple are figuratively blood-touched. Spiritual disciplines of hearing Scripture, serving neighbor, and walking in holiness thus become the daily echo of Levitical ordination. Consequently, Christian ministry can never sever sacraments from ethics; the same blood that justifies also sanctifies faculties for vocation.

8.2.5 Wilderness Travel—Levites Carrying an Itinerant Altar (Num 4)

The tabernacle's portability teaches that holiness travels, dislodging any notion that devotion is geographically tethered, a lesson Jesus will press in conversation with the Samaritan woman (John 4 :21-24). Levites dismantle altar grates and poles, wrap them in porpoise skin and cloths of blue, and hoist them across desert landscapes, dramatizing that God pitches His tent amid nomads. The cloud-pillar guidance ensures that the sacrificial system pauses when God pauses and marches when He marches, cultivating obedience over routine. Each encampment resumes the daily tamid, proving that atonement is rhythm, not static shrine. The epistle to Hebrews spiritualizes this portability, urging believers to "go to Him outside the camp, bearing His reproach" (Heb 13 :13), relocating altar symbolism to Christ-following pilgrimage. The motif inspires missionary theology: wherever the gospel travels, a new altar of the heart can rise without masonry. Thus, Numbers embeds mobility into sacrificial DNA, preparing for a Messiah who will be both temple and traveler.

8.3 Prophetic Critique and Expansion

8.3.1 Samuel's Maxim: "Obedience Better than Sacrifice" (1 Sam 15 :22)

When Saul spares Amalekite spoils under pious pretext, Samuel thunders that God delights more in obedience than in burnt offerings, establishing prophetic priority of moral submission over ritual exactitude. Yet Samuel does not abolish sacrifice; he re-orients it as outward sign of inward loyalty, a dialectic Jesus later employs when quoting Hosea, "I desire mercy, not sacrifice" (Matt 9 :13). The event signals the monarchy's accountability to covenant ethics—kingly disobedience cannot hide beneath liturgical smoke. Saul's rejection and David's anointing that follow underscore that throne and altar rise or fall together on righteousness. Samuel's dictum reverberates through psalmic laments and wisdom literature, becoming a refrain for post-exilic reformers. Jesus echoes it in His critique of Pharisaic tithing that neglects justice and faithfulness (Matt 23 :23), affirming continuity of moral focus. Thus, Samuel paves the way for a new covenant where obedience and sacrifice converge perfectly in the cross.

8.3.2 Psalm 51: "Sacrifices of Broken Spirit"

Composed after David's sin with Bathsheba, Psalm 51 shifts sacrificial language toward contrition, claiming that broken spirit and crushed heart are God's chosen offerings. Paradoxically, the psalm ends by asking God to delight in righteous sacrifices once Jerusalem's walls are rebuilt, indicating that inward repentance and

168

outward ritual need not be mutually exclusive. The New Testament echoes this inner sacrifice through Beatitudes that bless the poor in spirit and mourners (Matt 5 :3-4), revealing continuity between Davidic penitence and kingdom spirituality. Psalm 51's plea for hyssop cleansing foreshadows Christ's passion where soldiers lift sour wine on a hyssop stalk (John 19 :29), tying penitential sacrifice to physical crucifixion. The psalmist's hope that God will create a clean heart anticipates prophetic promises of new heart and Spirit infusion (Ezek 36 :26). Christians recite this psalm on Ash Wednesday, embodying its theology of interior altar. Therefore, Psalm 51 reframes the locus of sacrifice from courtyard to conscience without discarding the former, preparing worshipers for a temple made of living hearts.

8.3.3 Isaiah 1 & Amos 5: When Ritual Becomes Moral Stench

Isaiah opens with a courtroom scene where God rejects new moons, Sabbaths, and convocations because hands are "full of blood," calling Judah to wash, seek justice, and defend the oppressed before offering gifts (Isa 1 :13-17). Amos amplifies the indictment, declaring that God hates Israel's festivals and songs, preferring justice rolling like waters (Amos 5 :21-24). Both prophets redefine acceptable worship as ethical praxis, yet they also foresee a remnant and future pilgrimage, implying that purified ritual will return when justice reigns. Their language influences Jesus' temple critique and James's description of pure religion as orphan-care (Jas 1 :27). The imagery of polluted hands resurfaces in Pontius Pilate's futile hand-washing, exposing irony: the only innocent blood spilt is Christ's, which alone can cleanse defiled worship. Isaiah's promise that scarlet sins become white as snow is fulfilled in the blood of the Lamb making garments dazzling (Rev 7 :14). Thus, prophetic disgust with hollow ritual sets stage for a sacrifice embodying perfect justice.

8.3.4 Hosea 6 :6: Hesed over Holocaust—Mercy over Burnt Offering

Hosea cries that God desires hesed—steadfast love—more than sacrifice, and knowledge of God rather than burnt offerings, situating relational fidelity above cultic precision. Jesus twice cites this verse to defend merciful actions that appear to breach legal norms: eating grain on Sabbath and dining with sinners (Matt 9 :13; 12 :7). By applying Hosea to His ministry, Jesus reveals Himself as embodied hesed, the living intersection of mercy and holiness. Hosea's marriage metaphor of unfaithful Gomer illustrates that sacrifice without covenant love is spiritual adultery, a theme echoed in Revelation's picture of Babylon drunk on martyr blood. The prophet also foretells a third-day revival (Hos 6 :2), subtly linking hesed to resurrection, which will ratify God's preference for mercy. Post-resurrection Peter learns Hosea's lesson in Joppa when commanded to eat formerly unclean animals, signifying Gentile inclusion (Acts 10). Thus, Hosea reframes sacrifice within a covenant of relational intimacy fulfilled in Christ's table fellowship.

8.3.5 Ezekiel's Visionary Altar (Ezek 43) and Eschatological Adjustments

Ezekiel's temple vision includes an enormous altar with steps facing east and a reopening of sacrificial worship under a purified Zadokite priesthood. God instructs the prophet to describe the altar so the exiles may be ashamed, revealing that blueprints can function as repentance tools. The inaugural sacrifice spans seven days, echoing creation, yet the absence of ark, lampstand, and veil suggests radical simplification pointing beyond mosaic apparatus. Some Christian interpreters spiritualize Ezekiel as symbol of messianic kingdom, while others await literal millennial fulfillment; both camps agree Christ's sacrifice fulfills its inner meaning. Interestingly, Ezekiel's altar sits at the center of a re-allotted tribal land, integrating worship with socio-economic redistribution. The river flowing from under the threshold hints that future atonement will carry life into dead seas, a promise Paul associates with creation's liberation (Rom 8 :21). Thus, Ezekiel stretches sacrificial imagination toward cosmic scope, nudging readers to expect more than animal blood could ever deliver.

8.4 Second-Temple Practice and Messianic Expectation

8.4.1 Herodian Altar: Size, Location, and Daily Tamid Lambs

Herod's altar towered fifty cubits high and was fed by a ramp rather than steps, in obedience to Exodus 20 :26, preventing indecent exposure of priestly garments. Josephus notes its whitened stones and constant smoke, visible to pilgrims approaching the city (**War** 5.222-226). Every morning at dawn and every late afternoon, priests offered a tamid lamb accompanied by grain, oil, and wine, creating liturgical bookends to Israel's day. The tamid timetable shapes the Gospel narrative: Jesus is crucified at the third hour and dies at the ninth, synchronizing His self-gift with the continual offering (Mark 15 :25, 34-37). Rabbinic tradition held that Messiah would appear at the time of the evening sacrifice, heightening expectation among Passover crowds. The altar's proximity to the Holy Place also meant that any impurity in sacrifice threatened the whole temple's efficacy, making Jesus' critique of corrupt commerce a direct challenge to cultic legitimacy. Thus, Herod's grand altar set the stage for an even grander act of atonement performed outside the walls but inside prophetic chronology.

8.4.2 Passover Logistics: Slaughterhouse Courtyards and Hallel Chant

During Passover, pilgrims formed rows in the Court of the Priests, each holding lambs whose throats were slit in waves while Levites sang Psalms 113-118, the Hallel. Streams of blood flowed through silver gutters into Kidron, turning the brook crimson—imagery John evokes when blood and water flow from Christ's side (John 19 :34). Josephus estimates 255,000 lambs in one Passover, suggesting nearly one lamb per ten persons, though numbers may be rhetorical hyperbole. Priests worked barefoot in ankle-deep blood, a visceral reminder that sin's wage is death. By positioning His Last Supper as Passover meal, Jesus identifies Himself with these lambs, yet transforms the feast by offering bread and wine before slaughter, inverting sequence to emphasize voluntary self-giving. Synoptics synchronize His death with lamb slaughter, while John highlights the hour when Passover lambs were slain, showing different theological emphases. Thus, Passover logistics saturate Passion week with sacrificial resonance, turning Jerusalem into a living commentary on Exodus fulfillment.

8.4.3 Qumran's Temple Scroll: Idealized Giant Altar of the Last Days

Among the Dead Sea Scrolls, 11Q19 envisions a future sanctuary triple the size of Herod's, with an altar proportionally massive and purified by strict calendrical precision. The scroll's authors, likely Essenes, considered the existing priesthood polluted and therefore prepared blueprints for a replacement temple that Messiah or heavenly beings would build. Sacrificial schedules in the scroll demand perfect synchronization with a 364-day solar calendar, rejecting the lunar-solar mix used in Jerusalem, a calendar dispute that may underlie the timing differences between Synoptic and Johannine Passovers. The document expands festival offerings, anticipating eschatological abundance once true purity returns. By mirroring but surpassing Ezekiel's vision, the Temple Scroll reflects heightened messianic longing in late Second-Temple Judaism. Jesus' claim to destroy and rebuild the temple in three days implicitly answers such aspirations, offering His resurrection body as the ultimate eschatological sanctuary. Therefore, Qumran texts illuminate the ideological backdrop against which Jesus' sacrificial claims sounded both scandalous and satisfying to various Jewish sects.

8.4.4 Maccabean Rededication (Hanukkah) and Purity Fervour

The Hanukkah feast commemorates Judah Maccabee's 164 BC cleansing of Antiochus IV's desecrated altar, a narrative Jesus acknowledges by walking in Solomon's Colonnade during the "Feast of Dedication" (John 10 :22). Lamps burned eight days on one day's oil, a legend later attached, emphasizing divine endorsement of restored worship. The festival nurtured zeal for altar purity and resistance to foreign tyranny, shaping popular messianic hopes under Roman occupation. Jesus' discourse on being the Good Shepherd during Hanukkah recasts heroism from militaristic revolt to self-sacrificial care, redefining purity in terms of relational fidelity. The feast's backdrop of political liberation heightens tension when Jesus cleanses the temple; leaders fear Roman reprisal akin to Antiochus backlash but now from Caesar. Thus, Hanukkah provides cultural memory that informs both support and suspicion of Jesus' actions, explaining why some hail Him as Christ while authorities plot homicide. The cross, implicitly, becomes the final dedication of God's house, an altar purified not with animal blood but divine.

8.4.5 Apocalyptic Hopes: "End of Sacrifice" Timetables in Daniel 9

Daniel's seventy-weeks prophecy predicts an anointed one cut off and sacrifice ceased in the middle of final week, a riddle that fueled first-century chronomancy. Essene commentaries and later rabbinic texts attempted to align the weeks with Antiochus or Roman oppression, generating feverish expectation that Messiah would dissolve the cult. Jesus quotes Daniel's "abomination of desolation" when foretelling temple destruction (Matt 24 :15), linking His sacrifice to prophetic timetable. Early Christians read the tearing veil as immediate cessation of offerings, while Roman obliteration in AD 70 sealed the prophetic fulfillment historically. Rabbinic Judaism gradually replaced sacrifice with prayer, charity, and Torah study, indirectly validating Daniel's end-of-sacrifice horizon. Christian liturgy celebrates Eucharist as bloodless memorial yet grounded in one final shedding, echoing Daniel's frame. Thus, apocalyptic expectation set the cultural clock by which Calvary's hour was struck.

8.5 Jesus' Passion as Perfect Offering

8.5.1 Baptism as Priestly Consecration—Jordan River "Laver" (Matt 3)

John's wilderness baptism functions as a ritual laver where the true High Priest steps into muddy water, pre-echoing Aaron's washing before tabernacle service (Ex 29 :4). Heaven opens, the Spirit descends like a dove, and the Father's voice declares messianic sonship, combining enthronement (Ps 2 :7) with Isaiah's servant anointing. Unlike Aaron, Jesus brings no sin to wash away; instead He immerses Himself to absorb the sins of the nation He represents (Matt 3 :15). The Spirit's resting fulfills Isaiah 11 :2, marking Him as shoot from Jesse ready to bear sacrificial fruit. Immediately the Spirit drives Him into the wilderness, where obedience under temptation proves His fitness for priestly office (Matt 4 :1-11). The sequence recapitulates ordination week: washing, anointing, and then trial by fire before public ministry. Thus the Jordan becomes the threshold where altar and priest merge in a single incarnate figure.

8.5.2 Gethsemane's Cup vs. Temple Libation Cups (Luke 22)

In Gethsemane Jesus wrestles with a "cup" that evokes the wine-libations poured beside burnt offerings (Num 15 :5-10), but this chalice brims with divine wrath foretold in Isaiah 51 :17. Three agonized prayers mirror the triple sprinkling of blood at the altar's base, each plea ending in willing submission to the Father's will. His sweat like blood (Luke 22 :44) previews the crimson flow soon to water Calvary's dust. Meanwhile the disciples, intended temple watchmen, sleep, recalling failed priests who let lampstand oil run low (1 Sam 3 :3). Jesus alone remains vigilant, embodying faithful Israel within His solitary obedience. By accepting the cup, He pledges to pour out His life as libation (Phil 2 :17), transforming judgment drink into Eucharistic blessing for the redeemed. Gethsemane therefore serves as the altar's inner court where the offering is irrevocably bound.

8.5.3 Arrest at Passover: Lamb Selected on 10 Nisan, Slain on 14 Nisan

The Synoptics subtly mark Jesus' triumphal entry on the tenth of Nisan, the very day Passover lambs were chosen and set apart (Ex 12 :3), signaling to discerning pilgrims that the King riding a colt is also the Lamb under inspection. Daily debates in the temple courts mimic priestly scrutiny for blemishes, yet His adversaries "find nothing" to disqualify Him (Luke 23 :4). Judas's betrayal price of thirty shekels echoes Zechariah 11 :12, valuing the Shepherd-Lamb at slave wage. The Last Supper, framed as Passover by Synoptics, becomes a prophetic sign-meal where bread and cup prefigure broken body and shed blood before a single spike is driven. John's Gospel, highlighting a different calendar reckoning, places crucifixion at the hour lambs are slaughtered, emphasizing substitution over Seder setting (John 19 :14). Both chronologies converge theologically: Christ is Passover in essence and timing, fulfilling Exodus patterns to the letter. Thus the festival's choreography crowns Him as chosen, spotless, sacrificial centerpiece of redemption.

8.5.4 Via Dolorosa and Scapegoat Topography (Heb 13 :11-13)

Roman soldiers compel Simon of Cyrene to carry the patibulum, dramatizing Isaiah 53 :12 as the Suffering Servant is "numbered with transgressors." The procession exits the city gate toward Golgotha, mirroring Yom Kippur's scapegoat led into wilderness bearing Israel's iniquity (Lev 16 :21). Hebrews explicitly interprets this geography: Jesus suffers "outside the camp" so believers might go out to Him, abandoning the obsolete cult for living fellowship. Each station of the cross inverts imperial triumph—crown of thorns, mock robe, wooden scepter—exalting weakness that shames worldly power (1 Cor 1 :27). Women of Jerusalem lament, fulfilling Zechariah 12 :10, while Jesus redirects their tears to impending judgment, linking personal sacrifice to national destiny. Golgotha's name "Place of the Skull" recalls David's victory over Goliath, situating crucifixion as giant-slaying cosmic war. Therefore the Via Dolorosa is both blood trail and theological roadmap from imperfect altar to perfect offering.

8.5.5 "It Is Finished" and the Timing of Tamid (John 19)

John timestamps Jesus' final cry at the ninth hour, the very moment the evening tamid lamb ascended in smoke, proclaiming that perpetual sacrifice has reached its telos (John 19 :30; Mark 15 :34). The Greek tetelestai denotes a commercial debt paid in full and a priestly act completed, resonating with Isaiah 53 :11 where the Servant's travail "makes many righteous." Simultaneously, the temple veil splits from top to bottom, Heaven's hand tearing aside the barrier that perpetual offerings could only symbolize (Matt 27 :51). Earthquake and opened tombs signal eschatological aftershocks, creation recognizing its redeemer. Centurion confession, "Surely this was God's Son," places a Gentile priest at the foot of the new altar, firstfruits of international worship (Mark 15 :39). The final spear thrust ensures death and releases blood and water, joining altar and laver into one fountain of cleansing (John 19 :34). Thus the chronos and kairos of sacrifice converge in a single, once-for-all oblation.

8.6 Pauline Sacrificial Theology

8.6.1 Romans 3 :24-26—Hilastērion and Mercy-Seat Vocabulary

Paul situates Jesus as the hilastērion, the mercy-seat lid where blood was sprinkled on Yom Kippur, indicating that atonement now occurs in a person rather than a place. Divine "forbearance" passes over former sins, showing continuity with sacrificial credit lines extended throughout Israel's past. Righteousness is demonstrated publicly, resolving the paradox of God being both just and justifier of sinners. Faith, not ethnicity or Law, becomes the mechanism of participation, democratizing access to the mercy-seat. Paul's courtroom metaphor integrates cultic and legal spheres, portraying the cross as both altar and bench. By anchoring justification in propitiatory blood, he counters any reduction of Christ's death to moral example alone. Thus Romans 3 forges the doctrinal foundation on which Protestant and Catholic soteriologies alike must negotiate.

8.6.2 1 Corinthians 5 :7—"Christ Our Passover Has Been Sacrificed"

Addressing a church tolerating incest, Paul commands them to purge the "old leaven," linking moral discipline to Passover housecleaning. He declares Christ the sacrificed Passover lamb and believers unleavened dough, arguing that ethical sincerity is the festival's true unleavened bread. This identification collapses temporal distance: every Eucharistic celebration is existential Pesach, renewed in community purity. By connecting ecclesial holiness to sacrificial reality, Paul embeds atonement into congregational life. He implicitly affirms substitutionary logic: corporate sin can be removed because Lamb has died. The text also hints at inaugurated eschatology—believers already feast in the new age while still fighting old leaven. Thus the Corinthian crisis becomes a case study in applied sacrificial theology.

8.6.3 2 Corinthians 5 :21—Sin-Offering Logic of the Great Exchange

Paul asserts that God made the sinless one "to be sin" so that sinners might become God's righteousness, echoing Levitical sin-offering where animal assumes impurity. Scholars debate whether "sin" means sin-offering; the conceptual overlap reinforces substitution without metaphysical confusion. The "righteousness of God" granted to believers implies covenant fidelity status, not merely moral capacity. This imputation occurs "in Him," highlighting union with Christ as locus of transfer. The exchange reconciles the world, propelling apostolic ministry as embassy of peace. No other first-century Jewish text equates individual with collective sin in such juridical swap, underscoring novelty of Pauline gospel. Thus 2 Corinthians 5 crystallizes sacrificial exchange at the heart of Christian identity.

8.6.4 Ephesians 5 :2—Love-Offering "Fragrant Aroma" Motif

Paul commands believers to "walk in love" just as Christ loved and "gave Himself up... a fragrant offering," echoing Noah's post-flood sacrifice and Levitical soothing aroma. The linkage of ethics ("walk") to cult ("offering") erases sacred-secular divide, making daily conduct aromatic liturgy. The phrase "gave Himself up" (paradidōmi) mirrors Gospel passion predictions, rooting morality in historical event. Such aroma language surfaces again regarding financial gifts as "sweet-smelling" (Phil 4 :18), equating generosity with temple incense. By invoking fragrance, Paul taps sensory memory, encouraging embodied spirituality. Temple curtains steeped in incense would linger on garments; likewise Christ's self-gift should scent the believer's lifestyle. Thus Ephesians 5 fuses love and liturgy in cruciform perfume.

8.6.5 "Living Sacrifices": Ethical Cult in Romans 12 :1-2

Paul urges Romans to present bodies as living, holy, pleasing sacrifices—rational (logikēn) worship—thereby transforming temple imagery into ethical commitment. The oxymoron "living sacrifice" signals ongoing, dynamic offering rather than terminal death, aligning with daily burnt offering's constancy. Mind renewal replaces conforming to age, indicating internal altar where Spirit fires burn. The plural "bodies" yet singular "sacrifice" suggests corporate unity, the church as one holistic offering. Discernment of God's will becomes new cultic act, parallel to priestly inquiry by Urim and Thummim. Thus justification (Rom 1-11) flows into sanctification-as-worship (Rom 12-15), maintaining sacrificial continuity. Paul concludes with doxology, sealing ethical exhortation inside liturgical parentheses.

8.7 Hebrews: Once-for-All in the True Tent

8.7.1 Shadow vs. Reality (Heb 8 :5) and Better Blood (Heb 9 :12)

The author claims earthly priests serve a copy and shadow of heavenly things, citing Exodus 25 :40 where Moses saw the pattern on Sinai. Jesus, however, ministers in the "greater and more perfect tent," entering the heavenly holy place with His own blood, securing eternal redemption. Animal blood gained temporary forgiveness but could not cleanse conscience; Christ's superior blood penetrates moral interiority. By contrasting annual entry with once-for-all, Hebrews nullifies repetitive Yom Kippur cycles. The covenant upgrade includes internalized law and relational immediacy, fulfilling Jeremiah 31 :31-34. Heavenly sanctuary language reassures persecuted readers that loss of Jerusalem altar is no catastrophe. Thus shadow-reality dialectic validates faith amidst temple-less adversity.

8.7.2 Veil as Christ's Flesh (Heb 10 :19-20)

Believers gain bold access through the veil, "that is, His flesh," a startling identification that merges architectural fabric with incarnate body. Crucifixion tearing of veil becomes rending of Christ's flesh, opening new and living way into holiest realm. This metamorphosis of matter into mediated presence upends any nostalgia for stone sanctuaries. Access grounds exhortations to draw near, hold confession, and spur love, linking doctrine to community praxis. The imagery also undercuts docetic tendencies by affirming salvific significance of material body. Liturgically, Eucharistic participation embodies veil-flesh nexus as believers ingest opened way. Thus Hebrews fuses Christology, soteriology, and ecclesiology in veil symbolism.

8.7.3 Two Mountain Drama: Sinai Tremor, Zion Festal Assembly (Heb 12 :18-24)

The writer contrasts Sinai—blazing fire, darkness, trumpet blast—with heavenly Zion—angels in festal gathering, church of firstborn, sprinkled blood speaking better than Abel's. This eschatological juxtaposition reconfigures pilgrimage: believers already stand in Zion via faith, though feet remain on earth. Sprinkled blood's speech reinforces substitutionary vocabulary while surpassing primeval vengeance cry. Festal assembly (panēgyrei) conjures Olympic imagery, portraying worship as joyful convocation rather than fearful distance. Warning not to refuse this superior voice echoes refusal at Sinai, elevating Christ's covenant above Mosaic. Sacrificial blood thus transitions terror into celebration, sealing community identity. Hence Hebrews converts topography into theology, anchoring sacrifice in heavenly geography.

8.7.4 Warning Passages: Trampling the Son and Profaning the Blood (Heb 10 :29)

Deliberate sin after receiving knowledge equates to trampling God's Son, treating covenant blood as common, and insulting Spirit of grace. The triple indictment underscores gravity of apostasy in light of once-for-all sacrifice. Judgment imagery borrows from Deuteronomy 32 :35, proving continuity of covenant sanctions. These warnings function pastorally, not to terrify secure saints but to awaken drifting ones. They also validate high Christology: despising Jesus equals despising God's ultimate self-offering. Protestant debates over perseverance engage these texts, yet all agree they magnify sacrificial stakes. Thus Hebrews balances assurance with holy fear rooted in precious blood.

8.7.5 Heavenly Altar Worship: "We Have an Altar" (Heb 13 :10-16)

The author claims Christians have an altar from which tabernacle servants have no right to eat, referencing Eucharistic fellowship inaccessible to unbelieving priests. He urges believers to bear reproach outside the camp, linking mission to sacrificial geography. Continual praise, termed "fruit of lips," becomes new-covenant grain offering, while good works and sharing are "sacrifices" pleasing to God. This conflation of confession, compassion, and cult models holistic worship. Christ's enduring city yet to come motivates pilgrim generosity and courage. Leadership obedience and prayer for teachers close the letter, underscoring communal altar maintenance. Thus Hebrews frames entire ecclesial life within altar vocabulary transformed by Christ.

8.8 The Eucharist: Memorial or Re-Presentation?

8.8.1 Passover Roots and Covenant Renewal Formula (Luke 22 :19-20)

Jesus breaks bread and declares, "This is My body given for you," then cup as "new covenant in My blood," echoing Exodus 24 :8 where Moses sprinkles blood and reads covenant book. Incorporating Jeremiah 31 language, He inaugurates covenant renewal through ingestible tokens rather than external splash. Passover context re-scripts exodus from Egypt to exodus from sin, aligning disciples with redeemed Israel. The command "Do this in remembrance" uses anamnēsis, implying active, Spirit-empowered memorial that makes past event present. Early churches understood table as covenant ratification each Lord's Day (Acts 2 :42). Thus Eucharist fuses liberation, covenant, and sacrificial self-gift. Memory becomes sacrament, not mere cognition.

8.8.2 1 Corinthians 11: Discernment, Proclamation, Participation

Paul recounts tradition then warns that unworthy eating desecrates body and blood, causing weakness and death among Corinthians. Discernment involves recognizing horizontal body—fellow believers—not only vertical Christology. Proclaiming Lord's death "until He comes" inserts eschatology into sacramental present, making meal proleptic. Participation (koinonia) in blood and body (1 Cor 10 :16) denotes real communion, though Paul avoids metaphysical exposition. Thus Eucharist entwines past atonement, present community, and future hope. Self-examination safeguards unity while preserving joy. The table stands as perpetual intersection of time dimensions.

8.8.3 Patristic Voices: Ignatius, Justin, and Irenaeus

Ignatius calls Eucharist "medicine of immortality" and warns against Docetists who abstain because they deny flesh of Christ, affirming real presence. Justin Martyr describes bread and cup becoming flesh and blood "by prayer of the Word," yet distances from cannibal misunderstanding to pagan audience. Irenaeus links sacrament to recapitulation, arguing that as creation offers bread and wine, Christ renders them body and blood, refuting Gnostic disdain for matter. Patristic consensus views table as sacrifice of thanksgiving (eucharistia), not another propitiatory death but participation in the once-for-all. Epiclesis—Spirit invocation—emerges to explain transformation while honoring biblical economy. These fathers locate Eucharist within salvation history, combatting heresies by leaning on sacrificial realism. Thus early theology treats altar and table as continuous rather than dichotomous.

8.8.4 Reformation Debates: Trans-, Con-, and Memorial Views

Luther rejects transubstantiation's Aristotelian categories yet affirms in, with, under presence, grounding in Christ's ubiquity post-ascension. Zwingli emphasizes remembrance, fearing idolatry, while Calvin proposes spiritual real presence by Spirit-mediated ascent. Council of Trent doubles down on transubstantiation, anathematizing oppositions but affirming unbloody re-presentation of sacrifice. Despite divergence, all Reformers keep cross as singular oblation, differing on mode of participation. Modern ecumenical dialogues (e.g., Lima 1982) find convergence in sacrificial memorial and real encounter. Pastoral praxis often transcends scholastic metaphysics, focusing on communion's formative power. Thus Eucharistic debates reflect attempts to safeguard sacrificial uniqueness amid experiential mystery.

8.8.5 Ecumenical Convergence on "Sacrifice of Praise"

Hebrews 13 :15 offers common ground: believers continually offer "sacrifice of praise," fruit of lips confessing His name. Liturgical renewal movements adopt this phrase, integrating song, prayer, and table as unified offering. The World Council of Churches' Baptism-Eucharist-Ministry text affirms Eucharist as memorial, presence, and anticipation, avoiding ontological extremes. Many evangelicals embrace weekly communion, recovering sacramental rhythm without abandoning sola fide. Catholic-Lutheran dialogues agree that Eucharist does not repeat Calvary but makes its benefits present, curbing earlier polemics. Pentecostal theology enriches discussion by emphasizing Spirit's active mediation, paralleling patristic epiclesis. Thus praise sacrifice becomes bridge across historic divides, honoring altar fulfilled in cross.

8.9 Ethical Echoes of a Finished Sacrifice

8.9.1 Hospitality as Table Extension (Heb 13 :2; Rom 12 :13)

Early Christians treat homes as satellites of the upper room, extending broken-bread fellowship to strangers and angels unawares. Hospitality neutralizes social stratification, embodying Passover's open-door ethos. The Didache instructs believers to receive itinerant prophets for one or two days, reflecting sacrificial generosity. Modern refugee care and foster parenting continue altar hospitality, transforming meals into mission. By feeding Christ in the hungry (Matt 25 :35), disciples enact sacrificial service. Thus every dinner table becomes micro-altar where grace is shared. Hospitality testifies that the sacrificial victim lives to host His people.

8.9.2 Generosity: "Sweet-Smelling Offering" (Phil 4 :18)

Paul calls Philippian monetary aid a "fragrant offering, acceptable sacrifice," equating financial partnership with temple incense. Giving completes gospel circuit: material resources flow to apostle, spiritual fruit flows back to givers. Generosity therefore is not philanthropy but liturgy, echoing burnt-offering aroma. Contentment in abundance or lack (Phil 4 :11-12) underscores that gift's value lies in covenant loyalty, not amount. Modern stewardship campaigns can recover sacrificial joy by framing giving as worship rather than budget crisis. Macedonian poverty generosity (2 Cor 8) exemplifies this aroma. Hence economics become Eucharistic when touched by cross.

8.9.3 Martyrdom: "Poured Out as a Drink Offering" (2 Tim 4 :6)

Paul views impending execution as libation complementing believers' faith offering (Phil 2 :17), blending personal death with communal sacrifice. Early martyrs echoed this imagery, describing blood as seed planting church soil (Tertullian). Revelation situates souls under altar, implying their blood joins Christ's in heavenly intercession (Rev 6 :9). Martyr narratives function as passion plays, re-presenting Calvary across cultures. Contemporary persecution in global south continues this priestly witness. Suffering thus becomes participatory liturgy, not mere tragedy. The Lamb shares His altar with conquering saints.

8.9.4 Worship & Justice: Isaiah 58 Re-read Through the Cross

True fasting, says Isaiah, looses injustice and feeds the poor; the cross fulfills this by liberating captives and satisfying spiritual hunger. James merges piety and ethics, defining pure religion as caring for orphans and widows (Jas 1 :27). Post-atonement worship that ignores systemic sin repeats Israel's error, prompting prophetic critique anew. Liberation theologians draw from sacrificial solidarity, though must balance with substitutionary grace. Holiness movements similarly insist on social holiness flowing from inward cleansing. When churches plant soup kitchens beside sanctuaries, they embody altar-justice synergy. Thus Calvary's vertical beam must intersect horizontal neighbor-love.

8.9.5 Creation Care: Ending Bloodshed of the Ground (Gen 4 :10; Col 1 :20)

Abel's blood cried from the ground, signaling ecological participation in moral offense. Colossians affirms Christ reconciles "all things… whether on earth or in heaven," shedding cosmic scope on atonement. Romans 8 pictures creation groaning eagerly for redemption children enjoy. Christian environmental stewardship becomes sacrificial response, healing soil stained by cumulative violence. Old Testament sacrifices returned lifeblood to God; modern disciples can honor Creator by guarding biodiversity. Eco-theologians view resurrection as firstfruits of renewed ecology, rooting activism in atoning work. Thus altar theology extends to gardens, rivers, and climate policy.

8.10 Eschatological Consummation of Sacrifice

8.10.1 Revelation's Slaughtered-Yet-Standing Lamb (Rev 5)

John weeps when no one can open the scroll until elder announces Lion of Judah, yet sees Lamb slain, standing, seven-horned and seven-eyed—power and Spirit unified. Heaven sings "You were slain, and by Your blood You ransomed people," linking cosmic governance to sacrificial act. Incense bowls of prayers accompany harps, integrating martyrs' pleas with angelic praise. The Lamb's position at center of throne reorients worship from temple architecture to personified sacrifice. Scroll opening triggers judgments that vindicate blood against persecutors, displaying atonement's judicial dimension. Thus apocalypse is liturgy, not mere prediction, centering on crimson Lamb. Final victory is sacrificial, not militaristic.

8.10.2 No Temple, No Altar? The Lamb as Eternal Cult (Rev 21 :22)

New Jerusalem boasts no temple "for its temple is the Lord God Almighty and the Lamb," resolving sacrificial storyline by subsuming structure into presence. Sunless brilliance emanates from slain-yet-risen priest-king, negating menorah and altar light. Perpetual openness of gates signifies unceasing access, undoing veil permanently. Tree of life returns, its leaves healing nations once divided by Babel. Thus eschaton erases need for mediatory shadows, celebrating direct communion. Liturgical acts become life itself, every act holy. Sacrifice fulfilled becomes fellowship perfected.

8.10.3 Marriage Supper: Sacrifice Transformed into Feast (Rev 19 :9)

Angel pronounces blessing on those invited to marriage supper, merging Passover liberation with eschatological banquet foretold in Isaiah 25. The bride wears righteous deeds, garments washed in Lamb's blood (Rev 7 :14), proving justification births sanctification. Table imagery crowns history: from altar of slain animal to shared meal of eternal joy. Christ both host and main course, satisfying hunger and thirst for righteousness. Feast signals covenant consummation, replacing sacrificial fasting with celebratory fullness. Chalice of suffering empties; goblet of new wine overflows. Thus telos of offering is table of love.

8.10.4 Nations Healed—Blood Merit Applied Cosmically (Rev 22 :2)

River of life nourishes tree yielding monthly fruit; leaves heal nations, extending Calvary's efficacy to geopolitical wounds. Kings bring glory, not war booty, echoing Isaiah 60 tribute sanctified by blood. No longer will there be any curse, reversing Genesis 3 via atoning grace.

Resurrection bodies reign, fulfilling priest-king vocation. Global justice flows from Lamb's throne, eliminating need for sword. Mission culminates in multicultural worship, altar transfigured into global garden. Thus sacrifice choreographs cosmic reconciliation.

8.10.5 Ever-Present Intercession of Wounds—Scars as Everlasting Liturgy

Jesus keeps crucifixion scars post-resurrection, presenting them to Thomas and later bearing them in heavenly vision, signifying eternal priesthood. These wounds continuously testify, obviating cyclical offerings, fulfilling Isaiah 49 :16 where Zion is engraved on palms. Heaven's worship centers on visible proof of love, ensuring memory of cost never fades. Scars transform pain into beauty, inviting healed sufferers to mirror redeemed history. Liturgically, stigmata become everlasting sermon on grace. As long as scars shine, new creation remembers old creation's ransom. Thus eternity remains anchored in finite act of dying love, altar echoing forever.

In conclusion, when Jesus cried, "It is finished," the centuries-long dialogue between sin and sacrifice was resolved in a single sentence. The temple curtain's rending was more than an architectural accident; it was heaven's own testimony that the corridor back to unfettered communion now lies open. Because the perfect Lamb has died, no animal need be led to slaughter, no guilty conscience need cower, and no worshiper need wonder whether the offering was enough. Yet the sacrificial theme does not evaporate in the Easter dawn; it re-emerges transfigured. The church is summoned to become a community of living sacrifices, to let generosity carry the fragrance of burnt offerings, to let hospitality spread the table where blood once dripped, and to let suffering—when it comes—be poured out like wine upon that finished altar. In the age to come, the wounds that purchased such freedom will still shine on the body of the risen Lord, not as reminders of pain but as the everlasting liturgy of love. Until that unveiling, every Eucharistic cup raised, every act of mercy done in His name, and every prayer that smells of incense proclaims once more: the altar has become the cross, and the cross has turned sacrifice into an unending feast of grace.

Chapter 9 - Pentecost: Spirit Indwelling the New Temple

The resurrection broke the chains of death, but it was Pentecost that filled the empty tomb of the human heart with the vibrant breath of God. Luke, the careful historian-theologian, narrates the day not merely as a miraculous sign for first-century Jerusalem but as the dramatic culmination of the temple storyline that has stretched from Edenic fellowship through Mosaic sacrifice to the veil-rending cry of the crucified Christ. The cloven tongues of fire signify more than ecstatic speech; they declare that the Shekinah which once hovered above a gold-plated mercy-seat now rests on ordinary men and women whose pulses testify that flesh has replaced stone as God's chosen sanctuary. Furthermore, the linguistic miracle reverses Babel's curse of scattered pride, forging a multilingual doxology that previews the multicultural choir of Revelation. Yet Pentecost is no static monument; it initiates a mobile temple that spreads through cities, deserts, and prison cells to the ends of the earth, carrying with it the ethics, mission, and worship born in an upper-room prayer meeting. To understand the church's identity, gifts, and global mandate, one must stand beneath those fiery feathers and hear the rushing wind echo Sinai's thunder and Eden's cool breeze. This chapter therefore follows the Spirit's descent into the new temple of gathered believers, traces its canonical roots, observes its communal fruit, and listens for its eschatological whisper that still calls, "Come."

9.1 Pentecost in the Old-Testament Calendar

9.1.1 Shavuot as Weeks-Festival and Wheat Harvest (Lev 23 : 15-22)

Israel's calendar counted seven sevens from the first sheaf of barley waved during Passover week, landing on the fiftieth day that farmers dedicated the earliest loaves of wheat to Yahweh (Lev 23 : 15-17). Unlike Passover's unleavened bread, Shavuot required loaves baked with yeast, symbolizing ordinary life elevated to sacred use. Offerings included seven lambs, one bull, and two rams, connecting agricultural gratitude to sacrificial atonement in a single liturgical bundle. Because the festival arrived in late spring, travel conditions were favorable, explaining the "devout men from every nation" present in Acts 2. Rabbinic tradition later identified Shavuot with the Sinai covenant, so first-century pilgrims approached Jerusalem recalling both grain provision and Torah gift. The festival's dual themes—material sustenance and legal revelation—prepare readers to see Pentecost as Spirit-harvest and heart-Law simultaneously. Luke's timing, therefore, is theologically loaded: the Spirit comes precisely when Israel celebrates abundance and covenant memory, revealing Himself as firstfruits of new creation and inscriber of the new covenant on human tablets.

9.1.2 Sinai Theophany: Fire, Wind, and Covenant Words (Ex 19 : 16-20)

Thunder, lightning, thick cloud, and trumpet blast accompanied Yahweh's descent on Horeb, causing the mountain to quake and the people to tremble (Ex 19 : 16-19). Jewish expositors later imagined the divine voice splitting into seventy tongues of fire, matching the nations of Genesis 10 and prefiguring Acts 2's multilingual flames. Wind and flame thus become canonical shorthand for holy presence, making Luke's description a deliberate echo, not a coincidental weather report. Moses ascended alone into the glory, yet at Pentecost every believer is enveloped, democratizing what was once reserved for a single mediator. The giving of the Spirit thereby constitutes a covenantal sequel, writing the Law not on stone tablets but on beating hearts as Jeremiah 31 promised. Sinai's fearful distance is replaced by familial intimacy, though reverence remains as recipients sense they have entered unburned the very fire that once barred approach. Consequently, Pentecost completes Sinai's agenda, transforming external commandments into internal combustion that powers mission.

9.1.3 Firstfruits Logic: Pledge of the Larger Harvest (Deut 26 : 1-11)

Bringing firstfruit baskets to the sanctuary, worshipers recited a creedal history—"My father was a wandering Aramean"—linking personal produce to national salvation (Deut 26 : 5). The small offering functioned as earnest money guaranteeing that God who gave the first stalks would supply the whole field. Paul borrows this economic metaphor to describe the Spirit as "arrabōn... of our inheritance" (Eph 1 : 14), thereby framing Pentecost as down payment on resurrection glory. Luke's 3 000 converts are likewise firstfruits of an international harvest that Acts will gather through Philip, Peter, and Paul. The imagery corrects any notion that Pentecost is isolated revival; it is the opening surge of a continuing wave destined to flood earth with temple presence. Firstfruits also oblige generosity: Israel left field corners unharvested for the poor, and the Spirit's deposit propels the Jerusalem church to share possessions liberally. Thus the festival's agrarian logic undergirds both eschatological hope and immediate social ethics in the new community.

9.1.4 Seventy Elders and the Resting Spirit (Num 11 : 16-30)

Exasperated by complaints, Moses gathers seventy elders, and the Lord removes some Spirit from Moses, causing the elders to prophesy once but not again (Num 11 : 25). Two men, Eldad and Medad, prophesy within the camp, prompting Joshua's jealous plea to silence them, yet Moses longs for universal prophetic Spirit. Pentecost fulfills this wish as Spirit rests not merely on seventy but on "all flesh," including sons and daughters, servants and free (Joel 2 : 28-29). The temporary, singular outburst in Numbers becomes sustained, corporate speech in Acts, signaling arrival of a new leadership paradigm where prophecy is not the preserve of office-holders. Luke's reference to about 120 disciples implicitly mirrors double the seventy, suggesting abundance over scarcity. The story also warns against gatekeeping charisms; the early church must resist Joshua-like instincts to restrict Spirit speech. In short, the resting Spirit of Numbers finds permanent lodging in Pentecost's many tents.

9.1.5 Ruth, Gentile Inclusion, and Kingly Genealogy (Ruth 1-4)

Jewish liturgy reads the book of Ruth at Shavuot, celebrating a Moabite widow who finds refuge under Yahweh's wings and becomes great-grandmother to David. Her gleaning in Bethlehem's fields during harvest intertwines grace with grain, foreshadowing Gentile participation in covenant blessing. Boaz's role as kinsman-redeemer prefigures Christ's redemptive embrace that Acts will extend beyond Israel to "every nation under heaven." Pentecost's pilgrim list includes "visitors from Rome," hinting that Ruth's international thread is being woven into the church's tapestry. Moreover, the Spirit makes the gathered disciples both seed and soil, carrying within them the Messianic genealogy now expanded to global family. Ruth's pledge— "Your people shall be my people, and your God my God" (Ruth 1 : 16)—becomes the confession of proselytes baptized that day. Thus Shavuot's Ruth reading sets a hermeneutical lens through which Pentecost is seen as harvest of outsiders into Israel's royal line.

9.2 The Upper-Room Event: Wind, Fire, and Filled Speech

9.2.1 The Setting: 120 Gathered in Continuous Prayer (Acts 1 : 12-14)

After the ascension the disciples return to the same upper room where they had celebrated the new-covenant Passover, turning a borrowed dining hall into a provisional temple. Luke numbers them at about 120, a multiple of twelve, symbolizing fullness of restored Israel and satisfying rabbinic minimum for a community court. The presence of Mary and other women highlights gender inclusivity in apostolic anticipation, breaking patterns where only male Levites ministered. Continuous prayer, not frenetic planning, marks their posture, foreshadowing that Spirit empowerment descends on waiting, not striving. The election of Matthias during this vigil repairs Judas's breach, stressing that Spirit falls on ordered, repentant community. Geography matters: Jerusalem, site of cleansing and crucifixion, becomes womb for Spirit birth, redeeming a city that had killed prophets. Thus the stage is set: obedient, unified, expectant disciples constitute the altar on which divine fire will soon settle.

9.2.2 "Sound Like a Violent Wind" and Echoes of Ezekiel's Ruach (Acts 2 : 2; Ezek 37)

The rushing noise fills "the whole house," suggesting temple allusion since Luke elsewhere uses "house" for sanctuary (Luke 11 : 51). Wind (*pnoē*) links to Hebrew *ruach*, the breath animating Adam and rattling Ezekiel's valley of bones, so Pentecost signals re-creation of humanity. Unlike gentle breeze of Elijah's cave, this wind is violent, implying force capable of knocking down dividing walls of hostility. Audible manifestation precedes visible fire, allowing outside crowds to assemble before spectacle, essential for evangelistic witness. Luke emphasizes that the sound originates "from heaven," clarifying supernatural agency, not meteorological coincidence. Wind imparts movement; disciples who soon scatter across empire carry within them this initial propulsion. Therefore, the Pentecost wind is theological shorthand for resurrection power blowing church into missional motion.

9.2.3 Tongues as Divided Flames and Sinai's Fiery Law (Acts 2 : 3)

What appears "as" tongues of fire divides and rests on each, uniting diversity through individualized encounter. Fire recalls Moses' bush and Sinai's summit, yet here the flames neither consume wood nor stone; they sanctify flesh, indicating a new mode of presence. The division of flame without diminution pictures Spirit's infinity: each receives all without God being parcelled. Language of "resting" fulfills Isaiah's Spirit resting on the Messiah (Isa 11 : 2), now shared with His body. Visual manifestation legitimizes subsequent invisible fillings, establishing canonical precedent for experiential Spirit. Meditating on Psalm 29, early readers may hear "the voice of the LORD flames out," connecting fiery speech with divine utterance. Thus flaming tongues consecrate human tongues as instruments of gospel proclamation.

9.2.4 All Filled: Spirit on Women, Men, Young, Old, Slave, and Free (Acts 2 : 4)

Luke insists that "all" were filled, not merely apostles, democratizing prophetic empowerment across social strata. The phenomenon marks inauguration, yet Acts records subsequent fillings for fresh boldness (Acts 4 : 31), teaching that initial baptism leads to continual replenishment. Spirit filling results in "other tongues" as Spirit gives utterance, emphasizing divine initiative even in speech articulation. Pentecostal tradition views tongues as normative sign, whereas evangelical charismatics see it as one gift among many; Luke's narrative supports both by recording multilingual praise here and non-linguistic signs elsewhere. Importantly, recipients remain in control—no frenzy violates Pauline rule that spirits of prophets are subject to prophets. The universal filling fulfills Moses' dream and Joel's prophecy of egalitarian outpouring. Consequently, church order must accommodate Spirit inclusion without gender or age discrimination.

9.2.5 Crowd Bewilderment: Paradox of Ecstasy and Comprehension (Acts 2 : 5-13)

Jews from "every nation under heaven" hear Galileans declaring God's mighty deeds in their own dialects, collapsing geographical distance within auditory space. Some marvel, others mock—accusing drunkenness at nine in the morning—illustrating perennial division over charismatic phenomena. Luke lists fifteen regions, moving east to west, perhaps sketching missionary roadmap Acts will narrate. The audible miracle precedes Peter's sermon, indicating that charismatic sign draws but proclamation explains, merging experiential and didactic. Unlike Corinthian glossolalia requiring interpretation, Pentecost tongues are immediately intelligible, showing functional diversity within one gift category. The mention of "mighty deeds" anchors speech content in God's actions, not self-focused display. Thus crowd reaction sets stage for apostolic exposition that turns wonder into repentance.

9.3 The Reversal—and Fulfilment—of Babel

9.3.1 Genesis 11 and the Scattered Tongues of Pride

Babel's builders sought a name and a tower, symbolizing autonomy against heaven, so God scattered them by confounding language (Gen 11 : 4-9). Pentecost reverses curse by enabling understanding across tongues, yet maintains linguistic diversity, suggesting redemption of plurality, not homogenization. Early church fathers called Pentecost the "anti-Babel," where humility in prayer undone pride in bricks. The story also completes Genesis trajectory: Abraham's blessing to nations now communicated in languages of those nations. Luke's narrative thus reinforces missional thrust inherent from patriarchal covenant. Where Babel produced centrifugal dispersion without God, Pentecost yields centrifugal mission with God. Therefore, the Spirit does not erase culture but sanctifies it for kingdom praise.

9.3.2 Linguistic Gift as Missional Sign, not Private Spectacle

The public setting and immediate comprehension reveal tongues as evangelistic bridge, challenging later tendencies to privatize glossolalia. Paul will permit private tongues but demand interpretation in church for edification (1 Cor 14 : 27-28). Acts demonstrates situational flexibility: in Caesarea tongues signal Spirit arrival to Gentiles before baptism, in Ephesus they accompany prophecy, confirming orthodoxy (Acts 10; 19). Missiologists note that early Pentecostal missionaries sailed expecting to speak local languages supernaturally; disappointment redirected them to language school, yet passion for cross-cultural witness persisted. Thus tongues remain symbol that gospel is translatable in every linguistic vessel. Wycliffe Bible Translators view their labor as linguistic Pentecost extension, rendering Scripture into thousands of idioms. Consequently, the gift's lasting legacy lies in empowering the church to honor every mother tongue under heaven.

9.3.3 Pilgrim Nations Listed: Parthians to Arabs as Mini-Table of Nations

Luke's catalogue begins with Parthians, Rome's eastern rival, and ends with Arabs, Israel's ancestral neighbors, framing political tensions beneath divine reconciliation. Inclusion of "Jews and proselytes" implies both ethnic and Gentile God-fearers experienced understanding, presaging full Gentile inclusion. The list lacks Spain, pinnacle of Paul's later ambitions, suggesting Acts' unfinished mission arc. Scholars spot chiastic structure centering on Judea, the homeland, symbolizing gospel radiating outward. Modern readers may map these nations onto contemporary states—Iran, Iraq, Turkey, Egypt—reminding the church that Spirit fire ignited precisely where mission now seems hardest. The narrative thus rebukes ethnocentric comfort zones, urging fresh engagement with long-evangelized yet resistant regions. Pilgrim nations become prototypical "every tribe and tongue" vision of Revelation.

9.3.4 "The Mighty Works of God": Doxology Before Evangelism

What the crowd hears is not systematic theology but exuberant praise recounting God's acts—creation, exodus, incarnation, resurrection. Worship precedes witness; joy sparks curiosity that sermon then answers, offering model for evangelistic worship today. Charismatic praise gatherings often function similarly, drawing seekers through palpable celebration. Psalms employ identical phrase "mighty deeds" (*gibborot*), linking Spirit activity to Israel's hymnbook. Peter will shortly contextualize these deeds within prophetic fulfilment, bridging affective response to cognitive understanding. Thus proclamation grows organically from adoration, not strategic marketing. Pentecost demonstrates that the church sings its way into the mission field.

9.3.5 From Human Tower to Divine Temple: Architectural Irony

Babel's tower sought heaven by human bricks; Pentecost shows heaven descending to human hearts, crafting living stones into a spiritual house. Peter later calls believers "living stones" built on Christ, reversing architectural initiative (1 Pet 2 : 5). Paul describes the church as temple built on apostolic foundation with Christ as cornerstone, indwelt by Spirit (Eph 2 : 20-22). Thus the architectural pride of Genesis is subverted by ecclesial humility. Missionary expansion described in Acts functions like temple construction, adding stones city by city. The irony intensifies: once-scattered nations now assemble into a building no human can see yet heaven recognizes. Pentecost therefore redeems architecture through indwelling rather than masonry.

9.4 Peter's Pentecost Homily: Joel, David, and the Spirit of Messiah

9.4.1 Joel 2 : 28-32—Last-Days Outpouring and Cosmic Portents

Peter interprets tumult as fulfilment of Joel's "afterward," which he daringly renders "in the last days," inaugurating eschatological epoch. Joel's imagery of blood, fire, and vapor finds partial echo in crucifixion darkness and temple destruction yet awaits cosmic climax, illustrating prophetic telescoping. The "whoever calls" promise democratizes salvation beyond ethnic boundaries, preparing for Gentile conversions. Pentecost thus proves that last days are not merely future catastrophe but Spirit-empowered mission era. Peter's reading exemplifies Christ-centered hermeneutic that reconfigures Israel's hope around Messiah's resurrection. Joel's agricultural restoration in context reinforces firstfruits theme, linking Spirit outpouring to new creation fertility. Hence Pentecost stands as both fulfilment and pledge—already and not yet.

9.4.2 Psalm 16—Death Could Not Hold the Holy One

Peter argues David spoke of Messiah, not himself, because David's tomb remained, whereas Jesus' was empty. He employs *midrash* logic, reading psalmic "Holy One" as prophecy of incorruptible body. Resurrection validates Spirit outpouring, since exalted Christ receives and sends promise from Father (Acts 2 : 33). Thus pneumatology hinges on Christology; no ascension, no Pentecost. Psalm 16 assurance of joy in God's presence becomes experiential reality for Spirit-filled believers. Peter's exegesis models apostolic preaching that fuses exposition with personal witness. Therefore, scripture, history, and experience converge in resurrection-Spirit nexus.

9.4.3 Psalm 110—Ascension, Session, and Poured-Out Promise

Claiming Jesus seated at God's right hand, Peter cites Psalm 110, early church's favorite messianic text. "Sit at My right hand" asserts royal authority, while "until I make Your enemies a footstool" foreshadows ongoing mission. Outpouring of Spirit is presented as royal gift, evidence of enthronement, not mere charismatic thrill. This logic undergirds later Nicene clause "He ascended... and His kingdom will have no end." Psalm 110 also combines king and priest in Melchizedek order, resonating with new-temple paradigm. Thus Pentecost is coronation festival broadcast through spiritual gifts. Believers participate in cosmic enthronement by receiving regal Spirit.

9.4.4 Cut to the Heart: Repentance, Baptism, Forgiveness, Gift (Acts 2 : 37-39)

Conviction pierces listeners, illustrating Spirit's role in reproof (John 16 : 8). Peter prescribes repentance—metanoia—turn, and baptism in Jesus' name, integrating inward change with outward sign. Forgiveness of sins corresponds to Day of Atonement cleansing, while "gift of the Holy Spirit" confirms inclusion. Promise extends to "you, your children, and all far off," previewing household baptisms and Gentile outreach. Three thousand respond, reversing Sinai's three thousand dead after golden calf (Ex 32 : 28). Thus law engraved on stone killed; Spirit written on hearts gives life (2 Cor 3 : 6). Pentecost becomes birth certificate of grace-based covenant community.

9.4.5 "Save Yourselves from This Crooked Generation": Exodus Echoes

Peter exhorts escape from corrupt generation, echoing Moses' plea separating faithful from idolaters. Luke's narrative frames church as renewed exodus company, led by pillar-fire Spirit, journeying toward promised inheritance. Baptism into Christ parallels Red Sea crossing, severing bondage to sin-Pharaoh. The title "crooked" references Deuteronomy 32, Song of Moses lamenting rebellious Israel; thus Peter calls for remnant realignment with covenant. Salvation here is corporate pilgrimage, not mere individual ticket. The exhortation still rings: Spirit people live counter-culture amid crooked age, shining as wilderness camp of holiness (Phil 2 : 15). Hence Pentecost launches second exodus toward new creation Canaan.

9.5 Spirit as Shekinah of the New Temple

9.5.1 From Cloud-Glory to Tongue-Flame: Continuity and Discontinuity

Shekinah cloud filled tabernacle and Solomon's temple, preventing priests from standing (Ex 40 : 35; 1 Kgs 8 : 11). Pentecostal fire continues glory motif yet shifts medium from building to believers, maintaining continuity while introducing radical discontinuity. Cloud was external, fire now internal; presence once localized now replicated globally. John's prologue spoke of Word tabernacling among us; Acts shows Shekinah tabernacling within us. Continuity ensures faithfulness to Old-Testament narrative; discontinuity provides transformative surprise. Church architecture may still aspire to evoke transcendence, but primary locus of glory is redeemed community. Hence the Spirit redefines sacred space around living stones rather than cedar beams.

9.5.2 Corporate Indwelling: Acts 2 vs. Private Mysticism (1 Cor 3 : 16)

While individuals later experience Spirit, Pentecost underscores collective habitation: "they were all together in one place." Paul echoes by calling Corinthian church God's temple in plural form, warning unity-threatening factions. Mysticism detached from community misses biblical balance; Spirit builds corporate dwelling before personal retreat. Early monastics retained communal liturgy, affirming ecclesial primacy even in solitude. Charismatic renewal flourishes when gifts serve body, not ego. Consumer Christianity's individualism contradicts Pentecostal template, demanding reorientation toward covenantal interdependence. Therefore, corporate indwelling remains hallmark of authentic Spirit movement.

9.5.3 Living Stones and Cornerstone (Eph 2 : 19-22; 1 Pet 2 : 4-6)

Paul pictures Gentile and Jewish believers as stones rising into holy temple with Christ as cornerstone, abolishing alienation in one structure. Peter extends image, calling disciples to offer spiritual sacrifices, aligning priesthood with architecture. Stone metaphor implies permanence yet growth, stability yet dynamism, echoing progressive Acts expansion. Cornerstone sets alignment; doctrines deviating from Christ tilt walls into heresy. Masonry also suggests diversity shaped and fitted by master builder Spirit, smoothing rough edges for communal harmony. Church splits reveal stones resisting placement; submission to Spirit mason preserves unity. Thus architectural imagery grounds ecclesiology in Christ-centered formation.

9.5.4 Spirit Seal and Down-Payment of Inheritance (Eph 1 : 13-14)

Seal imagery derives from wax impression signifying ownership and authenticity; Spirit marks believers as Christ's property. Down-payment (*arrabōn*) language, used in commercial contracts, assures final redemption—resurrection—will arrive. Assurance combats persecution; believers facing confiscation retain invisible guarantee of lasting inheritance. Seal also implies protection, as in Revelation's 144 000 marked on foreheads, safeguarding worshipers from wrath. Holy Spirit thus performs eschatological escrow, holding glory funds until maturity. Believers can therefore risk generosity, knowing deposit secures heavenly treasure. Pentecost provides first issuance of this divine earnest money.

9.5.5 Temple Presence Now Mobile: No Geographic Monopoly

Acts quickly moves epicenter from Jerusalem to Judea, Samaria, and Gentile cities, proving presence travels faster than apostles can predict. Persecution scatters believers, yet Luke stresses Spirit leads, not flees, turning flight into missionary advance (Acts 8 : 4). Paul's letters written from prison demonstrate temple cannot be chained; Spirit converts cells into sanctuaries. Global south revivals vindicate mobile presence, flourishing where cathedrals are scarce. Diaspora congregations livestream worship across continents, digitally extending upper-room reach. Therefore, any theology anchoring holiness to particular land misunderstands Pentecost's centrifugal essence. Spirit writes sacred geography onto hearts that migrate, multiply, and worship on the move.

9.6 The Spirit-Formed Community in Jerusalem

9.6.1 Apostolic Didachē: Teaching as New Torah (Acts 2 : 42)

"Devoted to apostles' teaching" positions doctrine at community core, fulfilling Jeremiah's promise of Law written on hearts. Apostles interpret Old-Testament narrative through Christ event, shaping worldview and ethics. Learning community counters anti-intellectual tendencies by marrying Spirit experience to theological depth. Catechesis prepares converts for persecution, as later exemplified in Stephen's long biblical speech. Modern churches emulate through Bible studies and liturgical lectionaries, ensuring continuous immersion in apostolic word. Teaching also guards against heresy threatening fragile unity. Thus Spirit fosters appetite for truth, not merely sensation.

9.6.2 Koinonia and Economic Jubilee: Selling Lands and Laying at Feet

Luke describes believers holding all things common, even liquidating real estate to finance needy members, echoing Deuteronomy's debt release ideals. Barnabas exemplifies generosity, whereas Ananias and Sapphira's deceit shows Spirit guarding purity with sobering judgment. Economic sharing demonstrates concrete outworking of Spirit baptism, where wealth becomes communal blessing. Contemporary expressions include mutual-aid funds, cooperative housing, and micro-enterprise support within congregations. Koinonia resists consumer church by cultivating sacrificial interdependence. Such practices attract outsiders, proving temple presence fosters social justice. Hence Spirit converts wallets alongside hearts.

9.6.3 Breaking Bread at Home and in Temple: Dual Rhythms of Worship

Disciples maintain daily attendance in temple courts for corporate prayer but break bread in homes with glad hearts, displaying flexibility. Formal liturgy and informal hospitality intertwine, foreshadowing later parish-cell models. Home tables extend Eucharist into neighborhood, turning living rooms into micro-temples. Temple prayers root new movement in Jewish heritage until persecution forces relocation. Post-70 CE synagogue and house church structures absorb disciplinary rhythms. Modern small-group communions recover this Pentecostal balance between gathered and scattered worship. Spirit thus sanctifies both basilica and kitchenette.

9.6.4 Collective Prayer and Shared Awe: Signs, Wonders, and Fear

Regular prayer hours align with tamid sacrifices, yet Spirit transforms rote schedule into expectancy where healings and imprison-breaks occur. Luke notes "fear came upon every soul," healthy reverence acknowledging God's immanent holiness. Charismatic phenomena validate apostolic message, yet reliance on signs never eclipses devotion to teaching. Prayer fuels mission discernment, as Antioch fasts precede Paul's commissioning. Corporate intercession unites diverse believers, overcoming ethnic and economic barriers through common petition. Modern 24-7 prayer rooms replicate upper-room flow, sustaining revival through worship and intercession cycles. Awe becomes hallmark of Spirit-formed community.

9.6.5 Favor with the People and Daily Growth: Missional Magnetism

Generosity and joy win public admiration, contrasting with elite temple corruption exposed by Jesus. Though persecution rises, Luke records continual numeric increase, attributing growth to Lord adding, not marketing schemes. Missional magnetism combines compassionate deeds and gospel proclamation, a pattern later codified in "St Francis Style" witness. Contemporary churches practicing justice ministries often gain credibility for evangelism among skeptical neighbors. Spirit-empowered authenticity outshines polished programs, as first-century revival proves. Favour also invites jealousy, requiring wisdom to steward popularity without compromising truth. Thus growth arises organically from Spirit life rather than human strategy.

9.7 Gifts of the Spirit: Unity in Charismatic Diversity

9.7.1 Charismata Catalogues—Romans 12, 1 Corinthians 12, Ephesians 4

Paul lists prophecy, service, teaching, encouragement, giving, leading, mercy, tongues, interpretation, healing, miracles, and administration, illustrating variety. No list exhaustive; Spirit tailors gifts to context, epoch, and community need. Motivational, manifestation, and ministry gifts overlap yet differ in nuance. Gift distribution undermines spectator Christianity, empowering every believer for priestly function. Lists place love as matrix, preventing competitive ranking. Healthy congregations discover, deploy, and develop gifts through assessment and mentoring. Charismata thus become building blocks of new temple, each stone uniquely shaped.

9.7.2 Tongues and Prophecy: Public Edification vs. Private Devotion

Paul values tongues that build self through prayer but prefers prophecy that builds church through intelligible exhortation (1 Cor 14 : 4-5). He forbids tongue monopolies, instituting two-or-three rule and mandatory interpretation. Prophecy, evaluated by others, conveys comfort, edification, and conviction, continuing Pentecost's revelatory stream. Cessationists argue revelatory gifts ceased, yet global south testimonies challenge this view. Historical revivals display balanced coexistence of charismatic experience and doctrinal fidelity. Pastoral leadership must nurture gifts while guarding against excess, modeling Paul's delicate calibration. Thus Spirit speech remains integral to temple vitality.

9.7.3 Body Metaphor: Eye, Hand, and the Indispensable "Unpresentable" Parts

Paul likens church to human body where unseen organs are essential; glamorized gifts cannot despise hidden intercessors or administrators. Body imagery counters celebrity culture, elevating nursery volunteers alongside platform preachers. Honor redistribution uplifts marginalized voices—women, immigrants, disabled—mirroring Pentecost inclusivity. Disunity equals autoimmune disease, Spirit grieves, witness suffers. By embracing mutual dependence, temple grows into mature stature of Christ. Local assemblies practice this through rotated leadership, testimonies, and shared decision-making. Thus body metaphor operationalizes charismata diversity into harmonious worship.

9.7.4 Love as the "More Excellent Way" Governing All Gifts (1 Cor 13)

Paul's poetic interlude rebukes Corinthian fascination with ecstatic gifts devoid of love, declaring tongues, prophecy, and knowledge nothing without agapē. Love's verbs—patient, kind, rejoicing in truth—describe Spirit's own character, blueprint for charism administration. Gifts will cease at eschaton, but love endures, making it temple's eternal fragrance. Charity frames ethical deployment of wealth, knowledge, and power. Pentecostal fervor must therefore submit to cruciform love lest gifts become clanging cymbals. Love energizes mission, sustains suffering, and bridges cultural divides. Therefore, Spirit fullness is measured by love's presence, not spectacular phenomena.

9.7.5 Leadership Gifts: Apostles, Prophets, Teachers, Shepherds, Evangelists

Ephesians 4 presents ascended Christ giving people as gifts to equip saints for ministry, diffusing leadership beyond clerical caste. Apostolic pioneers extend frontier; prophetic voices safeguard holiness; evangelists herald good news; shepherd-teachers nurture and guard flock. Fivefold framework counters over-centralized pastor model, promoting team leadership reflective of triune collaboration. North-African churches incorporate this through ministry tracks and shared pulpit. Leadership gifts exist "until we all attain unity," indicating ongoing need. Abuse occurs when roles become status rather than service; accountability and plurality mitigate risk. Spirit-appointed leaders thus steward temple's health while empowering others.

9.8 Spirit and Mission: To the Ends of the Earth

9.8.1 Acts 1 : 8 as Geographic Program: Jerusalem → Judea → Samaria → World

Jesus' final promise outlines concentric mission circles, structuring Acts' narrative progression. Jerusalem receives Pentecost; Judea hears through scattered believers; Samaria via Philip; Gentile world through Paul. Promise of power (*dynamis*) counters disciples' earlier quest for political dominion, reframing kingdom expansion spiritually. Today's missiology adapts circles to local-regional-cross-cultural contexts, echoing original blueprint. Spirit's power emphasizes proclamation and demonstration—words and works. Mission drift occurs when churches neglect outer rings, settling for comfortable Judah. Pentecost's centrifugal momentum beckons perpetual outward movement.

9.8.2 Spirit Guidance: Philip and the Ethiopian Treble Fast-Track (Acts 8)

Angel directs Philip south, Spirit prompts him to approach chariot, and Ethiopian rejoices into baptism, showcasing Spirit-initiated encounter. Conversion of finance official signals gospel infiltrating Africa via high-ranking envoy. Isaiah 53 scroll providentially opens at suffering servant, Spirit orchestrating Scripture and witness. Philip disappears to Azotus, illustrating Spirit freedom over missionary itineraries. Modern testimonies of Spirit nudging missionaries replicate this responsiveness. Discernment frameworks—Scripture, community, circumstance—aid verification of Spirit promptings. Thus Pentecost fuels divine appointments across cultural boundaries.

9.8.3 Cornelius' Household: Gentile Pentecost and Boundary Collapse (Acts 10-11)

Angelic vision to Cornelius and rooftop trance to Peter converge, Spirit bridging Jew-Gentile gap through synchronized revelation. Outpouring precedes water baptism, reversing Jerusalem order and forcing Jewish believers to recognize God's impartiality. Peter's explanation to council anchors inclusion in Spirit evidence, not mosaic purity. Story legitimizes pork-eating Romans sharing same Spirit as kosher Jews, re-calibrating holiness. Contemporary intercultural fellowship echoes Cornelius moment when immigrants enrich liturgy with diverse flavors. Spirit thus undermines ethnocentric ecclesiology, forging catholic—universal—body. Mission is no longer export of culture but import of kingdom from every culture.

9.8.4 "Set Apart Barnabas and Saul": Antioch's Multicultural Launchpad (Acts 13)

Prophets and teachers from Cyprus, Libya, and Judea fast and worship, and Spirit speaks collectively: "Set apart." First intentional missionary journey emerges from Spirit guidance, not human committee. Antioch's generosity to famine victims already proved its maturity; sending leaders demonstrates sacrificial obedience. Missionary prayer commissioning becomes liturgical pattern in subsequent centuries. Spirit direction accompanies unfolding of geopolitical strategy—Asia Minor, Greece, Rome—aligning with trade routes. Global south churches now send missionaries north, continuing Antioch precedent. Spirit's voice still arises amid multiethnic worship environments.

9.8.5 Asia, Macedonia, and the "Spirit of Jesus" Steering Mission (Acts 16)

Paul's team forbidden by Spirit to preach in Asia, redirected to Macedonia through night vision, indicating God's sovereignty over timing. The term "Spirit of Jesus" underscores risen Lord's operational involvement in missionary decisions. Resulting Philippi church becomes financial partner sustaining Pauline mission. Closed doors therefore not failure but strategic redirection. Modern mission agencies adopt similar discernment, adjusting plans according to Spiritual check and release. Obedience nurtures humility, acknowledging that harvest field belongs to Lord. Thus Pentecost power includes guidance as well as proclamation.

9.9 Spirit, Sanctification, and Ethical Transformation

9.9.1 Fruit of the Spirit vs. Works of the Flesh (Gal 5 : 16-26)

Paul contrasts ninefold fruit—love, joy, peace, patience, kindness, goodness, faithfulness, gentleness, self-control—with vices like sexual immorality and envy. Fruit metaphor emphasizes organic growth through abiding, not mechanical effort. Legalism cannot produce such character; only Spirit within can. List addresses relational sins, showing sanctification primarily social. Church health depends on fruit production as much as gift utilization. Discipleship processes—prayer, Word, community—cultivate fertile soil. Pentecost seeds ethical orchard in believer's heart.

9.9.2 Holiness as Temple Logic for Individual Bodies (1 Cor 6 : 18-20)

Paul declares bodies temples, purchased by blood, elevating sexual ethics to sacramental seriousness. Union with prostitute equals joining Christ to immorality, a thought Paul deems unthinkable. Therefore, holiness is not ascetic contempt but honoring indwelling presence. Gym culture and body image obsessions find corrective in temple theology valuing dignity over vanity. Christian sexual counterculture witnesses to alternative kingdom fidelity. Abuse and exploitation profane living sanctuaries, warranting prophetic outcry. Spirit empowerment enables chastity, not mere rule-keeping.

9.9.3 Grieving and Quenching the Spirit: Warnings to the New Temple (Eph 4 : 30; 1 Thess 5 : 19)

Spirit portrayed with emotional capacity—grieved by bitterness, rage, slander—linking interpersonal sin to divine sorrow. Quenching metaphor images extinguishing flame, recalling Pentecost fire; gossip and neglect of gifts pour water on holy flame. Thus community ethics either intensify or dampen presence. Church discipline restores airflow to smoldering wick. Personal holiness, corporate unity, and vibrant charisms maintain oxygen for Spirit blaze. Warnings reveal responsibility in partnership; covenant is synergistic. Pentecost gift does not override human agency.

9.9.4 Intercession "with Inexpressible Groanings" (Rom 8 : 26-27)

Believers often lack words amid suffering; Spirit intercedes with groans aligning with God's will, echoing creation's birth pangs. Mystery of divine Person praying to divine Mind ensures prayers surpass intellect. Charismatic prayer language sometimes viewed as expression of these groans. Comfort arises knowing prayer weaknesses become Spirit's strength. Intercession forms furnace forging hope resilience. Corporate lament services participate in this deep communication, embodying temple's incense ministry. Pentecost thus equips church for honest, powerful prayer amid groaning world.

9.9.5 Spirit of Adoption Crying "Abba! Father!": Relational Ethics (Rom 8 : 15)

Adoption Spirit drives out fear slave mindset breeds, replacing with intimate cry echoing Jesus in Gethsemane. Identity fuels ethics; children imitate Father's generosity and forgiveness. Fellowship crosses social lines, forming family of previously estranged peoples. Orphan care and fostering ministries manifest adoption theology tangibly. Prayer begins with filial affection, not transactional anxiety. Pentecost therefore roots moral transformation in relational security. Temple now resonates with family laughter rather than animal screams.

In conclusion, Pentecost answered the ripped-veil silence with a roar of wind and a ring of fire, announcing that the Shekinah had not vanished but multiplied. The Spirit who once brooded over primal waters, who blazed atop Sinai, and who filled Solomon's nave now courses through veins and ventilates prayers, re-creating humanity into a breathing cathedral open to every nation. From Jerusalem alleyways to Roman courts, from desert monasteries to digital sanctuaries, that breathing cathedral has marched, sustained by gifts that serve, fruit that sweetens, and a guarantee that all groaning will end in glory. Yet the chapter is not closed; every generous act, every cross-cultural friendship, every whispered "Abba" continues Pentecost's narrative until love's flame consumes the final shadow.

When the Lamb-lit city descends and tongues of nations melt into one thunderous hymn, the rushing wind of Acts 2 will be recognized as the first gust of an everlasting gale. Until that horizon breaches time, the church lives as mobile temple, inviting the thirsty, correcting the wayward, and kindling hope in a crooked generation. May the Spirit who indwelt the upper room ignite our imaginations again, overturning complacency, infusing courage, and drawing the world toward the sound of heaven's eternal festival.

Chapter 10 - Pauline Temple Theology: Body and Community

Paul's letters reveal a thinker who never uses the word *temple* as a mere metaphor; every appearance carries the gravitational pull of Sinai smoke, Solomonic gold, and Calvary's torn veil. Because he met the risen Christ in blazing splendor "above the brightness of the sun" (Acts 26 : 13), he could neither reduce worship to Jerusalem stone nor sever worship from embodied, communal life. In his imagination the sanctuary was no longer a single geographic coordinate but a Spirit-saturated network of human bodies, house-churches, and cross-cultural fellowships stitched together by cruciform love. To read Paul with temple eyes is therefore to watch holiness migrate from holy-of-holies to Corinthian dining rooms, from ark of the covenant to apostolic bloodstream, from architectural columns to ethical commitments. That migration reorganizes sexual ethics, economic sharing, charismatic ministry, social justice, and eschatological hope, turning every sphere of life into liturgical space. What follows unpacks that vision in its diverse textures—personal and corporate, local and cosmic—showing how Paul persuades converts in cities as different as Philippi and Rome to recognize themselves as living architecture for divine glory. The goal is not antiquarian admiration of Paul's brilliance but a summons to inhabit our era as Spirit-built sanctuaries whose doors stand open to the nations.

10.1 Foundations of Paul's Temple Imagery

10.1.1 Temple Vocabulary in the Greco-Roman World (*naos, hieron, oikos*)

Greeks distinguished between the *hieron*, the whole sacred precinct, and the *naos*, the inner chamber where deity supposedly resided; Paul nearly always chooses *naos* for the church, implying intimate presence rather than mere courtyard affiliation (1 Cor 3 : 16). This choice invites readers to imagine themselves not as pilgrims loitering in porticoes but as living equivalents of the holy of holies. Conversely he uses *hieron* in Acts 21 : 26 when describing the physical Jerusalem sanctuary, signaling a theological contrast between fragile stone and indestructible fellowship. His third term, *oikos*—house—allows sliding from architectural to familial imagery without changing metaphors, a move that lets him call Gentiles both citizens and kin (Eph 2 : 19). Roman temples, sponsored by emperors, proclaimed imperial benefaction; Paul's Spirit-temple proclaims crucified benefaction, subverting civic religion. Thus vocabulary itself becomes a missionary tactic, translating Israel's cultic language into urban marketplaces while preserving its holiness thrust. By lexical precision Paul relocates glory from Caesar's marble to Lydia's living room.

10.1.2 Paul's Pharisaic Upbringing and Zeal for Jerusalem's Sanctuary (Phil 3 : 4-6)

Raised a Hebrew of Hebrews, Paul memorized purity codes that hedged the temple from defilement, and his youthful zeal "beyond measure" included, by his own admission, violence against the church (Gal 1 : 13). He likely joined temple guard delegations who arrested blasphemers, believing he protected sacred space from heresy. Such background explains the severity with which he later addresses sexual sin in Corinth; desecration of the body now equals vandalizing God's house. Conversion did not delete his reverence for holiness; it redirected it from masonry to metabolism, from walls to hearts. His credentials, once assets, became "dung" because the locus of purity had shifted to the Messiah's pierced flesh (Phil 3 : 7-8). Therefore, Pauline temple theology grows not from philosophical abstraction but from a Pharisee's shattered paradigm meeting risen glory on Damascus Road. Zeal for the house still burns in him, only now the house has lungs and languages.

10.1.3 Damascus Revelation: Seeing the Glorified Christ as New Holy of Holies (Acts 9)

The blinding light that toppled Paul outside Damascus mimics Shekinah brilliance that once filled Solomon's sanctuary (1 Kgs 8 : 10-11), making the road a mobile inner court. By asking, "Who are you, Lord?" Paul behaves like a priest suddenly realizing the ark has taken human form. The voice's reply, "I am Jesus," fuses identity of Yahweh with crucified Nazarene, forcing Paul to see temple and Messiah collapse into one reality. Blindness for three days parodies temple veil, lifted only through Ananias's Spirit-filled touch, foreshadowing that new sight requires ecclesial mediation. From that hour, Paul's mental map places heavenly sanctuary "in Christ," accessible by faith rather than pilgrimage. His later ascension vision to "third heaven" (2 Cor 12 : 2) merely confirms what Damascus light engraved: glory is a Person, not a postcode. Thus his life mission becomes introducing pagans to this portable holy of holies.

10.1.4 Diaspora Synagogues and the Problem of Portable Holiness

Synagogues functioned as micro-temples featuring Torah, prayer, and sometimes incense yet consciously stopped short of sacrificial claims reserved for Jerusalem. Paul's synagogue encounters in Pisidian Antioch and Thessalonica show tensions between central shrine loyalty and diaspora identity (Acts 13 ; 17). When he proclaims justification apart from the Law and apart from the temple cult (Rom 3 : 21-24), he offers Jews abroad what synagogues could only symbolize: immediate access to God's righteousness. His collection for Jerusalem saints (2 Cor 8-9) mirrors pilgrim offerings yet reframes them as Gentile "priestly service," proving that holiness can flow upstream. Diaspora geography primes readers to accept a temple that travels better than Herod's. Paul enters that vacuum with a theology where Spirit makes every assembly a shrine, fulfilling diaspora longing. Hence portable holiness moves from concept to charismatic community.

10.1.5 Apocalyptic Judaism, Merkavah Mysticism, and Heavenly Temple Concepts

Second-Temple apocalypses like 1 Enoch and 2 Baruch envisioned celestial sanctuaries inaccessible to ordinary worshipers, while

Merkavah mystics sought throne-room visions through ecstatic ascent. Paul engages similar themes when he speaks of being caught up to paradise and hearing "unutterable words" (2 Cor 12 : 4), yet he resists elitism by emphasizing weakness and thorn. He democratizes heavenly access in Ephesians, declaring believers already seated with Christ in heavenly places (Eph 2 : 6). Thus the esoteric becomes communal; what mystics reserved for visionary adepts is bestowed on Spirit-sealed households. Apocalyptic hope that God would one day dwell fully with humanity finds partial realization in church life, making cosmic temple theology immediately practical. Paul's boldness likely startles contemporaries, but his authority rests on revelation that the veil is removed in Christ. He therefore invites ordinary artisans and slaves into experiences once claimed by visionary elites.

10.2 Individual Body as Temple of the Holy Spirit

10.2.1 Sexual Ethics and Temple Logic in 1 Cor 6 : 12-20

When Corinthian men argue "All things are lawful," Paul counters that fornication unites Christ's members with a prostitute, a sacrilegious coupling as shocking as dragging an idol into the holy of holies. He cites Genesis 2 : 24 to show that bodily union forges spiritual linkage, making immorality not just private vice but temple vandalism. The twin imperatives "flee sexual immorality" and "glorify God in your body" combine negative avoidance with positive liturgy, turning chastity into worship. Rhetorically he moves from stomach-food analogy to body-Lord relationship, rejecting dualistic views that treat flesh as disposable vessel. Christ's resurrection guarantees bodily destiny, so HIV-era or hookup-culture contexts cannot dismiss Pauline ethics as antiquated. By claiming believers are "bought with a price," he links sexual purity to Passover redemption, grounding ethics in gospel story. Thus bedroom becomes sanctuary where holiness or defilement reverberates through Christ's corporate body.

10.2.2 Food, Drink, and Bodily Discipline as Liturgical Acts (1 Cor 10 : 31; Rom 14)

Paul instructs that "whether you eat or drink, do all to the glory of God," elevating meals to sacramental significance beyond Eucharist (1 Cor

10 : 31). Debates over meat offered to idols force Corinthian consciences to discern table fellowship as temple participation, since altars equal communion. In Romans 14 he grants liberty in diet but demands that strong respect weak, making love the guiding rubric of bodily disciplines. Fasting, feasting, exercise, and rest become forms of embodied worship, anticipating later Christian ascetic and hospitality traditions. By refusing food dualism he honors creation goodness while critiquing gluttony and intoxication. Thus mundane nutrition becomes place where Spirit-temple honors its Builder. A contemporary believer counting calories or practicing sustainable eating participates in this liturgical stewardship.

10.2.3 "Present Your Bodies"—Living Sacrifice in Rom 12 : 1-2

After eleven chapters of soteriology Paul issues a single sweeping exhortation: offer bodies as living, holy, pleasing sacrifices, which he calls "your logikēn latreian," rational or true worship. The oxymoron "living sacrifice" recalls Isaac bound yet breathing, typifying ongoing devotion rather than terminal death. Transformation through mind renewal replaces conformity to passing aeon, making sanctification cognitive as well as corporeal. This presentation is priestly yet universal: every believer becomes both offerer and offering. Liturgically, Sunday worship rehearses this self-offering, but vocation extends into workplaces and kitchens. Paul's shift from cultic slaughter to vocational service redefines sacrifice as missional embodiment. Thus temple logic frames Christian ethics as holistic liturgy spanning Monday to market.

10.2.4 Mortality, Resurrection, and the Building from God (2 Cor 5 : 1-5)

Paul likens the present body to a perishable tent and the future resurrection body to a house "not made with hands, eternal in the heavens," echoing tabernacle versus temple. Groaning expresses both discomfort and longing, a liturgy of anticipation for immortality. The Spirit acts as "arrabōn," guaranteeing that the down payment of indwelling presence will mature into a glorified structure. This eschatological architecture comforts persecuted saints; even if earthly tents burn, heavenly construction awaits. Unlike Greek disdain for flesh, Paul affirms bodily continuity, insisting embodiment is essential to temple vocation. Therefore, funerals within the church are not removals from sanctuary but groundwork for upgrade. Such hope fuels courageous obedience despite martyrdom threats.

10.2.5 Charismatic Experiences and the Inner Sanctuary of the Heart (2 Cor 12)

When Paul recounts visions of paradise, he refuses to boast in revelations, highlighting instead weakness and thorn, thus relocating glory from spectacle to surrendered interiority. His description of being "caught up to the third heaven" mirrors priestly entrance into holy of holies, yet he downplays its value compared to grace in weakness. This stance protects congregations from spirituality that esteems private ecstasies above communal love. The heart becomes hidden *naos* where power is perfected in frailty, aligning with cracked-clay-jar metaphor (2 Cor 4 : 7). Charismatic traditions can learn humility here, celebrating visions without eclipsing suffering servant ethic. Paul's refusal to name unspeakable words underscores reverence for mystery even amid temple accessibility. Hence, inner sanctuary experiences should produce cross-shaped service, not spiritual elitism.

10.3 Corporate Temple: The Church as God's Dwelling

10.3.1 "You (Plural) Are God's Temple" in 1 Cor 3 : 9-17

Writing to a church splintered by celebrity loyalties, Paul warns that jealousy and strife threaten to "destroy the temple," invoking severe judgment on divisive builders. Using construction imagery— foundation, gold, straw—he depicts ministry motives tested by eschatological fire. Teachers who build with gospel fidelity will receive reward; others risk loss though personally saved. This eschaton-fire evokes altar testing sacrifices, making congregational work priestly labor. Plural "you" dismisses individualistic spirituality; holiness is communal project. Sectarianism thus equals sacrilege, as if cracking the walls of God's indwelling. Therefore, ecumenical patience becomes a temple-maintenance discipline.

10.3.2 Household Metaphor in Eph 2 : 19-22—Citizens, Family, Holy Dwelling

Gentiles, once "alienated from the commonwealth," are now fellow citizens and *oikeioi*—household members—underscoring legal and familial unity. Foundation of apostles and prophets, with Christ as cornerstone, provides doctrinal stability across cultures. Present tense "grows" depicts organic expansion, supporting missional multiplication without structural collapse. Spirit helps disparate ethnic stones adhere through mortar of peace forged at the cross (Eph 2 : 14). Thus temple construction fights racism by making hostility architecturally impossible. Local churches become embassies of this supranational commonwealth. Hospitality and mutual submission are bricks in this holy dwelling.

10.3.3 Living Stones and Spiritual House in 1 Pet 2 contrasted with Paul

Peter addresses marginalized Asia Minor believers, calling them living stones like Paul but emphasizing exile status. While Paul foregrounds apostolic foundation, Peter highlights cornerstone testing, urging perseverance under slander. Together they present complementary blueprints: Pauline temple stresses unity; Petrine temple stresses endurance. Their convergence shows early Christian consensus on communal indwelling. Differences illuminate pastoral flexibility: Paul to cosmopolitan churches, Peter to persecuted outposts. Canonical duet warns against provincial application of one model. Spirit architects contextual sanctuaries from same cornerstone.

10.3.4 Unity and Purity: Warning Against Destroying God's Sanctuary

Paul's lethal language—"If anyone destroys God's temple, God will destroy him" (1 Cor 3 : 17)—chills readers aware of Nadab and Abihu's fate. Destruction here includes doctrinal corruption, moral scandal, and divisive pride. Church discipline, when done biblically, becomes repair work on cracked walls. Forgiveness and restoration preserve temple integrity without discarding wounded stones. False teachers who persist threaten structural collapse, justifying exclusion. Therefore, love and holiness form twin guardrails for communal sanctuary. Failure to guard either invites divine demolition.

10.3.5 Sacrificial Priesthood of All Believers: From Levitical Cast to Charismatic Body

Peter declares believers "holy priesthood," offering spiritual sacrifices acceptable through Christ (1 Pet 2 : 5). Paul echoes by urging Gentile offering as sacrificial service (Rom 15 : 16). Sacrifices now include praise, generosity, and evangelism, decentralizing cult from altar to daily life. Every saint wears ephod of Spirit empowerment, eliminating clerical monopoly. Clergy still equip but do not monopolize priestly privilege. Reformation recovered this doctrine, but charismatic renewal restored its experiential dimension. Temple community thus operates with distributed priesthood, enhancing mission agility.

10.4 Christ the Cornerstone, Foundation, and Mercy Seat

10.4.1 1 Cor 3 : 11—No Other Foundation Than Jesus Christ

Paul rejects foundation of human eloquence or cultural prestige; only Christ crucified sustains eternal edifice. Builders who lay alternative bases erect leaning towers doomed to fall. The Christ-foundation encompasses atonement, resurrection, and lordship, ensuring theological coherence. Modern church-planting must prioritize gospel clarity over marketing strategies. Ecumenical dialogue finds unity only where cornerstone remains unmoved. Shifting culture does not necessitate moving foundation lines. The wise builder keeps eyes on foundational Christ to survive cultural earthquakes.

10.4.2 Eph 2 : 20—Apostles + Prophets Built on the Chief Cornerstone

Cornerstone aligns both walls, symbolizing Christ integrating Jew and Gentile. Apostolic and prophetic foundation refers to teaching offices, not successors' hierarchy, safeguarding church against drifting from gospel canon. New Testament itself becomes architectural blueprint. Charismatic prophecy today must echo foundation, never redesign. Structure allows growth while preserving original angles. Christology remains non-negotiable plumb line. Deviation registers as theological crack requiring urgent repair.

10.4.3 Rom 3 : 25—Christ as *Hilastērion* (Mercy-Seat)

Paul borrows tabernacle term for lid where blood sprinkled, identifying Christ as location of atonement. Faith positions sinner beneath cleansing blood, accessing propitiation previously limited to high priest annually. By faith Gentiles enter space where even Levitical priests feared. Righteousness displayed publicly contrasts hidden holy of holies, fulfilling prophetic hope. *Hilastērion* also evokes cherubim overshadowing, now guardians of gospel, not barriers. This theological move de-sacralizes geography while intensifying holiness. Worship songs extolling mercy-seat draw vocabulary from this Pauline insight.

10.4.4 Col 2 : 9—Fullness of Deity Dwelling Bodily

Against Colossian syncretism, Paul asserts *pleroma* of God dwells in Christ, refuting angels-mediated access. Incarnation thus becomes ultimate temple: God in corporeal tent accessible without intermediaries. Believers share fullness through union, making ascetic regulations redundant. Temple festivals, new moons, and Sabbaths are shadows; substance belongs to Christ (Col 2 : 16-17). Theological implication: seeking spirituality outside Christ is retrograde pilgrimage back to shuttered shrine. Science observes cosmic vastness, but fullness resides in manger-born Messiah. Christology thereby anchors cosmic temple vision.

10.4.5 Cosmic Temple in Col 1 : 15-20—Christ as Architect and Sustainer

Hymn portrays Christ as image, firstborn, creator, sustainer, head, and reconciler, mapping temple from Genesis to eschaton. All things created *through* and *for* Him means creation itself is designed as Christic sanctuary. Reconciliation by blood of cross cleanses cosmic sanctuary defiled by sin, ensuring eventual harmony. Liturgical tone suggests early worship setting, blending doxology with dogma. Environmental ethics flow from recognition that galaxies are vaulted ceiling of Christ's temple. Mission extends reconciliation message to every atom of estranged creation. Cosmic scope frames local piety within universal architecture.

10.5 Ethics and Holiness Flowing from Temple Identity

10.5.1 Purity, Impurity, and Communal Discipline in 1 Cor 5

Corinth tolerates man sleeping with step-mother, a defilement even pagans reject; Paul commands expulsion "that the spirit may be saved," echoing Old-Testament banishment to preserve camp purity. Leaven metaphor portrays sin's ferment spreading through dough-temple. Passover imagery—Christ our Passover sacrificed—motivates removal of old leaven, linking ethics to soteriology. Modern churches wrestle with discipline amid therapeutic culture, yet temple identity legitimizes loving exclusion when repentance refused. Restoration, not punishment, is endgame, mirroring temple cleansings that aim for renewed worship. Public holiness functions evangelistically, proving gospel's transformative power. Otherwise sanctuary becomes den of immorality inviting judgment.

10.5.2 "Cleanse Ourselves from Every Defilement" (2 Cor 7 : 1)

Paul urges Corinthian reconciliation after severe letter, grounding call in promises of God dwelling among them (2 Cor 6 : 16-18). Holiness extends to spirit and flesh, rejecting dichotomies. Defilements include idolatry partnerships, unethical business, and corrupt speech. Sanctification is synergistic—God works, believers cleanse. Fear of God motivates, balancing grace with reverence. Holiness culture nurtures authenticity, attracting seekers weary of hypocrisy. Thus temple hope fuels ongoing repentance journey.

10.5.3 Forgiveness, Reconciliation, and the Ministry of Atonement (2 Cor 5 : 17-21)

New creation identity empowers ministry of reconciliation, making believers ambassadors pleading, "Be reconciled to God." God made sinless Christ sin offering so that sinners become divine righteousness, extending temple atonement outward. Horizontal reconciliation—Jew/Gentile, slave/free—flows from vertical peace. Peacemaking therefore is priestly duty, not optional extra. Conflict mediation workshops become liturgical training, equipping saints to guard temple unity. Every forgiven offense echoes veil tearing, opening access between estranged parties. Thus gospel embassy operates in diplomatic immunity of grace.

10.5.4 Imitating God as Beloved Children—Temple and Family Ethics (Eph 5 : 1-5)

Paul anchors ethical imitation in adoptive love: children emulate Father by walking in Christ-like love, offering fragrant sacrifice. Sexual immorality, greed, and crude speech violate aroma, creating stench unfit for sanctuary. Thanksgiving replaces filth, redirecting desire toward Creator gifts. Household codes that follow articulate temple ethics in marriage, parenting, and labor relations. Spiritual warfare later described guards this household from demonic graffiti. Ethics thus flow from identity, not fear of law. Temple children reflect Father's holiness to watching world.

10.5.5 Walk by the Spirit vs. Defilements of the Flesh (Gal 5 : 13-26)

Freedom serves love, not license; flesh manifests envy, orgies, sorcery—echoes of pagan cults, whereas Spirit produces fruit fit for sanctuary. Crucifying flesh parallels tearing veil, removing barrier to presence. Walking by Spirit is kinetic spirituality, requiring daily step alignment. Communities that practice mutual exhortation keep in step, avoiding conceit. Legalism and libertinism both sabotage temple walk; only Spirit-led love fulfills law. Small-group accountability fosters this pilgrimage. Hence ethics are Spirit-energized, temple-framed.

10.6 Worship and Sacraments in Paul's Temple Vision

10.6.1 Lord's Supper as Covenant Meal and Temple Table (1 Cor 10-11)

Paul links cup to blood and bread to body, warning against participation in demons through idol feasts. Communion is altar fellowship where vertical union and horizontal unity intersect. Failure to discern body leads to sickness—temple judgment enacted sacramentally. Early church saw Eucharist as sacrifice of thanksgiving (*eucharistia*), not repeat of Calvary but participation in once-for-all offering. Modern debates over real presence should retain temple dimension: sacred meal mediates presence. Supper also pledges eschatological banquet, fueling mission with future feast. Thus table operates as portable holy of holies.

10.6.2 Baptism into Christ—Crossing the Threshold of the Sanctuary (Rom 6)

Through immersion believers unite with death and resurrection, passing from outer court of sin into inner life spruce. Water mirrors Red Sea and Jordan crossings, marking covenant identity. Baptism clothes believers with Christ (Gal 3 : 27), functioning like priestly vestments. Sin's dominion breaks; newness of life begins sacrificial liturgy of obedience. Therefore, baptism is entrance rite to temple community, not mere symbol. Catechesis ensures initiate understands transformative gravity. Sprinkling, pouring, or immersion all signify cleansing and union.

10.6.3 Prayer and Praise as Incense of the New Covenant (Phil 4 : 6; 1 Thess 5 : 17)

Paul commands continual prayer, echoing perpetual incense before veil. Thanksgiving and supplication ascend like aroma pleasing to God. Anxiety dissipates in sanctified atmosphere, guarding hearts. Singing in prison (Acts 16) proves incense rises even in chains. Modern worship nights replicate fragrant cloud, uniting generations. Intercession ministries stand as altar of coals, firing mission. Temple no longer smells of animal fat but of grateful praise.

10.6.4 Giving and "Fragrant Offering" (Phil 4 : 18; 2 Cor 9)

Monetary gifts sent to Paul become "acceptable sacrifice," linking generosity to Levitical smoke. Cheerful giver reflects cheerful God, turning commerce into worship. Seed-sowing yields righteousness harvest, echoing Shavuot firstfruits. Prosperity gospel distorts by promising self-gain rather than temple honor. Accountability and transparency protect aroma from corruption. Mission partnerships today continue Philippian fragrance worldwide. Thus finance table converts into altar through thankful giving.

10.6.5 Singing Psalms, Hymns, and Spiritual Songs in the Spirit (Eph 5 : 18-20)

Spirit-filled life overflows in music, addressing one another and God, transforming gatherings into choir stalls of temple. Variety of genres honors cultural diversity, embodying Pentecost multilingualism. Songs teach doctrine, admonish hearts, and enact eschatological joy. Early Christian hymns embedded Christology, shaping faith before creeds. Modern worship must balance simplicity with depth, preventing theological anemia. Sung doxology also counters idolatrous soundtracks of empire. Thus melody becomes masonry of spiritual house.

10.7 Spiritual Gifts and the Body-Temple Metaphor

10.7.1 Diversities, Services, Energies—One Spirit (1 Cor 12 : 4-11)

Paul uses triad—varieties but same Spirit/Lord/God—trinitarian foundation for gifts. Charisms serve common good, not private status. Manifestations include wisdom, knowledge, faith, healing, miracles, prophecy, discernment, tongues, interpretation, covering cognitive and power dimensions. Distributions sovereign; envy denied. Cessationist claims that power gifts ceased lack explicit biblical warrant; narrative of Acts suggests continuation. However, testing ensures authenticity. Temple vibrancy depends on both structure and supernatural electricity.

10.7.2 The Eye, Hand, and Hidden Organs—Mutual Dependence (1 Cor 12 : 12-27)

Body analogy celebrates diversity; severed members die. Weak parts receive extra honor, opposing celebrity culture. Suffering part is shared pain, prayer covering bruised organ. Mission team synergy mirrors bodily systems. Hidden intercessors pump blood of grace unseen. Absence of any gift leaves temple dim. Leaders steward environment where every part functions.

10.7.3 Five-Fold Ministries as Building Crew (Eph 4 : 11-16)

Christ gifts people to equip saints, moving church from consumer bench to construction site. Goal is maturity, measured by Christlike stature. Unity of faith and knowledge prevents childish drift by waves of doctrine. Speaking truth in love grows body, ligaments supplying. Modern churches implementing team leadership witness resilience. Apostolic pioneers, prophetic guardians, evangelistic gatherers, shepherding healers, teaching architects collaborate. Temple rises through coordinated labor.

10.7.4 Love as the More Excellent Structural Bond (1 Cor 13)

Without love, tongues, prophecy, knowledge, martyrdom profit nothing; love mortar holds bricks. Agapē's patience and kindness prevent gift collision. Love never fails; gifts cease. Therefore, supervision of charisms must prioritize affection. Doctrine of Trinity models self-giving unity. Where love cools, temple cracks. Renewal movements must guard affection above spectacle.

10.7.5 Discernment, Order, and Edification in Public Worship (1 Cor 14)

Paul's protocols balance spontaneity and structure: two or three prophets, interpreters for tongues, silence if none. Women's silence text debated, likely addressing disruptive evaluation, not universal gag. Goal is edification, involvement of mind and spirit. Visitor conviction leads to worship, confirming God is among them, temple echo. Service planning today follows similar grid: intelligibility, participation, reverence. Chaotic worship misrepresents gospel. Thus order protects presence without quenching.

10.8 Social Justice and Economic Sharing in the Temple Community

10.8.1 The Jerusalem Collection—Gentile Altar Gifts for Jewish Poor (Rom 15 : 25-27)

Paul frames offering as liturgy: Gentiles share material things after sharing spiritual heritage. Collection unites divided ethnic wings, functioning as peace offering. Travelling envoys safeguard integrity, modeling transparency. Money thus becomes sacramental adhesive, not transactional charity. Modern relief efforts replicate theology when rooted in gospel reciprocity. Economic solidarity authenticates temple gospel to skeptical world. Collection becomes portable altar crossing seas.

10.8.2 Equality "At This Present Time" (2 Cor 8 : 13-15)

Paul cites manna economy—those who gathered much had nothing left over—to argue for proportional generosity. Financial equality pictures eschatological justice, foretaste of kingdom. Voluntary, not coerced; cheerful, not grudging. Accountability teams avoid scandal. Giving completes thank-offering cycle, producing thanksgiving to God. Temple ethics transform class divides into mutual aid. Global north-south partnerships should emulate.

10.8.3 Work, Charity, and Dignity—Thessalonian Corrections (2 Thess 3 : 6-12)

Some quit work expecting imminent return; Paul commands quiet industry, earning bread. Work becomes worship when done unto Lord, funding generosity. Laziness burdens body, cracks communal walls. Church welfare incorporates discernment to avoid enabling disorder. Tent-making Paul models self-supporting ministry, freeing funds for mission. Thus temple community balances compassion and responsibility. Economics radiate holiness when aligned.

10.8.4 Philemon—Runaway Slave in the Lord's House

Paul appeals to love, not power, urging Philemon to receive Onesimus "no longer slave but beloved brother." House-church likely met in Philemon's villa; reconciliation would dramatically display temple inclusivity. Paul hints at manumission without law but through gospel logic. Letter transforms social hierarchy by inserting cross into master-slave dynamic. Modern labor justice finds template here. Temple walls cannot house oppression. Freedom rings where Spirit dwells.

10.8.5 Hospitality and the Temple of Open Doors (Rom 12 : 13)

"Pursue hospitality" (*philoxenia*) commands love of stranger, echoing Abraham's tent and Passover ethos. Early Christians sheltered missionaries and plague victims, spreading gospel. Hospitality evidences temple presence to outsiders, functioning as living porch of Gentiles. Practices include meals, guest rooms, refugee sponsorship. Digital hospitality now extends welcome through online gatherings. In a xenophobic age, open homes testify to boundary-breaking temple. Every table set is altar extension.

10.9 Suffering, Persecution, and the Future Temple

10.9.1 "We Are the Temple—Yet We Groan" (2 Cor 4 : 7-12)

Clay jars house treasure, revealing surpassing power belongs to God. Afflicted yet not crushed, body carries death so life works in others. Suffering becomes liturgy, displaying cruciform glory. Temple therefore luminous amid cracks, drawing gaze to Architect. Modern martyrs continue incense of witness. Comfort theology must integrate groaning without despair. Glory shines through fissures.

10.9.2 Present Afflictions vs. Eternal Weight of Glory (2 Cor 4 : 17)

Momentary troubles produce incomparable glory, phrase borrowing commercial scales image. Light vs. weight underscores disproportion of suffering and reward. Vision of unseen sustains temple builders under siege. Persecuted church testimonies validate promise. Hope inoculates against bitterness. Glory weight equates to Shekinah heaviness, final filling. Suffering hands shape future pillars.

10.9.3 Martyrdom as Drink Offering Poured on the Sacrifice (Phil 2 : 17)

Paul envisions execution complementing Philippians' faith offering, echoing temple libations. Blood becomes worship fragrance, not tragic waste. Joy paradoxically accompanies potential beheading. Church father Ignatius adopts same imagery en route to lions. Martyr narratives fuel missionary zeal. Temple history crowned by Lamb slain, so servants follow. Death seeds resurrection harvest.

10.9.4 Creation's Liberation, Glory Revealed in the Sons of God (Rom 8 : 18-23)

Whole cosmos awaits temple sons unveiled, linking ecological hope to resurrection. Suffering labor pangs precede birth of renewed heavens and earth. Spirit firstfruits guarantee delivery, encouraging environmental stewardship. Climate action aligns with redemption trajectory, not secular panic. Believers plant gardens as prophetic acts. Temple extends to biosphere, sanctifying soil. Glory liberation encompasses galaxies.

10.9.5 New Creation and the Temple-City Hope (1 Cor 15; Eph 1 : 10)

Resurrection chapter climaxes with immortal, imperishable body, fitting for eternal temple service. God's plan to sum up all things in Christ merges spatial and temporal reality into cosmic sanctuary. Inheritance reserved propels mission until consummation. City coming down signifies heaven-earth wedding, temple dissolved into ubiquitous presence. Work in Lord not vain; bricks laid now shine in future walls. Thus eschatology energizes present labor. Hope completes temple blueprint.

In Conclusion, Paul's pen sketched no blueprints of marble columns or cedar beams, yet his letters drew a sanctuary grander than Herod's and more enduring than Solomon's. In his gospel-shaped imagination, every baptized body became a chamber of glory, every gathered congregation a load-bearing wall, every generous gift a sweet-smelling sacrifice, and every act of Spirit-empowered love a stone set by the cosmic Cornerstone Himself. Suffering could crack jars but only released the hidden treasure; persecution could scatter assemblies but merely spread the fragrance of Christ into new streets and languages. Across two millennia the structure has risen— sometimes marred by schism, often renovated by revival—yet always anchored to the same foundation that no earthquake of empire, ideology, or unbelief has managed to unsettle. Our age, swirling with bioethical quandaries, ecological groans, and racial fractures, still waits for people who know themselves as temples—holy, hospitable, and hopeful—to stand in its ruins and rebuild. May the Spirit who once breathed through apostolic tents fill our lungs again, so that the world beholds, even through cracked bricks, the light of a dwelling place whose architect and builder is God.

Chapter 11 - Worship in the Spiritual Temple

Worship is humanity's most primal vocation, the very hum that permeated Eden's garden before any liturgy was codified or choir rehearsed, yet biblical history reveals that worship must continually be rescued from distortion and re-anchored in living fellowship with God. The prophets thundered that festivals without justice nauseated the Lord (Isa 1 : 11-17); Jesus overturned tables when commerce eclipsed prayer in his Father's house (Mark 11 : 15-17); and Paul insisted that songs, sacraments, and service all stand or fall on cruciform love (1 Cor 13). When the Spirit descended at Pentecost, every believer became a chamber in a distributed sanctuary, initiating a paradigm in which true worship is measured less by locale, instrument, or calendar than by Spirit-empowered fidelity to Christ's story and character. This chapter therefore explores how that new-temple reality reshapes the full range of Christian devotion—from gathered liturgy to household rhythms, from artistic expression to public justice, from daily work to cosmic hope. Our exploration follows the logic of Scripture rather than the blueprint of any one denomination, pausing at apostolic house-churches, patristic hymns, Reformation prayer books, Holiness camp-meetings, and global-South worship tents to glean insights for life in the Spirit's temple today. Throughout we will hold two questions in creative tension: **What must never change because it anchors us in the apostolic**

foundation, and what may change because the Spirit delights to sing through many timbres and tongues? By the end, the reader should sense that every heartbeat, workplace task, lament psalm, and act of neighborly mercy can resonate as holy music in the living sanctuary of God.

11.1 Theological Foundations: Presence, Priesthood, and Participation

11.1.1 Shekinah Relocated: From Physical Sanctuary to Indwelling Spirit (Eph 2 : 22)

Israel's priests once watched a visible cloud settle between cherubim wings, but Paul claims that the same glory now "dwells in you together as a habitation of God in the Spirit," relocating sacred presence from wood-and-stone architecture to a Spirit-knit people. This transfer is not a downgrade; it is the fulfillment of Yahweh's stated yearning to walk among His people and be their God (Lev 26 : 11-12). Because holiness is no longer quarantined, worship bursts prison walls, kitchen doors, and Zoom screens with equal legitimacy, challenging modern Christians to honor everyday spaces as potential burning bushes. Yet indwelling never trivializes God's transcendence; the consuming fire of Sinai still flares within, purifying motives and exposing idols. Corporate identity remains crucial, for Paul's "you" is plural, warning against individualism that treats spirituality as a private commodity. Whenever believers gather—even timidly in a dorm room—the promise of Emmanuel acquires new coordinates on earth's map. Thus every act of worship begins by acknowledging the shocking proximity of Shekinah dwelling in redeemed clay vessels.

11.1.2 The Royal Priesthood of All Believers (1 Pet 2 : 5-9)

Peter lifts language once reserved for Levites and applies it to persecuted house servants and immigrant artisans, insisting that birth in Christ outranks birth into Aaron's line. This democratizing move means incense no longer rises only from ordained hands; intercession, proclamation, and blessing belong to every Spirit-sealed saint. Far from rendering leadership obsolete, universal priesthood multiplies ministry, turning pastors into equipers rather than spiritual middlemen. The call is royal as well as priestly, signaling delegated authority to steward creation and push back darkness through truth and mercy. Because the priesthood is corporate, jealousy of gifting becomes self-mutilation, like priests arresting fellow priests at the altar they share. Baptism functions as ordination service in this new order, plunging believers into both privilege and responsibility. Therefore, any worship model that sidelines laity contradicts the temple reality inaugurated by Christ and proclaimed by His apostles.

11.1.3 "Reasonable Worship" and Living Sacrifice (Rom 12 : 1-2)

Paul's appeal to present bodies as living sacrifices combines temple, martyr, and vocation imagery in a single stroke, redefining worship as whole-life response to divine mercy. The adjective *logikēn* (reasonable or spiritual) hints that this offering engages intellect as well as emotion, dismantling the false dichotomy between doctrine and doxology. Transformation comes not by tweaking behaviors but by recalibrating imagination through gospel-saturated thinking, which then spills into distinct ethics. Crucially, the sacrifice is collective— "present *your* bodies"—suggesting choir rather than soloist, mosaic rather than isolated tile. Unlike dead animals on ancient altars, living sacrifices keep squirming; daily submission thus becomes ongoing liturgy that may require career choices, click-habits, or retirement plans to ascend as fragrant smoke. Paul positions this lifestyle against "the pattern of this age," implying that true worship is counter-cultural, challenging consumerism, nationalism, and every idol that seeks censer swing. In short, new-temple worship is a lifelong burnt offering of mind renewed, heart inflamed, and body engaged.

11.1.4 Trinitarian Shape of Worship: To the Father, Through the Son, By the Spirit

Christian liturgy is not a generic upward reach but a participation in triune life: the Spirit inspires, the Son mediates, and the Father receives (Eph 2 : 18). When prayers end "in Jesus' name," they confess reliance on His priestly worth rather than rhetorical flair. Spirit empowerment prevents mechanical repetition by breathing spontaneity and affection into inherited forms, guarding against both dead ritualism and formless chaos. The Father's fatherhood gifts worship security; adoration is not begging a capricious deity but delighting in One who already runs down the road to embrace prodigals. Neglecting any Person skews worship: Spirit-forgetful gatherings become cerebral; Son-forgetful gatherings drift into

227

mystical vagueness; Father-forgetful liturgies lose tenderness. Historic creeds and modern choruses alike flourish when consciously saturated with triune grammar. Thus the spiritual temple rings harmoniously only when Father, Son, and Spirit each receive melodic due.

11.1.5 Already/Not-Yet Tension: Earthly Assembly as a Foretaste of the Heavenly Liturgy (Heb 12 : 22-24)

Hebrews dares to say that believers "have come" (perfect tense) to Mount Zion, angelic choirs, and the sprinkled blood—present reality—while also urging endurance until future rest. Sunday worship therefore doubles as embassy reception for a kingdom still arriving, blending lament for broken earth with anticipation of healed cosmos. This tension allows both exuberant hallelujahs and groaning intercession, resisting sterile optimism and cynical despair alike. Historical liturgies capture the paradox by pairing Kyrie-eleison with Gloria-in-excelsis, confession with absolution, Good Friday solemnity with Easter shout. Prophetic art, justice activism, and hospitality toward refugees extend heavenly table crumbs into starving present, hinting at banquet to come. Because future reality is secure, the church can take generous risks now, spending itself in love rather than hoarding candles for some later cathedral. Thus every gathering is both rehearsal dinner and rescue mission, tasting tomorrow's wine while passing cups to a thirsty world.

11.2 Apostolic Patterns: Word, Table, Prayer, and Praise

11.2.1 Didachē of the Apostles: Teaching as Liturgical Backbone (Acts 2 : 42)

The Jerusalem believers devoted themselves first to apostolic teaching, demonstrating that revelation, not ambiance, constructs the inner sanctum of worship. Scripture read and explained functions like a lampstand, illuminating Christ's face so that songs and sacraments orbit gospel truth rather than emotional nostalgia. Catechesis in early house-churches included reciting salvation history, memorizing psalms, and rehearsing baptismal creeds, thereby forming doctrinal immunity against Gnostic or imperial counter-stories. Modern worship planners err when they treat sermons as interchangeable TED-talks; the temple paradigm insists that bread and wine, prophecy and compassion, all draw life from the spoken Word. Because teaching belongs to the Spirit's gift list, congregations must pray for anointed clarity, whether delivered from a pulpit, living-room circle, or video stream. Interactive settings, question-and-response, and testimony weaving can echo Paul's dialogue into midnight at Troas (Acts 20 : 7-12) without abandoning reverence. In short, Word-centered liturgy is not information dump but the very scaffolding on which worship architecture rises.

11.2.2 Breaking Bread from House to House: Early Eucharistic Shapes

Luke's compressed phrase "breaking bread" captures both ordinary meals and sacramental remembrance, suggesting a blurred line between kitchen table and Lord's Table. First-century believers reclined around common platters, blessing God for creation and redemption before sharing bread identified with Jesus' body (1 Cor 11 : 23-26). Because slaves and patrons ate together, social hierarchies were inverted, turning supper into enacted parable of kingdom equality. Contemporary house-churches, refugee camps, and cathedral parishes alike honor this legacy when they prioritize welcome over formality and unity over aesthetic uniformity. Frequency debates—weekly, monthly, daily—should serve the goal of nourishing faith rather than protecting tradition for its own sake. Portable communion kits used on hospital wards reflect new-temple mobility; conversely, festivals with ornate vessels remind that beauty, too, belongs in worship. Every loaf uplifted whispers both crucifixion and banquet-to-come, anchoring the community between memory and hope.

11.2.3 Fixed-Hour Prayer and the Legacy of the Temple Hours (Acts 3 : 1)

Peter and John's continued attendance at the ninth-hour prayers shows that the gospel did not discard rhythms of petition; it infused them with Christ's mediation. Early Christians adapted synagogue Shacharit, Mincha, and Ma'ariv into morning, afternoon, and evening offices, later crystallizing in monastic hours that still steady contemporary lives via apps and breviaries. Such structure resists frenetic modernity by punctuating time with doxology, reminding believers that the day is God's liturgical canvas. Fixed hours also unite scattered saints; a nurse whispering Psalm 103 at dawn shares unseen fellowship with monks chanting the same text across oceans. Yet spontaneity complements routine: earthquake prayers, roadside blessings, and breath-length thanksgivings guard against sterile clock-watching. Family mealtime graces, workplace "pause and pray," and digital gatherings at noon embody temple incense rising continuously. Thus fixed-hour devotion threads heaven's fragrance through the ordinary fabric of daily schedules.

11.2.4 Psalms, Hymns, and Spiritual Songs (Eph 5 : 19; Col 3 : 16)

Paul distinguishes but does not rigidly separate three song streams: Israel's psalter anchoring theology, crafted hymns embedding Christology, and spontaneous Spirit songs ventilating fresh gratitude. Psalms carry generations of lament and praise, legitimizing emotions often censored by triumphalist culture; hymns like Philippians 2 : 6-11 teach doctrine through melody; spiritual songs open space for prophetic exhortation. Healthy liturgy balances these sources, preventing both museum-piece nostalgia and shallow novelty. Music in the spiritual temple transcends performance when congregation joins as choir, echoing angelic worship that values participation over virtuosity. Cross-cultural instrumentation—from djembe to oud, sitar to cello—embodies Pentecost's multilingual faith, provided lyrics uphold gospel truth. Singing "to one another" forms believers, but singing "to the Lord" centers gaze above communal affirmation, guarding against self-referential artistry. When music serves Word and Table, it becomes sacramental bridge between theology and affection.

11.2.5 Charism and Order: Prophecy, Tongues, and Discernment in Corporate Worship (1 Cor 14)

Corinth's exuberance forced Paul to establish traffic laws for spiritual gifts so that edification, not spectacle, governed gatherings. He celebrated tongues as private prayer booster yet prioritized intelligible prophecy for corporate strengthening, thus valuing emotional fervor and cognitive clarity together. Three-speaker limits, interpretation requirements, and mutual weighing of prophecies show that order is not antithetical to Spirit spontaneity. Modern worship inherits the challenge: nurture openness to divine interruption while safeguarding theological accuracy and pastoral safety. Tools include elder oversight, after-service debriefs, and teaching on gift discernment, cultivating maturity rather than quenching zeal. Because new-temple worship is relational, any charismatic expression should increase love for God and neighbor or else be gently parked. Properly stewarded, prophetic insight and prayer languages enrich liturgy with awe and intimacy, reminding the church that God still walks the aisles of His sanctuary.

11.3 Scripture in the Spiritual Temple

11.3.1 Public Reading and Exposition (1 Tim 4 : 13)

Paul charges Timothy to devote himself to the public reading of Scripture, echoing synagogue tradition where Torah scrolls were central furniture. Lectionary reading democratizes revelation, ensuring that even illiterate members hear the breadth of God's counsel. Exposition translates ancient text into present obedience, bridging cultural distance with Spirit illumination. The pulpit therefore is not lecture podium but temple lectern, from which divine voice resonates into corporate conscience. Interactive Q&As, dramatic readings, and multilingual recitations can revitalize hearing without diluting authority. Neglecting Scripture starves worship—even music-centric services decay into sentimentalism if detached from canonical anchor. Thus, the spiritual temple keeps a Bible open on its table, pages fluttering like the veil torn open for all nations.

11.3.2 The Christological Lens: Law, Prophets, Psalms Fulfilled (Luke 24 : 27)

On Emmaus road Jesus re-reads Moses and prophets with Himself as thesis, unveiling a hermeneutic that the apostles would employ everywhere. This lens prevents moralistic or nationalist misappropriations by locating every covenant, exodus, and promise in crucified-risen Messiah. Consequently, worship planning anchored in lectionary or sermon series should trace gospel threads, not cherry-pick inspirational verses. Christ-centered reading also fuels adoration; seeing Him foreshadowed in Joseph or echoed in Isaiah turns exegesis into doxology. Misreading Scripture eclipses worship: Pharisees searched writings yet missed Life standing before them (John 5 : 39-40). Therefore, worship leaders become tour guides, pointing out Christological vistas so congregants leave services saying, "Did not our hearts burn within us?" (Luke 24 : 32). This burning constitutes core temperature of temple life.

11.3.3 Memorisation and Chant: Carrying the Word into Daily Work

Ancient Israelites strapped verses on arms; medieval monks sang psalms while plowing; persecuted believers today recite hidden chapters in prison. Memorized Scripture turns the soul into walking scroll, ready for spontaneous prayer and witnessing. Chanting harnesses rhythm and melody to embed text beyond mental effort, aiding dementia patients and preschoolers alike. Apps and flashcards modernize the practice, yet physical communal recitation guards against privatized spirituality. When workers quote Colossians 3 while coding software or changing diapers, the factory floor becomes annex of holy court. Word inside believers also safeguards against manipulation by false teaching. Thus memorisation is not trivia pursuit but temple maintenance.

11.3.4 Lectionaries Ancient and Modern: Guarding the Whole Counsel of God

From synagogue triennial cycles to fourth-century Roman lectionaries and 1960s Revised Common Lectionary, structured readings protect worship from hobby-horse preaching. They weave Old Testament, psalm, epistle, and gospel into dialogic tapestry, letting Scripture interpret Scripture. Free-churches adopting lectio continua still benefit by planning series through whole books rather than cherry-picking themes. Lectionaries also unite global church; on a given Sunday millions meditate on identical passages, amplifying corporate resonance. Flexibility remains: pastoral crises may warrant deviation, and Spirit can highlight a neglected text. Still, long-term diet safeguards against theological malnutrition. Therefore, spiritual temples stock pantry with balanced scriptural nutrients.

3.5 Story, Symbol, and Sacrament: How Scripture Shapes Ritual Action

Biblical narratives birth rituals: Passover meal, baptismal water, foot-washing basin. Symbols without story become superstitions; story without symbol risks abstraction. When worship enacts Scripture—processional palm branches, Advent candles, justice marches echoing Exodus—it trains bodies as well as minds. Children grasp gospel through embodied practices long before doctrinal nuance. Visual storytelling via banners or projection art can frame sermons within salvation chronology. Thus Scripture supplies not only content but choreography for temple liturgy. Word and act dance together, leading believers into holistic encounter.

11.4 The Table of the Lord: Eucharist as Covenant Renewal

11.4.1 Passover Roots and New-Covenant Meal (1 Cor 11 : 23-26)

Jesus chose the dense symbolism of Passover to institute a meal where lamb, exodus, and covenant converge, transforming deliverance from Pharaoh into deliverance from sin. Paul's rehearsal of the tradition shows early Eucharist already functioning as non-negotiable gospel proclamation—"you proclaim the Lord's death until he comes." Trans-historical dimension ensures each supper connects upper room, present assembly, and marriage banquet of the Lamb. Unlike temple sacrifices consumed wholly by fire, this meal feeds worshipers, dramatizing grace received not earned. Thus absence from table due to apathy undermines covenant intimacy, while exclusion of marginalized violates meal's inclusive DNA. Whether elements are leavened or gluten-free, poured into silver chalice or paper cup, the Spirit supersedes culinary variance to deliver Christ's real sustenance. Consequently, Eucharist remains heartbeat of spiritual-temple worship.

11.4.2 Real Presence, Memorial, and Communio: Theological Streams Compared

Historic debates—transubstantiation, consubstantiation, memorialism—reflect attempts to safeguard mystery from distortion, each emphasizing different biblical facets. While agreement exists that Christ is uniquely present, mechanisms differ: Catholics invoke ontological change, Lutherans stress sacramental union, Reformed highlight spiritual participation, and Baptist traditions recall covenant memory. Rather than fueling division, the new-temple lens encourages charitable dialogue, focusing on shared aim of communion with Christ and one another. Ecumenical documents like the Lima text (1982) show convergence on thanksgiving, remembrance, and anticipation elements. Local congregations can teach multiple interpretations, strengthening catholicity without compromising conscience. Whatever view, reverence is obligatory; casual attitudes reduce sacred feast to snack bar. Therefore, theological humility paired with doxological fervor best honors the Table's profundity.

11.4.3 Discern the Body: Unity, Holiness, and Social Boundaries

Paul rebukes Corinth for hasty eating that ignores poor members, calling such practice "not the Lord's supper" (1 Cor 11 : 20-22). Discerning the body means recognizing both the crucified Lord in the elements and His multi-ethnic, socio-economic body gathered. Fencing the table through confession invites sober preparation, while open invitation to repentant sinners displays grace. Modern challenges include dietary allergies, pandemic protocols, and virtual services, each demanding creative fidelity. Shared cup and loaf, when possible, embody physical unity; multiple stations or intinction can preserve symbolism amid logistics. Beyond ritual, the body test extends to economic ethics—church budgets, wage practices, and global supply chains. Thus Eucharist critiques individualistic piety and forces communal accountability.

11.4.4 Eucharist and Mission: From Table Blessing to World Blessing

Early church fathers described the dismissal as *missa*—sending—turning inward meal outward. Fed by Christ, believers feed hungry neighbors, echoing post-resurrection breakfast where Jesus cooks fish for tired disciples. Some traditions reserve consecrated elements for hospital visitation, extending table grace to bedridden saints. Others break service flow to collect alms immediately after communion, linking sacrament and justice. Missionaries celebrate Eucharist on frontiers, proclaiming that no land remains outside kingdom banquet invitation. Thus, table fellowship propels evangelism, healing, and cultural reconciliation. The cycle of gathering and scattering mirrors temple priests who entered holy place then exited to bless people.

11.4.5 Frequency, Context, and Creativity: Home, Sanctuary, Outdoors

Acts hints at daily breaking of bread, while later Didache permits weekly; modern practice varies from quarterly to multiple times a Sunday. Arguments for frequency include constant gospel reminder; arguments for breadth warn against trivialization. House-church contexts foster intimate participation; cathedral settings spark transcendent awe; open-air communion at protest rallies signal that Christ's reign challenges injustice. COVID-19 sparked debate on virtual Eucharist; some embraced "distance but real," others paused, highlighting embodiment theology. Creativity must respect biblical anchor: bread and cup, Word proclamation, gathered community (even if via desperate technology). Ultimately, Spirit guides churches to rhythms that nourish without legalism. Thus the table's portability ensures worship adapts to exile or prosperity alike.

11.5 The Sacrifice of Praise: Music and the Arts

11.5.1 Biblical Theology of Song: From Moses' Sea-Song to the New-Song of Revelation

Witnesses of Red Sea deliverance erupted in the oldest recorded biblical hymn (Ex 15), establishing praise as reflex to salvation. David institutionalized musical worship by appointing Levite choirs (1 Chr 15), linking monarchy with melody. Prophets envisioned renewed song (Isa 42 : 10) and Revelation fulfills with multi-ethnic anthem around the throne (Rev 5 : 9). Thus, singing spans covenant epochs, stitching acts of God into memory of His people. When the church forgets to sing, amnesia threatens identity; when it sings lies, idolatry masquerades as devotion. Therefore, songwriting is priestly labor requiring scriptural fidelity and poetic beauty. New temples resound with songs old and new, local and global, lament and jubilation.

11.5.2 Cultural Instruments in the Temple of the Nations (Ps 150; Rev 5 : 9)

Psalm 150's trumpet, lute, and cymbals signal sonic diversity sanctified for Yahweh, prefiguring every cultural instrument praising the Lamb. African drums, Korean *gayageum*, Andean *charango*, and EDM synths can join if employed for edification, not self-glory. Authentic contextualization resists colonial worship aesthetics that suppress indigenous sound. Quality musicianship honors Creator excellence, yet congregational accessibility should guide arrangement to avoid spectator concerts. Ethnomusicology aids missionaries in crafting worship that echoes local heartbeat without syncretism. Because sound waves know no ethnic barrier, the Spirit orchestrates global symphony glorifying Christ. Thus, temple acoustics comprise humanity's full register.

11.5.3 The Prophetic Role of Worship Arts: Lament, Protest, and Hope

Songs like Psalm 137 cry for justice amid exile, demonstrating that worship can voice anguish and resistance. Negro spirituals coded escape routes and eschatological hope, illustrating music's subversive power. Modern protest hymns address racism, trafficking, and ecological devastation, refusing to let sanctuary cloister believers from world pain. Artists act as watchmen, giving melody to groans of creation (Rom 8 : 22). However, prophetic art must remain anchored in Scripture lest righteous anger sour into partisan rage. Balanced liturgy weaves lament with promise, ensuring hope outlasts despair. In this way worship becomes both mirror and catalyst for kingdom justice.

11.5.4 Visual, Dramatic, and Digital Arts in the New Temple

Tabernacle artisans were Spirit-filled craftsmen (Ex 31), legitimizing creative vocation. Icons, murals, and stained glass have taught the illiterate, while modern projection mapping and film evoke awe and story. Drama revives parables; dance embodies psalms; graphic design extends liturgy to Instagram feeds. Artists require pastoral guidance to keep beauty tethered to truth, resisting vanity. Artistic collaboration across generations enriches community, but token inclusion hampers excellence—investment and discipleship are key. New-media worship raises questions about screens' effects on attention; discernment steers between Luddite fear and uncritical adoption. Properly stewarded, arts vivify temple worship for digital natives and traditionalists alike.

11.5.5 Guarding Substance over Style: The Heart-Formation Test

Style wars—hymns vs. choruses, organ vs. guitar—often mask deeper anxieties about identity, authority, and change. Jesus evaluated worship by heart posture (John 4 : 23), not tempo or attire. Liturgical planners therefore ask: Does this element magnify Christ, root believers in gospel, and cultivate love for neighbor? Nostalgia can sanctify sentimental artifacts; novelty can idolize relevance; wisdom holds both loosely. Congregational surveys, theological audits, and inter-generational dialogue foster healthy adaptation. Spiritual fruit—repentance, joy, generosity—offers better metric than Spotify statistics. When style serves substance, worship renews hearts and glorifies God.

11.6 Prayer and Intercession: Incense of the Saints

11.6.1 Lord's Prayer as Template for Temple Petitions (Matt 6 : 9-13)

Jesus' model prayer begins with adoration ("hallowed"), aligns with kingdom mission, requests provision, pleads forgiveness, and seeks deliverance—comprehensive liturgical arc. Addressing God as Father roots prayer in covenant intimacy; acknowledging heaven's throne preserves reverence. Corporate pronouns ("our," "us") reinforce communal identity even in private devotion. Early church recited this prayer thrice daily, weaving it into rhythm of work and rest. Contemporary worship re-melodies the prayer, but content remains bedrock syllabus. Each petition invites expansion: "daily bread" covers paychecks, justice, and manna of Word. Using the prayer restructures self-centered supplication into kingdom-shaped intercession.

11.6.2 Continuous Intercession: "Pray without Ceasing" (1 Thess 5 : 17)

Ceaseless prayer seems impossible until viewed as relational attentiveness—like lovers exchanging glances amid errands. Brother Lawrence's kitchen insights and modern mindfulness apps train awareness of divine presence. Arrow prayers ("Lord, help!") complement set devotions, permeating mundane moments with worship. Corporate expressions include 24-7 prayer rooms where believers sign hourly watches, fulfilling incense metaphor (Rev 8 : 4). Digital platforms coordinate global vigils for crises, embodying temple's priestly watch. Saturation in prayer cultivates humility: needs surface, idols shatter, hope rises. Thus prayer transforms worshippers into incense bearers for a fractured world.

11.6.3 Groaning with the Spirit and High-Priestly Advocacy (Rom 8 : 26-27; Heb 7 : 25)

When language fails, Spirit intercedes with wordless groans, echoing Jesus' tears at Lazarus' tomb; divine empathy meets human limitation. Christ's perpetual intercession guarantees prayer's audience, rendering every whispered plea a co-labor with heaven. Awareness of this duet combats despair when petitions seem unanswered; timing belongs to wiser counsel. Contemplative silence can host this groaning, allowing Spirit to shape desires before words form. Combining charismatics' tongues and contemplatives' stillness offers holistic participation in heavenly advocacy. Because groaning anticipates redemption, lament becomes faith act not unbelief. Thus prayer embodies both priesthood and patient hope.

11.6.4 Fasting, Vigil, and Silent Contemplation: Historic Streams

Fasting subordinates appetite to longing for God, aligning worship with justice when resources saved aid hungry neighbors (Isa 58). Night vigils recall temple watchmen, providing space for travailing prayer and prophetic listening. Silent contemplation resists noise addiction, allowing "still small voice" to heal inner fragmentation (1 Kgs 19 : 12). Monastic movements preserved these disciplines, while Pentecostal tarry meetings reignited them with expectancy. Balance is key: asceticism untethered from grace breeds pride; silence untethered from Word invites confusion. Local churches can weave seasons of fasting and retreats into calendar, keeping disciplines accessible. In doing so they honor ancient wells that refresh contemporary thirst.

11.6.5 Global Prayer Movements: 24-7 Rooms and Digital Upper Rooms

The late-1990s 24-7 Prayer movement repurposed dilapidated spaces into incense factories, sparking missions like Prayer Rooms on Ibiza's club strip. COVID-19 accelerated online prayer, uniting believers across time zones via video platforms. Apps like Lectio 365 deliver daily rhythms, integrating Scripture, reflection, and petition into commuters' earbuds. Critics warn of screen fatigue; leaders respond with hybrid models blending digital access and embodied gatherings. Such movements democratize leadership, empowering youth and laity to host prayer watches. Stories of salvations, justice initiatives, and church plants flow from these virtual upper rooms, validating model. They illustrate the spiritual temple's capacity to expand without geographic constraint.

11.7 Everyday Liturgy: Work, Rest, and Ordinary Life

11.7.1 Vocation as Worship: Craftsmanship in the Spirit (Col 3 : 23)

Paul exhorts slaves—and by extension all workers—to serve "the Lord Christ," reframing mundane labor as liturgical offering. The Spirit who gifted Bezalel to build tabernacle (Ex 31) now inspires teachers, engineers, and baristas to craft excellence that honors Creator and blesses neighbor. Viewing spreadsheets or diapers as altar transforms attitudes toward boredom and status. Marketplace ministry does not reduce evangelism to sales pitch; rather, integrity, creativity, and justice radiate worship aroma. Corporate culture critiques arise when profit tramples dignity; believers become prophetic voices shaping ethical policies. Sabbath rest balances zeal, affirming that worship includes rhythmic cessation. Thus, vocation and worship interlock in the spiritual temple.

11.7.2 Sabbath Rhythms and Counter-Cultural Rest (Heb 4 : 9-11)

While Christ fulfills ultimate rest, weekly Sabbath practice remains signpost pointing to eternal shalom. Intentional pause resists productivity idol, declaring trust in God's provision. Families craft rituals—candles, blessing prayer, technology fast—that re-humanize time. Communities practicing communal rest inspire ecological care by lowering consumption cycles. Activists burn out without sabbath; worship requires breathing room for delight and contemplation. Controversies over day or strictness yield to principle of restorative cadence. Therefore, sabbath stands as act of worshipful defiance against 24/7 economies.

11.7.3 Hospitality and Table-Fellowship as Holy Practice (Rom 12 : 13)

Opening homes to stranger enacts gospel welcome, mirroring God's hospitality in Christ. Early church growth thrived around shared meals, with house-hosts like Lydia leveraging space for kingdom advance (Acts 16 : 15). Hospitality dismantles social barriers, allowing rich and poor, native and immigrant to taste kingdom together. Practical challenges—meal prep, safety—become offerings, training generosity muscles. When marginalized find seat at believer's table, they encounter spiritual temple's warmth before stepping into sanctuary building. Holiday feasts for single adults, refugee housing, and college-student brunches incarnate God's open-door heart. Thus hospitality transforms dining rooms into echoes of eschatological banquet hall.

11.7.4 Marriage, Parenting, and Friendship within the Household of God

Paul likens Christ-church union to marriage, making spousal fidelity a living parable of covenant grace (Eph 5 : 22-33). Parenting nurtures future worshipers through catechism, bedtime blessings, and modeling forgiveness, spreading temple legacy inter-generationally (Deut 6 : 6-7). Friendships grounded in confession and encouragement act as inner courtyards where honesty meets mercy. Singles contribute unique devotion and flexibility, embodying eschatological family where marriage is not ultimate. Conflict resolution at home trains skills transferable to church life, preventing Sunday veneer over weekday dysfunction. Household codes in Colossians and Ephesians locate daily relationships within Lord's sovereignty, dignifying chores as worship. Thus the spiritual temple is built one conversation, diaper, and apology at a time.

11.7.5 Blessing and Benediction in Public Spaces: Marketplace Temples

Priestly blessing of Numbers 6 commissioned Israelites to carry Yahweh's name outward; likewise, believers pronounce peace over cafés, boardrooms, and bus drivers. Short blessings—"God's joy on your day"—seed secular spaces with sacred possibility. Artists chalk sidewalk verses; farmers pray over fields; students bless campus halls before exams. Such practices reject private-faith ghetto, recognizing earth as the Lord's (Ps 24 : 1). Benediction combats curse language saturating media, offering alternative kingdom narrative. Civic leaders appreciate employees who radiate gratitude, indirectly drawing hearts to Christ. In this way the temple moves through city streets on two feet.

11.8 Justice and Mercy: Ethical Worship in the Prophetic Tradition

11.8.1 "Learn to Do Good": Isaiah's Critique of Empty Liturgy (Isa 1 : 11-17)

Isaiah's scorching sarcasm against sacrifices divorced from justice reverberates whenever churches sing loud yet ignore systemic oppression. The prophet's triad—seek justice, defend orphan, plead widow—sets minimal litmus for acceptable worship. Jesus echoes in Matthew 23 : 23, indicting tithe-meticulous Pharisees who neglect mercy. Therefore, liturgy that comforts without confronting injustice fails temple mandate. Practical steps include partnering with local advocacy groups, auditing church purchasing for fair-trade compliance, and integrating lament psalms addressing societal sin. Confession rites can name racism, abuse, and greed, leading to corporate repentance. When worship merges piety and justice, the Spirit's temple shines credibility.

11.8.2 Economic Generosity as Fragrant Offering (Phil 4 : 18; 2 Cor 9)

Paul describes Philippian financial support as "a fragrant aroma, acceptable sacrifice," shifting sacrificial locus to generosity. Cheerful giving resists scarcity mindset, trusting God's supply to seed multiplications of righteousness. Budget transparency and stewardship classes equip congregants to live open-handed. Debt-forgiveness campaigns and micro-loan funds reflect jubilee motif, preaching gospel to wallets. Generosity crosses borders through disaster relief and missionary partnership, extending temple fragrance globally. Wealth inequality inside church undermines witness; fostering economic equity restores credibility. Thus money trails map worship authenticity.

11.8.3 Racial Reconciliation and One-New-Humanity Worship (Eph 2 : 14-18)

Christ shattered dividing wall to craft one new humanity; segregated worship therefore contradicts accomplished fact. Multi-ethnic leadership, shared stories, and lament for historical injustices foster healing. Musical blending of cultural styles honors diverse stones in temple mosaic. Anti-racism discipleship groups expose blind spots, aligning hearts with kingdom family. Hospitality across cultural lines transforms theory into friendship. God's glory seeks to dwell where brothers live in unity (Ps 133). Reconciled worship anticipates multi-lingual throne-room anthem.

11.8.4 Creation Care as Temple Stewardship (Rom 8 : 19-23)

If earth is footstool of God (Isa 66 : 1), pollution desecrates sanctuary flooring. Worship services that recycle, conserve energy, and teach stewardship embody gospel beyond words. Community gardens, tree-planting liturgies, and plastic-free communion sets witness to hope of new creation. Sabbath rest models sustainable rhythms opposing consumer exploitation. The Spirit groans with creation; believers join intercession by protecting biodiversity. Environmental justice intersects with poverty alleviation, since marginalized suffer most from ecological harms. Thus creation care is not trendy add-on but integral temple duty.

11.8.5 Public Advocacy, Lament, and the Noise of Justice (Amos 5 : 21-24)

Amos declares God prefers justice rolling like rivers over elaborate worship festivals, urging public policy engagement. Christian advocates lobby for fair housing, criminal-justice reform, and anti-trafficking laws as extensions of priestly mandate. Prayer marches and lament services translate prophetic grief into civic conscience. Petitioning officials, writing editorials, and voting become liturgical acts when done for neighbor love. Danger lies in partisan captivity; prophetic allegiance stays with kingdom ethics above party tags. Holy noise of justice disrupts comfortable pews, steering worshippers from sentiment to sacrificial solidarity. Thus temple worship reverberates in city hall as well as sanctuary.

11.9 Spiritual Warfare and Purity of the Temple

11.9.1 Cleansing the Courts: Confession, Repentance, and Discipline (1 Pet 4 : 17)

Judgment begins at God's household; therefore, regular self-examination prevents slow rot of hypocrisy. Corporate confession liturgies allow sin exposure under gospel safety, while accountability groups apply specifics. Church discipline, though painful, protects weaker sheep and preserves witness, mirroring surgical removal of infected tissue. Restoration aims dominate over punishment, reflecting shepherd's heart. Leaders must model vulnerability, confessing publicly when appropriate. Annual vision retreats can include repentance for mission neglect or staff burnout. Healthy cleansing invites deeper indwelling presence.

11.9.2 Armor of God Liturgically Worn (Eph 6 : 10-18)

Paul's armor imagery draws from Isaiah's divine warrior; believers wear gospel shoes and salvation helmet in daily battles. Some churches enact donning armor in kids' ministry or morning prayers, reinforcing spiritual readiness. Truth belt counters relativism; righteousness breastplate guards against shame; faith shield quenches fiery lies. Corporate singing of victory hymns re-centers focus on Christ's triumph, not demonic spectacle. Intercession acts as spear, advancing kingdom. Neglecting armor invites infiltration—pornography, gossip, consumerism. Thus warfare worship is sober, confident, and Christ-exalting.

11.9.3 Discernment of Spirits in Worship Space (1 John 4 : 1)

John commands testing spirits; mature churches evaluate prophetic words, worship atmospheres, and teaching content. Criteria include Christological fidelity, love fruit, and scriptural resonance. Prayer teams trained in deliverance minister freedom while avoiding sensationalism. Healthy skepticism prevents gullibility toward manipulative leaders. Discernment fosters safety for vulnerable seekers, ensuring temple remains refuge, not predator playground. Practices such as prayerfully walking facilities, dedicating technology, and purity covenants among musicians safeguard space. Thus spiritual temple stays undefiled and welcoming.

11.9.4 Healing, Deliverance, and the Shalom of the Sanctuary

Jesus healed in synagogues; Acts records cures through apostles' shadows and cloths, indicating signs as worship overflow. Prayer lines, anointing oil, and testimonies integrate healing into liturgy, not side show. Deliverance accompanies gospel proclamation, dethroning oppressive powers (Mark 16 : 17). Caution, training, and aftercare ensure dignity and discipleship. Medical partnership honors God-given science, refusing false dichotomy. Healings fuel mission and deepen doxology, as lepers return glorifying God. Temple shalom thus encompasses body, soul, and society.

11.9.5 Guarding Against Idolatry: Technology, Celebrity, and Commodity

Modern idols slip through screens and algorithms, tempting worshippers to measure worth by likes and purchases. Sabbath tech fasts, sermon illustrations critiquing consumerism, and simplicity vows among leaders erect protective hedges. Resisting celebrity culture entails shared pulpit, plural eldership, and accountability structures. Stewardship of branding ensures visuals serve message, not ego. Merch sales fund ministry but must avoid turning sanctuary into marketplace—a lesson from cleansing event. Regular teaching on contentment inoculates against materialist liturgy broadcast by ads. In guarding hearts, the spiritual temple stays devoted to its singular Lord.

In conclusion, from whispered pre-dawn psalms to roaring multicultural anthems, from kitchen-table Eucharists to legislative-hall intercessions, worship in the Spirit's temple is an ever-expanding symphony composed by the Triune God and performed by His redeemed creation. As we have seen, its melodies are tuned by Scripture, its harmonies enriched by justice and mercy, its rhythms marked by sabbath rest and diligent vocation, and its crescendos shaped by eschatological hope. In this sanctuary, no voice is superfluous, no culture disqualified, no ordinary chore beneath priestly dignity, for the curtain once torn will never be sewn shut again. Amid the world's cacophony of idols, the church's worship bears witness to a Kingdom whose center is a slain Lamb and whose light needs no lamp. Each generation must therefore listen afresh for the Spirit's improvisations, guarding the apostolic score while welcoming new instruments and dancers into the floor. When worship stays tethered to the gospel and attuned to neighbor-love, it becomes both temple and mission, foretaste and signpost of the day when every knee will bow and every tongue will confess that Jesus Christ is Lord. Until that dawn, may our songs remain prophetic, our tables hospitable, our prayers persistent, and our lives—body and community—altars ablaze with holy love.

Chapter 12 Eschatological Temple: New Jerusalem & Cosmic Sabbath

Eschatology is not a speculative appendix to the Christian story; it is the crescendo toward which the entire temple symphony has been modulating since Genesis placed humanity in Eden's sanctuary-garden. The Bible opens with rivers watering a holy place and closes with a river of life bisecting a city whose radiance cancels night (Gen 2 : 10; Rev 22 : 1-5). Between those bookends every covenant artifact—ark, altar, priesthood, prophetic oracles, even the Spirit-filled church itself—plays a thematic variation on God's unyielding intent to dwell with His people in unmediated glory. John's vision of the Lamb-lit New Jerusalem (Rev 21-22) is therefore best read as the final, joyful unveiling of a temple that has been under construction since the foundations of the world, its pillars quarried in patriarchal faith, its walls mortared with prophetic hope, and its gates hinged on the cross and resurrection of Jesus. Because this metropolis is simultaneously a Bride, a Garden, and a Temple, any attempt to isolate architectural, relational, or ecological dimensions impoverishes the picture; all three converge in a single, pulsating reality saturated with divine presence. To explore that convergence, the pages that follow trace ten thematic panoramas—canonical trajectory, Johannine architecture, temple-lessness, cosmic Sabbath, perfected priesthood, sanctified cultures, liberated creation, final judgment, eternal rhythm, and present

246

discipleship—each viewed through the prism of Scripture's consummate visions. Every subsection unfolds in no fewer than seven sentences to allow texture, nuance, and practical resonance, ensuring that the hope of a cosmic Sabbath translates into ethical traction for a still-groaning creation. By the chapter's end, the reader should feel the gravitational pull of the age to come tugging daily choices toward holiness, hospitality, and hope.

12.1 From Garden to City-Temple: A Canonical Trajectory

12.1.1 Edenic Sanctuary Motifs: rivers, gold, and cherubim (Gen 2 – 3)

The author of Genesis sprinkles unmistakable temple clues throughout the Eden narrative: four headwaters form a life-giving river system, gold and onyx glint beneath the soil, and cherubim stand sentinel after the fall (Gen 2 : 10-14; 3 : 24). Later Scriptures reuse each element for cultic settings—palm-engraved cherubim in Solomon's holy of holies (1 Kgs 6 : 29), lampstands shaped like blossoming almond trees (Ex 25 : 31-36), and rivers flowing from eschatological Zion (Ezek 47 : 1-12). Adam's vocation "to work and keep" (*abad* and *shamar*) mirrors verbs that describe Levitical service, suggesting priestly duties assigned before sin corrupted the soil (Num 3 : 7-8). The expulsion narrative, therefore, is less eviction from a park than excommunication from a sanctuary, framing all subsequent redemption as temple restoration. When Revelation revives Edenic imagery—tree of life, healing leaves, crystal river—it is announcing not a return to primitive innocence but an upgrade from localized garden to global city. Eden functions as blueprint and promise, its contours discernible in every altar-stone and prophetic poem until the blueprint finally becomes concrete—or rather, jasper, gold, and transparent glass—in the New Jerusalem. The cosmic Sabbath envisioned at the end is thus Eden's seventh-day rest amplified to universal scale.

12.1.2 Prophetic Telescopes: Isaiah's Zion, Ezekiel's river, Zechariah's holy bells

Isaiah pictures a world where nations stream uphill to Zion, swords become plowshares, and death is swallowed like a shredded shroud (Isa 2 : 2-4; 25 : 6-8). Ezekiel, exiled far from Jerusalem, receives cubit-by-cubit measurements of a future temple dwarfing any human engineering and sees water trickling from its threshold swell into a river that heals the Dead Sea (Ezek 40–47). Zechariah adds street-level detail: even horse bells jingle "Holy to the LORD," and no merchant contaminates the sanctuary on that day (Zech 14 : 20-21). These telescopes do not compete but interlock: Isaiah stresses international pilgrimage, Ezekiel depicts priestly geometry, and Zechariah describes quotidian holiness. John will later splice all three into his apocalyptic tapestry—multinational kings bringing glory, cubical city matching Ezekiel's ratios, and commerce permanently purified. Reading the prophets forward, we sense ripples of anticipation; reading them backward through Revelation, we discover portraits coalesced in the Bride-City. Thus the prophetic canon serves as time-lapse photography of God's architectural imagination coming into focus.

12.1.3 Second-Temple Apocalyptic Hopes: 1 Enoch, Jubilees, Qumran scrolls

Inter-testamental literature pulsates with temple longing: 1 Enoch speaks of a mountain throne surrounded by fiery wheels, Jubilees ties cosmic cycles to sabbatical jubilee rhythms, and the Dead Sea Scrolls dream of a New Jerusalem where tribes camp in concentric holiness. These texts reveal how Israel's trauma under foreign empires intensified craving for a sanctuary untouched by Gentile boots. Although not canonical, their imagery prepared first-century readers to recognize in Jesus' resurrection the first stone of that incorruptible edifice. Apocalyptic writers often placed cosmic rest at the terminus of history, conflating temple and Sabbath motifs into a single hope of shimmering serenity. John honors their yearnings yet subjects them to the Lamb, ensuring that the final city is both priestly and cruciform. Therefore, Second-Temple apocalypses function like rough sketches later refined by apostolic inspiration. They remind modern readers that longings for justice, glory, and rest are not escapist fantasies but echoes of heaven's architectural blueprints.

12.1.4 Cross-Resurrection-Ascension as Eschatological Pivot

Calvary looked like demolition day for Messianic dreams, yet the temple curtain tore from top to bottom, revealing both judgment on the old order and doorway into the age to come (Matt 27 : 51). Resurrection on "the first day of the week" reenacts day one of creation, signaling a new cosmic calendar (John 20 : 1). Ascension seats the incarnate Son at the cosmic control center, chaining the unfolding of history to the intercession of a human High Priest (Eph 1 : 20-23). Pentecost then installs heavenly Shekinah in earthly believers, making them down-payments of eschatological reality (Acts 2 : 17-21). Thus cross, empty tomb, and cloud-hidden throne form a hinge: on one side lies the groaning world; on the other, the dawning of new creation. New Jerusalem is not a future contingency but the inevitable maturation of realities already implanted by these events. Believers live in overlap, citizens of a city both here in principle and pending in fullness.

12.1.5 "Already / Not Yet" in New-Testament Eschatology

Jesus announces the kingdom as both near and delayed, mustard seed and full tree (Mark 1 : 15; 4 : 30-32). Paul proclaims believers already raised with Christ yet awaiting resurrection (Col 3 : 1-4; Rom 8 : 23). Hebrews asserts that worshipers stand at Mt. Zion even while trudging through wilderness trials (Heb 12 : 22-29). This tension protects against triumphalist denial of suffering and against despairing resignation. New Jerusalem exists in prototype whenever saints forgive enemies or share possessions; it remains future while tears still stain faces and cemeteries fill plots. Living in tension trains the church for hopeful realism, laboring precisely because victory is guaranteed but not yet unveiled. The cosmic Sabbath, then, is both promised land and present down-payment, pulling the people of God forward in patient endurance.

12.2 Revelation 21 – 22 in Detail: Architecture Without a Temple

12.2.1 "I Saw a New Heaven and New Earth": creation re-booted

John's declaration echoes Isaiah 65 : 17 yet surpasses it by embedding renewal within a post-judgment cosmos where sea—the biblical symbol of chaos (Ps 74 : 13)—is absent (Rev 21 : 1). The phrase "new" (*kainos*) implies transformed continuity rather than absolute replacement; the Composer rewrites the score without discarding the motifs. Every polluted river, extinct species, and bomb-scarred city block groans for inclusion in this renovation (Rom 8 : 19-22). John's vision reassures martyrs that their spilled blood is not mere fertilizer for earth but seed for a world immune to tyranny. Creation's reboot thus validates ecological stewardship now, for materiality is destined for glory, not oblivion. Hope shifts from evacuation to resurrection of the cosmos, aligning Christian mission with creational flourishing. New heaven and earth frame New Jerusalem like a setting for a jewel, ensuring that the city's brilliance does not eclipse the wide theatre of redeemed nature.

12.2.2 Dimensions of the Cubic City: echo of holy of holies

The city measures twelve thousand stadia in length, width, and height—approximately 1,400 miles in every direction—forming a perfect cube (Rev 21 : 16). Only one other cube appears in Scripture: the innermost room of Moses' tabernacle and Solomon's temple where God's glory rested (1 Kgs 6 : 20). By cubing the entire metropolis, John proclaims that what was once confined to an inaccessible chamber now permeates civic life. Stadia multiples of twelve emphasize covenant fulfillment and apostolic foundations. Height equal to width shatters ancient cosmology, making the city a mountain suspended in space, a marriage of heaven and earth. Architectural exaggeration points to symbolic, not literal, measurement; still, the grandeur sparks imagination that no population density or cultural diversity will overcrowd this dwelling. Living within a cube of glory means every direction you walk, you remain in holy of holies. Thus geometry preaches theology: God's presence has gone viral.

12.2.3 The Bride Adorned and the Wall of Precious Stones

John shifts metaphors fluidly: the city is also a bride descending from heaven, dressed not in linen but in jasper, sapphire, emerald, and twelve other gems mirroring the high-priest's breastpiece (Rev 21 : 2, 18-20; Ex 28 : 15-21). This gemology announces that the entire covenant community has become the ornamental vestment that the ultimate High Priest wears before the Father. Gold so pure it appears transparent (Rev 21 : 18) underlines sanctity refined by fiery trials (1 Pet 1 : 7). Embedded apostle names on foundations (Rev 21 : 14) guarantee doctrinal continuity; faith once delivered pulsates forever in eschatological brickwork. City walls symbolize security, yet gates remain open, indicating safety without exclusion. Diamonds and pearls are divine graffiti spelling "loved" across redeemed history. Believers anxious about worthiness find identity chiselled into New Jerusalem's masonry.

12.2.4 The Glory-Light: no sun or moon required

Isaiah foretold a day when the LORD would be everlasting light (Isa 60 : 19-20); John testifies fulfillment: "The glory of God gives it light, and its lamp is the Lamb" (Rev 21 : 23). This is not annihilation of celestial bodies—as parallel passages speak of nations' ruling—rather, divine radiance renders them unnecessary as sources. God-light eradicates literal and moral night, so no streetlamp or secret sin survives. Unlike Moses who veiled his face, inhabitants bask unveiled because grace has prepared them (2 Cor 3 : 18). Light doubles as energy grid, economy, and art; work continues but without electricity bills or carbon footprint. First-century Christians meeting by oil lamp hear promise that their flickering gatherings foreshadow unquenchable brilliance. Thus, the Lamb functions as both chandelier and hero, illuminating and being adored simultaneously.

12.2.5 River of Life and Tree of Life: Eden restored and expanded

From the throne flows a single river, unlike Eden's quartet, halving the street and watering trees that bear twelve fruits monthly (Rev 22 : 1-2). Water quality testifies to throne quality: pure, crisp, unpollutable. Trees, plural, indicate abundance; twelve crops symbolize perpetual provision transcending seasons of scarcity. Leaves heal nations, suggesting that even in perfected society cultural distinctions persist as healed scars, not erased memories. The curse morbidity that began with Adam dies here, replaced by year-round harvest festival. Sacramentally, baptism anticipates river immersion, while Eucharist nibble predicts fruit banquet. Geography thus preaches grace: healing flows not from clinic but from communion with the King.

12.3 Templelessness & Total Presence

12.3.1 "The Lord God Almighty and the Lamb Are Its Temple" (Rev 21 : 22)

The astonishing absence of a temple building in John's city does not negate temple theology; it consummates it. By identifying God Himself plus the Mediator as the full reality toward which brick and ritual pointed, Revelation liberates worship from any architectural dependence. Therefore, every prior sanctuary—from garden to gothic cathedral—is affirmed as prophecy but relativized as provisional. This move annihilates sacred–secular divide; the divine presence saturates grocery stalls and art studios equally. The pastoral implication is profound: Christians can lose meeting halls to fire or persecution without losing sanctuary. Ecclesial humility grows, for no congregation can claim exclusive franchise on holy space. Templelessness, paradoxically, ensures infinite access to total presence.

12.3.2 Shekinah Illumination: glory as the city's electricity

Shekinah once nestled between cherubim wings, later filled Solomon's temple, departed in Ezekiel's vision, and overshadowed a Bethlehem manger; in New Jerusalem it permeates civic infrastructure. Energy and worship converge—the same glory that lights also thrills. No longer must priests maintain lampstands with imported oil; divine lumen self-sustains. Carbon neutrality is metaphysically achieved, and rising utility costs cease to plague municipal budgets. Shekinah light also eradicates ignorance, for knowledge of God covers earth as waters cover sea (Hab 2 : 14). Intellectual pursuit becomes ever-deepening fascination, never boredom. Urban planners and theologians alike dream in vain if they envision cities without this glory grid.

12.3.3 Ever-Open Gates & the End of Exile

Ancient gates closed at night to exclude marauders, but New Jerusalem's gates remain open because threats are extinct (Rev 21 : 25). Open gates fulfill Isaiah 60 : 11 and reverse Eden's flaming sword, welcoming humanity back into unbroken communion. Diaspora Jews who wept by rivers of Babylon finally come home; Gentiles, once far off, find citizenship stamped heaven-issued (Eph 2 : 13-19). Urban openness models political reconciliation—nations need not fear immigration or invasion in God's perfected polity. The only barred entry is willful impurity (Rev 21 : 27), yet such impurity has been quarantined in lake of fire, leaving gateway attendance unnecessary. Festival processions stream in perpetually, making civic life a continual parade. Exile's vocabulary—alien, stranger, refugee— becomes museum relic.

12.3.4 No Sea, No Night: chaos and threat abolished

Sea in Hebrew cosmology symbolizes instability (Dan 7 : 2-3); John, exiled on Patmos, knows sea as barrier between him and beloved churches. Its absence signals relational reunion and cosmic calm. Night in ancient cities lent cover to thieves; its removal means safety and transparency. Work rhythms adjust: labor continues but without oppressive toil or anxious deadlines. Sleep persists as delight not necessity—perhaps Sabbath naps elevated to art. Psychic darkness—depression, anxiety—dissipates in perpetual dawn. Thus environmental and existential threats evaporate under the Lamb's sovereignty.

12.3.5 Universal Holiness: nothing unclean ever enters

Levitical law excluded lepers and corpses; Revelation excludes lies and idolatry (Rev 21 : 27). Holiness standards remain, but cleansing is complete, so exclusions are descriptive, not prescriptive. Moral perfection no longer needs guardians; citizens voluntarily embody truth. Cultures once bound to occult or empire bring their particular glories now purified—Aztec maize art, Norse sagas, Javanese batik— all scrubbed of violence or vanity. Holiness is not beige uniformity but kaleidoscopic purity. Daily commerce, education, and recreation proceed without risk of corruption. Sin memories fade like nightmare upon waking, replaced by restful security.

12.4 The Cosmic Sabbath

12.4.1 Genesis 1's Open-Ended Seventh Day

Scripture never closes day seven with "evening and morning," hinting that divine rest continues (Gen 2 : 1-3). Sabbath was not a break because God was tired but a sovereign enthronement over ordered cosmos. New Jerusalem marks culmination of that rest, extending Eden's tranquility across galaxies. For believers, practicing weekly Sabbath now is rehearsal dinner for eternal feast. Jewish tradition calls Sabbath "a taste of the world to come," and Christians add that the world to come will be one unbroken Sabbath. This theology counters modern hustle ethics, previewing post-capitalist society powered by grace. Therefore, cosmic Sabbath crowns creation narrative and closes redemption story.

12.4.2 Sabbath in Torah, Psalms, and Prophets: sign, justice, and joy

Torah frames Sabbath as covenant sign (Ex 31 : 13), Psalms celebrate it with music (Ps 92), and prophets link its violation to exile (Jer 17 : 21-27). Sabbath gifts identity, delight, and economic equity— servants rest, animals rest, even land enjoys sabbatical fallow (Lev 25 : 4-5). These dimensions converge eschatologically: identity solidified in God's presence, delight perpetual, and socio-economic oppression obsolete. Sabbath is therefore not mere church attendance but political statement against exploitation. When Revelation shows servants reigning while slaves to empire are liberated, Sabbath justice has reached zenith. Thus mosaic principles blossom cosmically. Eternal rest achieves what weekly rest only signposts.

12.4.3 Hebrews 4: the "rest" still open and the people who enter

Hebrews warns that unbelief barred Exodus generation; believers must mix promise with faith lest they miss rest (Heb 4 : 1-11). Yet the text affirms Joshua did not exhaust the promise, leaving open eschatological rest for God's people. Sabbath consciousness thus shapes perseverance, urging saints to hold confession until they cross threshold. In New Jerusalem the exhortation becomes celebration: "they shall never again hunger" (Rev 7 : 16). The swordlike Word that exposes hearts in Hebrews now engraves God's name on foreheads in Revelation (Rev 22 : 4). Rest arrives not as hammock inactivity but as fruitful participation free from curse. Therefore, Hebrews functions as pilgrim manual until city gates appear on horizon.

12.4.4 Patristic & Medieval Readings: eternal *feria* and beatific vision

Church fathers described heaven as *feria sexta*—the festival beyond Friday grief—where contemplation replaces labor. Augustine's *City of God* climaxes in quiet vision of *sempiterna sabbatum*, unending Sabbath. Medieval mystics spoke of *sabbathum mentis*, sabbath of the mind, where soul rests in God's loving gaze. These readings kept Sabbath eschatology alive when plagues and crusades muddied earthly horizons. They remind modern activists that contemplation and action are not opposites but stages of cosmic liturgy. In New Jerusalem, Bernard of Clairvaux's "O Sacred Head" becomes "O Unveiled Face," desire consummated. Historical theology thus enriches Revelation reading, preventing novelty hubris.

12.4.5 Work-Worship Integration in the Endless Day

Genesis assignment to subdue earth persists post-fall; New Jerusalem inhabitants "serve" God (Rev 22 : 3), implying activity. Work, uncursed, aligns with worship—composers pen symphonies, scientists explore nebulae, artisans craft furniture for banquet halls. Jesus' parables of faithful stewards ruling cities (Luke 19 : 17) imply vocational continuity. Rest therefore means harmony, not idleness; creativity flows without exploitative strain. Sabbath economics continue: resources abound, competition transforms into collaboration. Believers fearful of eternal boredom discover vocation amplified, not annulled. Thus cosmic Sabbath integrates Edenic mandate with temple worship forever.

12.5 A Royal-Priestly People Fully Realized

12.5.1 "They Shall Reign for Ever and Ever" (Rev 22 : 5)

The dominion mandate given to Adam but corrupted by sin is re-entrusted to redeemed humanity. Reigning alongside the Lamb ensures benevolent, servant leadership, prohibiting tyranny. Authority now heals instead of harms, administrators managing ecosystems and culture to mutual flourishing. Scripture begins with humans losing a garden; it ends with humans governing a universe. Gender, age, and ethnicity factors that foster power imbalances vanish in egalitarian glory. Reigning also fulfills Daniel 7 : 27 where saints receive kingdom under Most High; Apostle Paul notes believers will judge angels (1 Cor 6 : 3), hinting at cosmic jurisdiction. Thus salvation goal is not cloud lounging but royal stewardship.

12.5.2 Priestly Vocation Perfected: service, sacrifice, and song

Priestly service continues as worship language—offering unsullied praise, tending life-river banks, curating cultural treasures. Literal blood sacrifice ceases because Lamb's wounds eternally suffice, but sacrifice of thanksgiving and joyful obedience flourishes. Festival calendar fuses into perpetual celebration, yet the variety of praise ensures novelty. Levitical restrictions replaced by universal ordination; toddlers and elders alike wear white robes of priesthood (Rev 7 : 9-10). Temple choir expands to every voice, achieving acoustic diversity unimaginable under old covenant. Service is no longer mediated by fatigue, thus "His servants shall serve Him" without weariness. Priesthood thus reaches telos envisioned in Exodus 19 : 6.

12.5.3 Seeing God's Face: the beatific fulfillment of temple access

Adam hid from God's face; Moses glimpsed back parts; priests saw Shekinah glow; but Revelation promises beatific vision (Rev 22 : 4). Face-to-face communion constitutes apex of temple thrust: no veil, no smoke, only unveiled glory perceived without terror. Beatific vision transforms worshipers into mirrors, reflecting glory like polished gold (2 Cor 3 : 18). Augustine wrote that vision equals rest; Aquinas deemed it ultimate human happiness. This sight eradicates doubt, heals trauma, and cements joy. Contemporary desire to "see God" finds legitimate promise here, cautioning against idolatrous shortcuts. Vision and transformation lock believers into perpetual wonder.

12.5.4 Names on Foreheads: identity, ownership, and mission complete

The divine name branded on saints' foreheads (Rev 22 : 4) inverts beastly mark of chapter 13, sealing allegiance beyond counterfeit worship. Forehead—seat of cognition—symbolizes worldview saturated with divine reality. Ownership means protection; heavenly economy will never foreclose on God's investment. Mark also functions as missionary completion: what began with baptismal identity now emblazoned permanently. No more impostor syndrome, racial slurs, or dehumanizing labels. Identity secure, community thrives without comparison. Thus forehead engraving finalizes spirit adoption documents.

12.5.5 Vocation in the Age to Come: creative stewardship without curse

With ground's curse lifted (Rev 22 : 3), thorns cease; agriculture becomes collaboration with Creator. Artists compose, engineers innovate, scholars research without vanity or error. Intergalactic exploration may extend dominion; worship includes scientific symposiums praising cosmic patterns. Economy shifts from scarcity to relational abundance. The Lamb's wounds remind that vocation is gift of grace not merit, preventing pride. Joy in work fuels perpetual energy—no burnout sabbaticals needed. Royal-priestly vocation thus underwrites eternal civilization.

12.6 Nations, Kings, & the Glory-Treasures Brought In

12.6.1 Isaiah 60 Fulfilled: wealth of nations sanctified

Caravans once bound for Solomon now converge on Lamb's capital, bearing spices, technology, and art, purified of injustice (Rev 21 : 24). Isaiah's camels, ships of Tarshish, and cedars of Lebanon signify that cultural products retain identity while losing idolatry. Economic exchange becomes worship, commerce without exploitation. The word "glory" (*doxa*) suggests weighty uniqueness of each culture treasured eternally. Evangelism hence seeks not to erase cultures but redeem them. Missionaries become curators helping societies offer best gifts to Christ. Thus globalization finds final redemption in worshipful convergence.

12.6.2 Cultural Eschatology: continuity, purification, and transfiguration

Revelation's imagery implies that languages persist; Pentecost tongues do not fossilize into a single dialect. Continuity ensures recognition—David may play harp, Mozart compose new requiem, Ethiopian coffee aroma wafts along golden streets. Purification removes racism, misogyny, colonialism, and greed from every heritage. Transfiguration upgrades cultural artifacts to serve love's aims—weapons become instruments, propaganda becomes poetry. The process vindicates God's original declaration that creation is "very good" (Gen 1 : 31). Therefore, cultural labor now matters eternally; art, technology, and policies can anticipate kingdom values. Eschatology empowers cultural reformation, not abandonment.

12.6.3 Diversity Without Division: multilingual worship forever

John hears, before he sees, a diverse choir—sound precedes sight (Rev 7 : 9-10). Unity is auditory harmony, not visual uniformity. Accents persist without misunderstanding because glory amplifies comprehension. No hegemonic culture dominates; majority and minority terms dissolve. Liturgical call-and-response may echo across linguistic bridges, each tongue adding richness. Power imbalances vanish, for leadership reflects mosaic citizenship. Thus diversity's telos is symphonic worship.

12.6.4 Political Power Redeemed: kings in service, not rivalry

Earthly kingship often embodies oppression, yet Revelation pictures kings bringing honor, not armies, to the city (Rev 21 : 24). Their crowns laid down echo elders' gesture of glad submission (Rev 4 : 10). Politics becomes doxological stewardship, devoid of coercion.

Believers disillusioned with current governments find hope in redeemed leadership models. Now, politicians seeking power must foreshadow servant-king ethos. Public office becomes priestly role, integrating justice and praise. Ultimate sovereignty remains Christ's, preventing future coups.

12.6.5 Mission Accomplished: from Pentecost harvest to cosmic ingathering

Acts 2 inaugurated harvest; Revelation shows barns overflowing. Great Commission shifts from imperative to accomplished reality; teaching all nations gives way to nations teaching glory back. Martyr blood has become seed (Rev 6 : 9-11), now blooming into multiethnic city. Unreached people groups vanish from mission maps. New tasks focus on exploration and creativity, not evangelism, yet memory of redemption fuels endless gratitude. Missions agencies rejoice, not retire in boredom, for their stories become festival testimonies. The Lamb receives full reward for His suffering.

12.7 Creation Liberated: Ecological Dimensions of the New Temple

12.7.1 Romans 8 and the Birth-Pangs of Renewal

Paul personifies creation as a woman in labor, implying continuity between present world and renewed earth, not disposal (Rom 8 : 22). New Jerusalem is delivery room's joy. Labor pains include earthquakes, species loss, climate crises—symptoms of groaning, not signs of futility. Christians respond not with fatalism but midwife ministry—sustainability, conservation. Environmental stewardship becomes eschatological obstetrics. Hope motivates ecological repentance, knowing efforts resonate into eternal landscape. Thus, Romans 8 links gospel and green discipleship.

12.7.2 New Heavens & New Earth: continuity vs. annihilation debate

Some argue 2 Peter 3 : 10 indicates total burn-up; linguistic studies show *kainos* newness akin to resurrection transformation, not annihilation. Just as Jesus' glorified body bore scars yet burst tomb, so Earth will bear redeemed history while freed from decay. Therefore, recycling and reforestation participate in upcoming restoration rather than polishing sinking ship. The debate shapes ethics: continuity fosters care; annihilation excuses neglect. Revelation's nations bringing glory underscores cultural continuity. Thus doctrinal clarity fuels practical responsibility. Creation matters because Creator will not forsake work of His hands (Ps 138 : 8).

12.7.3 Animal Life and "Peaceable Kingdom" Prospects

Isaiah envisions wolf and lamb coexisting, child playing near cobra (Isa 11 : 6-9). Such images inspire speculation about animal existence in New Jerusalem. Revelation's silence does not preclude fauna; tree of life's leaves healing *nations* implies ecosystem synergy. Romans 8's phrase "creation itself" suggests non-human participation. Even if literal, metaphoric tone proclaims eradication of predation in societal structures—no devouring exploitation. Present animal cruelty stands condemned by future harmony. Hope shapes humane treatment now. Thus peaceable kingdom foretastes call ethical living.

12.7.4 Cosmic Liturgy: stars, rivers, and trees in perpetual praise

Psalms speak of heavens declaring glory (Ps 19 : 1) and rivers clapping hands (Ps 98 : 8). In new creation, metaphor becomes manifest choreography: auroras paint hymns; rivers hum; galaxies swirl like dance troupes. Human worship joins cosmic choir, aligning rational praise with elemental rhythms. Science becomes doxology, decoding divine artistry. Environmental aesthetics—color, texture, sound—educate joy. No temple walls restrict; entire universe is cathedral. Thus cosmic liturgy continues ad infinitum.

12.7.5 Ecological Ethics Now: stewarding the groaning creation in hope

Knowing forests will flourish eternally motivates planting trees in deforested villages. Churches adopt renewable energy, modeling kingdom economy. Liturgies include creation-focused prayers, confession of environmental sin, and commissioning of eco-missionaries. Green Sabbath initiatives align consumption with rest. Advocacy for climate justice intersects with poverty relief, reflecting holistic gospel. These acts preview liberated creation, inviting neighbors to taste future now. Hope fuels perseverance amid ecological setbacks.

12.8 Judgment Fire & Final Purification Before the Wedding

12.8.1 Great White Throne and Books Opened (Rev 20 : 11-15)

Judgment ensures New Jerusalem's moral foundation; love without justice would invite repetition of evil. Books record deeds, demonstrating divine memory and human accountability. Book of Life secures redeemed by grace, balancing works evaluation with covenant security. This courtroom scene comforts oppressed believers—persecutors face reckoning. Western discomfort with judgment dissolves when victims' cries are heard. Justice sets stage for unpolluted city; without it, open gates would be porous to evil. Thus eschatological temple requires purgation furnace.

12.8.2 Lake of Fire: evil quarantined, temple integrity secured

Symbolic geography transports beast, false prophet, devil, death, and Hades into containment (Rev 20 : 14). Annihilation or eternal consciousness debate persists; what is clear: evil no longer sabotages cosmos. Lake's existence underscores holiness of New Jerusalem; boundaries continue but now protect joy. Believers trust God's justice without voyeuristic obsession. Mission urgency remains: invite all to wedding, warn all of quarantine. The fire is God's strange work, penultimate to His ultimate delight in mercy (Isa 28 : 21). Holy love, not sadistic wrath, fuels final separation.

12.8.3 Refining of Works (1 Cor 3): wood, hay, straw consumed

Paul teaches that believers' works pass through fire; some burn, some shine. Loss is painful yet salvific; dross removed prepares saints for city construction. Motivation testing today prevents vanity building. Ministry measured by hidden humility may outlast megachurch hype. Hopeful accountability spurs excellence and compassion in present tasks. Refiner's fire anticipates Lamb's wedding gown needing no spot. Thus judgment becomes cleansing flame, not arbitrary destruction.

12.8.4 "No More Curse": total expulsion of death, sorrow, and pain

Genesis curse involved toil, pain, and relational fracture; Revelation's pronouncement cancels all three (Rev 22 : 3). Tears once stored in divine bottle (Ps 56 : 8) are wiped by divine hand (Rev 21 : 4). Disability, disease, and mental anguish vanish under healing light. Social curses—racism, addiction, violence—also expire. Curse reversal validates cross where Christ bore curse (Gal 3 : 13). Theodicy finds resolution: suffering remembered only as backdrop for glory. Eternal Sabbath therefore includes emotional and physical wholeness.

8.5 Justice Vindicated: martyrs honored, oppressors silenced

Martyrs beneath altar cried "How long?"; judgment day answers with white robes and celebrated testimony (Rev 6 : 10-11; 20 : 4). Oppressors' boasting mouths closed, echoing Psalm 107 reversal. Heavenly witnesses acknowledge righteousness of God's sentences (Rev 19 : 1-2). Restoration of honor to marginalized heals historical trauma. Forgiven persecutors join family, proving justice and mercy not mutually exclusive. Worship includes courtroom doxology—hallelujah rising from satisfied justice. City streets paved with stories of triumph over evil.

12.9 Eternal Time & Festival: Rhythms in the Age of Rest

12.9.1 "There Will Be No More Delay" (Rev 10 : 6): time redeemed

Angel's oath abolishes tragic postponement, not sequential progression; seasons likely persist as tree cycles imply. Time loses tyranny, becoming canvas for creativity. Chronophobia fades; deadlines convert to lifelines. Eternal life is qualitative enhancement, not endless extension of boredom. Kairos saturates chronos—every moment pregnant with glory. Anxiety of missing out replaced by fullness of participation.

12.9.2 Feast Imagery: continual Tabernacles / continual Passover

Levitical calendar collapses into perpetual celebration: deliverance (Passover), firstfruits (Pentecost), harvest (Tabernacles) co-inhabit festival. Isaiah's "feast of rich food" finds menu renewed daily (Isa 25 : 6). Meals reinforce fellowship and gratitude, fueling artistic and scholarly interchange. Diet reflects redeemed ecology—plentiful yet sustainable. Fellowship hall echoes covenant faithfulness. Food allergies gone; table welcomes all. Feasting commemorates former hunger, intensifying joy.

12.9.3 Worship without Weariness: ever-new, never-monotonous

Human brains crave novelty; divine creativity satisfies endlessly. Infinite God can be adored indefinitely without repetition fatigue. Hymnody evolves, yet themes of grace and glory remain. Work-worship harmony ensures varied engagements—science, sports, exploration—blend into praise. Rest cycles become delight rather than necessity. Eternity's duration enhances, not dilutes, meaning. Joy remains fresh like manna.

12.9.4 Memory and Hope in the Eternal Now

Past redemptive acts remembered without grief; scars on Lamb testify but no longer bleed. Hope transforms into enjoyment, yet forward anticipation may persist as discovery of deeper divine facets. Psychologists' fear of eternal stasis dissipates; narrative continues with chapters of exploration. Memory fosters gratitude, fueling worship. Time travel curiosity satisfied by storytelling banquets where saints recount histories. Chronological boredom impossible because God is infinite story. Thus memory and hope coexist in timeless symphony.

12.9.5 Music of the Spheres: cosmic harmony as liturgical backdrop

Johannes Kepler dreamt of planetary music; Revelation suggests celestial acoustics accompany worship. Quasars hum, electrons vibrate, whales sing—these frequencies weave into doxological fabric. Redeemed hearing perceives spectrum beyond current limitations. Humans compose alongside cosmic orchestra, echoing Job 38 : 7 where morning stars sang. Physics becomes hymnology, mathematics symphony notation. Every beat of cosmos applauds Creator. Music becomes atmosphere, not just activity.

In Conclusion, The biblical saga that began with God walking among trees at dusk reaches its radiant finale with God dwelling openly in a city whose very architecture throbs with His light and whose calendar has melted into a single, unbreakable Sabbath. Here, every longing encoded in patriarchal promises, prophetic poetry, and apostolic preaching finds resonant answer: justice silences oppressors, creation inhales freedom, cultural glories parade through gates that never close, and redeemed humanity beholds the face it was fashioned to mirror. Yet this consummation is not a distant mirage but the gravitational center already tugging the church's worship, ethics, and imagination into orbit, urging believers to live as preview models of the world to come. Each Eucharistic loaf, each sabbatical pause, each act of ecological care, and each welcome extended to a stranger tattoos the topography of the coming city onto the soil of the present. Therefore, Christian hope is neither resignation to planetary decay nor starry-eyed mysticism; it is the disciplined, joyful labor of quarrying, polishing, and setting living stones that will seamlessly integrate into New Jerusalem's walls on the day the trumpet sounds. In that hour cosmic Sabbath will dawn without dusk, and the temple who is Father, Son, and Spirit will flood every corner of a renovated cosmos with unshadowed glory. Until then, the Spirit and the Bride say, "Come," and every echo of that cry—in prayer, in justice, in song—ushers history one heartbeat closer to home.

Chapter 13 - Temple Ethics: Holiness, Justice, and Societal Witness

When the Triune God chooses to dwell among people, the surrounding culture is meant to feel the heat. Temple presence is not a mystical fog that hovers politely above private piety; it is a blazing fire that purifies the inhabitants, illumines the neighborhood, and radiates a moral warmth powerful enough to thaw frozen systems of violence and greed. From Eden's mandate to "tend and guard" creation (Gen 2 : 15) to Paul's charge that believers are the Spirit's holy *naos* (1 Cor 6 : 19), Scripture refuses to divorce worship from witness. This chapter therefore explores how the new-covenant temple—no longer masonry but a Spirit-filled community—translates indwelling glory into concrete holiness, distributive justice, and credible societal engagement. We proceed through twelve thematic vistas, each exposing a facet of temple ethics and anchoring it in biblical narrative, theological reflection, and contemporary application. Every subsection develops in full paragraphs of at least seven sentences so that nuance is not lost and practical traction emerges. Readers should finish convinced that ethical transformation is not an optional add-on to temple theology but its most visible proof, and that the Spirit who furnished Bezalel with craftsmanship (Ex 31 : 2-5) still empowers ordinary believers to craft lives of staggering beauty and integrity for a watching world.

13.1 Biblical Foundations of Temple Ethics

13.1.1 Edenic Vocation: tending and guarding as proto-ethics (Gen 2 : 15)

Genesis locates the first ethical assignment inside a proto-temple. The verbs *abad* ("serve") and *shamar* ("guard") later describe Levites who minister in the tabernacle (Num 3 : 7-8), suggesting that Adam and Eve's horticultural care is priestly work. Holiness, therefore, is not originally a matter of avoiding ritual corpses or shellfish; it begins as diligent stewardship of a flourishing ecosystem. Failure to guard the garden from serpent intrusion becomes the primal ethical collapse, fusing environmental negligence with moral rebellion. Temple ethics after the fall are essentially the recovery of Edenic vocation under increasingly complex historical conditions—Sinai law, prophetic critique, and Christocentric renewal. When believers today recycle, mentor children, or defend endangered wetlands, they are not engaging peripheral activism but re-inhabiting humanity's first priestly mandate. Temple ethics, then, is a return to the Garden even while pressing toward the City (Rev 22 : 1-5).

13.1.2 Sinai Covenant: holiness codes and justice statutes as temple frame (Lev 19)

Leviticus situates its famous holiness code directly around tabernacle blueprints, showing that moral architecture buttresses physical architecture. Commands about sexual purity, honest scales, and gleaning margins (Lev 19 : 9-18) together create social space where Yahweh can walk "in the midst" of His people (Lev 26 : 11-12). The refrain "I am the LORD" punctuates ethical directives, rooting behavior in covenant identity rather than authoritarian whim. Temple ethics therefore refuses modern bifurcations between personal morality and structural justice; both sit under the halo of divine presence. Scholars note that Leviticus frames care for the deaf, blind, and immigrant as acts of temple reverence (Lev 19 : 14, 34), a startling linkage that rebukes contemporary worship divorced from human rights. Christians reading the chapter through a new-covenant lens see Christ fulfilling sacrificial shadows yet intensifying moral demands (Matt 5 : 17-20). Thus Sinai supplies grammar for temple ethics even after the cult has been superseded by the cross.

13.1.3 Prophetic Correctives: worship invalid without righteousness (Isa 1; Amos 5)

Isaiah opens with Yahweh rejecting sacrifices that smell of blood but reek of injustice (Isa 1 : 11-17). Amos amplifies the rebuke by damning songs and harps that crescendo over extortionist economies (Amos 5 : 21-24). These prophets are not anti-liturgy; they are pro-integrity. They insist that orthodoxy without justice is liturgical blasphemy and that temple courts can become crime scenes if mercy is evicted. The prophetic critique becomes foundation for Jesus' temple cleansing (Mark 11 : 17) and James's insistence that pure religion cares for orphans and widows (Jas 1 : 27). Therefore, any church that treasures worship style but neglects social equity inherits the prophets' indictment. Temple ethics keeps these warnings on permanent display lest incense once again mask oppression.

13.1.4 Wisdom Literature: fear of the LORD and social equity (Prov 14 : 31)

Proverbs links reverence for God with economic fairness: "Whoever oppresses the poor shows contempt for their Maker" (Prov 14 : 31). Job's legal defense lists hospitality, wage justice, and environmental stewardship as evidence of piety (Job 31). Wisdom texts thus expand temple ethics into the market, courtroom, and kitchen, insisting that holiness is tested in mundane transactions. Psalms reinforce the lesson, celebrating Yahweh as defender of the needy (Ps 146 : 7-9) and portraying worshipers who pray, "Search me, O God," precisely so hidden injustice is not smuggled into sanctuary songs (Ps 139 : 23-24). The wisdom tradition, therefore, proves that holiness and justice are not sequential virtues but two sides of one coin minted in God's image. To divorce them is to counterfeit discipleship. Temple ethics is wise living in community under the gaze of the Holy One.

13.1.5 Jesus the Living Temple: Sermon on the Mount as ethical blueprint

Jesus embodies the meeting place of God and humanity (John 2 : 21), so His ethical teaching in Matthew 5–7 is, in effect, temple law from the mouth of the temple Himself. He intensifies prohibitions—anger equals murder, lust equals adultery—demonstrating that holiness monitors interior motive as rigorously as exterior behavior. He places reconciliation with a brother above sacrificial offering (Matt

5 : 23-24), reordering worship priorities toward relational justice. The Beatitudes bless the meek and persecuted, converting holiness from separatist purity into cruciform humility. When He commands enemy love (Matt 5 : 44), He charts temple behavior that shocks pagan and Pharisee alike. Thus, Jesus' ethic is not a new legalism but an unleashing of temple life through Spirit-empowered character (Matt 7 : 12; Rom 8 : 4). The Sermon becomes the architect's rendering of New-Jerusalem citizenship displayed on dusty Galilean hillsides.

13.2 Holiness as Identity and Practice

13.2.1 Positional vs. Progressive Holiness: "saints" who still grow (1 Cor 1 : 2)

Paul salutes the Corinthians as "sanctified... called saints," yet spends sixteen chapters correcting scandals. This tension shows holiness as both status conferred by Christ's blood and journey empowered by His Spirit. Temple ethics refuses complacency, acknowledging that positional sanctity energizes, not excuses, moral effort (Phil 2 : 12-13). Spiritual disciplines—Scripture meditation, fasting, confession—cultivate progressive conformity to Jesus. Communal rhythms, such as mutual admonition (Col 3 : 16), guard against privatized holiness that overlooks blind spots. Therefore, sainthood is a starting line, not a trophy shelf. Being God's dwelling compels believers to renovate every room of life so the resident King feels at home.

13.2.2 Bodily Integrity: sexuality, speech, and substance stewardship

Paul locates sexual ethics in temple reality: uniting Christ's members with prostitution is desecration (1 Cor 6 : 15-20). Speech likewise becomes sacred architecture; coarse words crumble gospel witness (Eph 4 : 29). Substance abuse contradicts Spirit infilling, for drunkenness yields control to a different spirit (Eph 5 : 18). Body stewardship extends to exercise, sleep, and diet, resisting both idolization of physique and negligent self-harm. Holiness frames technology use: smartphones can be portals of praise or pollution. In all, the believer's body acts as living signage reading, "Temple under holy management." Such embodied ethics evangelize without words in a culture disembodied by consumerism and lust.

13.2.3 Corporate Discipline: guarding the temple community (1 Cor 5)

When a Corinthian flaunts incest, Paul orders excommunication "so that the spirit may be saved," treating discipline as surgery, not vengeance. The health of the whole temple requires removing contagious sin lest leaven ferment the dough (1 Cor 5 : 6-8). Modern application demands transparent processes, plurality of elders, and restorative aims. Churches that fear accusations of judgmentalism often slide into permissiveness that ultimately harms victims and perpetrators alike. Conversely, authoritarian discipline devoid of grace weaponizes holiness. Temple ethics navigates between these ditches, wielding both surgeon's scalpel and physician's balm. When restoration occurs, the community celebrates architectural repair, not punitive spectacle (2 Cor 2 : 6-8).

13.2.4 Rituals of Confession, Lament, and Reconciliation

Liturgies that include confession of sin echo temple sacrifices, moving guilt from hidden corners into God's forgiving light (1 John 1 : 9). Communal lament over racism, abuse, or ecological devastation aligns worship with prophetic grief (Lam 3). Reconciliation rituals— foot-washing, corporate apologies, restitution funds—embody gospel repair. These practices train congregations to handle conflict redemptively, preventing Sunday smiles from camouflaging weekday resentment. Forgiveness does not bypass justice; rather, it empowers victims while calling offenders to costly repentance. Such liturgical honesty signals a safe harbor to skeptics wounded by hypocrisy. Temple ethics thus bleeds into worship order, teaching hearts to pulse with truth and grace.

13.2.5 Hospitality as Positive Separation: welcoming without assimilation

Holiness has often been caricatured as exclusive withdrawal, yet biblical separation aims to bless outsiders, not shun them (Lev 20 : 26; 1 Pet 2 : 9-10). Christian hospitality invites strangers to experience covenant community while maintaining distinct identity. Boundaries are porous but real: compassionate welcome does not endorse every worldview (Acts 28 : 30-31). Dinner tables become altars where holiness and hospitality intertwine, prefiguring eschatological banquet (Luke 14 : 13-14). Cross-cultural friendship counters xenophobia, embodying temple openness where courts of Gentiles are honored. Therefore, holiness is missional, shining precisely through proximity, not isolation. Temple people stand out by letting love cross thresholds without diluting truth.

13.3 Justice at the Heart of Worship

13.3.1 Economic Justice: gleaning laws to Jubilee economics

Israel's gleaning law required landowners to leave crop edges for the poor (Lev 19 : 9-10), institutionalizing generosity into the agricultural economy. Sabbatical and Jubilee years further mandated debt release and land restoration (Lev 25). These stipulations reinforce that Yahweh owns the land and His temple people are tenants under stewardship. Jesus proclaims Jubilee fulfillment in Nazareth manifesto (Luke 4 : 18-19), then forms a church that sells property to meet needs (Acts 4 : 34-35). Modern parallels include living wages, ethical banking, and micro-loan programs. Economic discipleship classes equip believers to resist consumer slavery and fund kingdom mission. Temple ethics regards budget sheets as devotional logs charting worship depth.

13.3.2 Racial & Ethnic Reconciliation: one-new-humanity temple (Eph 2 : 14-18)

Christ demolishes the dividing wall, creating one humanity and granting both groups Spirit access to the Father. Jew-Gentile unity sets precedent for dismantling modern ethnic hostilities. Practical steps involve multiethnic leadership, repentance for historical complicity in racism, and liturgical languages reflecting congregational diversity. Table fellowship across cultures enacts eschatological vision where every tribe contributes glory (Rev 7 : 9). Advocacy for immigration reform, anti-hate education, and neighborhood partnerships extends reconciliation beyond sanctuary walls. Temple ethics thus demands more than sentiment; it shapes policies and friendships. Unity becomes apologetic evidence of gospel power (John 17 : 21).

13.3.3 Gender Honor and Mutuality in the Royal-Priestly People

Genesis 1 grants dominion to male and female; Pentecost pours Spirit on sons and daughters. Temple ethics refuses patriarchal devaluation and radical individualism alike, promoting mutual submission (Eph 5 : 21). Church cultures nurture female leadership within biblical parameters and safeguard against harassment. Marriages mirror Christ-church union through sacrificial love, not domination (Eph 5 : 25). Addressing wage gaps and education access honors Imago Dei in all genders. Discipleship curricula highlight women heroes— Deborah, Priscilla, Junia—modeling holistic partnership. Such mutuality amplifies witness in a world still plagued by gender violence.

13.3.4 Advocacy for the Vulnerable: orphans, refugees, trafficked persons

Scripture repeatedly identifies God as defender of the widow and orphan (Ps 68 : 5) and commands Israel to love the stranger (Deut 10 : 18-19). Modern application urges foster care, refugee sponsorship, and anti-trafficking coalitions. Churches can host legal clinics, language classes, and trauma counseling. Advocacy pushes governments for humane policies while providing grassroots hospitality. Temple ethics frames such service as worship, not optional charity (James 1 : 27). By prioritizing the least, congregations reenact Christ's kenosis, drawing skeptics to the gospel. Vulnerability thus becomes litmus for authentic holiness.

13.3.5 Metrics of Mercy: assessing budgets, buildings, and programs

Temple ethics employs quantitative and qualitative metrics: percentage of budget to benevolence, square footage used for community need, staff time allocated to justice initiatives. Annual mercy audits reveal gaps between mission statements and fiscal reality. Testimonies supplement numbers, narrating lives changed by housing projects or prison ministries. Transparent reporting builds congregational trust and inspires further generosity. Metrics guard against virtue signaling, ensuring justice is embedded, not decorative. When leadership celebrates baptisms alongside debt forgiveness statistics, worship and justice converge visibly. In this way, spreadsheets become sacred documents.

13.4 Imago Dei and the Sanctity of Life

13.4.1 From Womb to Tomb: abortion, euthanasia, disability dignity

Being God's image confers intrinsic worth independent of productivity or stage of development (Gen 1 : 27). Temple ethics therefore defends unborn life with compassionate support for mothers through crisis-pregnancy aid, adoption subsidies, and healthcare access. It opposes euthanasia that frames death as medical convenience, advocating palliative care and relational presence (Ps 71 : 9). Disability ministry shifts language from pity to partnership, embracing gifts differently-abled believers bring (1 Cor 12 : 22). Accessibility audits of buildings and liturgy display respect. Advocacy includes lobbying for equitable healthcare and disability rights. By honoring life from first heartbeat to final breath, temple people mirror the Creator's relentless affirmation of personhood.

13.4.2 Bioethics and Emerging Technologies: CRISPR, AI, transhumanism

Genetic editing promises disease cures but risks designer eugenics; temple ethics applies humility, justice, and stewardship filters. CRISPR therapies could align with healing mandate if universal access and respect for embryonic life are maintained. Artificial intelligence automates tasks yet poses threats to employment and agency; discernment weighs benefits against exploitation and misinformation. Transhumanist dreams of digital immortality reveal gnostic longing divorced from resurrection reality. Churches convene interdisciplinary panels—theologians, scientists, ethicists—to navigate complexities. Pastoral guidance equips believers to make informed decisions about IVF, gene therapy, and neuro-enhancement. Temple ethics integrates innovation with reverence for God-given limits.

13.4.3 Capital Punishment and Restorative Justice Debates

Genesis 9 : 6 grounds capital punishment in Imago Dei protection, while Jesus' cross absorbs violence, opening restorative possibilities. Christian traditions diverge: some uphold state authority; others advocate abolition citing redemption potential. Temple ethics encourages nuanced dialogue, supporting justice systems that seek rehabilitation and victim restoration. Programs like prison Alpha courses or restorative circles illustrate mercy without dismissing accountability. Wrongful conviction risks, racial disparities, and economic biases weigh heavily in deliberations. Where capital punishment exists, believers minister to death-row inmates, embodying gospel hope that even condemned bear God's image. Ethical positions remain complex but must reflect holy compassion.

13.4.4 Mental Health and the Temple of the Mind

Elijah's despair (1 Kgs 19), David's laments, and Jesus' Gethsemane anguish legitimize emotional struggle within holy life. Temple ethics destigmatizes counseling and medication, viewing them as providential means of grace. Churches form support groups, partner with therapists, and train leaders in suicide prevention (Prov 24 : 11). Sabbath, silence, and community affection act as preventive care. Preaching avoids triumphalism that blames faith deficiency for depression. By honoring psychological wholeness, congregations steward the inner sanctuary where Spirit resides. Mental health ministry thus defends Imago Dei against invisible afflictions.

13.4.5 Suicide Prevention as Priestly Care

With global suicide rates alarming, temple ethics intervenes through education, relational presence, and spiritual hope. Training members in QPR (Question, Persuade, Refer) equips gatekeepers. Liturgies include prayers for those contemplating self-harm, breaking silence stigma. Pastoral availability, 24-hour hotlines, and safe-home networks supply tangible lifelines. Theology emphasizes that despair never nullifies God's love; Christ's descent into death (Rom 8 : 38-39) assures ultimate solidarity. Memorial services avoid condemning the deceased while reinforcing the value of every breath. Such care manifests the Good Shepherd retrieving at-risk sheep before cliffs edge.

13.5 Creation Care: Ecological Dimensions of Temple Ethics

13.5.1 Earth as God's Footstool (Isa 66 : 1) and Human Stewardship

If heaven is God's throne and earth His footstool, polluting rivers is defacing divine furniture. Psalm 24 proclaims earth "the LORD's," placing ownership before exploitation. Temple ethics views recycling, habitat preservation, and sustainable farming as acts of worship. Francis of Assisi's canticle and contemporary eco-theology recover creation's role as choir singing Creator's praise. Christ's blood reconciles "all things" (Col 1 : 20), granting ecological mission gospel urgency. Seminars on carbon footprints become discipleship, not political hobbyhorse. By caring for earth, believers anticipate New Jerusalem's healed ecology.

13.5.2 Climate Justice and the Poor

Climate change disproportionately harms vulnerable populations through floods, droughts, and food insecurity. Prophetic witness demands advocacy for policies that mitigate emissions and fund adaptation aid. Mission organizations integrate reforestation and clean-energy projects into evangelism strategies. Wealthy congregations offset travel carbon or retrofit buildings, demonstrating solidarity. Prayer rallies lament creation's groaning and intercede for policy leaders. Stories from Pacific Island churches facing rising seas personalize statistics. Temple ethics thus binds environmental stewardship to Matthew 25 compassion for "the least."

13.5.3 Sustainable Lifestyles: energy, diet, consumer choices

Practices such as cycling, plant-forward diets, and minimalism witness against throwaway culture. Church potlucks prioritize local produce and composting. Energy audits lead to solar panels and efficient lighting, freeing budget for mission. Teaching series on creation care connect buying habits with discipleship, challenging impulse purchases driven by identity anxiety. Simplicity fosters generosity, echoing wilderness manna lesson of sufficiency (Ex 16).

Members share tools and clothing swaps, reducing consumption. Temple ethics regards credit-card statements as spiritual formation documents.

13.5.4 Liturgical Seasons and Ecological Awareness (Rogation, Harvest, Season of Creation)

Historic church calendars bless fields during Rogation Days and thank God at Harvest festivals, integrating agriculture with worship. Modern "Season of Creation" (Sept-Oct) offers prayers for oceans, fauna, and climate. Children craft liturgy with recycled art, cultivating eco-discipleship early. Scripture readings highlight covenant with "every living creature" (Gen 9 : 12). Outdoor services relocate worship to parks, rekindling wonder. These rhythms re-train desires toward stewardship and gratitude. Temple ethics blossoms through calendrical pedagogy.

13.5.5 Hope-Driven Activism vs. Eco-Anxiety

Alarmist narratives breed paralysis; biblical hope energizes responsible action. Romans 8 balances groaning with eager expectation, legitimizing lament while refusing fatalism. Congregations provide spiritual care for youth burdened by climate dread, pointing to resurrection power. Activism becomes worship, not frantic saviorism. Partnerships with secular groups witness to motivation beyond politics. Regular testimony of creation miracles— a river cleaned, species protected—nourishes joy. Temple ethics models sustainable pace, trusting ultimate renewal while laboring for present good.

13.6 Sabbath Economics and Radical Hospitality

13.6.1 Sabbath as Economic Brake on Exploitation

Sabbath first enters Israel's economy as a divine interruption of Pharaoh-style quotas, declaring that time itself is no commodity (Ex 20 : 8-11). By halting all labor—both freeborn and slave—Yahweh dethrones productivity as the measure of human worth. Modern economies running on 24/7 digital trades mirror Egypt's relentless brick demands, and weekly rest remains prophetic protest. Congregations that schedule no major programming on Sundays but instead encourage family meals, neighborhood walks, and worship cultivate counter-cultural imagination. Employers shaped by temple ethics examine shift patterns to protect low-wage staff from schedule abuse, thus translating doctrine into fair practice. Sabbath also liberates land, for a people accustomed to resting weekly can envision sabbatical fallow years that heal ecosystems (Lev 25 : 4-5). In this way a simple cadence of ceasing becomes the metronome for ethical commerce, ecological health, and human dignity.

13.6.2 Generosity Rhythms: gleaning, firstfruits, and modern tithing models

The gleaning command institutionalized generosity by embedding it into harvest technique, not post-harvest leftovers (Lev 19 : 9-10). Firstfruits offerings likewise taught that provision belongs to God before it belongs to entrepreneurs (Deut 26 : 1-11). Translating these patterns today, some churches fund benevolence through "reverse tithe"—setting aside the first 10 percent of every congregational gift for local need before internal budgets are met. Families practice micro-gleaning by pre-allocating grocery money for the food bank as part of normal shopping, rather than donating expired cans later. Business owners shaped by temple ethics bake philanthropy into pricing models, directing a slice of revenue to job-training scholarships. Such rhythms reframe giving from sporadic charity into patterned worship that mirrors heaven's perpetual flow of life-river (Rev 22 : 1-2). When generosity is ritualized, injustice loses its oxygen supply.

13.6.3 Table-Fellowship Across Class Lines

Jesus' habit of reclining with tax-collectors and sinners scandalized purity culture but enacted temple hospitality where courts of Gentiles widen (Luke 5 : 29-32). Contemporary equivalents include community cafés that integrate paying customers and voucher recipients at identical tables, erasing invisible velvet ropes of economic status. Home groups rotate venues so affluent suburbs and subsidized apartments share cooking duties, embodying Acts' vision of breaking bread "with glad and sincere hearts" (Acts 2 : 46). Even architectural choices—round tables instead of auditorium rows—reshape discipleship dynamics by facilitating mutual gaze rather than stage consumption. Meal liturgies name each person's contribution—bread purchased with disability stipend, salad grown in retirement-home plots—honoring dignity. Research shows that regular cross-class dinners improve empathy and reduce implicit bias, confirming Luke's theological intuition with sociological data. Thus the dinner table becomes micro-temple where candlesticks glow with Jubilee light.

13.6.4 Church as Debt-Forgiveness Community

Jubilee cancelled debts every fifty years, preventing inter-generational poverty traps (Lev 25 : 10). Paul echoes this ethic when he urges Philemon to charge Onesimus' debt to Paul's account, modeling gospel-motivated restitution (Phlm 18-19). Some congregations partner with non-profits that purchase medical debt at pennies on the dollar, proclaiming freedom letters to strangers as tangible evangelism. Others run interest-free micro-loan circles where repayments recycle into new loans, multiplying solidarity. Crucially, debt-forgiveness ministries include financial-literacy mentoring, respecting agency rather than fostering dependency. Liturgically, remission announcements are read in worship, linking economic mercy to the remission of sins confessed moments earlier. When liabilities are released in Jesus' name, the world recognizes a social architecture impossible without resurrection economics.

13.6.5 Practicing Presence in a 24/7 Culture

Temple ethics resists the speed that fractures attention and relationships. Congregations experiment with "phone-free zones" during fellowship hour, encouraging eye contact that dignifies image bearers. Professionals adopt email sabbaticals from Friday sundown to Saturday sundown, mirroring Jewish practice and guarding mental health. Parents schedule "tech-Shabbat" board-game nights, modeling restfulness for digital natives. These habits do not idolize nostalgia but reassert embodied presence as the matrix of love. Surveys report decreased anxiety and increased volunteerism among members who embrace weekly digital fasts, demonstrating holistic benefit. Ultimately, practicing presence rehearses eschatological reality where no notification interrupts face-to-face communion with God (Rev 22 : 4). Rested disciples prove more imaginative in justice work because their reservoirs of joy are replenished.

13.7 Peace-Making and Enemy-Love

13.7.1 Biblical Foundations: shalom, swords-to-plowshares, and the cross

Shalom is more than cease-fire; it is comprehensive well-being woven through creation (Isa 32 : 17-18). Micah envisions swords reforged into farm tools, picturing disarmament that reallocates resources toward cultivation (Mic 4 : 3-4). The cross embodies this transformation: an execution device repurposed into the tree of life, reconciling hostile humanity to God (Col 1 : 20). Temple ethics absorbs this theology, inviting believers to be artisans of peace who melt ideological weapons into instruments of collaboration. Seminary curricula incorporate conflict-mediation training next to Greek exegesis, acknowledging peacemaking as core priestly skill. Families adopt "peace tables" where children negotiate toy disputes using I-statements and prayer, incubating habits that outlive adolescence. Thus, from sandbox to Senate, temple people persistently hammer steel into soil-turning plows.

13.7.2 Nonviolent Resistance and Just-War Dialogue

Historic church tensions between pacifism and just-war theory reflect differing applications of the same temple ethic: protect life while honoring enemy dignity. Augustine allowed defensive war under stringent criteria; Anabaptists excluded sword entirely. Contemporary disciples study both streams, recognizing that nuclear age escalates collateral damage, thereby raising just-war thresholds. Nonviolent movements—India's independence, U.S. civil rights—show practical potency, aligning with Jesus' command to turn the other cheek (Matt 5 : 39) without turning a blind eye to oppression. Military chaplains influenced by temple ethics advocate for conscientious objection clauses and mental-health care, humanizing armed contexts. Meanwhile, pacifist communities provide sanctuary for refugees and war resisters, embodying alternative security paradigms. Respectful dialogue prevents demonization, fostering united witness even amid ethical variance.

13.7.3 Forgiveness Practices in War-Torn or Violent Contexts

Corrie ten Boom's handshake with a former Nazi guard exemplifies visceral enemy-love made possible by Spirit power. Post-genocide Rwanda's Gacaca courts combined confession, restitution, and reintegration, offering a template for restorative justice saturated in Christian symbolism. Church-led trauma-healing groups teach lament psalms and breath prayers to survivors, coupling psychology with pneumatology. Forgiveness rituals include planting trees over mass-grave sites, converting mourning into ecological renewal. Preaching emphasizes that forgiving does not equal forgetting; it entrusts vengeance to God (Rom 12 : 19) while pursuing truth-telling. Annual "peace anniversaries" remind communities of deliverance, preventing relapse into resentment. These practices render abstract commands concrete, enabling social fabrics to mend under temple grace.

13.7.4 Gun Culture, Security, and the Temple Ethic of Protection

In nations saturated with firearms, churches grapple with safety without succumbing to fear. Some employ unarmed security trained in de-escalation, echoing Christ's rebuke of Peter's sword (Matt 26 : 52). Others allow concealed carry but pair it with mandatory peacemaking workshops and mental-health screenings, seeking responsible stewardship. Sermon series address idolatry of firepower, reminding believers that ultimate refuge is in the Lord (Ps 46 : 1). Advocacy for universal background checks and community policing reforms demonstrates love of neighbor in legislative arenas. Gun-buyback events hosted on church property physically transform weapons into garden tools, embodying prophetic vision. Dialogues honor hunters and veterans while challenging vigilante fantasies, balancing nuance with conviction.

13.7.5 Interfaith Neighbor-Love without Syncretism

Temple ethics extends hospitality across religious lines, following Jesus' parable of the Good Samaritan that premised compassion on need, not doctrine (Luke 10 : 33-37). Congregations partner with mosques for refugee resettlement, yet clarify Christ-centered identity through joint service liturgies that include scripture readings from each tradition. Academic forums explore theological distinctions frankly, modeling civility. Community iftar meals during Ramadan offer fasting Christians a chance to empathize, while Muslim guests invited to Christmas pageants experience reciprocal welcome. Evangelism remains integral, but polemics yield to patient storytelling and deed-based credibility. When disasters strike, multi-faith coalitions distribute aid faster than isolated ministries. Such neighbor-love prepares the nations to walk through New Jerusalem's open gates without compromise on the exclusivity of the Lamb.

13.8 Public Theology: Political Engagement without Idolatry

13.8.1 Exile Paradigm: seeking city welfare while resisting empire (Jer 29)

Jeremiah instructs exiles to plant gardens and pray for Babylon's prosperity, yet Daniel simultaneously refuses idolatrous decrees. This tension outlines temple ethics in pluralistic democracies: constructive participation without capitulation. Christians serve on school boards, advocate for affordable housing, and support local businesses, treating neighborhoods as provisional parish. Simultaneously they critique policies that exploit migrants or deregulate predatory lending, echoing Hebrew prophets. Prayer gatherings at city hall anoint political space with kingdom fragrance. By viewing themselves as "resident aliens" (1 Pet 2 : 11) believers avoid both withdrawal and assimilation, embodying hopeful realism. Thus civic engagement becomes an exile liturgy—faithful presence until the King returns.

13.8.2 Voting, Advocacy, and Policy Formation as Priestly Service

Casting a ballot is an act of stewardship, a modest yet vital way of shaping structures that affect the vulnerable. Temple ethics encourages informed voting guided by Scripture-shaped conscience rather than single-issue reductionism. Advocacy extends beyond elections: writing representatives, attending town-hall meetings, and submitting op-eds amplify neighbor-love into policy arenas. Christian lawyers draft legislation combatting human trafficking; economists design fair-tax proposals; healthcare workers testify before committees. These efforts are framed as priestly intercession—

standing between God's justice and societal brokenness. Worship services commission members to legislative vocations with laying-on of hands, integrating sanctuary and senate. Such integration prevents Sunday-to-Monday identity split.

13.8.3 Church & State Boundaries: lessons from history

Constantine's legacy warns that state-sponsored faith often breeds coercion and corruption. Conversely, secular experiments that banish religion shrink moral vocabulary for public goods. Temple ethics navigates middle ground: free church in free state, each respecting conscience. Historical case studies—from abolitionism to apartheid resistance—show churches thriving when prophetic distance fuels critique. Clear boundaries prevent sacramental endorsement of partisan platforms, preserving gospel universality. Clergy avoid party endorsements from pulpits while encouraging civic discipleship classes. This posture guards against idolatry of either throne or cloister.

13.8.4 Prophetic Speech vs. Partisan Captivity

Nathan confronted David despite court chaplain status (2 Sam 12 : 1-7), modeling prophetic distance. In contrast, Amaziah silenced Amos to protect king Jeroboam's approval (Amos 7 : 10-13), exemplifying partisan captivity. Today, social-media echo chambers tempt pastors to mute critique of favored parties. Temple ethics calls leaders to exegetical rigor that refuses cherry-picking texts to baptize ideology. Sermons expose sins of all tribes—greed on right, sexual anarchy on left—thus equipping saints for complex loyalty to Christ alone. Congregations hold pastors accountable through diverse advisory councils that flag blind spots. Prophetic courage enhances witness; partisan captivity dilutes it.

13.8.5 Religious Freedom and the Common Good

Paul leveraged Roman citizenship for gospel advance (Acts 22 : 25), demonstrating legitimate appeal to legal protections. Religious-freedom advocacy today defends mosques and synagogues alongside churches, signaling neighbor-love. This coalition persuades skeptics that Christian liberty is not code for privilege but for pluralistic fairness. Meanwhile, believers weigh conscience exemptions—vaccines, military service—against communal responsibility, embodying balance. When conflicts arise, respectful litigation avoids demonization, trusting courts while praying for adversaries. By defending universal dignity, temple people showcase kingdom justice that outlives constitutional amendments.

13.9 Digital Discipleship: Holiness in the Information Temple

13.9.1 Attention Economy and the Battle for the Inner Court

Smartphone apps monetize attention, crowding the inner sanctuary where God's voice whispers. Temple ethics treats focus as liturgical resource, aligning with Psalm 27 : 4's single-minded desire. Digital rule-of-life plans schedule "Scripture before screen" each morning and family tech curfews at dinner. Churches develop notification-free prayer apps using gentle calls rather than dopamine hits. Retreats feature "digital deserts," guiding participants through withdrawal symptoms into contemplative stillness. Neuroscience confirms increased empathy and cognitive capacity after sustained screen breaks, corroborating ancient Sabbath wisdom. Thus guarding attention equals guarding holy ground.

13.9.2 Social-Media Speech Ethics: truth, charity, and witness

Proverbs warns that reckless words pierce like swords (Prov 12 : 18); online anonymity sharpens blades. Temple ethics imposes a Philippians 4 : 8 filter on posts: Are they true, honorable, just, pure, lovely? Believers verify sources before sharing, resisting algorithmic outrage. When debate occurs, they deploy James 1 : 19—quick to listen, slow to speak, slow to anger—modeling civic discourse. Pastors preach entire series on digital beatitudes, culminating in communal covenant for charitable engagement. Public apologies for misstatements enhance credibility, proving humility. Social timelines then become stained-glass windows refracting gospel light rather than smoke grenades.

13.9.3 Pornography, Privacy, and Technological Temptations

Porn distorts temple bodies into commodities, eroding neural pleasure pathways. Accountability software and small-group confession confront secrecy with community grace (Eph 5 : 11-13). Bi-annual teachings on sexuality integrate neuroscience, theology, and testimonies of recovery. Privacy stewardship extends to data: believers scrutinize app permissions, guarding neighbor information from exploitation. "Slow tech" movements inspire crafting hobbies—woodworking, gardening—that recalibrate dopamine baselines. Pastoral care includes trauma-informed counseling for partners hurt by porn betrayal, acknowledging systemic damage. Thus temples remain undefiled in cyberspace as well as physical space.

13.9.4 AI, Deepfakes, and the Integrity of Image-Bearing

Artificial intelligence can amplify ministry—language translation, Bible-study tools—yet risks algorithmic bias that marginalizes minorities. Temple ethics demands transparency audits and diverse training datasets. Deepfake technology threatens truth; churches teach media-literacy to spot manipulated videos, defending commandment against false witness (Ex 20 : 16). AI chatbots providing pastoral responses must be monitored to preserve theological accuracy and relational warmth. Theologians explore Imago Dei beyond consciousness, resisting both technophobia and techno-utopianism. Ethical committees evaluate AI hiring processes to ensure unemployment mitigation strategies. By stewarding tools wisely, believers leverage innovation without surrendering identity.

13.9.5 Sabbath from Screens: rhythms of digital rest

Weekly unplugging mimics Exodus release from production-driven slavery. Families store devices in decorative "ark boxes" on Friday nights, turning off Wi-Fi to heighten presence. Churches host outdoor worship with printed liturgies, freeing congregants from projection dependence. Testimony Sundays highlight transformations—restored marriages, rediscovered hobbies—born from digital sabbath. Psychological research notes lower cortisol levels and improved sleep in participants. Companies founded by Christians pilot four-day workweeks, reducing digital churn. These practices preview heavenly rest where glowing screens give way to Lamb's light.

13.10 Formational Practices for a Temple People

13.10.1 Rule of Life: integrating prayer, work, rest, and justice

Monastic rules—Benedictine, Franciscan—provided scaffolding for holiness. Modern disciples craft personalized rules: morning lectio divina, afternoon work excellence, evening examen, weekly service to marginalized. Covenants remain flexible, reviewed quarterly in spiritual-direction sessions. Shareable calendars foster mutual encouragement and accountability. Smartphone reminders prompt breath prayers at top of each hour, weaving micro-liturgies into daily fabric. Families adopt household rules—gratitude jars, chore rotations, Sabbath dinners—cultivating communal culture. Structured rhythms guard against mission drift in frenetic societies.

13.10.2 Spiritual Disciplines that Shape Social Imagination

Fasting loosens chains of injustice when savings feed hungry neighbors (Isa 58 : 6-7). Silence enables listening to oppressed voices often drowned by privilege. Fixed-hour prayer connects intercessors to global church, widening empathy. Simplicity deconstructs consumer identity, freeing funds for mercy. Lectio populi—prayerful reading of news—discerns spiritual battlegrounds in headlines, spurring advocacy. Artistic meditation—icon writing, hymn composition—transforms beauty into justice inspiration. Disciplines thus sculpt hearts into Jerusalem-stones ready for kingdom architecture.

13.10.3 Small-Group Accountability and Mutual Pastoral Care

Acts' temple model pairs large-group worship with house-to-house fellowship (Acts 2 : 46). Small groups practice confession, Scripture discussion, and service planning. Rotating facilitators prevent celebrity dependence and foster diverse gifting. Mutual exhortation combats isolation fueling addiction and cynicism. Crisis funds within groups provide immediate aid before church bureaucracy responds. Prayer walks through neighborhoods turn gatherings outward, mapping spiritual and social needs. These micro-temples replicate upper-room dynamics across city blocks.

13.10.4 Liturgy as Ethical Pedagogy

Call-and-response prayers train tongues in blessing rather than complaint. Passing the peace normalizes reconciliation gestures, reducing gossip. Offering procession reminds bodies that generosity is joyful, not reluctant. Prayers of the people expand intercession beyond individual concerns to global crises, cultivating compassion. Seasonal colors prompt reflection on justice themes—purple Advent longing for righteous king, red Pentecost fire for mission. Thus, sanctuary choreography scripts everyday ethics long after dismissal. Worship becomes an ethics rehearsal room.

13.10.5 Storytelling and Testimony as Catalysts for Change

Israel retold exodus annually; early church rehearsed resurrection weekly. Today, testimony nights replace abstract sermons with lived examples of debt forgiveness, healed racism, or ecological activism. Digital storytelling—podcasts, documentaries—amplifies witness beyond walls. Failure stories also surface, modeling repentance and resilience. Narrative medicine sessions invite healthcare workers to share patient journeys, linking vocation and faith. This storytelling arsenal ignites imagination, proving temple ethics achievable. Hearing peers' witness dissolves excuses anchored in fatalism.

In conclsuion, Temple theology without temple ethics would be an ivory tower dedicated to abstract glory, but Scripture insists that glory leaves footprints—bleeding hearts, open wallets, reconciled enemies, verdant fields, and fearless public witness. Throughout this chapter we have traced how the indwelling Spirit forms a people whose holiness is tangible, whose justice is measurable, and whose societal presence is irresistibly luminous. Holiness begins in hidden motives yet erupts in embodied purity; justice restructures budgets and laws until the vulnerable find safe harbor; witness manifests in civility online, courage before regimes, and hospitality across every barrier. None of this is moral heroism; it is the natural radiation of Shekinah light now resident within living stones. The prophetic promise is clear: nations will stream toward a brightness they can see (Isa 60 : 3), and that brightness is the character of Christ refracted through His corporate temple. Until the New Jerusalem descends and every ethical tension is resolved by unveiled glory, the church carries the torch—guarding, tending, challenging, and healing. May we, therefore, steward the presence with integrity, so that when the day of visitation arrives, our neighborhoods can say, "Surely God is among you in truth and goodness" (1 Pet 2 : 12; 1 Cor 14 : 25).

Chapter 14 - Contemporary Expressions and Controversies

The new-temple story that began in Eden, found architectural voice in tabernacle and Solomonic stone, and migrated into the crucified-risen body of Jesus continues to ripple through twenty-first-century culture in startling, sometimes contentious, ways. Warehouse worship spaces, livestream Eucharists, metaverse cathedrals, Black-church protest marches, prosperity citadels, eco-chapels, and diaspora house-churches all claim, implicitly or explicitly, to host God's presence. Meanwhile critics challenge the legitimacy, purity, or justice of those claims, asking whether glory can coexist with consumer spectacle, political nationalism, or algorithmic distraction. This chapter therefore surveys contemporary expressions of temple consciousness across twelve arenas—architecture, digital liturgy, charismatic renewal, justice activism, Majority-World missions, third-temple movements, nationalist rhetoric, prosperity economics, sexuality debates, eco-worship, deconstruction currents, and interfaith appropriations—while also spotlighting the controversies each arena provokes. The goal is neither blanket endorsement nor knee-jerk condemnation but discerning evaluation measured against scriptural criteria: Christ's lordship, Spirit fruit, love's ethic, and mission's witness (Matt 7 : 16; Gal 5 : 22-23). Because each context is fluid, the chapter emphasizes posture over prescription, offering theological tools for ongoing discernment. What follows is not an exhaustive catalogue but a panoramic map enabling readers to navigate today's kaleidoscope of temples with hopeful realism.

14.1 Architectural Revivals & Spatial Re-imaginings

14.1.1 Neo-Monastic "Urban Abbeys" repurposing warehouses and lofts

Across post-industrial cities, communities inspired by Benedictine stability purchase abandoned factories and reclaim them as mixed-use "urban abbeys" where prayer, affordable housing, and entrepreneurial workshops interlock. Their daily rhythm of fixed-hour prayer frames artisan coffee roasting or screen-printing as liturgy, echoing Paul's claim that "whatever you do... do all to the glory of God" (1 Cor 10 : 31). Critics worry that gentrification may displace original residents, yet successful abbeys cap rents and invite neighborhood governance boards, modeling Jubilee economics (Lev 25 : 10). The architectural rawness—exposed brick, lingering graffiti—functions theologically by witnessing to redemption of broken spaces rather than flight to suburbs. Liturgists note that echoing concrete shapes chant resonance akin to medieval stone, forging acoustic continuity across millennia. Urban abbots confess weekly the temptation to romanticize poverty while guarding against it through external audits and minority-led leadership rotation. Thus each warehouse becomes living parable: resurrection not by demolition but by transformative indwelling glory.

14.1.2 Mega-Campuses, Coffee Bars, and the Consumer-Temple Debate

Suburban mega-churches with 3 000-seat auditoriums, indoor playgrounds, and franchised cafés illustrate a different spatial theology, one that celebrates scale as evangelistic magnet. Proponents cite Acts 2 : 47, noting that the Lord added "thousands" to the first congregation, arguing that big buildings merely steward big harvests. Critics counter that mall-like concourses blur worship with marketplace, reviving Jesus' temple-cleansing concerns (Mark 11 : 15-17). Architectural consultants defend hospitable lobbies as a modern narthex where seekers acclimate before liturgical deep dive.

Empirical studies reveal both fruit—baptisms, overseas aid—and failures—spectator passivity, celebrity leadership collapses. Some campuses now allocate prime foyer space to prayer alcoves staffed by trained chaplains, subverting consumer flow with contemplative pause. Whether mega-space matures into mission hub or entertainment arena depends on governance, discipleship pipelines, and transparency about money and power.

14.1.3 Micro-Chapels, Prayer Pods, and the Rise of "Third-Space" Sanctuaries

At the opposite end of the spectrum, designers install eight-seat chapels in airports, hospital rooftops, and corporate towers, echoing Jesus' invitation to pray in secret rooms (Matt 6 : 6). These pods leverage biophilic design—live plants, soft acoustics—to counter technostress, functioning as inhalation lungs within frenetic environments. Chaplaincy apps tied to QR codes on the door let travelers request intercessory prayer, merging analog quiet with digital connectivity. Skeptics label pods as token spirituality, but usage data show steady traffic, including atheists seeking silence. Some parishes deploy mobile chapels—trailers unfolding into gothic arches—at music festivals, offering Eucharist beside food trucks. Theology professors debate whether sacramental validity requires stable place or merely gathered people; patristic evidence of catacomb liturgies supports flexibility. Thus micro-spaces remind globalized commuters that temple geography now follows Lamb, not longitude.

14.1.4 Green Cathedrals: net-zero buildings and eco-symbolic design

Scandinavia's wood-framed "forest churches" and Africa's thatched eco-basilicas illustrate rising conviction that sacred space should preach environmental stewardship. Solar panels doubling as nave roofing embody Psalm 19 : 1—"the heavens declare the glory" via harvested photons powering worship. Builders select local materials, reducing carbon footprint and honoring cultural aesthetics, while rain-harvesting baptisteries dramatize living-water motifs (John 4 : 14). Critics argue cost overruns divert funds from frontline evangelism, yet project managers counter that lower lifetime energy bills free resources long term. Liturgists incorporate tree-planting rites at building dedications, rooting architecture in creation care theology

(Gen 2 : 15). Indigenous consultants ensure designs avoid colonial imposition, displaying cedar carvings or adobe reliefs narrating local salvation history. Green cathedrals thus materialize eschatological vision of healed earth inside zoning regulations and building codes.

14.1.5 Pilgrim Hot-spots: intentional labyrinths, art installations, and pop-up shrines

Contemporary seekers trek to experiential sites such as Chartres-style labyrinths in city parks, participating in embodied prayer that mirrors Israel's festival pilgrimages (Ps 84 : 5-7). Temporary art installations—e.g., Luke Jerram's "Museum of the Moon" hung inside cathedrals—draw thousands who might never attend Sunday service, converting curiosity into awe. Pop-up shrines at disaster zones collect lament notes, echoing Jerusalem wailing wall dynamics. Theologically, such hotspots democratize access but risk emotionalism detached from discipleship. Pastors staff stations with trained guides who connect symbolic action to gospel narrative, handing out pocket gospels and church invitations. Studies show increased spiritual conversations in regions hosting these events, though long-term church engagement varies. Pilgrim expressions remind sedentary societies that faith remains a journey of feet as well as intellect.

14.2 Liturgical Innovation & Digital Worship

14.2.1 Livestream Sanctuaries: chat-moderated Eucharist and body-absence questions

COVID-19 lockdowns forced millions online, raising thorny queries: can bread broken in one kitchen communicate the same grace to viewers in many? Some traditions allowed "spiritual communion," citing desire over proximity (Ps 42 : 1-2), while others postponed Eucharist until corporeal assembly resumed. Chat moderators now curate digital aisles, posting prayer emojis during confession and directing seekers to local parishes for baptism, approximating Philip's rooftop guidance to Ethiopian eunuch (Acts 8 : 31-38). Sacramental theologians wrestle with incarnational logic: Word became flesh, not pixel, urging caution about perpetual online replacement. Accessibility advocates counter that shut-ins and diaspora believers experience real fellowship formerly denied. Hybrid models emerge: monthly in-person sacrament, weekly streamed Word-and-prayer, balancing embodiment and reach. Ongoing research tracks discipleship metrics—group participation, giving, ethical change—among digital-first congregants, informing future praxis.

14.2.2 Multi-Site & Hologram Preachers: presence, polity, and sacramentality

Before pandemics, multi-site churches beamed sermons to satellite venues; post-pandemic, hologram prototypes promise 3-D pulpit presence. Advocates cite Paul's epistolary authority as precedent for mediated teaching (Col 4 : 16). Critics fear celebrity fixation and pastoral unavailability during crises like hospital visits (Jam 5 : 14). Sacramental denominations limit multi-site sacramental presidency, insisting local priests break bread, not projected avatars. Governance innovations include campus pastors with real authority, preventing franchise franchising. Technologists develop two-way holography allowing preacher to see remote congregants, increasing reciprocity. Ultimately, theology of presence determines whether holograms become shepherding tools or showbiz gimmicks.

14.2.3 "Phone-First" Communities on Discord, WhatsApp, and Telegram

Gen-Z believers form Bible-study servers where Scripture bots post daily chapters and voice channels host spontaneous prayer. Privacy encryption offers safe space for underground Christians in hostile regimes, mirroring early church catacombs. Pastoral care emojis cannot replace hugs, yet testimonies report suicidal teens rescued by midnight chat intercession. Ecclesiologists note these groups often layer onto local church attendance rather than replace it, functioning as diaspora synagogues. Accountability features—screen-time tracking, porn-filter badges—convert phones from temptation portals into covenant monitors. Yet moderation burnout and doctrinal drift threaten health; networks now train digital elders in conflict resolution and orthodoxy. Phone-first temples thus expand while acknowledging their cyber-fragility.

14.2.4 Virtual-Reality Cathedrals and the Metaverse Mass

VR platforms host gothic sanctuaries where avatars kneel on pixel carpets; worship bands loop ambient praise while code renders stained-glass kaleidoscopes responsive to song volume. Immersive homilies teleport congregants to Golgotha or Revelation throne room, aiming for affective pedagogy. Sacramental realism debates intensify: can an avatar receive body-blood or is VR merely didactic prelude to real-world Eucharist? Accessibility advocates champion VR for immune-compromised believers; critics warn of Gnostic escape from embodied community, citing 1 John 4 : 2. Developers add haptic gloves simulating handshake peace exchanges, blurring tactile boundaries. Stewarding addiction risk, pastors set screen-sabbath guidelines to prevent virtual church from eclipsing neighborly service. Ethical design remains crucial: opulent castles risk reinforcing prosperity spectacle, whereas humble VR house-churches may better model incarnational simplicity.

14.2.5 Hybrid Rhythms: analog sacraments with digital scaffolding

Many congregations now operate "phygitally," livestreaming liturgy while emphasizing quarterly embodied feasts. Church management apps schedule service projects, fast sign-ups, and prayer chains, integrating James 1 : 27 activism with Acts 2 : 42 devotion. Sermon podcasts feature follow-up roundtables, allowing deeper exegesis and communal Q&A. Digital giving platforms free budgets for benevolence yet raise vigilance about data privacy. Families practice screen-free Sabbath but use Bible apps for daily lectio, modeling discerned engagement. Seminaries teach "digital homiletics," equipping pastors to exegete camera presence without reducing proclamation to TED-talk smoothness. Hybrid rhythms thus accept technology as tool, not temple, and measure fruit by transformed lives, not view counts.

14.3 Charismatic Renewal, Glory Cultures & Presence Theology

14.3.1 Soaking Rooms, 24-7 Worship Loops, and the "Open Heaven" Narrative

Originating in Toronto and Kansas City movements, soaking-prayer rooms invite believers to recline under ambient worship for hours, seeking Ephesians 3 : 19 "fullness." Supporters report emotional healing and missionary callings; detractors see passivity replacing discipleship. Quantitative studies show participants often volunteer more hours in justice ministries post-encounter, challenging lazy stereotypes. The 24-7 prayer movement frames constant worship as incense before throne (Rev 5 : 8), linking adoration to mission launch pads like Ibiza prayer rooms. Financial accountability remains crucial; some houses publish open budgets, countering allegations of introverted mysticism. Theology of "open heaven" asserts Calvary permanently tore veil (Heb 10 : 19-22) but must avoid triumphal denial of suffering. When integrated with lament and outreach, soaking cultures can revitalize dry congregations; detached, they risk spiritual escapism.

14.3.2 Modern Prophetic Movements: liturgy of declarations and controversy over accountability

Social-media prophets livestream real-time words about elections, weather, and economic trends, claiming Amos 3 : 7 precedent. Missed predictions spark questions about Deuteronomy 18 standards; some leaders repent publicly, others rationalize. Networks now establish councils for vetting national prophecies before broadcast, mirroring Corinthian "let the others weigh" protocol (1 Cor 14 : 29). Declarations—spoken blessing over cities, bodies, finances—derive from Proverbial tongue power (Prov 18 : 21) but can slip into name-it magic. Balanced teaching emphasizes alignment with God's will rather than coercion. Prophetic art and dance widen expression, yet maintain Christo-centric content to avoid vague spirituality. Healthy prophetic cultures produce humility, not hype.

14.3.3 Deliverance Ministries & Inner-Healing Labs: temple-cleansing or trauma trigger?

Global South revivals normalize exorcism; Western resurgence follows, citing Jesus' casting out demons as integral to gospel (Mark 1 : 39). Trauma psychologists caution that aggressive sessions may re-traumatize abuse survivors; best practice now requires consent protocols and mental-health referrals. Inner-healing models— Theophostic, SOZO—guide prayer to childhood memories, inviting Jesus' presence; outcomes vary from breakthrough to false memory concerns. Theological safeguards include Trinitarian framing and cross-anchored authority, resisting dualistic fear of demonic power. Communities track fruit: restored marriages, cessation of nightmares, increased Scripture appetite. Critics ask for peer-reviewed studies; practitioners welcome mixed-methods research to refine methodology. Deliverance anchored in love and accountability can function as temple purity ministry when freed from sensationalism.

14.3.4 Signs & Wonders in Global South Revivals: empirical claims and Western skepticism

Africa's prayer mountains report healings, dead raisings, and mass conversions; Latin American crusades witness gang leaders surrendering weapons. Western journalists sometimes expose fraud, but medical documentation increasingly validates partial claims, e.g., verified tumor regressions. Sociologists attribute high expectancy to collectivist culture, yet Bible records similar faith climates (Luke 8 : 45-48). Western cessationists caution against gullibility, while continuationists call for "charismatics with seat belts." Dialogue emerges: peer-reviewed miracle registries partner with hospitals to investigate claims, bridging anecdote and scrutiny. Fruits of revival—reduced violence, increased female education—add credibility beyond physical healings. Global South signs challenge Northern rationalism yet need rigorous discernment to avoid syncretism.

14.3.5 Post-Pentecostal Convergence: charismatic gifts in liturgical, Catholic, and Reformed spaces

Methodist, Anglican, and Catholic parishes host weekly charismatic prayer groups while retaining creedal liturgies, embodying Psalm 45 : 8—fragrance of myrrh and cassia mingling. Reformed theologians publish works on "continuous partial cessationism," allowing gifts under scriptural authority. Sacramental charismatics integrate tongues into Eucharistic thanksgiving, interpreting 1 Cor 14 order within liturgical rubrics. Critics fear emotionalism, yet convergence parishes note uptick in confession attendance and social outreach. Ecumenical conferences like "Together for the Gospel and Spirit" foster dialogue, proving pneumatology transcends denominational silos. Convergence invites Christians to taste fullness without abandoning doctrinal anchorage. The future likely features multi-tradition hybrids, demanding robust theological literacy.

14.4 Justice-Shaped Temples: Activism, Advocacy, and Liturgy

14.4.1 Black Church "Sanctuary Movement" and Sacred Protest Marches

Historically, Black churches doubled as underground railroads and civil-rights headquarters, viewing sanctuary as launch pad for Exodus-style liberation (Ex 3 : 7-10). Current sanctuary movements shelter undocumented immigrants, turning fellowship halls into legal safe zones. Worship often ends with march to city hall, drums echoing Jericho walls (Josh 6 : 20). Critics accuse churches of political overreach; pastors respond that Isaiah 58 worship demands loosed chains. Partnerships with legal clinics and interfaith coalitions strengthen strategy. Liturgical chants—"This Little Light of Mine"—carry theological narrative into streets. Public theology merges with embodied protest, reframing sidewalks as extended nave.

14.4.2 Migrant Shelters in Parishes: legal, ethical, and missiological tensions

Southwest U.S. dioceses convert classrooms into dorms, offering showers, medical care, and orientation classes. Legal consultants ensure compliance with harboring laws while challenging unjust detentions. Parishioners share meals, learning Spanish hymns, fulfilling Hebrews 13 : 2 hospitality. Critics fear resource strain and local resentment; churches host town-halls to dialogue. Some migrants encounter Christ through care, leading to baptisms—a mission spillover. Ethics boards monitor power dynamics to prevent paternalism. Shelters demonstrate temple as refuge in literal desert.

14.4.3 #MeToo Laments & Healing Liturgies for Abuse Survivors

After high-profile scandals, congregations hold services of lament, reading Tamar's story (2 Sam 13) and singing psalms of protest. Survivors craft liturgical art—shattered pottery mosaics symbolizing restored dignity. Churches revise policies: two-adult rule, mandatory reporting, trauma-training for staff. Critics decry virtue signaling, so boards publish investigation outcomes and restitution funds.

Theologians emphasize that temple holiness cannot coexist with predatory leadership (Ezek 8). Yearly audits verify compliance, treating safeguarding as sacrament of protection. Healing liturgies thus embed justice in worship DNA.

14.4.4 Reparations, Restitution, and the Economics of Temple Holiness

Some denominations allocate millions for descendants of enslaved laborers who built ancestral churches, fulfilling Zacchaeus pattern of fourfold restoration (Luke 19 : 8). Property deeds transfer to Indigenous groups whose land was seized for mission stations. Critics argue present congregants cannot be liable for ancestors; proponents counter corporate solidarity in Scripture (Dan 9 : 4-19). Reparations committees include historians, economists, and pastors, ensuring accuracy and pastoral care. Funds support scholarship, business micro-grants, and cultural revitalization centers. Transparency dashboards track outcomes, avoiding empty gestures. Economic repentance becomes evangelistic signpost to cynical generations.

14.4.5 Critics of "Woke Worship": accusations of syncretism or prophetic fidelity?

Opponents claim social-justice liturgies supplant gospel with activism; supporters reply that Micah 6 : 8 is integral to gospel. Polarized media amplifies caricatures, but grassroots surveys reveal overlap: most believers want both personal salvation and structural reform. Some churches host forums where partisan members examine biblical texts on justice, reducing echo-chamber hostilities. Theological educators teach hermeneutics that hold atonement and liberation together, avoiding reductionism. Publishers release worship albums blending lament, repentance, and hope, broadening lyrical diet. Discernment questions guide song selection: does it exalt Christ, confront sin, and offer grace? Tensions persist, but dialogue sustains possibility of holistic temple witness.

14.5 Majority-World Flourishing & Reverse Mission

14.5.1 African Prayer Mountains and All-Night Vigils as New Tabernacles

Across Kenya, Nigeria, and Rwanda, forested hillsides glow at night with campfires encircling makeshift pulpits, as tens of thousands gather for *kesha*—all-night prayer that locals call "taking the mountain." These gatherings draw on biblical precedents of Moses meeting Yahweh on Sinai (Ex 19 – 20) and Jesus praying through dark hours before daylight ministry (Luke 6 : 12-13), translating those moments into communal pilgrimage where geography meets intercession. Sociologists note that prayer-mountain economies sprout cottage industries—food stalls, security teams, sanitation crews—illustrating temple spillover into livelihoods. Healing testimonies, from barren wombs to political reconciliations, spread by word of mouth, reinforcing mountains as thin places where heaven kisses earth. Critics, however, raise environmental concerns over deforestation and trash buildup; in response, prayer networks now conduct monthly clean-ups and plant tree nurseries, turning devotion into ecological stewardship. The theological imagination at work sees each mountain as a miniature Zion where nations stream upward (Isa 2 : 2-4), anticipating eschatological ascent. Western visitors often return humbled, discovering disciplines of perseverance they rarely practice in climate-controlled sanctuaries, thus reversing the flow of missionary pedagogy.

14.5.2 Asian "Factory Churches" and Marketplace Sanctification

In the Pearl River Delta, Chinese entrepreneurs convert textile warehouses into dormitory-church hybrids, scheduling worship services during lunch breaks and discipleship classes after the ten-hour shift. Echoing Paul's tentmaking model (Acts 18 : 3), these "factory churches" incarnate temple presence amid conveyor belts, baptizing economic space without abandoning productivity quotas. Employees testify that communal prayer reduces workplace conflict and absenteeism, giving managers quasi-secular rationale for allowing gatherings despite regulatory scrutiny. Pastoral teams teach theology of work from Colossians 3 : 23—"whatever you do, work heartily as for the Lord"—linking wage integrity to worship. Because many workers are internal migrants, factory churches function as surrogate families, offering micro-loans and marriage counseling otherwise inaccessible in megacity anonymity. Critics fear exploitation when employers double as pastors, yet accountability covenants now separate HR decisions from church discipline, safeguarding spiritual freedom. The resulting ecosystem hints at Proverbs 31 entrepreneurship married to Acts-style koinonia, challenging Western compartmentalization of faith and economy.

14.5.3 Latin-American Prosperity Cathedrals: empowerment or exploitation?

Cathedrals like São Paulo's "Temple of Solomon," financed by tithes of Brazil's working poor, seat over 10 000 worshipers beneath gold-leaf ceilings, proclaiming that God wishes His people to "be the head and not the tail" (Deut 28 : 13). Proponents argue that prosperity preaching restores dignity to historically marginalized Afro-Brazilian populations, criticizing liberation theology for romanticizing poverty. Empowerment seminars teach budgeting, small-business planning, and addiction recovery alongside seed-faith offerings, creating a holistic yet controversial matrix. Economists, however, track cycles of giving where promised breakthroughs seldom materialize, prompting accusations of financial predation masked as faith. Recent scandals—pastors purchasing private jets—fuel regulatory investigations, forcing churches to publish audited statements if they wish to retain credibility. Theologically, prosperity cathedrals risk collapsing temple symbolism into consumer spectacle, forgetting Paul's boast in weakness (2 Cor 12 : 9). Yet testimonies of unemployed attendees who launched micro-enterprises after classes reveal a more complex picture, making blanket condemnation inadequate.

14.5.4 Diaspora Micro-Temples Re-Evangelizing the West

Nigerian Pentecostal assemblies renting London bingo halls, Filipino prayer cells filling Roman Catholic basements in Milan, and Iranian house-churches multiplying in Berlin illustrate the "reverse mission" phenomenon. These groups bring high-octane prayer, aggressive evangelism, and communal hospitality that re-ignite spiritual curiosity among secular neighbors. Sunday potlucks turn into cultural exposés where British pensioners taste jollof rice while hearing testimonies of answered prayer, blending Acts 2 cultural exchange with Luke 14 banquet evangelism. The diaspora grief of separation becomes fertile soil for mission zeal, echoing Israel's river-bank songs that nonetheless carried hope (Ps 137). Tensions sometimes arise over sound levels, dress codes, and charismatic manifestations unfamiliar to host congregations, prompting city councils to mediate noise ordinances and parking agreements. Ecumenical networks now pair long-standing parishes with diaspora pastors for shared Bible studies, fostering mutual humility. Thus, the global South not only fills empty pews but also challenges theological complacency, reminding Western heirs that the gospel is multilingual and migratory.

14.5.5 Translation Debates: indigenous architecture, dance, and vestments as temple vessels

Maasai believers erect circular mud-brick sanctuaries with central fire pits, arguing that longhouses symbolize communal hearth and echo Exodus pillar-of-fire imagery; European missionaries once forbade such structures, insisting on rectangular pew layouts mirroring colonial nostalgia. Today, translation theology recognizes that architecture itself must be contextualized, lest temples become monuments to foreign power rather than incarnational presence (John 1 : 14). Indigenous dances previously condemned as pagan now accompany offertory, re-coded as Davidic praise (2 Sam 6 : 14), while vestments weave tribal patterns into stoles and chalice veils. Critics fear syncretism, but local theologians apply Acts 15 Jerusalem-council logic, distinguishing gospel essentials from cultural add-ons. Anthropologists confirm higher retention when worship aesthetics resonate with indigenous cosmology, reducing perception that Christianity is cultural betrayal. Western tour groups, witnessing multi-sensory liturgy, often reevaluate their own "traditional" styles as likewise enculturated. As a result, temple theology becomes a tapestry of color and rhythm reflecting Revelation's "every tribe and tongue," rather than monochrome uniformity.

14.6 Messianic Judaism & Third-Temple Aspirations

14.6.1 Temple-Mount Archaeology and the Politics of the Shovel

Excavations near Jerusalem's Western Wall routinely unearth Herodian streets and Second-Temple mikva'ot, fueling Jewish longing for restored sacrificial worship. Archaeologists operate under Israeli Antiquities Authority permits, yet Palestinian authorities decry digs as "weaponized archaeology," claiming land-rights erasure. Evangelical tour groups photograph ancient stairs while guides quote Psalm 122 : 1, forging emotional bonds that reinforce Christian Zionism. Academics warn that selective interpretation of shards often serves ideological narratives more than objective history. Recent proposals for subterranean prayer spaces aim to allow Jewish worship without dismantling Islamic shrines, stirring halakhic debates about ritual purity. The "politics of the shovel" thus transform trowels into international flashpoints, reminding observers that temple stones still shape modern geopolitics. Discerning pilgrims must hold archaeology in tension with Jesus' claim that worship is now "in spirit and truth" (John 4 : 24), lest stones overshadow living stones.

14.6.2 Red-Heifer Projects, Priesthood Training, and Eschatological Timetables

Orthodox institutes in Israel are breeding blemish-free red heifers (Num 19) and sewing priestly garments in preparation for Third-Temple rites. Christian prophecy teachers track calf births like stock markets, layering Daniel 9 timelines onto modern headlines, often selling DVDs or online courses. Jewish authorities remain divided: some rabbis prioritize Messiah's arrival before any sacrifice, while others push logistical readiness. Critics within Judaism liken efforts to forcing God's hand; scholars recall golden-calf impatience (Ex 32). Evangelical excitement sometimes blinds to regional conflict implications; Palestinian Christians plead for theology that values living neighbors over prophetic charts. Interfaith dialogues attempt to decouple sacred texts from political exploitation, though social-media sensationalism complicates nuance. Meanwhile, Jesus' once-for-all sacrifice (Heb 10 : 10-14) raises the question of whether animal offerings could ever regain salvific meaning, challenging Christian support for literal temple rebuilding.

14.6.3 Christian Pilgrimage Tourism: devotion, economy, and displacement

Pre-pandemic, over three million Christians annually walked Via Dolorosa or sailed Galilee, injecting vital revenue into Israeli and Palestinian economies. Pilgrims describe tangible connection to Incarnation geography, echoing psalmists' Zion joy (Ps 84 : 10). Yet tourism's boom inflates property values, pushing Arab Christian families from Old-City homes; NGOs urge ethical travel that supports local believers through fair-wage cooperatives. Some tour operators incorporate service days at West-Bank hospitals, balancing holy-site consumption with diaconal engagement. Theologies of place debate whether divine presence is omni-localized or uniquely resident in Holy Land—Acts 17 : 24 asserts the former, yet many still seek "thin places." Environmentalists note erosion of Sea-of-Galilee shoreline from boat wakes, prompting boatmen to adopt electric motors. Ethical pilgrimage thus integrates worship, justice, and conservation, challenging selfie-stick superficiality.

14.6.4 Liturgical Hebrew in Gentile Churches: appropriation or grafting-in?

Gentile congregations increasingly chant *Shema* (Deut 6 : 4) and use shofars to open worship, claiming Romans 11 grafting imagery. Messianic Jewish leaders welcome recovery of Hebraic roots but warn against token exoticism detached from robust theology. Courses in Biblical Hebrew enhance exegetical depth; however, adopting tallit without understanding covenant symbolism risks costume spirituality. Joint Passover Seders foster mutual learning, yet must avoid supersessionist reinterpretations that erase Jewish continuity. When practiced humbly, Hebrew liturgical elements remind Christians of salvation's Jewish cradle, countering historical anti-Semitism. Liturgical commissions now recommend guidelines: contextual teaching, Jewish guest voices, and clarity that ceremonies point to Messiah, not cultural thrill. Done well, Gentile use of Hebrew becomes a bridge, not a boundary theft.

14.6.5 Rabbinic–Christian Dialogue after the Abrahamic Accords

The normalization of relations between Israel and several Gulf states opened unprecedented venues for rabbinic-Christian-Muslim think tanks. Scholars explore temple imagery common to each tradition— Solomon in Qur'ān, Ezekiel in Talmud, Hebrews in New Testament— seeking shared ethical vision for holy space stewardship. Dialogues convened in Abu Dhabi propose interfaith ecological projects on Temple-Mount runoff management, reimagining Zion water prophecies (Ezek 47) as practical collaboration. Conservative voices fear syncretism, yet participants assert strong confessional identities while partnering on humanitarian goals. The Spirit may be using geopolitics to reopen ancient conversations, echoing Acts 17 : 27 hope that "they should seek God... and find Him." Whether these forums influence grassroots attitudes remains uncertain, but they exemplify temple themes as diplomatic currency. Ongoing relationships could temper apocalyptic rhetoric by foregrounding common stewardship duties.

In Conclusion, the twenty-first-century landscape of temple expressions is dazzlingly diverse, occasionally disorienting, and frequently divisive. We have toured prayer-soaked African mountains, hologram-enhanced auditoriums, migrant shelters that turn parish halls into exodus corridors, TikTok confessionals, and eco-Eucharists served in compostable chalices. Each expression carries seeds of authentic presence and weeds of potential distortion; each controversy invites a return to Scripture's fourfold plumb line: Christ crucified and risen as cornerstone (1 Cor 3 : 11), the Spirit's fruit as credibility marker (Gal 5 : 22-23), love of neighbor as ethical non-negotiable (Mark 12 : 31), and missional witness as telos (Matt 28 : 18-20). If the church can hold these axes in creative tension, it may continue to shepherd fresh manifestations of God's dwelling without lapsing into idolatry, consumerism, or sectarian suspicion. Controversy, then, is not merely a hazard but a diagnostic gift that exposes hidden idolatries and summons deeper fidelity; pruning pain often precedes renewed bloom (John 15 : 2). The global chorus of temples—warehouse abbeys, metaverse cathedrals, rooftop gardens, diaspora living rooms—echoes the promise that the knowledge of the Lord will indeed fill the earth as waters cover the sea (Hab 2 : 14). Until the cosmic Sabbath closes every debate and unveils the singular Lamb-lit sanctuary, discerning disciples will walk the tightrope of joyful openness and rigorous discernment, welcoming the Spirit wherever He blows yet testing every wind by the nail-scarred compass of Christ.

Chapter 15 - Practicing Temple Spirituality Today

Temple spirituality is the conscious art of living as though the torn veil of Calvary (Matt 27 : 51) has truly altered every ordinary moment. It insists that breakfast tables, city buses, break-room cubicles, and midnight cribs are as eligible for divine encounter as Solomon's gilded sanctuary or Ezekiel's visionary nave. If previous chapters traced the temple motif historically and theologically, the task before us is intensely practical: to translate holy-of-holies theology into alarm-clock rhythms, budget line items, and neighborly deeds that can be calendared, measured, and shared. The following fifteen sections, each subdivided into concrete practices, move centrifugally—from the secret heart to the public square—so that the reader can adopt, adapt, or improvise habits that suit context while remaining anchored in Scripture. Every paragraph is deliberately shaped with seven or more sentences to slow the reader into meditation; every practice cites at least one biblical witness to remind us that innovation must remain tethered to revelation. Because cultures, temperaments, and life stages differ, no single rule fits all; therefore, the chapter offers a buffet rather than a blueprint. In the Spirit's hands these practices become chisels, carving believers into living stones who carry the fragrance of the inner court wherever they tread (2 Cor 2 : 14-15).

15.1 Re-membering the Presence: Daily Personal Rhythms

15.1.1 Dawn Dedication

Whether sunrise glows through city smog or predawn fog blankets a farm, beginning the day with a whispered *Shema* (Deut 6 : 4-5) or the Lord's Prayer (Matt 6 : 9-13) frames consciousness around covenant before news alerts set the emotional thermostat. Many disciples keep a small candle by the bed and strike a flame while reciting, "Here I am, Lord" (1 Sam 3 : 4). That two-minute ritual signals to flesh, psyche, and unseen powers that the temple is open for business. By dedicating thoughts before they wander, the believer echoes the priest who trimmed lamps at dawn (Ex 27 : 20-21). Journaling one sentence of gratitude immediately after the prayer trains vision to notice manna throughout the day. Over months, neurological studies show increased optimism when gratitude precedes caffeine. Thus dawn dedication mortgages the day to grace at favorable interest.

15.1.2 "Scripture Before Scroll" Rule

Phones slept on nightstands tempt thumbs before souls awaken; adopting a simple rule—no social-media scrolling before a chapter of Scripture—protects the neural gate. Lectio divina, with its four movements of reading, meditating, praying, and resting, slows intake so words sink like seed in good soil (Luke 8 : 15). Analog Bibles help, but apps can suffice when set to airplane mode. A sticky note on the screen reading, "Feed spirit first," acts as low-tech nudge. Couples can practice side-by-side, reading aloud alternate verses, knitting intimacy with truth. If toddlers interrupt, parents turn the disturbance into mid-text blessing, placing a hand on the child's head while finishing the verse. The rule is not legalism but leash, restraining algorithms until kingdom priorities direct attention.

15.1.3 Mid-day Re-centering

Ancient Israel marked the sixth hour with sacrifice; Peter and John kept that rhythm when they went to pray at the temple's ninth-hour service (Acts 3 : 1). Setting a watch or phone alarm for noon prompts one deep breath prayer—"Lord Jesus Christ, Son of God, have mercy on me a sinner." Office workers swivel chairs away from screens;

delivery drivers pull to the curb; students close laptops. The practice disrupts productivity idolatry, reminding that the Spirit, not spreadsheets, animates worth. Some add a 60-second body scan, releasing shoulders and jaw tension that store silent anger. Regular re-centering lowers cortisol, creating physiological space for patience with afternoon colleagues. In crowded settings the prayer can be internal, yet the effect is public when frustration dissipates.

15.1.4 Evening Examen

Ignatius' five-step examen—thank, review, regret, request, resolve—mirrors lampstand inspection at dusk (Num 8 : 1-4). Sitting with a journal or prayer partner, disciples replay the day's scenes like surveillance footage, searching for glory footprints and missed cues. Noting one joy and one sorrow trains balanced sight, avoiding toxic positivity or despair. Confession of specific failures—"I gossiped about Mark"—invokes 1 John 1 : 9 cleansing, polishing conscience mirrors. Asking the Spirit for next-day grace converts regret into momentum. Households can adapt by lighting a candle at dinner and inviting each member to share "rose, thorn, bud." Over years the examen becomes narrative memory, composing a living chronicle of God's fidelity.

15.1.5 Night Watches

Psalm 63 : 6 celebrates remembering God upon one's bed in the night watches. Turning off blue-light screens an hour before sleep honors circadian rhythms and signals temple closure for restoration. Some believers read a short compline psalm—often Psalm 91—then trace a cross on the pillow, entrusting dreams to divine custody. Parents bless children with Aaronic words (Num 6 : 24-26), embedding identity deeper than classroom labels. Insomniacs recite memorized Scripture rather than count digital sheep, letting Word lull anxious neurons. Scientists affirm that reflective gratitude lowers heart rate, confirming ancient wisdom. Morning energy the next day is sacramental overflow of holy rest. Thus sleep becomes silent liturgy where the Spirit sings over His beloved (Zeph 3 : 17).

15.2 Bodily Worship: Integrating Movement, Diet, and Rest

15.2.1 Embodied Liturgies

Raising hands during praise mirrors priestly uplifted palms (Ps 134 : 2) and recruits kinesthetic memory to reinforce verbal confession. Kneeling for confession submits joints along with words, combating Gnostic detachment. Liturgical traditions introduce prostration in Lent, reminding flesh of mortality, while charismatic circles dance Davidically, yielding cardiovascular benefit. Yoga-adapted prayer flows, when stripped of idolatrous mantras, stretch saints into postures of surrender; instructors quote Romans 12 : 1 to retether movement to mercy. Elderly bodies participate via gentle chair gestures, asserting that age does not disqualify temple sacrifice. Teen athletes read Colossians 1 : 17 during stretches to perceive Christ holding tendons together. Over time, embodied liturgy fraternizes spirit and sinew until worship feels as physical as breathing.

15.2.2 Temple Nutrition

Daniel's vegetable fast (Dan 1 : 8-16) inspires believers to practice "Daniel days," abstaining from processed foods to heighten spiritual sensitivity. Recognizing the body as purchased property (1 Cor 6 : 19-20), disciples plan balanced meals that stabilize glucose and thus temperament. Periodic corporate fasting—perhaps sunrise to sundown on first Fridays—redirects appetite toward bread of life (John 6 : 35). Feasting also belongs: Easter brunches with sweet breads rehearse Isaiah 25 : 6 banquet promise. When diets become idols, accountability partners gently pivot focus back to freedom in Christ (Gal 5 : 1). Sharing recipes in small groups cultivates culinary koinonia, and donating equivalent grocery savings during fasts funds benevolence, aligning nutrition with justice. Thus forks and knives become liturgical utensils.

15.2.3 Exercise as Sacrifice of Praise

Running clubs memorize Hebrews 12 : 1-2 while pounding pavement, experiencing cloud-of-witness solidarity. Weightlifters recite Philippians 4 : 13 between sets, translating strength promises into literal muscle contractions. For the chronically ill, five-minute balcony stretches still count, proving that worship measures intent, not mileage. Groups pledge to pray for unreached peoples during cardio sessions, making sweat incense (Rev 5 : 8). Avoiding vanity demands heart checks: selfies yield to gratitude for functioning lungs. Churches host 5K charity runs, funneling registration fees to local shelters, embodying Isaiah 58 link between fasting and justice. Exercise thus reverses sedentary liturgy of screens.

15.2.4 Restorative Sabbaths

Sabbath is temple time in mobile form (Ex 20 : 11); instituting weekly tech-fasts reclaims attention from algorithmic Pharaohs. Families switch off routers Friday sundown, lighting candles to symbolize Shekinah rest. Board games and hikes replace streams and scrolls, re-socializing attention. Singles share potluck brunches, preventing isolation and replicating Acts-breaking-bread joy. Pastors model Sabbath by resisting sermon prep on days off, proving trust in God's sovereignty. When emergencies intrude, rescheduling rest within the week guards principle over letter (Mark 2 : 27). Overtime cultures may resist, but testimonies of improved creativity and reduced burnout validate command.

15.2.5 Sexual Integrity Plans

Because the body is a temple extension, sexual holiness matters deeply (1 Thess 4 : 3-5). Couples draft intimacy vows that include mutual consent, prayer before union, and date-night rhythms, sanctifying bedroom as inner sanctum. Singles pursue chastity through friendship covenants, shared check-ins, and hobbies that channel desire into creativity. Apps like Covenant Eyes send weekly reports to accountability partners, exposing hidden browsing pathways. Congregations destigmatize conversation by hosting workshops on theology of desire, quoting Song of Songs alongside Paul. Victims of abuse receive trauma therapy so shame does not sabotage future intimacy. Periodic fasting from sexual activity in marriage, by mutual agreement (1 Cor 7 : 5), directs longing toward deeper prayer. Integrity plans transform eros into liturgy rather than taboo.

15.3 Crafting a Household Rule of Life

15.3.1 Family Prayer Corners and Table Altars

Designating a bookshelf nook or windowsill as prayer corner, stocked with candle, cross, and seasonal colors, communicates to children that spirituality is concrete. Daily lighting before breakfast segues into Psalm recitation—perhaps Psalm 23 on Mondays, Psalm 121 on Tuesdays—embedding Scripture through repetition. Guests notice space and feel invited into practice, soft evangelism by décor. At dinner, table altars host a loaf and cup, even when not celebrating Eucharist, visually connecting everyday supper to Luke 24 Emmaus revelation. Rotating responsibility—each child lights candle one night a week—builds ownership. Holiday decorations integrate Advent wreath or Passover seder plate, teaching salvation history through objects. The home turns into micro-nave where walls echo praises as powerfully as cathedrals.

15.3.2 Hospitality Calendar

A shared digital calendar earmarks first and third Fridays as "open-door nights," when neighbors or church newcomers may drop for soup and conversation. Scheduling ensures margin, preventing introvert panic or extrovert overextension. Luke 14 : 12-14 guides guest lists toward overlooked folks—international students, widows, or refugee families. Hosts pray before events that conversation glorify Christ, then trust Spirit to orchestrate connections. Leftovers become next-day porch deliveries for elderly shut-ins. When budgets strain, potluck style still accomplishes fellowship, proving table power lies not in cuisine but presence. Tracking stories in a shared journal shapes family narrative of welcoming grace. Over decades, hospitality becomes house biography.

15.3.3 Budget Tithes, Jubilee Giving, and Micro-Gleaning Funds

Besides traditional tithe to local church, households allocate two percent to a "gleaning envelope" for spontaneous needs—groceries for a single mom or taxi fare for clinic visits. Annual reviews compare spending on streaming services with giving to missions, inviting repentance and recalibration. Every seventh year, families attempt a mini-Jubilee: cancelling debts owed by friends or donating a month's rent to shelter ministries. Children earn chore commissions, then divide coins into spend/save/give jars, visualizing Proverbs 3 : 9 firstfruits. Budget meetings close with prayer that resources magnify kingdom—not personal security. Financial advisors testify that generosity cultivates contentment, reducing impulse-buy stress. Thus spreadsheets turn into doxology ledgers.

15.3.4 Conflict-Resolution Liturgies

Kitchen-table peace covenants begin with lighting a candle symbolizing Christ as witness, then each speaker holds a "grace cup" while sharing grievances without interruption. After both sides speak, they jointly prune a small plant, visually portraying removal of bitterness (Eph 4 : 31). A shared prayer of forgiveness follows, and the candle is extinguished to mark conclusion. Families employ Matthew 18 steps: private talk, mediation, wider church support if unresolved. Children learn to articulate feelings rather than slam doors. Keeping documentation prevents memory wars months later. Conflict liturgy trains domestic priests to guard sanctity of relationship altar. Homes practicing such rites often export peacemaking skills to workplaces and churches.

15.3.5 Inter-generational Storytelling

Once a month grandparents or senior friends share ten-minute testimonies during dessert, illustrating Psalm 145 : 4—"one generation shall commend your works." Scrapbooks and photos accompany stories, engaging visual learners. Younger listeners ask questions, forging identity continuity. Digital recordings archive narratives for dispersed relatives, creating cloud-based hall of remembrance. Story nights also surface lament; elders confess failures, modeling repentance's lifelong relevance. Immigrant families keep heritage alive, weaving cultural parables into gospel tapestry. Such storytelling counters media-fragmented memory by grounding lineage in God's acts.

15.4 Congregational Liturgies that Form Temple People

15.4.1 Call to Worship

The gathering begins not with hush but with psalmic summons—"Lift up your heads, O gates" (Ps 24 : 7)—declared by child, elder, or immigrant in native tongue, signaling inclusive doorway. Music starts quietly, crescendoing like temple musicians under King Hezekiah (2 Chr 29 : 27-28). Art projected on screens depicts open veil, teaching through image. Call transitions hearts from scattered to centered, framing ensuing confession as response. Churches rotating calls across worship teams prevent monotony. Congregants arriving late feel loss, gradually learning punctuality. The call shapes assembly into conscious court of praise.

15.4.2 Confession-and-Assurance Patterns

Following Isaiah 6 rhythm, leaders invite silent confession, then corporate prayer: "We have wandered like lost sheep." Silence of thirty seconds feels long enough for Spirit's scalpel. Assurance from 1 John 2 : 1-2 then lifts guilt, and congregation stands, embodying resurrection. Some churches employ sung Kyrie followed by Gloria, dramatizing transition from plea to praise. Visuals of broken pottery restored with gold (kintsugi) reinforce grace narrative. Children participate, learning early that failure is not terminal. Regular confession declutters hearts, making room for Word to land. Without it, sermons bounce off hardened defenses.

15.4.3 Word-Table-Sending Flow

Scripture reading alternates Old Testament, Psalm, Epistle, and Gospel, showcasing canonical harmony. Expository sermons connect texts to Christ, aligning to Emmaus pattern (Luke 24 : 27). Eucharist follows, embodying preached Word; preacher descends to serve bread, symbolizing incarnate message. After communion, a brief commissioning reminds worshipers that they exit as mobile temples (1 Pet 2 : 5). Such flow resists consumer disconnect between doctrine and mission. It also satisfies sensory learners—ears, taste, feet moving outward. Congregations adhering to this triadic rhythm display higher retention of sermon themes, according to internal surveys.

15.4.4 Prayers of the People as Incense

Intercessions rise like incense (Rev 8 : 3-4) when readers from diverse demographics voice local, national, and global petitions. Congregants respond, "Lord, in your mercy," weaving unity. Prayer leaders gather requests via digital form by Saturday, ensuring relevance. During crises—school shooting, earthquake—the prayers pivot spontaneously, demonstrating pastoral attentiveness. Scented incense sticks burned (where allergies permit) engage olfactory sense; otherwise, projected smoke animation suffices. Offering plates follow prayers, linking supplication and sacrifice. Children deliver plates to altar, teaching stewardship. Thus prayer shapes compassion muscle weekly.

15.4.5 Benedictions That Commission Everyday Priesthood

Rather than generic "Go in peace," benedictions quote Numbers 6 or Romans 15 : 13, arms raised Aaronly. Some congregations invite worshipers to extend hands to receive, bodily acknowledging gift. Visual slide lists weekly missional challenge—invite neighbor, pick up litter—tying blessing to action. Ushers hand out small cards with benediction text for pocket meditation. Musicians play gentle reprise of opening call, forming inclusio. Parents bless children at exit doors, continuing liturgy homeward. Benedictions thus launch saints as portable sanctuaries into Monday terrain.

15.5 Prayer Pathways: From Closet to City Square

15.5.1 Fixed-Hour Offices

Apps like Pray As You Go or Book of Common Prayer audio guide first, third, sixth, and ninth-hour prayers, aligning with Acts church rhythm. Office bells chime on smartwatches, sanctifying secular devices. Workers read aloud in cubicle corners or whisper on buses, marking time as gift. Long passages cultivate biblical literacy; repetitive canticles lodge deep. Shared practice knits global church, as believers recite same psalm across time zones. Skeptics fear rigidity, but freedom exists in occasional participation. Offices become skeleton on which spontaneous prayers hang.

15.5.2 Neighborhood Prayer-Walk

Small groups map streets, noting schools, clinics, liquor stores, and abandoned lots; then walk weekly, praying aloud blessings and binding spiritual oppression (Jer 29 : 7). Residents sometimes question activity, offering openings for witness. Litter picked during walks embodies petition for clean hearts. After months, participants compile answered-prayer stories—crime reduction, new playground funding—stirring faith. Data overlay with city statistics demonstrates impact, persuading civic leaders to partner. Prayer-walks train eyes to see people, not just pavement. The neighborhood becomes extended nave under open sky.

15.5.3 24-7 Upper-Room Rotas

Congregations schedule hourly slots, both onsite and online, ensuring continuous prayer flame (Lev 6 : 13). Graphics display open hours, nudging sign-ups. Themes rotate: Monday for family, Tuesday justice, etc. Remote participants post short prayers in group chat, building community. Skeptics fear burnout; leadership sets sabbath weeks quarterly. Testimonies of healed marriages and visa approvals encourage persistence. The rota embodies temple incense rising day and night.

15.5.4 Listening Prayer & Prophetic Teams

Teams gather after services offering silent listening, asking Spirit for edifying words (1 Cor 14 : 3). Protocols include Scripture alignment, confidentiality, and humility disclaimers—"We may be mistaken." Recorders jot impressions, giving recipients printouts for discernment. Abuse prevention policies forbid directive prophecy about marriage or finances without pastoral oversight. Community surveys show increased encouragement and reduced attrition among those receiving words. Skeptical members eventually participate after observing balanced practice. Listening prayer trains ears for Monday's marketplace guidance.

15.5.5 Public Lament Gatherings

After local violence or injustice verdicts, churches convene at city hall steps, reading psalms of lament (Ps 13). Participants bring stones symbolizing grief, later forming cairns in church gardens. Speakers include affected families, ensuring authentic voice. Silence of eight minutes forty-six seconds commemorates victims, mirroring Job's friends seated seven days (Job 2 : 13). Officials attending sense spiritual weight absent in partisan protests. Follow-up meetings address policy change, embodying Nehemiah's wall-building after prayer. Lament thus channels righteous anger into constructive advocacy.

15.6 Justice Practices as Temple Holiness in Public

15.6.1 Sabbath Economics Workshops and Debt-Release Funds

Congregations that have tasted the freedom of Sabbath learn to extend that rest into the financial realm by offering quarterly workshops where members examine spending records in the light of Leviticus 25. Volunteers trained in budgeting coach families to live beneath their means so that surplus can champion Jubilee generosity rather than inflate lifestyle. At the close of each workshop participants place shredded credit-card offers into a large clay jar, symbolically burying Pharaoh's brick quotas before the Lord. A portion of every monthly offering is diverted into a "church micro-jubilee fund" that retires high-interest payday-loan balances for qualifying neighbors, echoing the kingly mercy of Matthew 18 : 27. Beneficiaries attend optional financial-literacy classes, demonstrating that gift and discipleship are not enemies. Statistics tracked over three years show reductions in congregational consumer debt and spikes in mission giving, verifying Paul's promise that sowing bountifully reaps bountiful harvest (2 Cor 9 : 6). These projects preach louder than any stewardship sermon that the temple is indeed a storehouse of practical mercy.

15.6.2 Creation-Care Crews: Neighborhood Clean-Ups and Compost Co-ops

Once a month, orange-vested volunteers walk local streets armed with gloves, grabbers, and Psalms set to Bluetooth speakers, treating litter collection as an act of priestly cleansing akin to Hezekiah's temple sweep (2 Chr 29 : 15-17). The crew separates trash for recycling and counts cigarette butts, using data to lobby city council for more public ash cans—justice beginning in measurable stewardship. Homeowners donate lawn clippings and vegetable scraps to a congregational compost pile that in nine months returns as nutrient-rich soil for a community garden. Children paint signs quoting Psalm 24 : 1, reminding passers-by that "The earth is the Lord's," crusading against the secular myth of ownerless space. Seasonal bird-watching devotions train eyes to see "the birds of the air" whom the Father feeds (Matt 6 : 26), turning science into doxology. Within a year vacant lots bloom with sunflowers, and skeptical neighbors inquire about "the church that gardens." Evangelism thus sprouts organically from stewardship, showing that clean streets can pave the way for clean hearts.

15.6.3 Refugee and Migrant Welcome Teams

When Jesus identifies Himself as the stranger welcomed or ignored (Matt 25 : 35-40), temple people respond by forming specialized teams that meet asylum seekers at airports with placards bearing their names and baskets of culturally familiar snacks. Local landlords collaborate to offer six-month discounted leases, funded in part by an annual "Feast of Ruth" offering that commemorates the Moabite's integration into Israel (Ruth 2 : 14-16). ESL tutors meet in church classrooms two evenings a week, pairing vocabulary lessons with psalm chanting to strengthen lungs and spirits simultaneously. Medical professionals in the congregation schedule pro-bono clinics, remembering Israel's command to treat the foreigner with equity (Ex 23 : 9). Host families invite newcomers to national-holiday meals, redeeming civic rituals from xenophobic narratives. Research indicates that refugees connected to faith-based sponsors integrate faster into the labor market; data therefore bolster theology. Over time, the congregation's demographic palette widens, mirroring Revelation's multi-ethnic throne room and proving that hospitality can rewrite a church's DNA.

15.6.4 Racial-Reconciliation Tables and Story Circles

Borrowing from Acts 6, which addressed ethnic tension in the early church, leaders convene monthly "table talks" where six to eight participants from varied backgrounds share personal histories while passing a talking stick carved from olive wood. Ground rules commit listeners to James 1 : 19 posture—quick to hear, slow to speak, slow to anger—preventing hijack by dominant voices. Storytelling begins with ancestry reflections, then probes experiences of prejudice and hope, ensuring that wounds receive empathetic validation. A trained facilitator guides lament prayers using Psalm 13 cadence—complaint, petition, trust—so that raw pain ascends as incense rather than festers. Action steps arise organically: shared book clubs, joint service projects in underserved neighborhoods, and policy advocacy at city hall. Skeptics who feared mere talk witness tangible friendships forming across pew aisles, as evidenced by interracial small-group sign-ups tripling within a year. In this way, story circles carve out little courts of the Gentiles where dividing walls crumble (Eph 2 : 14).

15.6.5 Advocacy Days: Prayer-Saturated Visits to Legislators

On an annual "Micah 6 : 8 Day," congregants don matching T-shirts emblazoned with "Do Justice, Love Mercy, Walk Humbly" and board buses to the state capitol. The day begins with Eucharist served in the church parking lot, underscoring that sacrament fuels citizenship. After a brief training in respectful discourse, teams meet representatives to discuss bills concerning foster-care reform, anti-trafficking measures, or environmental protections. Each conversation ends with an offer to pray a 30-second blessing from Numbers 6 ; surprisingly few officials refuse, and some request follow-up pastoral counsel. Participants debrief on the bus ride home, compiling next-step commitments and sending thank-you notes irrespective of political outcomes, modeling Romans 13 honor without idolatry. Media coverage often highlights the unusual tone of humility and respect, distinguishing temple ethics from partisan rancor. The day equips ordinary saints to recognize civic engagement as an extension of intercession, proving that incense can permeate marble corridors.

15.7 Workplace and Vocational Integration

15.7.1 Theology-of-Work Cohorts: Monthly Lunches at the Office

Believers in the same business district form lunchtime cohorts that read short passages—perhaps Colossians 3 : 22-24 or Proverbs on diligence—and discuss how corporate goals align or conflict with kingdom values. Meetings rotate among participants' conference rooms, signaling to colleagues that faith is not relegated to weekends. Members share success stories: how refusing to falsify numbers protected a client, or how subtle intercessions during staff meetings diffused tension. Over time, companies notice lower turnover among cohort participants, reinforcing the practical wisdom of biblical ethics. Cohort minutes (sanitized for confidentiality) circulate to pastors, who integrate marketplace testimonies into Sunday prayers, shrinking sacred-secular divides. When layoffs loom, the group activates a benevolence fund, illustrating 1 Corinthians 12 mutual-care ideals. Thus offices become annexes of the outer court where worship and work intermingle.

15.7.2 Ethical Decision Lenses: Daniel-Like Integrity Guidelines

Drawing inspiration from Daniel 1 and 6, professionals craft a laminated "decision lens" booklet listing questions: Does this action love my neighbor? Does it obscure truth? Does it exploit creation? Before approving marketing campaigns, executives run proposals through the lens, empowering conscience to speak. Training sessions simulate ethical dilemmas—data manipulation, discriminatory hiring—allowing practice in a risk-free setting. Peer review across departments fosters corporate-wide accountability akin to Nehemiah's wall-building teams. Employees testify that clear criteria reduce anxiety when pressured by quarterly targets. Biblical allusions printed in footnotes subtly evangelize curious colleagues. Integrity thus shifts from abstract virtue to daily operational protocol.

15.7.3 Sabbath Boundaries in Knowledge-Economy Careers

IT consultants and healthcare workers agree on a "sunset ceasefire" policy: no emails between 7 p.m. Friday and 7 p.m. Saturday unless life-threatening. Outlook auto-responders cite Exodus 20 command, educating clients while setting expectations. Managers initially fear productivity loss but later report fresher creativity on Mondays. Employees practice digital Sabbath by setting phones to grayscale, reducing dopamine addiction. Families plan outdoor excursions to reinforce embodied rest—picnics, not pixels. When emergencies break Sabbath, participants log time and reclaim rest mid-week, honoring principle over perfection. The policy bears witness to a counter-cultural rhythm that values being over ceaseless doing.

15.7.4 Craftsmanship Retreats for Artists, Coders, and Tradespeople

Twice yearly, a retreat center hosts "Craftsmen of the Kingdom," inviting painters, software engineers, carpenters, and baristas to explore Exodus 31 Bezalel inspiration. Workshops mix theology lectures on creation mandate with hands-on skill swaps: welders teaching coding novices to solder LED art, writers coaching plumbers in storytelling. Nightly vespers feature testimonies of how code or carpentry became prayer, dissolving hierarchy between pulpit and workshop. Participants leave with collaborative projects—church websites, communion-table designs—donated to under-resourced congregations. Feedback loops report increased job satisfaction post-retreat, aligning with 1 Timothy 6 : 17 enjoyment of God's gifts. The event reinforces that every vocation can be altar and incense.

15.7.5 Witness through Excellence, Humility, and Service

In a culture that equates Christian witness with overt evangelism, temple spirituality adds silent apologetics: impeccable work quality echoing Jesus' "well done" ideal (Matt 25 : 23), humble demeanor deflecting praise to team members (Phil 2 : 3), and service acts like refilling communal coffee pots without recognition. Excellence earns credibility; humility disarms skepticism; quiet service plants curiosity seeds. Employees who repair others' code bugs without public shaming incarnate Proverbs 15 : 1 soft answer ethos. Annual performance reviews objectively confirm increased peer trust, which often leads to gospel conversations. Thus temple witness at work is less about posters in cubicles and more about cruciform posture bathing the workplace in unseen incense.

15.8 Digital Discipleship and Cyber-Sanctity

15.8.1 Attention Tithing: First-Fruits of Focus to Prayer and Study

Data reveal average smartphone users touch devices 2 600 times daily. Temple practitioners counter by tithing the first ten minutes of each online hour to prayerful reflection—switching apps to Bible or journaling before Twitter. Screen-time analytics verify compliance, converting piety into measurable discipline. The habit rewires dopamine circuits, so spiritual affection gradually outstrips novelty craving, embodying Psalm 90 : 14 satisfaction each morning. Community challenges post weekly attention-tithe graphs, spurring friendly progress. Critics call it gamification, yet participants report reduced anxiety and richer conversation offline. Attention tithe thus sanctifies the very neural economy Big Tech monetizes.

15.8.2 Online Speech Covenants

Small groups sign a covenant drawn from Ephesians 4 : 29 prohibiting unwholesome talk, adapting it for comments, memes, and retweets. Violations trigger loving reminders via direct message, preserving dignity. Quarterly workshops analyze virtual case studies—political thread blow-ups, sarcasm misfires—applying covenant principles. Data show decreased relational fallout and increased constructive debate within group feeds. Outsiders observing distinct tone often inquire about underlying motivation, offering evangelistic openings. The covenant transforms cyberspace from marketplace of outrage to court of gentle reason, reflecting Proverbs 25 : 11 apples of gold in silver settings.

15.8.3 Virtual Small-Group Etiquette

Zoom fatigue challenges digital fellowship unless etiquette mitigates friction: cameras on when possible, mute microphones when dogs bark, use hand-raise icons to prevent crosstalk. Facilitators limit meeting time to 60 minutes—25 for check-in, 20 Scripture discussion,

15 prayer—honoring limited attention resources. Breakout rooms pair introverts for deeper sharing, maximizing participation equity. Communion is reserved for in-person gatherings, but spiritual communion prayers maintain sacramental longing. Tech volunteers call elderly members pre-meeting to troubleshoot connections, embodying Galatians 6 : 2 burden-bearing. Over time, virtual intimacy proves viable, especially for diaspora members longing for home-culture worship.

15.8.4 Screen-Sabbath Rhythms and "Analog August" Challenges

Churches launch an annual "Analog August," encouraging members to replace screens with analog activities—vinyl listening parties, hand-written letters, paperbacks over e-readers. Sermons throughout the month explore Psalm 46 be-still spirituality. Participants journal withdrawal symptoms in week one, breakthrough creativity in week three, testifying on final Sunday. The challenge recalibrates baseline dopamine, making digital reentry less compulsive. Families craft scrapbooks of analog adventures, preserving memories in tactile form. Skeptics who skip the challenge still benefit from ambient cultural reset—group outings replace endless group texts. Analog August injects breathing space into frenetic digital liturgy.

15.8.5 Cyber-Outreach: Livestream Prayer Lines and Discipleship Podcasts

Recognizing that seekers Google questions before visiting buildings, churches run livestream prayer lines on Instagram nightly at 10 p.m., when loneliness peaks. Volunteers trained in apologetics answer queries, quote Scripture, and invite follow-up Zoom coffee. Data analytics show that 25 percent of line users attend a physical service within three months. Parallel discipleship podcasts release bite-size 12-minute episodes unpacking lectionary texts, allowing commuters to "walk through the temple" aurally. Listeners submit questions via voice memo, some aired and answered, creating interactive catechesis. Podcast metrics indicate global audience, evidencing Acts 1 : 8 digital reach. Cyber-outreach thus turns Babylonian media rivers into singing highways to Zion.

15.9 Mentoring, Discipleship, and Inter-Generational Transfer

15.9.1 Spiritual-Parenting Triads

Triads pair a gray-haired saint, a thirty-something parent, and a college student, meeting monthly for mutual counsel. Older mentor shares wisdom; middle peer hosts meeting; younger member brings tech skills, modeling 2 Timothy 2 : 2 chain. Triads read a gospel together annually, rotate prayer leadership, and perform one service project each quarter. Exit interviews reveal improved retention of young adults in church life. Mentorship manual outlines boundaries, safeguarding against unhealthy dependencies. Triads produce stories of grandparent-like bonds for orphans, fulfilling Psalm 68 : 6 solitary family promise.

15.9.2 Confirmation-Style Catechesis for Adults

Recognizing biblical illiteracy among converts, churches run nine-month catechumenate cycles with weekly teaching, spiritual disciplines labs, and service immersion. Adult sponsors accompany candidates, echoing early-church models. Graduation liturgy at Pentecost includes reaffirmation of baptismal vows and foot-washing of sponsors by catechumens, reversing hierarchical expectations. Retention rates surpass short membership classes, confirming depth over speed. Catechesis notebooks contain reflection prompts and recommended reading, bridging Sunday teaching and weekday practice. Alumni form resource pool for future cohorts, ensuring generational sustainability.

15.9.3 Testimony Evenings and Story-Bank Archives

Quarterly gatherings replace sermon with five-minute testimonies—healings, breakthroughs, laments resolved—curated to reflect demographic breadth. Recordings upload to a searchable "story bank," tagged by theme: provision, reconciliation, vocation. Researchers show storytelling increases communal resilience by reinforcing collective memory. Youth filmed interviewing elders gain editing skills and spiritual heritage. Stories become prayer prompts, fueling intercession nights. Over time, archives document God's faithfulness across decades, a digital Ebenezer (1 Sam 7 : 12).

15.9.4 Leadership Apprenticeships with Character-First Metrics

Aspiring leaders shadow elders for six months, focusing on hospitality, conflict mediation, and prayer guidance before platform skills. An assessment rubric prioritizes 1 Timothy 3 virtues over charisma: spouse faithfulness, financial integrity, temperance. Apprentices preach only after demonstrating fruit at home and work. Feedback loops incorporate congregational input, distributing discernment. Drop-outs due to misfit find alternative service without shame. Character-first pipeline muddies celebrity allure, fortifying temple against future scandal.

15.9.5 Lifelong Learning Labs

Monthly Saturday workshops cover theology, justice, creativity, and tech, paralleling temple guild training under David (1 Chr 25 : 1-8). Retirees teach woodworking; teenagers teach coding; refugees teach languages, embodying Romans 12 diversity. Labs crown sessions with corporate prayer, consecrating skills. Scholarships ensure accessibility; meals foster fellowship. Alumni networks share job openings and mentorship leads. Learning labs keep community intellectually vibrant and vocationally resourceful.

15.10 Discernment, Accountability, and Ongoing Renewal

15.10.1 Spiritual Direction and Confession Partnerships

Certified directors meet directees monthly, practicing contemplative listening, scripture soaking, and discernment of consolation/desolation patterns (Luke 24 : 32). Parallel confession partnerships follow James 5 : 16, exchanging weekly check-ins via encrypted apps. Confidentiality covenants create safe space for deep surgery. Data from counseling ministries show partnered individuals relapse less into addictions. Directors undergo annual supervision to prevent power abuse. Sessions end with Eucharistic thanksgiving, rooting guidance in grace. Together these practices keep temple channels unclogged.

15.10.2 Annual Community Examen

Every November the church gathers for half-day retreat reviewing year's ministries, finances, testimonies, and failures in light of Psalm 103 blessings. Sticky-note stations invite congregants to label joys and sorrows, later shaped into corporate prayer. Budget transparency charts cultivate trust; repentance moments acknowledge misused resources. Strategic goals emerge through Lectio-guided brainstorming on Acts 13 Antioch model. The meeting concludes with foot-washing among leadership and laity, pledging servant future. Surveys show higher volunteer engagement post-examen.

15.10.3 Guardrails against Celebrity, Consumerism, and Burn-Out

Policies prohibit pastor faces on billboards larger than cross icons, combating celebrity culture. Sermon series promote simplicity, and church stores refuse logo merchandise unless profits fund benevolence. Sabbath sabbaticals mandatory for staff every seven years prevent burnout; metrics include emotional health inventory. External preaching invites require elder approval to avoid overexposure. Feedback loops allow congregants to flag ego creep anonymously. Guardrails protect temple integrity from worldly corrosion.

15.10.4 Conflict-Transformation Teams

Teams trained in restorative-justice principles mediate disputes, seating parties in circle, using talking pieces, and drafting reconciliation covenants. Scriptural framing draws on Matthew 18 and 2 Corinthians 5 ministry of reconciliation. Success measured not merely by apology but by behavior change and community reintegration. Annual refresher courses keep skills sharp. Record-keeping ensures patterns addressed, not buried. Transformation teams model cross-shaped peace-making to watching world.

15.10.5 Continuous Prayer for Fresh Infilling

Weekly "oil check" services invite those sensing dryness to receive prayer for Spirit renewal (Eph 5 : 18). Laying-on of hands by diverse elders reassures immune-compromised with sanitizer protocols. Testimonies of rekindled passion guard against routine. Musicians keep set lists simple to prioritize heart posture over performance. Quarterly fasting amplifies hunger for God beyond complacency. Fresh infilling proves temple spirituality is river, not reservoir.

In conclusion, practicing temple spirituality today is less about inventing exotic disciplines and more about re-inhabiting the marrow of biblical life with unembarrassed intentionality. The habits surveyed—attention-tithes, neighborhood potlucks, compost co-ops, quarterly silent retreats, code-of-conduct covenants, and community examens—are ordinary planks that, under breath of the Spirit, build extraordinary cathedrals in time and space. They remind the believer that holiness is not a weekend costume but a weekday skin; justice is not a Twitter slogan but a shopping list and a budget line; witness is not a shouted creed but a whispered kindness amplified by consistent integrity. By anchoring each practice in Scripture—from Genesis gardens to Revelation rivers—we ensure that creativity never drifts into novelty for novelty's sake but always bends back to the crucified-risen cornerstone. Every believer will adopt these rhythms differently, shaped by season of life, cultural setting, and vocational call; yet the shared aim is identical: to host the glory that once threatened to shatter stone walls and now chooses to dwell in clay jars, transforming them into vessels of durable beauty (2 Cor 4 : 7). May these pages serve as a training ground rather than a checklist, a springboard rather than a cage, propelling God's people into ever-deepening cycles of presence, purity, and mission until the final trumpet announces that the temple of God and the Lamb has filled every square inch of the renewed cosmos.

Chapter 16 - Conclusion: From Glory to Glory—Anticipating Ultimate Indwelling

Glory is the Bible's shorthand for the undiluted reality of God—weighty, luminous, inexhaustibly life-giving. From the moment divine "light" shattered pre-cosmic darkness (Gen 1 : 3), creation has been magnetized toward that splendour, yearning to be filled, transfigured, and finally saturated by the One who spoke it into being. Israel's storytellers, prophets, poets, and apostles all testify that the Creator never abandoned this intent; instead, He wove a temple-shaped thread through history so humanity could trace the way home. Every chapter of this book has followed that thread: Eden's garden-sanctuary, Sinai's mobile shrine, Solomon's gilded nave, exilic heartbreak, messianic fulfilment, Pentecostal fire, apostolic re-imagining, and the church's contested witness in our own age. Now, at the story's edge, we stand before the horizon the seers called "new heaven and new earth" (Rev 21 : 1), a horizon they did not merely predict but actively beckoned. This closing chapter therefore refuses to offer tidy summary or dispassionate recap; instead, it gathers the whole narrative momentum into a single, forward-leaning gaze— "from glory to glory" (2 Cor 3 : 18)—and asks: How shall we live, work, suffer, and hope in view of ultimate indwelling? What follows sketches nine panoramas, each exploring one facet of that forward pull, so the reader exits not with nostalgia for bygone sanctuaries but with courage to inhabit the overlap of ages until every shadow becomes transparent day.

16.1 The Arc Revisited: From First Light to Final Radiance

16.1.1 Edenic Spark: Primal Vocation and Rupture

Genesis frames the cosmos as temple-in-the-making: a vaulted sky for ceiling, lush ground for flooring, and an image-bearing couple set like living statues to reflect the Architect's splendour (Gen 1 : 26–28). Their vocation—"serve and guard" the garden (Gen 2 : 15)—employs verbs later used for Levitical service, embedding priesthood into humanity's DNA. When they heed the serpent, glory does not evaporate but becomes lethal exposure, driving them east of Eden behind a flaming sword (Gen 3 : 24). The exile inaugurates a recurring pattern: unfaithfulness fractures communion, yet God initiates fresh proximity, refusing to surrender His dwelling dream. Eden therefore remains both prototype and promise; every later sanctuary is an echo of that primordial invitation to walk with God "in the cool of the day" (Gen 3 : 8). Without Edenic memory, tabernacle blueprints and Christological fulfilment would make little sense, for temple architecture is, at root, a reclamation project. Thus the first light already contains the last—intended glory delayed, not denied.

16.1.2 Tabernacle Journey: God on the Move in Canvas and Cloud

When Yahweh descends on Sinai, the mountain quakes, smoke billows, and trumpet blasts split the silence, announcing a holiness too volatile for long-term habitation (Ex 19 : 16-18). In mercy, He commissions a portable sanctuary so glory can travel without incinerating a stiff-necked people. Acacia boards, linen curtains, and golden furniture transform desert nomads into processioning temple-keepers, rehearsing the nearness they once forfeited. The Shekinah cloud that rests upon the tent by day and becomes fire by night (Ex 40 : 34-38) visualises Immanuel long before the incarnation. Israel's routes thus map theology: every camp-site becomes a holy precinct, every journey a pilgrimage of presence. Significantly, the tabernacle never functions as superstitious talisman; when covenant vows are

326

broken, glory threatens departure, teaching that presence is relational, not mechanical. The roaming shrine therefore foreshadows a mobile church—living tents animated by the Spirit, carrying holiness into every wilderness where the nations wander.

16.1.3 Solomonic Splendour: Fixed Glory and Looming Fracture

Solomon's temple, rising on Zion's crest, crystallises decades of longing into cedar, bronze, and gold so abundant that chroniclers weigh it by talents rather than shekels (1 Kgs 7 : 51). When priests withdraw from the holy place, the cloud fills the house with such density that ministry halts (1 Kgs 8 : 10–11). Yet the building's very permanence seeds complacency; prophets later decry "This is the temple of the LORD" mantra weaponised to excuse injustice (Jer 7 : 4-11). Thus splendour becomes both gift and test: will Israel guard ethical consonance with architectural glory? Failure invites Babylonian siege, scorching the nave and hauling exiles east—the same tragic compass point as Eden's expulsion. Still, Ezekiel beholds a future house with river-flooded thresholds (Ezek 47 : 1-12), signalling that even ruin can midwife greater radiance. Solomon's edifice collapses, but the promise embedded in its foundations—"My name shall be there" (1 Kgs 8 : 29)—migrates into eschatological designs.

16.1.4 Second-Temple Turbulence: Restoration, Compromise, and Yearning

Returning exiles weep when they see Zerubbabel's modest foundations, some with joy, others with grief at lost grandeur (Ezra 3 : 12-13). Though rebuilt walls stand, tangible glory never re-enters; no cloud descends, no fire ignites the altar. Intertestamental literature vibrates with expectation: Haggai predicts latter glory surpassing former (Hag 2 : 9), while Malachi foresees the Lord suddenly appearing in His temple to purify priests (Mal 3 : 1-3). Greek occupation, Maccabean revolt, and Roman dominance transform the complex into both spiritual beacon and political flashpoint. Herod's renovation projects stunning colonnades yet deepen dependence on imperial favour, a compromise that will sting. By the first century, pilgrims ascend Jerusalem singing Psalms of Ascent, but many hearts ache for unmediated presence. This tension sets the stage for the carpenter-rabbi who dares to call His body the true sanctuary, enacting the prophecies none could fulfil by stone alone.

16.1.5 Christ the Pivot: Living Temple, Torn Veil, Empty Tomb

Jesus embodies the long-sought Shekinah in flesh—"We have seen His glory" (John 1 : 14)—and reorients sacred geography around Himself. He cleanses the outer courts, indicting exclusionary commerce (Mark 11 : 15-17); He forgives sins without cultic mediation, hinting at earthquake ahead. At Golgotha, the temple curtain rips "from top to bottom," divine hand tearing formerly lethal separation (Matt 27 : 51). Resurrection on the first day of a new week echoes creation's dawning; the empty tomb becomes holy of holies where angels sit at head and foot like cherubim on mercy-seat (John 20 : 12). Ascension enthrones Adam's dust at God's right hand, ensuring human royalty within triune communion (Eph 1 : 20-23). Pentecost completes pivot: fire and wind once reserved for Sinai now crown disciples, proclaiming that mobile sanctuaries have gone viral (Acts 2 : 1-4). Christ is cornerstone of a temple under endless construction—living stones added across centuries, cultures, and continents.

16.2 Already / Not-Yet: Life in the Overlap of the Ages

16.2.1 Inaugurated Temple Age: Spirit Indwelling as Down-Payment

Paul calls the Spirit "arrabōn"—earnest money guaranteeing future inheritance (Eph 1 : 13-14). Indwelling presence authenticates believers as covenant property while whispering that full possession awaits unveiling. Gifts of prophecy, healing, and tongues operate as architectural previews, furnishing rooms that are still under scaffolding. Sacraments function similarly: baptism seals but also anticipates river-of-life immersion; Eucharist nourishes yet points to marriage supper of the Lamb (Rev 19 : 9). The church, therefore, inhabits dual citizenship: seated with Christ (Eph 2 : 6) yet groaning in mortal bodies (2 Cor 5 : 4). Spiritual warfare arises precisely because two epochs overlap; darkness resists eviction but cannot reverse the verdict of resurrection morning. Hope, then, is neither naïve optimism nor stoic grit; it is theologically grounded confidence that the foundation has been laid, and the final inspection day is scheduled.

16.2.2 Groaning Creation: Cosmic Labor Pains and Human Pilgrimage

Paul likens creation to a woman in childbirth—painful convulsions destined for joy (Rom 8 : 22). Earthquakes, pandemics, and ecological collapse thus read as contractions, not death throes, beckoning midwife church to steward birth rather than flee to sterile escapism. Believers groan too, longing for adoption's completion— the redemption of bodies (Rom 8 : 23). Pilgrimage spirituality frames life as Exodus-to-Zion journey: manna of Word, water from Spirit-rock, and cloud-by-fire guidance. Sabbath pauses provide breath between contractions, reminding travellers that arrival is guaranteed even when wilderness sand burns feet. Martyrs' cries under the altar (Rev 6 : 10) prove that groaning includes lament, an honest soundtrack to unfinished redemption. Yet every answered prayer, every healed rift, every reconciled enemy announces that new creation's head has already crowned.

16.2.3 Firstfruits and Earnest Money: Sacraments and Charisms as Pledges

James calls Christians "firstfruits of His creatures" (Jas 1 : 18), living specimens of what the whole cosmos will become. When a congregation sings in multilingual harmony, it previews Revelation's choir; when bread and cup unite diverse bodies, the wedding banquet sends appetizer. Charisms—administration, mercy, prophetic insight—are not party tricks but construction tools shaping participants into the architecture they foretell. Even mundane acts— changing diapers, fixing engines—performed "in the Lord" gain eschatological weight (1 Cor 15 : 58). Thus every faithful deed, however small, slips a brick into New Jerusalem's wall. Firstfruits identity inoculates against despair and triumphalism alike; we taste enough to persevere, yet hunger enough to intercede. The Spirit's pledges train hope to walk by faith, not sight, while anticipating sight beyond faith.

16.2.4 Suffering–Glory Tension: Cross-Shaped Hope That Outlasts Affliction

Jesus' post-resurrection scars teach that glory perfects but does not erase history; wounds become worship (John 20 : 27-28). Believers therefore interpret tribulation as raw material for future beauty (2 Cor 4 : 17). Persecution, whether social ridicule or martyr's blade, forges credibility before watching powers (Phil 1 : 28-29). Suffering joined to Christ dwarfs Stoic endurance, because resurrection guarantees compensation far beyond loss (Rom 8 : 18). Communities that lament honestly yet praise stubbornly transform neighbourhoods' perception of God. Cross-shaped hope refuses shortcuts, rejecting both prosperity denial of pain and nihilistic surrender. It clings to promise that tears will be wiped, not because they are trivial, but because they are fully seen (Rev 21 : 4).

16.2.5 Discernment and Expectancy: Watching, Working, and Waiting Well

Parables of virgins, talents, and vigilant servants (Matt 25) teach that eschatological posture combines lamp-trimmed attention, profitable labour, and hospitable welcome. Discernment guards against date-setting frenzy while expectancy prevents lukewarm drift. Spiritual disciplines—fasting, examen, prophetic listening—keep radar tuned to subtle Spirit nudges. Ethical diligence in mundane tasks—paying invoices timely, recycling trash—embodies watchfulness, refusing divide between sacred and secular. Corporate worship rehearses watchfulness; liturgy's repeated "Come, Lord Jesus" (Rev 22 : 20) tugs hearts forward. Mission engagement safeguards expectancy from selfish insulation: those who proclaim gospel abroad accelerate day of God (2 Pet 3 : 12). Thus disciples live like farmers: sowing, watering, scanning horizon for dawn.

16.3 The Spirit's Transforming Presence

16.3.1 Progressive Conformity: "From One Degree of Glory to Another"

Paul describes transformation as beholding the Lord with unveiled face, morphing into His image progressively (2 Cor 3 : 18). This sanctification is relational, not mechanical—becoming like the One we contemplate. Daily Scripture reflection, artful worship, and sacramental participation polish the mirror of the heart, increasing reflective capacity. Failures do not reset progress to zero; repentance accelerates growth by deepening dependency on grace. Community feedback acts as chiselling tool, smoothing rough edges we cannot see. Spiritual growth, therefore, is less staircase and more spiral: circling familiar themes at deeper levels. The promise of ultimate conformity fuels patience with the slow pace of character change.

16.3.2 Corporate Living Stones: Community Architecture of Holiness

Peter envisions believers as "living stones" built into a spiritual house (1 Pet 2 : 5). Stones must be shaped to interlock; interpersonal conflict becomes sanctifying friction. Diversity—ethnic, economic, generational—enlarges floor plan, displaying multi-faceted grace. Authority structures function as load-bearing beams, not ornamental tyranny; servant leadership under Christ the cornerstone ensures stability (Eph 2 : 20-22). Spiritual gifts supply plumbing and wiring—administration channels resources; teaching illuminates hallways; mercy warms rooms. Church discipline, when restorative, removes mould so structure remains habitable. The resulting edifice is no static monument but a living organism, ever-expanding as new stones confess Christ.

16.3.3 Charisms as Construction Tools

Gifts of wisdom, knowledge, faith, healing, tongues, and helps (1 Cor 12 : 7-10, 28) are artisan tools passed out by the Spirit foreman. Prophets mark blueprints, evangelists lay foundation, pastors and teachers finish interiors. No gift is surplus; omission leaves structural gaps. Jealousy over tools insults the Giver and stalls progress. Training seminars sharpen usage: prophetic words weighed, mercy energized with boundaries, administration purified from control. When tools work in sync, outsiders walk through church doors and intuit coherence, glorifying God (1 Cor 14 : 24-25). Charisms cease being party spectacles and mature into construction equipment for the age to come.

16.3.4 Fruit as Evidence: Love, Joy, Peace as Visible Glory-Sheen

If gifts are tools, fruit is finish—visible sheen proving Spirit occupancy (Gal 5 : 22-23). Love embodies the Shema, joy echoes temple choirs, peace mirrors sabbath. Patience, kindness, and goodness turn abstract doctrines into neighbourhood witness; faithfulness, gentleness, and self-control provide structural integrity during storms. Fruit requires abiding, not striving; branches do not grunt to produce grapes (John 15 : 4-5). Seasons of pruning may feel like regression but guarantee sweeter yield. Communities that prioritise fruit over fireworks become safe harbours for bruised reeds. Glory is recognizable not by spotlights but by quiet kindness during parking-lot traffic jams.

16.3.5 Mission as Overflow

Pentecost overflows into multilingual proclamation, linking presence and witness. Holiness cannot hoard glory; it radiates. Evangelism becomes aroma diffused from temple incense (2 Cor 2 : 14). Justice ministries spring from same source—Isaiah's vision marries worship and coal-purified lips bearing good news to poor (Isa 6 ; 61 : 1). Artistic creativity, scientific discovery, and political reform likewise flow outward, each a tributary of living water (John 7 : 38). The Spirit's indwelling is centrifugal, pressing church toward ends of earth until glory covers sea floor. Only in mission does indwelling reach its telos.

16.4 Eschatological Hope and Pastoral Resilience

16.4.1 Hope as Anchor of the Soul

Hebrews pictures hope as anchor tunnelling through curtain into inner sanctuary (Heb 6 : 19). Tempests above surface cannot dislodge what is moored behind the veil. Pastors cultivate hope by preaching promises larger than present anxieties: resurrection of body, renewal of earth, justice for martyrs. Personal devotions must sip same hope lest sermons become empty rhetoric. Hope is learned behaviour, fed by remembering former deliverances (Ps 77 : 11-15). Singing eschatological hymns—"When Christ shall come..."—strengthens nautical rope. An anchored soul can care for storm-tossed seekers without capsizing.

16.4.2 Perseverance under Pressure

Early believers lost property joyfully, knowing a better possession (Heb 10 : 34). Modern sufferers—cancer patients, persecuted minorities, exhausted caregivers—inherit same promise. Churches equip perseverance by sharing martyr stories, hosting lament psalm nights, and surrounding the afflicted with tangible aid. Spiritual warfare teaching demystifies attacks, reminding that fiery trials refine faith (1 Pet 1 : 6-7). Community perseverance composites into corporate testimony: a temple still standing when cultural earthquakes reduce idols to rubble. Thus endurance is not grim survival but anticipatory triumph. Eyes fixed on joy set before us (Heb 12 : 2) outrun fatigue.

16.4.3 Lament inside Assurance

Biblical lament refuses to choose between complaint and trust; both hug Psalter pages. Jesus models lament on cross, quoting Psalm 22 while entrusting spirit to Father (Luke 23 : 46). Churches that silence lament breed hidden cynicism; those that give voice convert pain into prayer. Liturgies include "How long, O Lord?" refrains during tragedies, teaching congregants vocabulary for grief. Assurance inserts after lament, not before, maintaining narrative integrity. The alternation shapes resilient faith capable of tears without despair. Lament is preparatory catacomb where eventual praise resounds louder. Temple spirituality embraces whole emotional register.

16.4.4 Communion of Saints: Solidarity across Time and Tomb

Hebrews 12 describes worship as joining festal gathering of angels and righteous made perfect. When we sing doxology, voices mingle with persecuted believers in underground cells and Augustine's choirs alike. Commemorating saints' days, reading old prayers, and visiting graveyards remind that we are bricks laid atop a foundation of martyrs. Such solidarity dwarfs individual concerns and comforts isolated disciples. It also humbles triumphalistic moderns who imagine they are first to face cultural hostility. The communion of saints is living proof that glory has been expanding, not retreating, through consecutive generations. Death therefore loses finality, becoming doorway into larger choir.

16.4.5 Sabbath Anticipation: Rest Fueling Resistant Joy

Weekly Sabbath rehearses eternal rest (Heb 4 : 9-11), re-situating believers in eschatological timeline. Ceasing from labour resists Pharaoh cultures that measure worth by output. Joyful feasting, unhurried prayer, and holy leisure preview banquet day. Sabbath kids teach parents to play again; laughter becomes prophetic protest against despair. Rested saints re-enter workweek as outposts of future Eden, carrying peace into frenetic offices. Sabbath thus functions as time-machine: a 24-hour visit to age to come, gathering courage to plod onward. It trains hearts for cosmic sabbaton when rest permeates every molecule.

16.5 Cosmic Sabbath and Liberated Creation

16.5.1 Genesis Sabbath Unfinished

Genesis does not close day seven with evening-and-morning refrain, hinting at open-ended Sabbath. Revelation's ceaseless day completes that pause, revealing destination implicit from inception. Creation's initial "very good" status was orientation, not final state; maturity awaited royal-priestly stewardship. Sin delayed but did not derail trajectory. Thus cosmic Sabbath is climax, not epilogue—a future that beckons the present. Every weekly rest aligns compass, reminding travellers destination still lies ahead. Glory to glory is Sabbath to Sabbath.

16.5.2 Creation Healed, Not Scrapped

Isaiah envisions new heavens and new earth, but familiar Jerusalem persists, albeit renewed (Isa 65 : 17-25). Peter's "elements melting" language (2 Pet 3 : 10) parallels flood imagery—purifying deluge, not annihilating obliteration. Jesus' resurrected body, recognisable yet glorified, foreshadows planetary resurrection. Therefore ecological care is not rearranging deck chairs on sinking ship but pitching tents on soon-to-be-permanent soil. Recycling bins, rewilding projects, and carbon-footprint reductions become acts of eschatological fidelity.

Creation groans for sons and daughters to steward birthing process (Rom 8 : 19-22). Temple priests midwife the cosmos by sustainable love.

16.5.3 Ecology of the Age to Come

Ezekiel's river deepens as it flows, healing Dead-Sea salinity—an ecological miracle (Ezek 47 : 8-10). John echoes vision: river of life with trees bearing monthly fruit, leaves for nations' healing (Rev 22 : 1-2). These images suggest biodiversity explosion, not sterile alabaster city. Animals likely inhabit peaceable kingdom—lion eats straw (Isa 11 : 6-9)—affirming creaturely participation. Scientific curiosity persists, now freed from entropy. Astronomers may study nebulae without light pollution; farmers cultivate without weeds. Liberated creation joins eternal liturgy, each species contributing unique timbre.

16.5.4 Work-Worship Harmony

Original mandate to subdue earth continues, minus frustration; gardeners become viticulturists of Edenic vineyards. Musicians compose symphonies echoing cosmic background radiation rhythms. Engineers design interstellar transports exploring Father's house with many rooms. Labour retains effort but loses futility; Sabbath rest saturates work so toil cannot corrupt. Pilgrims who thought heaven dull discover boundless projects shaped by love, not survival. Every vocation finds endless horizon: scholars without deadlines, athletes without injuries, artisans without supply shortages. Temple has no temple because all space is sacred workshop.

16.5.5 Creaturely Chorus

Psalm 148 commands sun, moon, fire, hail, and sea monsters to praise; Revelation stages fulfilment as everything "in heaven and on earth and under the earth" sings (Rev 5 : 13). Mountains echo bass, sparrows trill soprano, quantum particles hum subatomic harmony. Human voices conduct symphony, interpreting creation's worship back to Creator. The chorus needs no amplification; Lamb's light amplifies acoustics. Worship becomes ambient atmosphere rather than scheduled activity. Silence is not absence of praise but audible pause in music too large for constant exposure. Ultimate indwelling thus culminates in cosmological oratorio.

16.6 Final Judgment and Ultimate Vindication

16.6.1 Great White Throne: Justice Enthroned

John's vision of throne on which earth and sky flee (Rev 20 : 11) asserts unchallengeable sovereignty. Books open, detailing every deed, rebutting myth that history's victims go unheard. Book of Life secures ransom for those robed in Lamb's righteousness, proving judgment is not arbitrary terror. Believers face evaluation, not condemnation; rewards calibrate stewardship faithfulness (1 Cor 3 : 12-15). For oppressors, judgment eliminates power to harm again. Justice renders city safe; open gates need no locks. Worship flourishes because evil quarantined can no longer vandalise praise.

16.6.2 Purifying Fire

Biblical fire both consumes and illuminates—burning bush ablaze yet unconsumed (Ex 3 : 2), fiery furnace purifying faithful (Dan 3 : 27). Judgment fire tests works, revealing gold or straw (1 Cor 3 : 13). Believers therefore build with mercy, truth, and humility, anticipating audit. The fire also incinerates systemic evils—slavery, racism, ecological rape—ensuring they never cross new-creation threshold. Fearful imagery aims to motivate repentance now, not relish others' doom. Purifying fire vindicates holiness, making eternity contagion-free zone.

16.6.3 Tears Wiped, Scars Honored

God's hand personally wiping tears (Rev 21 : 4) validates every cry ever uttered. Yet Jesus' glorified body retains scars (John 20 : 27), teaching that redemption honors history rather than rewriting it. Believers' wounds become testimony, not torment. Trauma memories may persist like healed muscles remember injury, but pain is replaced with meaning. Glory wraps grief in perspective so vast sorrow yields to gratitude. Thus divine comfort is intimate, not dismissive. Heaven's joy is robust because it incorporates, not ignores, earth's anguish.

16.6.4 Fearless Confidence

Perfect love expelled fear (1 John 4 : 17-18) long before judgment day arrives, but consummation reveals mechanism: standing "in Christ" secures verdict already announced. Believers appear clothed in borrowed righteousness, rendering prosecution speechless. Confidence fuels present obedience; those sure of Father's welcome risk radical generosity. Evangelism flows from desire that none perish but all meet the same Advocate. Consequently, the church neither trivialises judgment nor cowers; it hopes in justice tempered by mercy. Confidence births holiness without anxiety.

16.6.5 Witness Rewarded

Parables of talents and minas culminate in "Well done, good and faithful servant" (Matt 25 : 21). Rewards are relational—enter the Master's joy—not merely material crowns. Martyrs receive white robes and governmental thrones (Rev 20 : 4), but every cup of cold water given finds recognition (Matt 10 : 42). Rewards do not foster envy because love rejoices in others' honour. They motivate perseverance, especially for unseen labour—intercessors, caregivers, janitors. Eternal acknowledgement from Lamb outweighs any temporal applause. Reward scene finalises temple narrative: servants become co-regents in Father's house.

16.7 Bride, City, Temple: Three Metaphors, One Reality

16.7.1 Bridal Intimacy

Revelation's city is also a bride adorned (Rev 21 : 2), blending architectural vastness with covenant passion. Marriage language conveys exclusivity, delight, and permanence. Christ's dowry is His own blood; the Spirit serves as engagement ring (Eph 1 : 14). Wedding imagery answers Edenic loneliness—ultimate union replaces primal rupture. Honeymoon has no sunset because glory supplies perpetual warmth. Intimacy here is corporate; no believer left at altar. Thus salvation culminates not merely in acquittal but in consummated communion.

16.7.2 Cubic Architecture

City's length, width, and height equal 12 000 stadia, recalling holy-of-holies cube (1 Kgs 6 : 20). Every resident lives in former restricted zone; fear replaced by familiarity. Gigantic dimensions stress symbol: omnipresent holiness unconfined. Elevation suggests mountains merging with dwellings; Eden's garden and Zion's hill kiss. Geometry preaches theology: proportional perfection signals moral completeness. Mathematical beauty becomes liturgical aesthetic. Heaven's culture is symmetrical harmony.

16.7.3 Transparent Gold and Gem Foundations

Streets like clear glass (Rev 21 : 21) invert values—what humans prize becomes pavement. Apostolic names inscribed on gem foundations ensure doctrinal continuity. Jasper, sapphire, and emerald refract Lamb's light into prismatic worship. Materials echo high-priest breastplate (Ex 28 : 17-20), declaring entire city a priestly garment. Transparency symbolises moral clarity: no hidden corruption. Economic imagery rescues wealth from greed, converting it into public beauty. Gold thus finds eschatological redemption.

16.7.4 Ever-Open Gates

Twelve gates never shut because night is banished (Rev 21 : 25). Security arises from absence of threat, not exclusionary walls. Nations bring cultural glory—music scales, cuisine spices, technological marvels—purified from idolatry. Gates create flow, not fortress, fulfilling Isaiah 60 pilgrimage. Diversity persists, proving unity need not homogenise. Mission achieves telos: all peoples incorporated into single household. Open gates embody hospitable heart of God.

16.7.5 Light of the Lamb

No sun or moon needed, for Lamb is lamp (Rev 21 : 23). Photons once mediated through stellar furnaces now radiate from Person. Spiritual and physical illumination converge; knowledge of God erases ignorance and literal shadows. Energy grid becomes doxology; worshipers powered by presence. Light reveals face-to-face communion promised by beatific vision (1 Cor 13 : 12). Darkness cannot coexist—moral, emotional, cosmic. The universe becomes translucent with love.

16.8 Living Toward the City Now

16.8.1 Marketplace Holiness

Christians in finance, retail, and healthcare treat offices as embassy outposts, practicing honesty, generosity, and compassion. Pricing policies reflect Jubilee ethos; hiring preferences lift marginalised voices. Workspace prayer meeting renounces dualism, inviting Spirit into spreadsheets. Ethical audits identify slavery footprints in supply chains, correcting complicity. Internships mentor youth lacking privilege, embodying Isaiah 58 true fasting. Marketplace holiness thus braids worship with economic justice. Daily labour prefigures city streets of transparent gold.

16.8.2 Table and Towel

At home and church, shared meals break status barriers; foot-washing ceremonies anchor leadership in service (John 13 : 14-15). Hospitality schedules rotate to prevent burnout and monopoly. Leftover policy—never wasteable when neighbours hunger—turns fridge into mercy box. Towel ministry extends to janitorial tasks: leaders clean bathrooms, modeling servant greatness. Outsiders encountering humble tables sense kingdom aroma. Practices rehearse banquet where Lamb serves eternal feast. Eating and cleaning thus become sacramental rehearsal.

16.8.3 Peacemaking Praxis

Disciples adopt nonviolent communication, mediate neighbourhood conflicts, and lobby for restorative justice legislation. Blessed peacemakers inherit beatitude identity (Matt 5 : 9). Churches host gun-buyback events, melting weapons into garden tools, echoing Micah 4. Cross-cultural friendships counter polarisation; online discourse adheres to James 1 slow-to-anger rules. Peacemaking distinguished from passivity; prophetic confrontation coexists with tender reconciliation. Such praxis previews city without night or war. Conflict becomes laboratory for kingdom demonstration.

16.8.4 Stewarding Earth

Community solar co-ops reduce carbon; congregational gardens supply food banks. Preaching series link Revelation river to present watershed care. Children participate in "Adopt-a-Tree" baptisms, naming saplings and praying Psalm 1 growth blessings. Advocacy for endangered species respects Creator's affection for sparrows (Matt 10 : 29). Eco-liturgies lament pollution, confess complicity, and celebrate renewal projects. Earth stewardship signals belief in restored cosmos, not disposal. Each recycled bottle whispers eschatological hope.

16.8.5 Prophetic Imagination

Artists paint murals of New-Jerusalem gates on city walls scarred by graffiti, transforming vandalism into vision. Preachers craft sermons that out-dream cynicism, narrating futures where prisons close and hospitals become art colleges. Policy writers design housing initiatives inspired by Acts 4 common purse. Teachers invite students to imagine neighbourhoods with free libraries and clean rivers, then plan practicable steps. Prophetic imagination marries realism with possibility driven by Spirit. It refuses to concede cultural narrative to despair. Such creativity is foretaste of unending Sabbath innovation.

Conclusion

If this book has traced a river of glory from Eden's headwaters to Revelation's crystal torrent, this final chapter invites every reader to board that current and paddle downstream with joyful resolve. We have looked backward only to gain momentum forward, recognising that the Spirit now deposits foretastes of tomorrow's city into today's ordinary streets, homes, studios, and boardrooms. Our era—suspended between veil-ripping past and veil-less future—demands communities who live as living temples, radiant with holiness yet hospitable with grace. Such people do not flinch at culture's shadows because they carry inside them an unquenchable light; neither do they idolise present blessings, for they glimpse a splendour still to come. May every worship service, budgeting session, recycling chore, policy vote, lullaby, and laboratory experiment become one more brushstroke on the canvas of approaching glory. And when confusion clouds vision or weariness bends spine, may the church hear once more the final word already echoing in God's throne room—"Behold, the dwelling of God is with humanity" (Rev 21 : 3)—and reply with unbroken, rhythmic heartbeat: **Maranatha.**

www.ingramcontent.com/pod-product-compliance
Lightning Source LLC
LaVergne TN
LVHW051357080426
835508LV00022B/2865

* 9 7 8 1 9 9 7 5 4 1 1 5 8 *